GH00976378

PICTURES
FROM
MY
MIND

ACKNOWLEDGEMENTS

The publishers and editors are grateful for the efforts of the following
individuals in making this anthology possible:

Richard Clark, Peter Jones, Greg Marsden, Thelma McGrath, Thomas McGrath,
Sandra Richards, Nicola Sydenham and Roger Thomas of Prontaprint, Paignton

PICTURES
FROM
MY
MIND

An Anthology
of verse from the
younger generation

Vanessa Sydenham
Editor

Steve Sydenham
Publisher and Managing Editor

Copyright © 1999 Poetry In Print
as a compilation

Individual copyright to poems
belong to the poet

Cover design and artwork
by Amanda Ross

All rights reserved
No part of this book may be
reproduced in any way without
express permission of the publisher
in writing

ISBN 0-9528964-4-3

Published by
Poetry In Print
PO Box 141
Paignton
TQ3 1YY

Printed In England
by Maslands Ltd, Tiverton

INTRODUCTION

Welcome to our first anthology of verse specifically for children and young adults. This came about as a direct result of a competition open to schools and we sincerely thank teachers and parents for their enthusiasm and for helping to make the competition and the anthology such a success.

Congratulations to the winners of the competition and to all of our young contributors, well done, a superb effort by all concerned. Most of the poems that appear within these pages are from young poets whose work is appearing in print for the first time and for many we are sure it will not be the last.

The competition was open to all ages and abilities and for some of the contributors an extraordinary effort was required simply to submit an entry. To these children in particular the excitement of seeing their work published means so much and we sincerely hope this will help to encourage them to write even more in the future. The comments made by their teachers has been most rewarding to all concerned at Poetry In Print.

Theories of what a poem should be are only of minor importance here. It is more important that the student has taken the time to write something, perhaps loosely poetic, but interesting and often unique. The editors have truly enjoyed putting this anthology together. The poems are written with such honesty and openness, coupled with a lively imagination and expression that can only come from young minds.

We wish all of our young contributors much success for the future and hope all of their dreams and aspirations come true in the new Millennium.

CONTENTS

First Prize Winners

Sandra Hallet, Totnes, Devon | **King Edward V1 Community College**
Katherine Barron, Aldershot, Hants | **Ash Manor School**
Sarah Biddlecombe, Danbury, Essex | **Danbury Park County Primary School**
Katherine Penn, Wickford, Essex | **Northcrescent Primary School**

Second Prize Winners

Luke Shaw, Bude, Cornwall | **Budehaven Community College**
Jenny Harding, Chesham, Bucks | **Dr. Challoner's High School**
Scott Herrington, Folly Hill, Surrey | **Hale Primary School**
Hannah West, Croxley Green, Herts | **Harvey Road Primary School**

Runners-up

Naila Aslam/ Woodley, Berks

Jesamine Cook/ Beacon, Cornwall

Geoffrey Gilbert/ Crewkerne, Somerset

Jodie Leebody/ Brookwood, Surrey

Elizabeth O'Hara/ Padstow, Cornwall

Amanda Weeks/ Rownthams, Hants

Samantha Allen/ Bridgwater, Somerset

Kyle Burford/ Lydney, Glos

Stephen Durant/ Bridgwater, Somerset

Rosalind Morgan/ Polstone, Beds

Stewart Peters/ Chandlers Ford, Hants

Harriett Walker/ Kintbury, Berks

Catherine Caller/ Cullompton, Devon

Simon Harris/ St. Day, Cornwall

Kimberley Moyle/ St. Day, Cornwall

Natalie Pluck/ Aylesbury, Bucks

William Spencer/ Harpenden, Herts

Daniel Wilson/ Cirencester, Glos

Katie Berrington/ Headington, Oxon

Joel Blatchford/ Tavistock, Devon

Emily Gadd/ Tolland, Somerset

Wilhelmina Gibbs/ St. Marybourne, Hants

Daniel Harvey/ Crewkerne, Somerset

George Passco/ Bridgwater, Somerset

Zoe Clarke/ Tongham, Surrey

Bradley Fricker/ Hemel Hempsted, Herts

Gemma Godfrey/ N. Baddesley, Hants

Phiona Maidment/ N. Baddesley, Hants

Arup Sen/ Ash, Surrey

Graeme Williams/ N. Baddesley, Hants

Joseph Buckley/ Rayleigh, Essex

Craig Deane/ Canvey Island, Essex

Ian Johnson/ N. Baddesley, Hants

Cherelle Morgans/ Canvey Island, Essex

Laura Shearer/ Marldon, Devon

Lucy Webb/ Ash Vale, Surrey

Abigail Colley/ Upper Hale, Surrey

Peter Jefferys/ Ivybridge, Devon

Naomi Nickerson/ Wellshead, Oxon

David Puddle/ Ducklington, Oxon

Eloise Turner/ Gretton Fields, Glos

Stephen Witham/ Aylesbury, Bucks

Beth Berry/ Chalfont St. Giles, Bucks

Lucy England/ Bodmin, Cornwall

Jenny Gale/ Winchester, Hants

Verity Grigg/ St. Austell, Cornwall

Gemma Harragan/ Waltham Abbey, Essex

Katherine Pendray/ Chalfont St. Giles, Bucks

First Prize Winners

Past Pity On The Left

Sweetness and innocence,
On the breach of fear.
Hope is just a corner
And she'll never reach there.
Hate's a mile stretch of highway
Bleak and in despair.
Time is just a sentence
Spent awhile inside.
Caught in her emotions,
She stops just past envy
Across the street from 'Why?'
And sits cross-legged
Upon the pavement - to cry.

Sandra Hallett (Age 15)

Trapped

A force from behind, yet greater within
I can find a way out.
I know how to begin.
My past in denial, My future untold.
I must endure. My unrepentant soul.
I will cloud the sins of trust I took.
Display a crisp blank page of life's long book.
Capture my dreams I once dismissed.
The path ahead a shower of bliss.

But the unforgiving taunt my revolt,
Conscience mocking every fault,
'Time will heal', many preach,
But who has suffered,
Of those who teach?
Ashamed to confess my deep down fear,
But I cannot keep trying to be sincere.
A familiar, savage, ungrateful trait,
An encouraging morsel of tempting bait,
A force from behind, yet greater within, I can find a way out
I now know how to begin.

Katherine Barron (Age 14)

First Prize Winners

The Air Raid

The piercing sound of a siren shot through my ear,
I stumbled fearfully to a shelter, crying with fear.
The woken baby was screaming angrily in my arms as
I ran,
To a small smelly shelter, shaped like a can
I fell into the shelter and was about to shut the door when
    BOOM!!!
Bombs were exploding like fireworks,
I was frozen, watching them falling swiftly and exploding deafeningly.
I screamed loudly and shut the door as the ground tumbled and shook,
I would rather have a life than a look.
I was petrified as I sat clutching the shivering baby, trying to calm her.
The tin all around us dangerously rattled,
As I fought frantically for my life in this terrible battle.
It went on forever and I cried until I was numb
Then it was silent.

Sarah Biddlecombe (Age 10)

If You.....

If you dance in the rain,
dance with me!

If you skip to school,
skip with me!

If you watch a play,
watch with me!

If you love and care about your family,
love and care with me!

If you have a secret,
share it with me!

If you are lonely,
I'll be there with you.

Katherine Penn (Age 7)

Second Prize Winners

The Fate Catalyst

You slain the devil with a toy sword,
"Your soul is mine" the devil roared,
It really hasn't yet sunk in,
The nightmare really did begin.

Better to burn out than fade away?
How we wish that you could stay,
But now you're gone and gone for good,
Can't heal our scars nor stop the blood.

A whole life was ahead of you,
But fifteen years and that was through,
Although whilst alive you would never admit;
Eventually your body would have to submit.

Your habit was to see your untimely demise,
Shame that death's the only prize.
You still live on – inside our souls,
But our hearts still manifest gaping holes.

The outcome: in reality, clearer than glass,
We lost our mate to a can of gas.

Luke Shaw (Age 17)

Dreams

I dream of many wondrous things,
Of fantasy worlds where angels sing,
Of hope and love and peace and care,
I dream of places and wish I was there.

But then there are nightmares that shatter my thoughts,
Of death and destruction and people distraught,
Of hate, pollution, war and despair,
I dream of places and I'm glad I'm not there.

But for once in my life I stood back and saw,
I'm living in a world polluted by war,
No love, no hope only hatred and spite.
I thought and I thought deep into the night.

My nightmares are reality; my dreams are just dreams,
I'm in a world where people adore mean,
They kill and they fight and it makes headline news,
Don't they realise?
Don't they understand?
In the end we all shall lose.

Jenny Harding (Age 14)

Second Prize Winners

My Friend Jake

When I was little aged about three
My friend Jake looked like me
Now my friend is bigger than me
He can do things easily
I've tried and tried and can't succeed
But I know he will be never as handsome as me.

In the bath, scrubbing his spots,
"Wow", he's got lots and lots!
Washing his hair flicking his curl,
He always gets lots of girls.

Now that I'm grown up and nearly a man,
My secret world has finally gone
Now I look and it's plain to see -
My friend Jake is really . . . .
Handsome old me!

Scott Herrington (Age 10)

January Trees

January trees have lost their leaves
And quite bare appear
Like knives in the drawer
Like hands in the straw
And their twigs like thorns on a bush
Their dull black branches sway in the wind
And their thin bare twigs as sharp as pins
They look like witches casting spells

Hannah West (Age 7)

Think Again

Galaxies intertwine
Centuries lost and found
Thoughtlessness on waves
Light bursting

Distance yearning to increase
Time and space
Knowing no bounds
Records broken

Ceaseless adventure
Time to exist
Life is fast
And invigorating

Reality or feelings,
Difficult to tell
Body is soaring
Mine or yours

Naila Aslam (Age 15)

A Game Of Chicken

I'm waiting,
Waiting for what,
The worst,
Trapped in the cold corridors of the hospital,
The trauma of the accident still haunts me,
I distinctively remember,
The thud of my friends head as it hit the road of tarmac,
Next the nurse is at my side,
My friend is dead,
The knives of depression hit me,
It's a whole year since that accident,
I can't cross a road due to my fear,
Why did I play that stupid game of chicken,
Now because of it my friend is dead,
But I can't run or hide from death,

Sian Abrahams (Age 11)

Sleepless Night

I lie in bed listening listening
Listening to the sounds of the traffic in the street
To the wind outside whistling, whistling
And listening to the sounds of the creeky plastic seat

I lie in bed fully awake
Hearing the sounds of the baby crying
The pitter patter of rain on slate
And the sound of voices never dying

I think of the best which I'll have tomorrow
I think of the fish in the dying creek
I think of my pencils someone had borrowed
I think about why I can't get to sleep

Jenny Allen (Age 12)

A Yearning

The call of the wind
Asks me
To follow its trail
In the misty night

The cry of the rain
Tells me
To search for its end
In the endless darkness

The shriek of the lightning
Orders me
To join in on the hunt
In the empty world

I, sit confused
Watched by the storm
A leaf in the mud

Saaiqa Aslam (Age 14)

Magic Door

Through that door
I would go back to the past
To see the brutal dinosaurs
No humans have seen before
I would see the meat eaters
Tearing other dinosaurs apart
With their ripping claws
And teeth sharper than spears
Stronger than a thousand men

Daniel Ackland (Age 9)

Clamouring Classroom

Chattering children
Blinking blinds
Waves of wood upon the table
Dancing minds
Ink pens leaking
Rocking chairs
Chalk squeaking
What a clamouring classroom

James Atkinson (Age 8)

Earth

The shimmering sea
Holds fish,
The wandering sky
Keeps birds,
The gloomy undergrowth
Grips the insects
And the plants
That help us live.

Robert Abbott (Age 10)

What Colour?

In December cold,
The sheep huddle in a fold,
This colour covers the hills,
As the cold milk falls and spills.

This colour is of potato mashed,
As pure and smooth like eggs being bashed,
My ice cream, vanilla flavour, Yum,
The cone and flake, that fills my tum,

The clouds in the sky up high,
This colour is only one little lie,
Now can you guess what colour I see?
It's not black, it's not red, it's white - just like me!

Anna Allan (Age 11)

Hot And Cold

With hot or cold stole from the sky,
You would freeze or burn and surely die.
But with persistence in your existence,
You will harness both and carry on.

On to the desert,
Cold and wet.
On to the desert,
How dead can you get?
On to the desert where death is served cold.
On to the space where land is not sold.

But to the other extent,
Where the air is bent,
And the cars wobble by in the heat.
Where the ants all hide and don't go outside,
For fear of burning their feet.
Where death shines down from the bright blue sky,
And on the wind more death blows by.
The bones of men,
Wind swept with chips,
Who drowned in the sand with dry parched lips.

Nathan Abbott (Age 14)

All Around Us

All around us
Flowers are blooming
Trees are blowing
And pushing out their buds

Leaves are greening
Children playing
With the Spring
That's coming

Inez Armstrong (Age 7)

Things That Go Bump In The Night!

Things that go bump in the night -
It might well be a ghost;
It just could be a thief,
Or even your granny with her false teeth!

Things that go bump in the night -
It could be your parents;
It might be a can,
Or it might be Robin, or Batman!

Things that go bump in the night -
They always give you a fright,
But don't be scared,
You've got your teddy bear to hold you tight.

Steven Alvey (Age 14)

What Am I ..

I am white and black
My enemy is boots
I usually come out in the winter
I live in a stadium
I am two years old
I wish I was big
I am round

I am a Football

Tom Adams (Age 7)

My Senses Poem

With my eyes I can see a helicopter flying
With my ears I can hear Father Christmas coming
With my nose I can smell mummy cooking bacon
With my tongue I can taste a hot dog
With my hands I can feel grass in a pot.

William Adams (Age 4)

Alien Footy

Aliens are football crazy,
Crazy for footy they are,
Are they the best though no,
No they're rubbish,
Rubbish or not,
Not easy to score with them though,
Though they are well and truly rubbish,
Rubbish or not,
Not no-one in the England football team
Would dare play against aliens.

Kier Abrahams (Age 7)

Christmas Tradition

Christmas is a time to cheer
It only comes round once a year
We decorate with wreaths of holly
To make the house feel warm and jolly
And on the night 24th of December
All Christians will remember
That Christ the Lord was born in a stable
He had no television and no cable
He only had the simple things in life
Made by Joseph and Joseph's wife
That tradition has been passed down and down
And every year it comes around

David Attwood (Age 11)

The Computer

The computer
Is not from Jupiter
The game Boldies
It never mouldies

The further you get
The harder I bet
You can't boil an egg
Or break a leg

On the internet,
Sometimes you bet
You look and look
And get hooked on a book

You can drive a kart
It can't eat a tart
It makes you stare
And gives out a glare

Peter Allen (Age 11)

Playgrounds

Tornado leaves crushing
Turning bins
Footballs twirling
Lonely skipping ropes
Trees standing alone
Leftover jumpers lying there
Black brown mud
Escaping litter
Puddles splashing

Kate Atkinson (Age 8)

Untitled

Sat alone in a room full of sadness,
Collecting together my melancholy thoughts
Wondering, did only I know madness,
Or was saneness something everyone sought?

Sometimes I want to lose myself inside,
And cry to ghosts that haunt my lonely dreams
But that would completely destroy my pride
And condemn other souls to hear my screams;

This insurmountable cloak of grief,
Enrobes me in its dark imprisonment
Where getting high is my only relief
And death row is where I must be sent!

No-one understands, why feelings I hide,
But to me, they're things I must keep inside!

Samantha Allen (Age 14)

A Strange Cover Teacher

A strange, new teacher taught us today,
She wouldn't let any of us have our way,
She had a little ginger cat,
Our usual teacher wouldn't do that.

We had a spellings test, we hate them,
We had some biscuits but the cat ate them,
She made us sit on a "Magic Mat",
Our usual teacher wouldn't do that.

Our usual teacher would be small and weedy,
But this strange teacher likes her foody,
She's tall and fat and plump all round,
She's like a big ball in our small playground.

A strange, new teacher taught us today,
She wouldn't let any of us have our way,
She had a little ginger cat,
Our usual teacher would NEVER have that!

Nicola Adams (Age 11)

Beach At Sunset

The golden beach with an orange and yellow sunset,
Singing birds going back to their warm twig beds.
Dark blue sea with the reflection of the orange and yellow sunset.
The smell of the salty sea,
The tide creeping up the beach to find
The left-overs that people have left behind
The jelly sea bobbing up and down with boats on.
The lighthouse flashing, flashing on and off, on and off.
The twinkling stars shining in the dark blue sky

Alison Albutt (Age 8)

A Shark Is . . . .

Deadly
Swimming silently towards you
Blood thirsty
Vicious teeth
Razor fin
Coming to eat you
Gliding through the sea
A killer coming towards you

Sophie Allen (Age 10)

The Millennium Bug

What is this millennium bug
Is it in the computer or under the rug
Is it slimy and scary with six hairy legs
Or does it just nibble and take up your megs.
Can you catch it and cage it and flush it away
Or is it in your computer and determined to stay
The year two thousand is coming so fast
That if you aren't careful it is going to blast
We must sort it out and get it all straight
The first of two thousand will be much too late

Andrew Armstrong (Age 9)

Red

Red is a joyful colour,
Brighter than any other,
There are red cars
Seen from afar,
It's most peoples' favourite colour.

My favourite colour is red,
Some people have a red head,
The colour is great,
It's my fave, until fate,
The colour I write of, is RED.

Tom Auger (Age 11)

What Am I?

My once green leaves lie brown on the floor
My crunchy, ripe fruit red as the rose smell sweeter than honey picked, gone.
My bare, empty branches with soft creamy snow lying on the top.
The sound of crisp golden leaves
Spinning around in mini whirlwinds
Landing silently on the stiff frosty grass.
The splash of puddles echoes through the icy autumn air.
The taste of the morning mist as the rich yellow sun lights up the dark, grey sky.
I am sad and lonely that my fruit has gone
But glad it's gone to good use I shall not be lonely for long.
Spring will be here soon and my fruit will grow back
And I will be bright and joyful once more.

Rebecca Ayers (Age 11)

Untitled

There was an old man from Leeds,
Who always finds he speeds,
He gets in his car
And goes very far
That funny old man from Leeds

David Armistead (Age 11)

The Rainbows

Red, yellow, green and blue
are the colours of the rainbow.
The rainbow sits upon a cloud,
the colours gleaming on the ground.

Orange, violet and indigo
are the colours of the rainbow.
The rainbow sits up in the sky,
the colours gleaming on a cloud so high.

That's all the colours of the rainbow,
and the colours of the sky,
and the colours that I like
so HIGH ... HIGH ... HIGH.

Samantha Ashford (Age 10)

Christmas

Crispy potatoes roasting in the aga
Hot chestnuts roasting in the fire
Rum, whisky, scotch and wine on the sideboard
In the living room, family laughter
Surprises in presents under the tree
Tree glitters with gold tinsel and red balls
Mum has perfume, dad has slippers
And Michael has a playstation, for me a surprise
Squirming basset hound puppy just for me

Sarah Akehurst (Age 11)

Creation

I like the rain when it is wet and we can do skids
I like the sun when it shines because my clothes get dry
I like the sky because it tells me the weather
I like the snow because you can make snowballs
I like rainbows when it's bright because we can play football
I like the wind when it's windy because our hats come off
I like space because it has lots of planets

Asim Akram (Age 8)

Raindrop

Here I go, here I go again,
Running down the window pane,
I roll down with a splish,
And drop with a splash,
When I hit the ground
I hit it with a bash,
I splosh down the gutter
And fall down the drain
Can you guess what I am?
Yes I am a drop of rain.

Guy Andrews (Age 11)

I Met A Monster

I met a monster
Walking down the street
I met a monster
He was really neat!

He was small and green
But furry
And his eyes were
Kind of blurry

I met a monster
Walking down the street
I met a monster
He was really neat!

Natacha Anderson (Age 11)

November The 5th

On November the 5th I can smell,
Smoky bonfires burning well

On November the 5th I can hear,
Fireworks banging clear

On November the 5th I can taste
The cold wind blowing onto my face

On November the 5th I can feel,
My warm gloves, as comfy as can be

On November the 5th I can see,
Tasty sausages, sizzling free

Elizabeth Allen (Age 8)

Growing Older

It must have been at least a week
Since I had that talk with my Dad
I was there over an hour in that room
Firstly he said about
Leaving cups and dishes and food
In my room.
It's the biggest room in the house
Why does all the junk end up in my room?
Everyone tells you to tidy up
Does anyone tell him to tidy up?
NO!
It's not fair.

Lee Anderson (Age 11)

There's Something In The Basement

There's something in the basement,
It's going round and round,
As I walk above it
It makes a splashing sound.

But don't be so frightened,
It really isn't mean,
It's only the spinning sound,
Of mum's old machine!

Kimberly Ashmead (Age 8)

When I Was Little

When I was a little boy
I never stopped to touch a toy
All I did was terrorised the house
Everyone wanted to leave even my pet mouse
All I did was screamed and cried
That may be the reason why my pet mouse died
Breakfast time was very yummy
But food did not go to my tummy
At breakfast time I made a mess
Mostly over my mum's dress

Joe Argent (Age 10)

Trapped

I was driving in my car down the road
I heard a big bang, it was my engine, it had blown

I started to spin round and round
My car did a flip landing roof to the ground

I had crashed my car in the street
My legs were trapped, I could not feel my feet

A person came to see if I was alive
The man was gobsmacked to see I had survived

When he went off to get some help
I felt a bit wheezy so I let out a yelp.
The Ambulance men came and this is what they said
"There is no use here the man is
Dead."

Chris Astell (Age 14)

Jet Plane

I went to the airport,
I saw a big plane,
It went up and down on to the lane,
I got on to it, it was very clean,
It was ready to go with a great puff of steam,
The engine's revving,
The Captain said "let's go",
The propellers were fast
How long would they last
But when I was there the propellers stopped,
I dropped my bags in surprise.

James Argent (Age 7)

Doctor, Doctor

Doctor, Doctor,
Tell me why?
Why's my belly,
Two feet high?

Doctor, Doctor,
Tell me please
Why my dog
Has knobbly knees?

Marcus Lee Appleby (Age 8)

Rose

I rose from my chair by the fire
I heard my name in the wind
It was the ghost of my true love
Come to get the rose of our past
As I walked to the window I felt
A sudden breeze touch my hand
Sadness was gone for now
I remember the rose is golden, red, blue
And silver with a red jewel
It smelled sweetly
I remember he gave one to the lady before me
I saw a bright light
I saw him in golden clothes
It touched my heart when he returned
The other half of the rose
He looked at me
Then I saw him go
My heart was pounding
I felt so happy
I will remember this night for years to come

Katie Allen (Age 8)

The Covered Candy Corner

There was a covered candy corner
That made my tummy rumble
It was too delicious, it made me crumble.
It walks around the crumble corner
I try to miss it but I can not resist it
But one day (happily)
I missed it
The next day I got out of bed
And had a bath and brushed my teeth
Went down stairs
Opened the door
Looked around the corner
And the crumble candy
Did not make my tummy rumble
It was gone
I was happy as can be
It did not make my tummy rumble any more.

Damon Andrew (Age 9)

One Eyed Zombie

It had one eye I don't know why
I ran and ran like a man
Through the city's evil heart
Don't look back or he'll squish your back
Like a ballet by day
By the end of a day you'll have no bay
Like a dragon day.

Peter Armson Smith (Age 10)

Fear

Fear is white plain and pale
It smells like tar being laid
It tastes mouldy and rotten
It sounds like stone is grinding
It feels like a lashing sword
It lives in your body

Charlotte Andrews (Age 10)

Love

Love is as red as a rose,
Love is a flower's pollen adrift in the air
Love tastes like the best thing in the world
Love is as quiet as a flower
Love feels like silk
Love lives in your heart

Luke Adams (Age 10)

Sneeky Jim

Sneeky Jim was bad
His friends thought he was fab
Once he played a joke
It made his grandma choke
Then he ran away
He went to his friends to play
His mum said no
So Jim had to go
He ran to the dump
Where he got a thump
By the dustman that didn't like him
Poor Jim

Nick Andrews (Age 10)

The Old Donkeys

The old Donkey plays outside,
He says hello and doesn't hide,
In the stable he's just as nice,
He only stays there when there's ice.

The old Donkey has a friend,
And she won't drive you round the bend,
She used to work on the beaches,
Now she stays and gobbles peaches.

The old Donkeys eat the hay,
In their field there are lambs in May,

Charlotte Allan (Age 10)

Animals

Tigers have lots of stripes,
But they don't like to chew pipes.

Monkeys like to hang around,
And they don't like to make much sound.

Dolphins are so grey,
And they like to swim by the bay.

Elephants are mighty strong,
And they're not very long.

Fish like to swim and play,
And they swim in the day.

Whales have big tails
And they don't have any nails.

Thomas Ackland (Age 9)

Guess Who?

It's big, it's grey, it lives in a jungle
    and has a very long nose.
It's yellow and black, buzzes all the summer time
    and sits on a big rose.
It's brown, it has big ears
    and climbs the trees
It's long, it can be even longer
    and it eats rats
It's colourful, it flies
    and it has wings.
Can you guess who they all are?

Anisah Ali (Age 8)

Foggy Morning

A gloomy dark day
The sky has fallen,
It wa spooky,
It's misty,
Like any day
It's damp
Look about
It's foggy everywhere,
The sky is blue
You can't see.

Natasha Ashman (Age 8)

Winter

Snowflake spinning in the sky,
Like a diamond in the night,
Wrap up warm hats and scarves,
Snow cold Christmas fun,
New Years Eve
Happy ending to the year

Natalie Andrews (Age 8)

Shopping From Hell!!

I was lost in an old, spooky shop
I went to look for my mum right in to a mop
In a forest of skirts
There were loads of turns
Where should I look?
I climbed on a hill of cheese
All I saw was a bag of peas
I started to cry for my mummy
Some people came feeling sorry
My mum came out of nowhere
My mum still says she didn't go anywhere

Ben Allen (Age 9)

A Summer's Life In A River

One summer's morning, the sun starts to rise
The frogs are leaping on the floating lily pads
Beavers gnashing and munching with their sharp teeth through the wood
Moss whirling above the rippling, reflecting, river.
Snakes slithering and swirling through the rocks and the moss
Herons waiting for fish to swim by .
Willows waving its leaves in the wind.
Reeds are cutting the children's playing fingers.
Boats halting by the old rotten lock.
Golden sunset waves slowly down.
Everything quietens
The river goes to sleep.

George Archer (Age 8)

The Monster Under My Bed

There's a monster living under my bed
Whose got a big fat hairy head
His breath smells like my dad's old socks
And he's as crafty as a sly old fox
He only comes out in the middle of the night
And never when the sun is bright
His nose is as red as his ruby red lips
And he is all wrinkled down to his finger tips
His hair is black as lumps of coal
And on his chin he's got a large brown mole
He only ever exists in my dreams
But he is so real to me it seems

Lewis Ash (Age 12)

My Monster

His teeth were sharp like pins,
His eyes like Lego,
His mouth was like a worm,
He was slimy.

Tim Beckett (Age 4)

Travel To The End

I will leave a thousand memories for you all to share,
I will write a box of stories
Which will soon be very rare,
I will let the paths unwind
For what it might have been. . .
These are the steps I'll follow on my . . .
Travel to the end.

Joanne Bowley (Age 14)

Elephant Footsteps

Hot sweat,
Shaking ground,
Suddenly I turn around,
A greeny light beams in my room,
Elephant footsteps
BOOM
BOOM
BOOM
The aliens are invading us,
Must tell someone,
Really must!
These mini martians from outer space,
Are invading all around the place.

Lauren Anthony (Age 9)

The Hot Dog

I went to watch Tottenham play,
I stepped on a hot dog,
The juice squirted out of the sausage,
I shouted "Dad Dad" but he didn't hear me.
So I scraped it off my shoe.
Then Tottenham scored I said "Hooray hooray"
But when it ended I stepped in some chewing gum.
I got in the car and saw the Millenium Dome,
So it ended up with me fast asleep in my bed.

Jordan Amner (Age 8)

Towards The Light

It's so much more peaceful outside the house
All your words and phrases behind the window
My own family shouting cursing one another.
These words of aggression
With my anticipation.
The house was calm, a homely world
But breaking glass makes my mind turn.
I feel myself breaking down inside.
My own flesh and blood the anger.
What is the final outcome today
Why do I care so much
The lights are on the house seems bright
But where in hell will I sleep tonight.

Outside the door sitting in the garden,
The roses bleed with fear
But I can worry for all of them.
The white door looks so cold
But broken ice must melt
Or my life will be pointless.

Alexander Brown (Age 15)

A Martian Sends a Postcard Home

Roads are rivers the cars are stones
Bouncing down the river
Bridges are centipedes
The pillars are giant hairy legs

Lanes are giant worms
The rugged skin on a worm
Is the jagged tarmac
On the lane

Lights are mechanical suns
The mechanical suns and lights
Both give off
A haze of bright light

Fire is hot water
The fire blisters skin and
Hot water scolds skin
From Mr. Moon

James Barnes (Age 12)

Spring

Silently gleaming
Silk smooth grass
Pouncing seas face the silent wind
Springing buttercups
Astonished trees
Uncountable colours
Growing excitingly patiently every day
Powerful light, dead rivers
Gleaming colours
Jagged edges silently stop
Glittering seas
Scampering mice
Glittering sites
Tranquil air
Rustling leaves lay silently still
Boiling bubbles
Day fresh sky
Sparkling light
Peaceful tunes
Camouflaged chameleons hiding in the tree
Silently . . . . . .

Samantha Baxter (Age 11)

Winter

Snowflakes glitter and shine,
Like the lovely sun shining,
As they fall and break
Like glass.
They are a sign of winter
And when they break
And when they melt
Snow is everywhere.
Shining.
So lovely and shiny.
They were once so shiny
But then they melt
And the snow turns to water.

James Robert Bettis (Age 7)

Phew!

On a cold day
On a really cold day
On a really really cold day
On a really really snowy day
There is nothing better
Than playing on my
Brand new
Red
Sparkling
Fast and speedy
Wooden sledge
Yippey!!!!!

Christine Batey (Age 6)

My Dream Bike

As I walk by my favourite shop
The dream machine catches my eye
I know I really should not stop
But I cannot walk by

I have to go inside the store
To stroke the glossy paint
I've never seen the likes before
I feel that I might faint

I go up to the smart salesman
And ask to try the bike for size
He says "My boy, of course you can
It's one of our best buys"

I really think this is so great
So how much is the bike?
He says "You can't afford this mate
You'd better take a hike!!"

Michael Barker (Age 12)

The Third Millennium

Space planes from Gatwick,
To holidays on planets made of chocolate,
Green tourists,
Fizzing cars that run on cola,
A robot that tidies your room,
A CD rom drive watch.

Knowledge chips in your ears,
So no need for schools,
Plasters that heal instantly,
Injections without needles,
A gun to fill the ozone hole,
And food for all the world.

James Boswell (Age 12)

Frost

Frost is freezing
Frost is white and cold
Frost we can skid on
Frost has smokey breath
Frost is freezing
Frost melts in the sun

Hannah Busbridge (Age 6)

The Beach

I drag my hands through the sand
People run into the sea, stabbing at the water.
There's a sudden sound, drums, a parade.
Everyone runs to see the exciting floats rolling in.
There are face-paints of palm trees and footprints in the wet sand.
"Have fun" the lifeguard's command,
Throwing the balls back to the boys and girls.
The boats sailing away on the sea.
The sun goes down, a bang of brightness,
Fireworks, pinks, greens, blues also yellows float in the sky peacefully.
The moving noise walks away, but there's one thing that stays with the sea
Which is me, the roaring waves folding in.

Sarah Beverstock (Age 11)

Weather Poem

Sparkly frost on the ground
Never stops glittering now.

Rain falling on the ground
For animals to drink, also flowers.

Wind curling through
Your cracks in the door.

Kiera Brown (Age 6)

Water Melon

Blood flows from a perfect sphere
Its glossy green surface parted
For the gain of one bite.
Soft tissues, creamy white, give way
Revealing perfect pink flesh
Dotted now and again by shiny black gems
Treasure uncovered from its tomb
Beautiful reflecting the pearlescent knives
As they take a bite

Kyra Bown (Age 14)

Summer Dreams

As the sun gleams through my bedroom window
I dream about the day ahead
I close my eyes I dream away
I picture a beach on holiday
Everyone's full of happiness and joy
Laughter of children fills the air
Volleyball, tennis, football, cricket
The games of the summer are enjoyed by all.

Georgia Bryan (Age 11)

The Weather

The rain came down
On the window pane
Drip drip drip
The sun comes out
And dries it all away
Thunder, lightning
Crash, Crash, Crash
Rain pouring down
And clearing again
A rainbow appeared
All was calm again

Claire Blaker (Age 11)

The Headless Ghost

Mist rolls in
The air is damp
The headless ghost clanks
His chains

Moans echo through the
Castle grounds
He glides, he slides
Through walls, through floors

His head under one arm
Blood curdling screams
His bulging eyes
"I will not rest"
"I'll seek revenge"
On those who killed

Michelle Button (Age 12)

A Tiger

If you want to see a tiger
You must go to the hot grassy plain

I know a tiger
Who's living down there
He's stripey, he's strong
He's scary he's got a lot of teeth

Yes, if you really want to see a tiger
You must go to the hot grassy plain.

Go down to the plain and say
Here pussy pussy
Here pussy pussy
And he'll come out
But don't stand there
RUN FOR YOUR LIFE!!!!

Richard Burgess (Age 7)

Fierce Forest

Walking in the forest,
Strange eyes stare at me.
"What if it eats me?"
"What if it strangles me?"
"What if it .....?"
"What if it......?"
I think to myself.
Scratching and squealing noises come from the darkness,
As I walk closer and closer to the edge of the forest
Light peering through the leaves.
Trees swaying in the terrifying wind,
Noisy, black bats come flying through the trees.
I sit up rubbing my eyes and realise it was only a dream . . .
Or was it?

Maria Blanco (Age 12)

Autumn

Leaves crunching.
The animals are hibernating.
I kick the leaves,
Conkers crack,
Hedgehogs rustling,
Squirrels are scuttling,
Swallows fly to Africa
When it gets cold.

Peter Joe Bennett (Age 5)

The Music Of The Spheres

A mist of evil lay there,
Before the Angel Dragon came,
But he swept away,
All the wars of the world,
With his hypnotic music.

The music is a blissful sound,
Heaven bound.

The melody of the eccentric dragon is heard,
Even in dreams.
For if dreams die,
Life will be like a broken-winged bird,
That cannot fly.

The music is brought to an end,
The dragon begins to change the tune,
And rhythm - his part of the deal.

When dawn breaks,
And the music is no more,
The world doth not quake,
But liveth in peace and in
Harmony with the Music of the Spheres.

Hilary Brewer (Age 11)

Image

Moonlight reflects on ocean,
Wave crashing over wave.
Froth and spray splash onto the rock
Into the dark stone cave.

Hoof print followed by hoof print
In the golden sand.
A horse galloping in the surf
Over the moonlight land.

Birds fly over the water
Fish swim the ocean floor
The waves gently lapping
Upon the lonely shore.

Oh can you not imagine
Can't you picture this wondrous sight?
This moody, dreamy image
Of the ocean on a starlit night.

Joanna Barker (Age 13)

Be Quiet

"Hello what's your ...?"
"Be quiet!"
"Sorry I was just ..."
"Be quiet!!"
"O.K. bye"
"Be quiet!!!"

"Hello my ..."
"Be quiet!"
"Go up to ..."
"Be quiet!!!"
"Do you want a smack"
"Be quiet, oops!"
OUCH!!!!

Thomas Brooks (Age 8)

Waterfall

Crashing
Rushing down the hill
Mighty animal
Roaring in rage
Carving crevices
In cool, hard rock
On the brink of
The rock
It bellows in pain
Then falls
Rolling
Tumbling over and over
Soaking everything
In a frosty spray
Overpowering noise
Fills the air
With a splash
It recedes into a surging mass
Then freeing itself
Carries on
Down the hill.

Katherine Bates (Age 11)

War

Back home in Britain,
The posters said:
It's your duty lad.

But now amid the dense barbed wire,
In this dead land of hate and fear,
Blood's the only coloured thing.

Our trench world
Is now one huge grave,
Full of lads who shan't grow old.

A young boy's head smashed like an eggshell,
No one seems to care,
Except a lonely woman.

Matthew Brooks (Age 13)

The Bee

I like to watch a lot of TV
On the screen there was a bee
The bee was laughing about me
I tipped the tea in the drain
When he was out it started to rain
The poor bee went down the lane
I went off on a plane

Joanne Blake (Age 14)

A Spider

I have legs as thick as rope
My body is fat as a snowman
My eyes are as fat as a pig
My mouth is like a golf ball
I eat humans and cake
I slurp human's blood

Adam Boulton (Age 8)

Lights Out

It's nearly 6 o'clock and it's getting rather dark
I'm sat here by the swings in the middle of the park.
At about this time of night I should be getting bright
But no matter how hard I try I can't make any light.

My mum says I should eat more greens if I want to be seen
But although I eat all my leaves to show I'm really keen,
I just don't seem to have the knack of lighting up the sky
Whilst I sit here gazing up as the stars go passing by.

I try and try all night long but don't think I will ever learn
To be able to make a light and be a brilliant glow worm.

But wait a minute who's that handsome bug I see
He is rather nice with a really bright glow and he is looking straight at me.
What is happening I feel embarrassed sort of glowing and alight?
My goodness I am glowing and oh so very bright!

Nia Baxter (Age 11)

Winter

The trees are bare
The frost is on the ground
The ground is crunchy
The floor is slippery
All the cars are icy
Rub your fingers on the car
They will get cold and hard

James Blackmore (Age 6¾)

The Dog Chased The Cat

Meow, meow a dog chased the cat.
Hiss, hissss don't do that
Screamed the cat.

Danielle Bowler & Adam Lewin (Age 6)

Hot Dog

I wanted one hot dog
You wanted another
We didn't get our hot dogs
So we killed each other!

Sam Beadle (Age 13)

The Caravan

Cool said the man
It's a big white caravan
I will live in it
And I will fry in it
But most of all I will fly in it

It has red wheels
And car deals is written all over
In a couple of years it will grow clover

Oh look it has one gear
And it cannot steer
For there is no steering wheel
Shall I call the old bill?

What shall I do?
I know, I'll sue
No that's no good
I know, I'll knock it up with nails and wood
Oh no it's gone cor it doesn't half pong
Now I'll have to sing a song

Philip Burton (Age 10)

Flames

Burning flames
Flickering bright
Dancing and twisting
At the peak of its life
Then it starts to fall
Hissing angrily
Soundlessly it dies, dies
Into a pile of ashes . . . . !

Adam Bonny (Age 12)

Go And Open The Door

Go and open the door
Maybe there's
A noisy House of Lords,
A bustling market
Or
A wet petrol station.

Go and open the door
Maybe there's
A blind one-eyed marble!
An ill headache pill!
Or
A drunk pencil case!

Go and open the door
Maybe there's
A bottomless pit,
A speaking pencil pot,
Or
A burnt book.

Edward Burgon (Age 9)

Goldilocks

While walking in he woods, she may look kind, but let's put that all behind.
For she is a cruel and nasty vandal, who comes across a vicious scandal
She enters a house without permission, just as if she's on a mission.
She eats their breakfast and spits it out, but enjoys the childs one without a doubt.
She sits on the chairs; then makes her way up the stairs.
She went to bed to rest her head. As she awoke she got a surprise,
Looking down at her were three bears eyes, up she jumped, and got out her gun,
She shot the bears one by one, then she had to run.
The police later arrived onto the scene, where Goldilocks had been.
She ran off the scene without a trace, a policeman caught up with her, and looked her in the face.
She took off her wig and made a confession, she then gave him the gun from her possession.
She stayed in jail, for just one year, until her conscience was completely clear.

Katie Barrett (Age 11)

The Pet Shop

We went to the pet shop
And bought a thin rat
It grew very fat and gave birth
There were three tiny babies
All covered in pink
And I saw one of them blink
And wink

We went to the pet shop
And bought a fat rabbit
That had a bad habit
Of biting its fur
We took it to the doctor
"Put him to bed" the doctor said

Harriet Louise Beckwith (Age 8)

All Around Us

Spring is lovely, daffodils beautiful
Yellow on top and a green stem on the bottom
Tulips blue and violets blue
Flowers are everywhere
Spring is sunny not raining at all
Most of the time I play football
Buds on trees turning into leaves
Three months in Spring
March, April, May
That means lots of weeks at school!
Yipee!!!

Joe William Brittain (Age 7)

23

Spooky!!!!

There it was sitting in its cave,
It had blood shot eyes,
Big bulging bright purple lips.

It was all slimy and had green skin
With the most disgusting brown spots,
Six gruesome grotty slimy legs, four gungy arms.

Five yellow claws it had on each and every arm,
Its blood was the colour of the deep blue sea,
The hair on it was long and spiky and also pink.

It was the most scariest, spookiest thing
I have ever seen in my whole life.

Charlotte Birkbeck (Age 10)

Afraid

I was afraid so I ran.
Walking behind me were two bony figures.
A cold shadow came upon me,
Screams were echoing through my head.
A voice told me to scream out loud.
Friends - no - only enemies were with me!
Run faster, I said.
Another scream came, bounding through my head,
I was scared and alone,
Do it, I said........
         I SCREAMED!

Jemma Beach (Age 11)

Nightmare!

It crawls through me towards the brain,
It drives me insane!
It crawls down my spine like a snake,
Suddenly my bed begins to move.
I find myself in a never ending hole,
I begin to go all dizzy,
Soon I find myself in darkness.
I begin to hear noises in my head.
I begin to feel strange.
It gets too much!
I try to wake up,
But I can't!

Kyle Burford (Age 12)

A Winter's Day

Fields of ice, glistening
Like the icing on cakes
In early morning dew
The wind comes gently, gently
Like a mother rocking her baby
Jack Frost creeps through the night
With wind in his hair
Like the sun moving from cloud to cloud
With a sea of magical frost behind
Covering trees and windows
With a magic wand
The afternoon comes slowly
Snowflakes appear from the sky
Like leaves in the Spring
Popping out of their buds
The night comes
All is quiet
Like the calm sea
With sea creatures slowly moving
Winter has crept its way in

Adam Brooks (Age 10)

Snowflake

I'm a chilly snowflake
A lovely shape and
When the sun comes out today
I'm surely going to
Melt away

Emily Bissett (Age 6)

All Around Us

When I went out in the wood
I saw a bird peeping and cheeping
From a nest
I saw some daffodils
Poking up from the ground
There are Spring songs
All around

Jessica Brown (Age 7)

Clowns

Clowns are funny clowns are smart
Clowns have red noses all about.
I like clowns they are silly,
They roll on the ground
And throw custard pies at each other.
They throw buckets of water and juggle with joy.
I wish I was a clown.

Duncan Branthwaite (Age 7)

Jasmine My Hamster

Jasmine Jasmine in your soft warm bed,
She snuggles up like a cat.
She runs on her wheel as fast as a car.
She loves her bright yellow cage,
She loves her warm bedding.
She crawls up the stairs like a worm,
She runs as fast as a van in her ball.
She loves her Vet we take her to,
She loves everybody in her family,
We love her too.
She plays like a cat, she plays with my rat.
She plays on the mat. She sits on the mat,
She sleeps on the mat.
That's what my hamster does.

Daisy Butler (Age 8)

The Brave And Strong

War breaks out
Recruit the young
Strong and fit, the war can be won.
Thousands march to the Somme
Unafraid to fight for the nation's pride.

Mud filled trenches lined our way,
Steep banked trenches, barbed wire blockades
Germans attacking both night and day
Never knowing which one will be your way.

Bodies lying face down in the mud
Limbs missing, torsos lying in blood
Cries for war, cries for HELP!
Cries of pain our poor boy's shout.

Thousands sent, hundreds return
Walking injured, they are the lucky ones
Remember them, so brave and strong
The heroes of the Somme.

Sophie Boobyer (Age 13)

Poverty

Not enough money,
People on the street,
Not enough food,
Beggars in a mood.
No-one doing nothing,
Just lying there.
Not even the government are helping the poor,
They are just dying,
And no one cares,
Just think for once about these people.

Badly behaved at school,
Got chucked out of home at 15,
Found my way into drugs,
Then into the police cells.
Oh, how no-one helps us:
Not even our family cares,
All we do is sit there,
Helpless, cold, alone, sad and poor.

Alison Bolt (Age 13)

Myself!

M y ambition is to be a solicitor.
Y ou don't know much about me.
S wimming is my favourite sport
E xcept for running round here.
L ove sport
F ind English fun!

Douglas Beattie (Age 9)

Tavistock River

Splashing through the rocky rocks,
Going down the waterfalls,
Shiny and glittery blue river.
By the bank are lovely flowers.
People running in and out of shops.
The river is shining in the sun.

Naomi Beckett (Age 6)

Cold

I went outside
It was cold
I went back in to get
My coat and gloves
I got my hat
I put it all on
I went back outside

Samantha Boucher (Age 6)

All Around Us

Poppies are red in the Spring
And chicks are bright
The grass is green in the sun
The sun is bright
And the sheep have babies
And the foxes come out of their dens
In Grass in the ground

Georgia Brafield (Age 6)

A Martian Sends A Postcard Home

A flickering flame from which a scream emerges,
It makes humans appear in strange blue outfits,
And sometimes it causes the eyes to flow.

A giant gliding bird with a monsterous roar,
Which makes you duck down,
And wave your branches as you chase it away.

A long black river that does not flow,
Except when nature interferes,
Then the black does run.

A strange shiny object in which you see your twin,
It only smiles at you if you smile at it,
Then when you go away it will not stay.

A box with fire and mist curling from the roof
In it humans stay when the blue disappears,
Then young humans scream from pictures they see.

Danielle Bradley (Age 12)

Listen

Listen to the wind blow
First fast and then slow
Listen to the sound of the sea
The waves rushing wild and free

Listen to the rain falling fast
And now the sun shines through at last
Listen to the stars in the night
So far away yet shining so bright

Silence has many sounds
Listen to life all around
Up to the heavens and down to the ground
Listen carefully and hear the sound

Listen to sadness and to pain
Listen to happiness and smile again
Listen to the night when it becomes morning
Listen to the beautiful dawning

Ediz Beyaz (Age 11)

Nannies

Nannies Nannies who likes them
Fat or slim or like a stem
In front of the TV with popcorn
Crunch Crunch Crunch
They go to bingo every night
Hoping to win cash or food
Nannies Nannies everywhere
Nannies Nannies in my hair
In the car with the radio on
Bang Bang Bang

Gary Barton (Age 11)

Hamster

A strange little thing
It's different in a way
Smaller than a dog
A big cage for a small thing
A tiny weeny fur ball

Laura Best (Age 11)

Boxers

B oxers are cuddly and they're cute
O ver the waves they jump,
X citing
E very time he wiggles that tail
R unning after a snail,
S plat! the snails dead ... poor thing!

Oh well .... that's Boxers!

Kimberley Buck (Age 11)

Leanne

She sits drawing, a quick sketch in five-minute break
before we hit the books again.
The pencil traces a line like a snake across the page
a white desert of endless flats,
from which a figure emerges.
She sits, and swirls the pencil slowly, with intent, deep in thought.
Her eyes, a soft, blue-grey are fixed on a point, close, near,
and yet her thoughts stretch a million miles away, up, with the
stars in the night sky.
A few final strokes and she sits back, smiles; satisfied.
She has finished what I can see to be
her thoughts on the day behind us.

Martin Baker (Age 14)

The Hole

There's a hole in the ceiling
Where the rain comes through
But on a sunny day
You get a good view
If someone came and mended it
That would be the end of it

Marc Barber (Age 17)

The Making Of The Ocean

The trickle of the stream in the dark dense forest
Runs down and around through the brown undergrowth
Collecting and building into a river with a flow,
A current and character

Still growing, digging away at the loose earth of the bank
Eating it away chunk by chunk taking it in its grasp
Reaching out like its hungry for more
Whisking it down and out of sight into the murky depths

Building bigger, wider and longer
The river refusing to stop, pours over the edge
Plunging down and away down to the river below
Beginning its quest to the ocean
Down round and finally fresh sea water hits

The trickle of a stream
The roar of the ocean

David Ball (Age 14)

The Vampire

A dark cloud passes overhead
Flashes of black and red
He passes over hills and mountains, searching

He approaches a small village
Slowly he enters
His mouth and hands are full of needles.

He leaps onto a window ledge
His eyes light up with joy
For in the room fast asleep is a little boy

His body seeps through the window
Like water would through paper
He creeps up to his bedside, mouth open, danger

He leans over him, his prey
Then as he reaches his neck
A light appears in the hall
He slinks away into the night
Cloak, claws, teeth and all

Sarah Brackpool (Age 14)

My Ant

I once had an ant which was very shiny,
He was so small,
I called him tiny,
He followed me around,
He fell to the ground,
He made a very little sound,
I fed him some ivy,
He got a bit lively,
He began to walk around,
He walked up my cup,
Onto the rim,
He toppled over,
He fell in,
Tiny swam around,
And he slowly drowned.

Robert Brown (Age 10)

All Around Us

Roses are red
Violets are blue
Flowers awake
So do you
Lavender, lavender bumble bee

Daffodils open
And bushes too
Snow is melting
Life is sprouting
Lavender, lavender bumble bee

Beth Berry (Age 6)

The Days Of The Week

Monday is money day
Tuesday is choosing day
Wednesday is Wedding day
Thursday is good-turn day
Friday is frying day
Saturday is natter day
Sunday is run day

Alex Bennett (Age 9½)

Winter

Winter is cold.
Snow comes down.
Some leaves get frosty on the trees.
When it's cold your fingers start to hurt.
When it's snowy
You can make a snowman
Snow is cold on your hands.
All the grass is white.

Lauren Blomfield (Age 6)

I Want A Puppy

I want a puppy that's playful
And gives joyful barks
Not sad, like a bleating sheep
On a busy farm.

I want a puppy to care for
To feed, that I can take to the
Park at the end of a lead

I want a puppy who will be my
Best friend and stay with me
To the bitter end.

But I won't wait any longer
I want one . . .
NOW!

Natasha Bass (Age 9)

I Know A Kangaroo

I know a kangaroo, a cuddly kangaroo.
He goes over the top with enthusiasm,
He gets extremely excited over the tiniest things.
He can then get some what confusing.
I call him 'Sir'.

I know a kangaroo, a musical kangaroo.
He bounces impetuously from idea to idea,
He tends to go a bit crazy.
He is quite small but still powerful.
I call him 'Sir'.

I know a kangaroo, a bouncy kangaroo.
He is sometimes exceedingly busy,
He is often rather frantic,
He is always unbearably enthusiastic!
I call him 'Teacher'.

Susannah Bedford (Age 12)

Paper Dart

Twisting, turning
In the air
Flying like a bird
Jumping, soaring
Lower lower
Down it goes
Gliding, swirling
Skimming the ground
Stopping!
Finally Stopped!!!

William Cathcart (Age 9)

Stars And Moons

I like the stars that shine every night
I like the moon that smiles and laughs

But

I like the dark, beautiful sky

Chloé Brunsdon (Age 8)

A Sad Moment

A sad moment is like looking at a photograph
of your family when they're dead
A sad moment is when your mum and your dad
are rowing and you're hoping they won't split up
A sad moment is when you're burying your hamster
in your back garden
A sad moment is when you're crying in bed and your mum
and dad has split up and you're crying for your mum to come back

Danny Bryson (Age 8)

Hope

Hope is pink,
It smells like perfume,
It tastes like ice-cream,
It sounds like sweet music,
It feels fluffy,
Hope lives with the angels.

Gemma Bradley (Age 9)

Harry Hedgehog

I'm Harry the hedgehog
Who lives in the lane
I love eating worms and bugs and snails
I have two sisters and one big brother
They love me so much, as much as my mother
There used to be six of us but now there are five
'Cos our father got killed while crossing the road

Zoe Batt (Age 8)

Dogs

Daring dogs,
Only dogs,
Gentle dogs,
Smelly dogs.

Laura Bailey (Age 9)

Footballers

There are hundreds of footballers around,
God knows where they are found.
Many of whom become a star,
And fame for them spreads afar.
Some earn more than ten thousand pound,
Just for kicking a ball around!
Like Gazza he's a God, he should be picked by Hod.
Or Andy Cole,
You can bet he'll put a hole in the back of the net!
And Beckham clearly the best,
He's one step better than the rest,
Or even Ginola . . . ., no, he always falls over.
But top of the tower,
Young Michael Owen, he's full of power,
His staggering runs, trouble even the big guns,
Like Stam and Keane, and to think he's only eighteen!
The future sure does look bright,
We'll give any country a fight,
If only the FA would keepout of scandal,
And only stick their noses into things they can handle!

Steve Bennett (Age 13)

Black Mamba

B ig and Beautiful
L ong and thin
A lways a danger
C oloured and marked
K ing of the snakes

M ighty and big
A s tall as could be
M aneater I fear
B ecause it is deadly as could be
A ustralia is where we can be found.

Benjamin Barker (Age 10¾)

Channel Hopping

"And they're winning 2-1"
"Bang goes the gun."
"And Henman's just won"
"He's got a hole in one."
"Here's one I made earlier."
"There's an outbreak of pneumonia"
"And we'll be singing three lions on the shirt"
"There's been a crash."
"Game, set, match."
"He's won it with a smash!"

Edmund Barter (Age 9)

Diamante

Day
Colourful, bright
Joyful, rushing, playful
Flowers, grass - black, calm
Shady, creepy, ghostly,
Gloomy, sleeping
Night

Zoe Banfield (Age 9)

Speed Freaks

The red car and the blue car had a race
All Red wants to do is stuff his face
It's so magically clean,
It's just like a dream
So smart old Blue
Did take the Milky Way
It's so chocolaty
With cream
That's just supreme!
So smart old Blue did take the Milky Way
Oh no the bridge is out,
Tell Red, he'd better look out ....
"Oh no! too late!"
That's why smart old Blue did take the
Milky Way.

Edward Bromilow (Age 9)

Fireworks

Fireworks are loud
And noisy.

Fireworks are big, beautiful,
And colourful.

Fireworks are fun
To have.

Fireworks are like,
Twirling flowers in the sky.

Fireworks are fun
To watch.

Fireworks are big sparks flying
And BIG explosions.

Emma Bartlett (Age 8)

Children's Chant

Working class
Noisy class
Clever class
Best class
Oh fun giver
Oh fun taker
What have you in store
For a bored child today?

Working class
Noisy class
Clever class
Best class
Oh fun giver
Oh fun taker
What have you in store
For a bored child today?

From my seat
I cast news
Of why my brother has the flu
Oh our class
I hope he is better
With colour in his cheeks
Oh our class

James Burgess (Age 9)

Black & White

Why can't black and white get along?
Why can't they both learn the song,
Of love, friendship, peace and trust,
Before they turn the world to dust.

They both know that they should be friends,
And about the wars which will never end.
The racist comments and deaths on the news,
The grief, the pain and the bad moods.

People need to have their say,
But not in this unnecessary way.
I may be young but I know what's what -
Some think it's funny, when I know that it's not.

Polly Bennett (Age 12)

In The Gloomy Forest

My horses hoofs stopped galloping
As I approached a derelict forest
I heard a twig break
Far off in the distance
I dare not step down from my horse
For I do not know who will be waiting there
My horse took a step back
And another and another
I drew my sword
At that second
And stepped off
But my horse ran off with fright.

David Barker (Age 10)

Loneliness

I'm tired I'm tired so very tired,
No-one to care,
I'm going on top of this world,
Sleepy but endless,
Sad and unhappy,
Don't know what to do.

Oh feeling like a cry baby,
Without a sigh don't feel wanted,
Don't feel wanted,
Oh I'm feeling sleepy,
But somewhere in these bones
I'm not so tired.

Matthew Bills (Age 8)

Blue

Blue blue I like blue
Blue is the colour
Of the sea and
The sky too
I love Blue

Rachel Bridle (Age 9)

Children's Revenge

My teacher is Mr. Arnold
He is ugly and old
Sometimes he breaths smoke
But he likes a joke
I will not be surprised the day he turns scaly and green
He is mean
He has a sharp tongue
To pierce your lung
He has high expectations
Like a cruel nation
He is very bold
But he is also going bald
He was born in hell
And grew up in a well
He is very kind but
He has two minds

I want a truce

Stephen Bailey (Age 10)

Foggy Morning Poem

One foggy misty, damp morning
In the garden very dark
It was so foggy
Damp and dark and unclear
You cannot see anything
And so misty as well
And gloomy it was so damp hard to see.

Sara Barry (Age 9)

Cat In The School Grounds

Cat in the school grounds,
Why is he there?
Running around, fur in the air
Jenny is sneezing, what a to do
Follow him now he's in the loo!
Gone through the window, in through the door,
Back in the playground he's having a tour!
We've cornered him now he won't run away
Robert and Zoe stop that, and hey!
He's in the classroom near the paints
On the toys, squashing the saints!
Where is he going? I don't know
Well start following go go go!
The headmaster, children caretaker too,
All head for this poor cat hullabaloo!
He's off at a run and speeding away
Out of the school grounds, gone for today.

Caroline Brown (Age 10)

Witchy Words

Witches, witches in the air,
Cat on broom and bright green hair.
Hat on head and crooked nose,
Bats are flying but no one knows,
Of the frightening things that make you shiver,
Make you shake, scream and quiver.

Petrified children run around,
As the witch lands on the ground.
Bewitching things start to happen,
As the witch stirs up a potion.
Frogs are jumping in the air,
Jumping so high they'll give you a scare.

Black magic forms and curses curse,
A black witch is definitely worse,
Than any goblin that makes you stutter,
Or a spell making wizard that makes you mutter.
Witches, witches in the air,
Be careful or they'll give you a scare.

Lucy Beedie (Age 12)

A Hamster

A wood nibbler
A cat hater
A day sleeper
A person biter
A bar chewer
A fast runner

Lewis Betty (Age 10)

Fireworks

Fireworks are bright and beautiful
You think nothing happens then BANG!

Fireworks are entertaining,
You look around and watch people DAZZLE!

Fireworks are fascinating,
You see people gaze and select their FAVOURITE!

Fireworks are colourful,
Like an illustration that's just SMASHED!

Fireworks are like an explosion,
Some ENORMOUS - Some SMALL.

Fireworks are fast,
Like they're having a race and then
　　　FALL
　　　　D
　　　　　O
　　　　　　W
　　　　　　　N

Sarah Burge (Age 8)

Spider

A drain-climber
A fly-eater
A web-maker
A sticky-creature
A long-hanger
A corner-dweller
A loft-finder
An incy-wincer

Joshua Beazley (Age 10)

Down In The Park

Down in the park where the green grass grows,
There lives a monster with a big brown nose,
It's slimy and green and slides sideways,
It wriggles and tosses, shouts and neighs.

Down in the park where the green grass grows,
There lives a monster with a big brown nose,
It's long bony arms grasp, clasp and clutch,
It's long bony arms catch too much.

Down in the park where the green grass grows,
There lives a monster with a big brown nose,
It rips down the fences and shouts nonsense words,
Everything scatters, even ducks and birds.

Down in the park where the green grass grows,
There lives a monster with a big brown nose,
There's a Paignton Zoo van, what's that doing here?
They're catching the monster!
They're getting pretty near . . . . !

Phoebe Blades (Age 10)

Haiku

Food

I ate my pudding up
And my dinner meal
But not my vegetables

Jason Bell (Age 10)

If You Want To See a Tiger

If you want to see a tiger
You must go down to the
Federation jungle in Russia.

I know a tiger who's living down there
He's creepy, he's swift,
He's strong, he's sly.

Yes if you really want to see a tiger
You must go to the
Federation jungle in Russia.

Go down to the long grass and
Say Oh handsome, Oh charming
Oh fierce, Oh strong, Oh wonderful
Oh King, Oh powerful

And out he will prowl but
Don't stick around RUN, RUN!
RUN AND CLIMB UP THE BIGGEST
TREE YOU CAN SEE!

Matthew Barrett (Age 8)

Science

Science is a dangerous job
Full of weird bits and bobs

A flaming splint got caught on
Martin's pants, yep he's gone.

Acid and iodine do not mix
Someone found that out Amy Pix

Methanol is always a danger
Near a flame 'bang' you're a stranger

Anthony Mcdoel was near a flame
And the colour black he became

So science needs beware
You're in for a scare!

Just remind yourself of my class
And you won't pay for the broken glass

Kayleigh Buckling (Age 12)

Autumn

Leaves floating to the ground
A bed of green, orange red and brown
Crunching through the soft, wet ground
With damp shoes.
Looking up into the sky,
And high, high up there are clouds like
The stuffing of pillows.
The wind is blowing very hard,
Oh no the wind has blown the old man's hat off.
Wrap up warm it's a very cold day.
On goes the coat, on goes the gloves,
On goes the hat and on goes the scarf.
Throwing leaves up in the air,
Landing on people's hair.
Going on a walk and watching squirrels,
Getting ready to hibernate for the winter,
It's time to go home now
Crunch, crunch, crunch through the leaves.

Alice Blackwell (Age 9)

Earth And Moon

The earth is quite flat,
And very bright and colourful.
It is so crowded,
We have a lot of water.
Our sea is very polluted,
With a lot of oil.
The earth is green, blue, white and brown.

The moon is very bumpy,
And very quiet.
It is cratered,
There are mountains on the moon.
The men bounce up and down instead of walking,
The moon is orange, grey, black and a little brown.

Rachael Burch (Age 10)

Foggy Morning Poem

It's a foggy morning today
I feel miserable today
It's like a swirly pattern
Fog, fog, fog, fog, fog, fog.
I feel very unhappy today
It looks magical
Fog, fog, fog, fog, fog, fog.
It's damp and gloomy
It looks cloudy
All the world is covered with fog
Fog, fog, fog, fog, fog, fog.

Kayleigh Louise Brown (Age 8)

The Dark

A dark blanket of silk
Creeping and wrapping around people,
Silently and quietly.
Tucking children into bed,
Keeping them warm.

A dark blanket of silk
Tip-toeing across the floor.
Covering everything in sight.
Watching children sleeping,
In their dreams the dark blanket,
Smiles at them slowly.

Janine Bolitho (Age 10)

My Pet

My pet is a cat
He's a little bit fat his
Name is Sammy he's
A little bit funny
He's got a fury tail that
Looks like a fork
And makes it look very
Short he lies on
His back with
His paws in the air he
Also has black and
White hair

Emma Blackman (Age 9)

The River

Flowing like a motorway
Splashing over rocks,
Riding to the deep blue sea,
Flowing over rocks.

Look, it's the sea!
Go faster go faster,
Hit the sea like a stone
We've made it let's rest.

Christopher Bradshaw (Age 10)

The Burning Flame

A candle is a burning delicacy swaying with
The rhythm of the wind.
A fit athlete,
A beaming burden of light
It's wax is a gentle waterfall
A dripping tap of silver moonlight.
Its flame is a burning scintillating star
Floating in the starlit midnight
It is the root of the world
Guiding people in the dark and magic
Hours of the night
Every four years leading swarms of Olympic stars
Its beauty reigns over all wonderful things
Standing tall and erect over the world

Helen Burn (Age 11)

My Broken Knee

I was running all around.
Then I fell onto the ground.
I screamed in pain and agony
Someone said, "have you hurt your knee?"
Slowly I limped inside.
"It really hurts" I cried,
In hospital I had an X-ray.
"It's broken" they said, "You can't go out to play",
I had a bandage and a crutch.
A wet plaster that was yucky to touch.
My knee will take six weeks to mend
I can't do P.E. because my leg won't bend.
I was in lots and lots of pain.
By Christmas it will be better again.

Melanie Babbage (Age 9)

Fireworks

Fireworks are fast,
Whizzing through the sky.

Fireworks are bright,
Glittering blue and red.

Fireworks are diamonds,
Sparkling in the sky.

Fireworks are swirling stars,
Glittering in the dark.

Fireworks are very loud,
As they zig-zag in the dark.

Fireworks are great!

Harriet Bryant (Age 8)

My Family

My Daddy is a bear
Because he is very tall,
My mummy is a butterfly
Because she flies around the house
Cleaning the house
I am a monkey
Because I jump around a lot
And my brother is a fox
Because he grasses a lot
I like my animal family

Christina Betts (Age 8)

Alliteration

(P)
A panda called
Polly has a pink
pig's head.

(T)
Tom's teddy
tickled toes
on Tuesday.

(E)
Edward's egg
has
enormous eyes.

(S)
Seven silly
sausages saw a
sticky snake.

Sophie Bright (Age 9)

Fear

Fear is like when you're sure you've done something but it hasn't been done.
Fear is like when you're in bed and everyone else is asleep and you hear the tap dripping.
Fear is when you think someone's down stairs and you see shadows.
Fear is when the lights flicker on their own.
Fear is when the phone rings and you pick it up and there's no-one on the line.
Fear is like when you're lost in a huge supermarket.
Fear is when someone's in hospital and came back from the dead.
Fear is rain tapping on the window in the pitch black night in bed.
Fear is when you think aeroplanes lights at night are UFO's.
Fear is like walking around a graveyard on your own.
Fear is like being buried alive.

Scott Bryson (Age 9)

Night

Night . . . . .
Is approaching
A big silky sheet that conceals the sun and clouds
Owls hooting
Foxes rummaging through dustbins
Silent trees
Sinister cats shuffle from pavement to pavement
Lights switch on
The moon shines like an enormous ball of electricity
And glows like a luminous glow worm
Thick misty clouds travel around the moon
Stars sparkle and twinkle in the sky like glitter
Some stars shoot across the sky in rainbow colours
The moon fades away
The silky sheet gradually disappears
The sun comes out, it is dawn
People get up ready to go to work
The lights turn off, it's a brand new day.

Charlene Louise Bettis (Age 10)

My Garden

At the back of the house
I have a garden
Which is as small as a child's toy
The swing has snapped
The trees are all gone
In the ragged old place at the back

The blustering bushes
In the back of the yard
Making a tremendous sound
The whispering wind
And the crying hound
All of these sounds
In the ragged old place at the back

Alex Bulman (Age 8)

A Foggy Morning

One foggy morning,
I woke up with a fright,
It was dark, cold and miserable,
Creepy, soggy and wet,
I yawned a big yawn and
Then got out of bed,
Looked out of the window,
It was icy outside and raining
Dark, no-one up yet
Yet it felt like someone was watching me
The grass was wet and frozen.

Amy Bills (Age 8)

Sunflowers

Sunflowers, sunflowers,
All year round
Never could be found
In USA or Francisco Bay
But there is a place
Where you might find
Some Sunflowers
In the sun.

Hannah Blacklaw (Age 8 ½)

Twister

A big black object
Spinning around and around
Taking everything!

It took their life,
Their home,
Their children, everything
Then went just as easy!

Chris Bamber (Age 11)

War Poem

Men line up to join the war
Some think it will be great
But when they get there
Terror and shock run through their mind
As they see men drop to the floor

The men go on fighting
Until the bitter end
When all hope is lost
The soldiers begin to retreat
With bodies laid upon the ground

Men fight within the barracks
As bullets and bombs
Are fired towards them
Men lay upon the ground
But have died with pride

As the few that survive trudge home
They are greeted with many celebrations
Yet to know that in a few years
They will have to trudge back
To the place where friends have died

Michael Bond (Age 11)

Bombay's Transportation

Swaying trains slither along,
A silky snake.
Buses clatter like a brake-less bike,
Down a bumpy track.
Wasp striped taxis squeal.
Roads weave in and out,
Like a dusty maze.
Boats bob up and down,
In a never-ending nod.

Joe Barnes (Age 10)

My Monster Poem

His hair is like a stiff old broom
His mouth is as dark as a damp old room
His ears are the size of a black hole
His nose is made of mole holes
His tongue is like a rattlesnakes
His teeth are stuck in the things he bakes
His breath is as bad as gone off food
His eyes are small and crude
His hands are as big as buses
His claws are as dirty as rusty crushes
His chest is as hairy as his knees
Not something you would like to squeeze
His skin is as rough as a rusty chain
You don't want to see the likes of him again

Steven Burton (Age 11)

34

The Swamp

Slurpy, slushy, steamy swamp.
Why do you make yourself so sinister
With your powerful embrace?
Why do you look as if you want
To swallow me whole?
Why are you there?
Do you maybe hide a secret?

You have slimy green lilly pads
Floating on your surface.
Are they your eyes?
I ask myself,
How many bodies do you hold?
I ask myself these things,
But I may never know.

Roxane Bradley (Age 10)

Safety Fireworks

Do not put fireworks in your pocket!
Burn your pocket!

Do not light a not gone off firework that did not work!
Sizzle your face like a sausage!

Do not take a pet!
Scare them to death!

Do not hold sparklers!
Without child gloves!

Do not make a bonfire!
Without checking for hedgehogs!
"Ou, ouch, my tiny feet!"

Holly Bull (Age 8)

A Baby

Like an unknown tale,
Like a ship that hasn't sailed,
Like a bird that hasn't flown,
A baby...

Like a rainbow that isn't seen,
Like a fish that hasn't swum,
Like a cat that hasn't scratched,
A baby...

Like a dog that hasn't barked,
Like an unwritten novel,
Like a new life,
A baby.

Joseph Buckley (Age 14)

Splash!

On a rainy day
On a really rainy day
On a really, really rainy day....
There's nothing better than
Putting on my wellies and
Splashing
Jumping
Kicking
Floating
Sploshing
In the rain
Yippee.

April Bennett (Age 7)

Wild Animals

Animals are fun, animals are sweet
Some I would really like to meet
Some as cute as small seals
But some of the sweetest are for meals
Tigers are out at night
With bats and cats give you a fright
Frogs and toads
Go hopping on the roads
Dogs give barks
With singing larks
Fast whales racing
Against slow snails
Cats miaow
Waiting, saying wow wow
Panthers blink
While prey is wanted by the minks
Some of the animals are pets
Some they go to the vets
But only when they're ill
Then YOU go home with a bill!

Erin Biss (Age 10)

My Dad

My Dad and I
Are very much alike
He likes discos and night life so do I

My Dad and I
We both go on holiday
We both swim together

My Dad and I
Love McDonalds
He and I pick the same things

My Dad and I
Hate watching football,
But, love playing it

My Dad and I
Always agree with each other
Even though we don't always know it

My Dad and I
Like to watch "Tom and Jerry" together
We like to watch films together too

My Dad and I are not always alike
He hates hair gel and my short hair
But I hate spicy food which he loves

Emily Byland (Age 10)

What Is Colour

Red -The colour of a wounded man
Blood dripping from his arm

Orange -The colour of a juicy fruit
So sweet, succulent and refreshing

Yellow -The colour of a bright star
Shining down on you

Green -The colour of fresh cut grass
With a sweet scent in the morning

Blue -The colour of the sea
So calm and gentle on this summer afternoon

Indigo -The colour of the royal robes
As they enter the hall

Violet -The colour of the small flower
As it glides in the steady wind

Rainbow -The colour of all of these
Put together makes the rainbow

Joshua Bromfield (Age 12)

Phew!

On a hot day
On a really hot day
On a really really hot day
On a really really boiling hot day ...

There is nothing better in the whole world than
Licking a
Lovely
Icey
Cold
Melting
Flakey
Ice cream
Mmmmmmmm.

Jenny Bantick (Age 7)

My Monster

He ate all my friends,
he had three legs,
four teeth,
six noses,
one thousand eyes,
Help!

Joel Blatchford (Age 5)

Pig

How does
a pig cry?
How does
a pig sleep?
How does
a pig smell?

How?

How?

Bethan Barrick (Age 8)

Christmas Is Getting Near

Christmas, Christmas is getting near,
Our favourite time of the year.
Sweets and treats,
And lots of sheets,
To keep us warm at night.

Christmas, Christmas is getting near,
Seeing presents under the tree,
Crackers going bang!
And then it's Christmas Eve.

Christmas is here,
Lets go down stairs,
Open our presents and say,
Hooray!

Rachel Bagshaw (Age 8)

What Is Purple?

Purple's fantastic
Purple's great
Purple's everywhere
Even on the gate

Lucy Charlton (Age 6)

Pigs

Pinky pig
Inky pig
Porky pig
Greedy pig
Fat pig
Sick pig
Aah!

Emily Bannister (Age 8)

Who Is My Best Friend?

Who lives in a big old house?
It has lots and lots of rooms
Who's favourite colour is purple?
Who plays with me?
Who gives me little treats?
And maybe sometimes a big one
I love my best friend
Jessica is her name

Laura Bennett (Age 6)

Winter

The snowman in winter
Is standing in the garden
The floor is cold
Snow drops on the snowman's nose
His nose drops off
The hedgehogs come out
The snowman begins to melt
The children are sad
The children cannot play
The ducks are gone
The pond is ice
The ducks cannot swim
The shops are closed
That's winter

Sam Brown (Age 7)

Rapunzel

Once upon a time, far far away there lived a lovely wife and her husband.
A child was to be born,
The wife ate the witch's lettuces.
The witch took the baby and made it hers,
She put her in a tower with no stairs,
Rapunzel thought nobody cares.
Until a prince appeared having climbed up her hair,
The prince did the same every day for a year,
But there in the tower Rapunzel had to stay.

Harry Babbington (Age 8)

November

No light
No sun
No-one to play
Just on my own all day
November

Jade Blythman (Age 8)

The Magic Box

I will put in the box
A leaping elephant that goes sh sh sh
With his big long trunk swooping towards me
With deep blue eyes, like river and rain water.
My box is like a rough piece of paper
With old wrinkly corners.
I will throw my box into a deep rough sea
So no-one can ever wreck it.

Zoe Brace-Day (Age 11)

Fireworks

Fireworks are explosions,
Massive bangs and huge noises.

Fireworks are bright,
Sparkles of light.

Fireworks are dangerous,
They could set you on fire.

Fireworks fly into the sky,
Booming, wooming, wasakazooming!

Fireworks are Catherine Wheels,
They spin round and round.

Tom Burlton (Age 8)

Me!

I'm relaxed,
I'm laid back,
I'm the type who likes to chat,
I'm not exactly skinny,
But then I'm not fat,
But don't look on the outside,
There's more to me than that!

I want to be quite famous,
So that everyone can see,
That I have got some talent,
Beneath what they see as me!

Sam Cunningham (Age 12)

My Monster

He had one big eye,
he had seven legs,
he had two mouths,
he was horrible.

Joshua Bullock (Age 5)

My Walk

I walk across the road
So many different smells
I see lots of flowers
I walk through the
Leaves that have fallen on the ground
Then on my way back home
I hear the birds talking to their friends.

I love my walk.

Holly Brittain (Age 8)

Judgement

You may really think you know someone,
You think you've seen them as they are,
But really you are unaware,
You haven't searched very far.

First impressions cling in your mind,
The way they act all day,
You do not know and have not seen,
They can act in a different way.

You can't judge a person by the colour of their skin,
Nor by their sex, intelligence or religion,
You can't judge a person if they're fat or thin,
Or if they made the wrong decision.

So basically what I am trying to say,
Is don't judge by what you first see,
Make sure you reach deep into their soul.
And see what they really can be.

Eleanor Barnard (Age 14)

First Day Nerves

I couldn't wait to go to school
As I reached the gate
I felt anxious
I felt fidgety
I was petrified waiting for my new teacher
I listened I didn't feel panicky anymore
I felt mature, delighted
I was with my friends again
For a first day it was great
It wasn't as fearful as I expected it to be

Katie Blewett (Age 10)

My Hamster

Butterscotch - my hamster
Best friend?
Maybe!
Sharp teeth,
Carpet nibbler,
Night exerciser,
Four legged sniffer,
Lick my finger when I need comfort,
Hide and seek player,
Dressing-gown-burrower,
Hiding, waiting to find a sleeve to come out of,
Best friend!

Kristina Bassett (Age 9)

Storm

The storm is a cat,
a wild wicked cat,
that sails across the skies.
She howls and purrs and dances wildly,
she stirs up the seas with a single paw,
she shakes her coat to make the winds.
She sails over islands and blows down the trees,
hissing and whistling to call the rain clouds,
crouching and purring and breaking down boats,
clawing and ripping the rocky old beaches,
seeing and sinking the fishermen's boats,
watching the trouble she's caused.
Pouncing on vessels and tossing them up,
crouching and jumping, playing and tossing,
making waves, whirlpools, winds and rain.
Then the storm's over.
She sleeps.

Rebecca Brandon (Age 9)

Bombay Streets

Roads, ever-winding ribbons of vehicles.
Rhino taxis on the rampage;
Pushy, impatient and short tempered.
Noisy serpent trains chug along.
Vine pylons tangle in and out.
Ant-like people mingle;
Dodging everywhere.
Bungalows share their hollow bellow,
The door their mouth;
Blinking windows either side their eyes.

Victoria Basham (Age 9)

Day Falls In To Night

SLOWLY, you walk down to the Fair,
SLOWLY, old age rocks in his chair,
SLOWLY, the boy falls to sleep,
SLOWLY, the man shears his sheep.

SLOWLY, I correct my sums so they're right,
SLOWLY, day falls in to night,
SLOWLY, your car rounds the bend,
SLOWLY, this poem comes to its end.

Matthew Bates (Age 10)

The Conker Poem

The trees blowing round and round,
Trees swaying, the leaves are falling in the sun,
The trees rocking as they sway,
Trees chasing beneath the sun.

The leaves are rushing then they're crushing,
The leaves are brown, red and yellow,
Crunching leaves falling to the meadow,
Delicate leaves falling from the sky.

The conkers fall to the ground,
Conkers smashing, others crashing,
Shiny conkers smooth and round,
But then they go all dark and dull.

The conker shell is green and spikey,
Hard on the outside, soft inside,
The case inside is like a silky bed,
The shell is prickly like a pin.

Smashing conkers as people play,
Swaying pendulum through the wind,
Some are playing, some are thrashing,
I flick my conker and crack another.

Sophie Anne Beecroft (Age 11)

A Bombay Day

In the east the giant sunflower sun rises . . .
An explosion of colour.
Spider taxis scuttle along the road,
Scaly as a lizards back.
Ant-like people take their morning walks.
In the town the snake train slithers by,
Weaving in and out.
In the west the giant Grape-fruit sun sets...
An explosion of colour.

Ceri Broussine (Age 10)

A Cat

My cat is as fat as a rhinoceros
And his breath smells of rotten oranges
And his cat food smells
His claws are very sharp
His legs are as thick as rope
He is as fat as an elephant
His nose is as red as tomatoes
He leaps like a Jaguar
He slurps his milk like a naughty school boy

Emma Bunton (Age 7)

Winter In Icing

A cake of winter,
So real you can see it move.
The icing setting on chocolate,
Like snow setting in muddy puddles.
And in the chocolate covered fields
Silvery threads between the sugar gate,
Like a spider webbing with his shiny string.
Children impatient to ice their cakes,
Like the busy drivers
Impatient to get to work.
Icing pond with plastic ducks,
Like models of dinosaurs in a museum.
On our cake there are whipped-up blizzards of icing,
Overpowering winter.
In reality small snow droplets
Have melted in the sun's radiance.
Boxing Day,
All is quiet,
No children playing or grown-ups shouting,
The cake has been eaten!

Philip Burley (Age 11)

Pollution

Pollution is so very bad,
I am so, very mad,
Put that litter in the bin,
You stupid kid,
You should be sinned.

The journey to work
Would be cleaner;
Use your bike,
And you'd be leaner,
No rev's, no gas,
Just a person walking past.

Bottles, cans and paper,
Don't just bin it,
Use your nature,
Then it would be a better place,
With a lot less waste.

Neil Buller (Age 13)

Summer

Sky as bright as the sea
Sea as bright as the sand
Sea - swish, swash

Bobbie-Jo Bremner (Age 8)

The Old Deserted House

There it is, just standing,
Standing there in the moonlight,
Moonlight drifting down,
To the old deserted house.

Not a sound to be heard,
Nothing stirred,
Silence surrounded,
The old deserted house.

Cobwebs, cobwebs, all around the walls,
In every little corner, of the deserted house.
Nests, old nests, each one empty,
Not even an egg, in the old deserted house.

Christmas edges nearer,
Snow drifts down peacefully,
Silver frost covers the grass,
All around, the old deserted house.

The windows are silver,
The slated roof has been decorated,
Just for Christmas,
OH! What a gorgeous old deserted house!

Kristina Braund (Age 11)

T-Rex

Watch T-Rex as he treks through
The dinosaur county causing havoc
And a terrible distress!

When he eats dino meat he makes
A terrible disgusting mess,
Causing every dinosaur to get
Into a stress

With killer jaws and thundering roars
As he rampages through the land
Eating raptors as his first course!

A little bit more stegosaurs,
As he fights with brontosaurs
Eating more and more
It's T-Rex

Frazer Considine (Age 13)

My Mum

My mum is a volcano
Lather spilling out
She screams like the world is dying
Covering the house with her warm glow
She is the noisiest volcano
You know when she is going to erupt
She is the hot water tap fuming to spill

Melissa Bollen (Age 11)

Millennium

Millenium, Millennium -
Next year it's 2000
We're having a party here at my house
With fireworks and lots of fun!

Millennium, Millenium -
I'm 10 but nearly 11
Next year it is Secondary School
With all those big high halls.

Millennium, Millennium -
We're saving up for our holiday
My mum's started buying economy!
And it's yuck, yuck, yuck.

Millennium, Millennium -
Will it be a disaster?
Will all the lights go out and computers crash on us?

Millennium, Millennium -
I'm lucky to be in one
Because I doubt it very very much I'll be in another

Sarah Burton (Age 10)

What Is In My Box

Is it a sparkly crystal
Or is it a golden horse
Kick it jump on it
Shake it up and down
Move it about
Oh! it's a mouse

Clarissa Chay (Age 5½)

No Mans Land

WAR!!!
War is horrible sad and
lonely.
The one and only
War is bad.
Lots of people dead.

PEACE
Peace is lovely
Like champagne,
Nice and bubbly.
No more sad,
No more lonely.

Ryan Backhouse (Age 12)

Autumn Leaves

Autumn leaves golden brown
Falling softly to the ground
Bare trees
No leaves
They've all floated to the ground
Winter is coming but autumn is still here
They both come once a year
Along with summer and spring
They all take turns in the ring

Katie Berrington (Age 7)

If Copper Was ....
Dedicated to my Welsh Springer Spaniel "Copper"

If Copper was a colour, orange he'd be
He's zippy and tangy and very juicy!
Like the fruit he is bursting with goodness and fun
And refreshing to see when my school day is done

If Copper was transport, a sports car he'd be
Forever in front, sleek, fast, at top speed
His face in the wind, his nose in the air
His ears flying high, he hasn't a care

If Copper was a hero, himself he would be
Because he's my puppy dog and very special to me
When I call he comes running as fast as he can
He just seems to know I'm his number one fan

If Copper was a drink, champagne he would be
He is fizzy and bubbly and always happy
When I come to the door, he sits 'till I'm in
Then pop, like a cork, we create such a din!

If Copper wasn't Copper, a bird he would be
Flying and swooping, just happy to be free
Yet when the night came, he would look for a nest
Somewhere warm, safe and cosy, my home would be best!

Elizabeth Barratt (Age 12)

I Can

I can cuddle,
Climb the stairs,
Stamp in a puddle
And eat a pear.

I can swim
Dress up as a fairy,
Tie a knot
And read a lot.

Tiggy Claydon (Age 5)

Parts Of My Body

I use my head to think,
I use my eyes to see,
I use my mouth to speak and taste,
I use my nose to smell sweet and horrid smells,
I use my ears to hear loud and soft sounds,
I use my hands to feel hard and soft, rough and smooth materials,
I use my feet to walk about,
And holding all these parts together is my body.

Sarah Bolton (Age 7)

Shopping On Saturday

"Come on Ellie its time to go"
"Go where" I shout
"You know where we always go"
"Oh yeah I know"
Down the town to the shops
Shopping, shopping until we drop
Carry this carry that
Do you think I match this hat
But what about me my cupboards bare
But of course she doesn't care
She's on her high horse
She's racing the town
She puts on make-up and looks like a clown
Time to go home she says in sorrow
But it doesn't matter there's always tomorrow.

Eleanor Checkley (Age 11)

Night

Asleep, dark,
Quiet, soundless, bed,
Moonlight, stars, alive, light,
Noisy, shouting, awake,
Sun, clouds

Day

Marie Clements (Age 9)

My Eyes Are.....

My eyes are black, white, green and blue.
Blue as the summer sky with the sun rising.
Blue as the salty water that I can see my reflection in.
Green as the grass stains on my football shorts.
Green as the icy green lollipop.
Black as my shiny cat's fur when she licks herself.
White as milk from a carton.
White as a polar bear rolling in the cold ice.

Josh Bragg (Age 7)

Easter Bunny

I saw an Easter Bunny
Knocking on my door.
The Easter Bunny hides the eggs.
What did I see?
Bunnies, bunnies.
I love bunnies.
I found the eggs
In my bed.

Nicola Cook (Age 6)

The Beginning Of The End

Slowly, step by step she neared the light
What had gone before was meaningless
The pain, the regrets, the sorrow, all gone
Suddenly things were in perspective
Death stood watching above and around
She feared
She knew
That for her this was the Beginning of the End

The hazy tunnel spun violently
Light flashing, beams of rainbow colours
Hold on, reach out, stay strong, won't be long
Faster and faster her heart did beat
Standing there frightened she knew nothing
She screamed
She froze
She finally knew that for her this was the end

Zoe Clarke (Age 15)

Toffee Apples And Sweets

Lights very bright and music loud,
Fun packed fun for everyone!
Lots of rides to go on,
First day stalls with lots of toys and sweets.
I couldn't believe my eyes! There were lights everywhere . .
Win lots of toys on the stalls,
Go on rides and have lots of fun,
Lots of rides for everyone!
There's a spinning wheel and a whirly woo,
Lots of fun for me and you.
I love the rides, I love the sweets,
But most of all I love the beats.
My mind kept saying you're having fun with everyone.
Everyone is happy, everyone is glad,
They're going on the bumper cars with lots of candy bars.
Toffee apples and lots of sweets, I like the bumper beats!
The bumper cars are noisy, the bumper cars crash!
But most of all I like the bumper bash!
The bash of the cars make me shiver,
The last of the cars make me slither!!

Alice Colligan (Age 7)

Rainbow Poem

Red is for a crafty fox all fluffy with sharp teeth
Orange is for oranges all juicy and round
Yellow is for daffodils bursting from the ground
Green is for pears all furry and ripe
Blue is for rain drops dripping from the sky into deep puddles
Indigo is for paintings on the walls making pretty patterns
Violet is for scented flowers growing bigger and bigger
But my favourite is silver because
I like watching dolphins diving into deep clear water

Madelaine Crossley (Age 6)

Phew!

On a cold day
On a really cold day
On a really really cold day
On a really really blistery cold day

There is nothing better than
Sitting by the hot crackling
Red, orange warm nice fire.

James Crocker (Age 7)

My African Adventure

Monkeys scratching
Crocodiles hatching

Lions roaring
Buffalo snorting

Hippo yawning
Sunny morning

Roads are bumpy
Cars are lumpy

Cheetahs are running
Leopards are sunning

Hot and dusty
Dry and crusty

Arabella Coggins (Age 5)

Holiday

When I went on holiday,
I had a lot of fun,
We went to the beach,
And had a lolly each,
I was a disco diva,
And then I caught a fever,
I stayed in bed all day,
And couldn't come to play,
I swam in the sea,
And forgot about my tea,
We had chips and fish,
A very nice dish,
I had a nice balloon,
It was taken by a baboon,
I sunbathed by the pool,
The boys thought that was cool,
I went to the fair,
And won a teddy bear,
That was my holiday,
Can I go again?

Rebecca Chaffey (Age 10)

Feelings

The texture of birdsong
Is sweet and cheerful
The sound of perfume
Is like roses being crushed

The taste of fear is like
Someone stabbing you in the back
The feel of darkness is
Like a black cloud swooping over you ·

The taste of dawn is
Dry and distasteful
The taste of air is
Breathless but calm

Faye Cramer (Age 12)

When I Grow Up

One day in the summer holidays, my dad came up to me
And asked me what I want to read at university.
I answered "books" he gave a sigh, put down his coffee cup
And told me I should write this list -
What I want to be when I grow up:
A professional musician, an authoress,
A dancer, a poet, a scientist,
A vet, a composer, an actress, a swimmer,
A charity worker, a sweet or toy shop owner,
Rich, famous, happy, generous, loved,
BUT,
Here's my most important thing,
Though for all of the rest I might strive,
When I grow up (if ever), then I'd like to be
Alive!

Judith Christian (Age 12)

Doggy

Doggy, doggy
Why can you fly?

Because I ate a
Baked bean pie.

Why oh why
Did my dog go to school?

Because he wanted
To go in the pool.

Craig Caldicott (Age 9)

I'm A Ray Of Sunshine

I'm a ray of sunshine
Warm and bright
When I'm shining
I look light
I'm a ray of sunshine
Long and light
I can make you
Feel alright

Adam Chaffey (Age 6)

Every Saturday

Every Saturday from August to May
A strange phenomenon
We put on our uniforms for the special day,
We go in cars, coaches and trains,
We travel all over England,
We sing and chant,
And everyone knows the words,
We go with heaps of hope and sometimes even fear,
When ninety minutes later the final whistle blows
We blame the ref,
We blame the ball,
We blame the weather,
We blame the pitch,
If we win we sing,
If we lose we moan,
But one things for sure,
We'll be back for more.

Nick Cooke (Age 12)

Trapped

I was driving in my car,
I wasn't going very far.
I had no clue what was about to happen,
All I heard was a little tapping.
I started to panic, I was scared,
Something like DEATH entered my head.
I felt so dizzy and I felt cold,
I realised my car was no longer on the road.
I knew at this moment I was going to die,
Because I was TRAPPED and no one drove by.
I was there for ages it seemed like years,
Then pain suddenly gave way to tears.
Then flashing lights is what I could see,
The emergency services were here to help me.
They took me to hospital where I wasn't alone,
And where I was warm and not freezing cold.
Now I'm at home and not at the wheel
This poem was done by a boy called Neil

Neil Carpenter (Age 14)

My Maths Lesson

When we had our maths lesson
We sat so very bored
We had to do algebra
Which makes me say "Oh Lord"
Now that algebra's over
We have to do a sum
My friend doesn't want to
His name is Thomas Lunn
The sum we have to work out
Is the square root of 59
I don't like doing sums
Tom says it's fine
Now the lessons over
We pack up and run
I'm glad that we have finished
The lesson wasn't fun

David Casson (Age 11)

My Secret Friend ?

I can hear you calling me
Even though I can't see you, I know you are there
You sit in your secret hiding place
So sweet, so lovely
You never let me down and you've always been there for me
Cheering me up and giving me comfort
When I feel sad
People say you are no good for me
What do they know?
I see you in my dreams and will always need you
You make me what I am
I'm coming for you now wait for me
My secret friend - chocolate

Stephanie Cresswell (Age 11)

First Day At School

"I don't want to go!"
"They Bully me!"
"I've missed the bus!"
None of my excuses work
I still have to go.

When I walk into the classroom
They laugh and jeer at me.
And when they are finally quiet
It is almost time to leave.

The first lesson went quite well
But the second - a nightmare
At last the day has come to an end
And when I get home
Someone asks if I had a good day
I say nothing.

Being a teacher is no fun!

Graham Claxton (Age 14)

This Is My Life

This is my life
How would you feel?
I know its cruel
So leave us all alone

I love my home and my family
So let me live my life to the full

My cubs look up to me
You don't care, you just call it fun

Life only comes once
I intend to complete mine
For all you bullies and murderers
Ending lives, who think it's a sport, it's unnecessary

Lauren Clarke (Age 12)

The Teacher's Scary

This teacher's scary,
She teaches me every day,
She looks at me real starey
In a scary kind of way

I can't be late for school
I don't like this at all
You really feel a fool
She makes you feel so small

The day is nearly done,
She's been nagging me all day
I haven't had much fun
It's 3.05 - HOORAY!

Gemma Childs (Age 11)

Autumn Trees

The wind is blowing,
Through the trees.
I can hear a rustling,
In the leaves.

Light brown, dark brown,
Everything is dead
Next month,
Animals have to go to bed.

The leaves shudder,
In the midnight darkness.
The winter is coming,
Winter is coming.

Jenna Cornwell (Age 9)

There Was A Young Lady From Ickenham

There was a young lady from Ickenham
Who went on a bus-trip to Twickenham
She drank too much beer
Which made her feel queer
So she took off her boots and was
Sick-in-em

Sam Cannell (Age 13)

Nature

Creepy crawly spiders
Wriggling and squirming
Early morning black bird
Busily chirping

Slimy snails slither
Along the leafy path
At the beach the sea worms
Are forming in their casts

Harvest mice all gathering
Enjoying autumn feasts
Some scorpions all stagger,
They're very deadly beasts

The swirling wind is blowing
The birds all gliding by
The butterflies all flutter
Looking lovely in the sky

Anna Cooke (Age 11)

The Bug

The bug breathes acid like a dragon
He is silent as a snake
With teeth like sharks

The Bug's hair is like the angry spikes of a porcupine
He is as fast as a cheetah
And has . . .
An appetite like a huge hog

Andrew Chaplin (Age 8)

Harvest Moon

The harvest moon
In the sky
Just as day begins to die.

It shines so brightly
It glows so great
It really has kept me awake.

Now I'm sad to say
It has to go,
I will really miss
Its bright red glow.

John Cordon (Age 11)

Valentine Sonnet

The day I spotted you, that way you looked,
Your hair so sleek and shining like the sun.
So kind, so sweet, I'm definitely hooked,
My heart does melt with swirls of gentle fun.

I dream of you all through the day and night,
My thoughts of you are strong as tectonite.
Your gentle smile that makes me laugh is bright,
As bright as stars that shine with all their might.

Those eyes I love, look down on me sweetly,
I love your voice, your lips, your gentle kiss.
The love moves fast through our hearts so quickly,
I never knew my life could be such bliss.

With hands and hearts we shall walk together,
The love of our lives will be forever.

Hayley Charlesworth (Age 13)

Mum

My Mum is the colour of a yellow daffodil,
Shining all the time.
My Mum smells like a red rose.
She tastes like a soft caramel.
She sounds like a soft sweet sound of a flute.
My Mum feels like a furry cat.
My Mum lives in my heart.

Samantha Cale (Age 11)

Parents

Parents, aren't they just a pain,
All they say is
Don't do this, don't do that.
Just make sure you put on
Your mack.

Mum can I have this.
No you can't have that.
Why can't I have that,
Ugh that's ugly.
No it's not.
Mum just buy me
The lot.

My parents are awful,
I don't know about yours.
But what I do know is,
I can't wait until
I leave home!

Lucy Collins (Age 11)

Hail

The frozen leaves are icy white,
The sky hard as stone,
The hail is thundering down now,
Noisy, as you sleep.

The cold wind, the east wind,
Running through the night,
Like a ranger on his mega motorbike.

The hail is strong
And heavy as weights,
The hail is invading all my mates.

Serena Skov Campbell (Age 9)

Cleopatra's Needle

Mist lay on the brown water of the Thames
Lazily, the soft, white, vapour
Drifted along the bankside
Suffocating the daisies in its path
No longer does it have the tendrils
Of heat before it
Wind was not in abundance
Nor was the sound of the hooters
Sirens, bells and
Traffic from the city
No longer does the heat beat
Down on the
Head of the daunting point
Of Cleopatra's Needle

Andrew James Clarke (Age 10)

Mystery Man

I'll describe this man as best I can,
His head is like an un-made bed.
Three crossed eyes, like squashed mince pies,
A nose as long as my garden hose.
His mouth it goes from north to south,
When he smiles it goes miles and miles.
His neck, oh heck, don't make me laugh!!
I've seen shorter ones on a giraffe!!
He has muscles on his shoulders, just like great big boulders.
His hands dangle like six frying pans.
His feet, so sweet, oh please, I almost hit his knobbly knees.
He's got a great big belly, that wobbles like jelly.
His skin is green, wet and slimy. Is it catching? Oh cor blimey!!
His hair is greasy, slick and set, oh my gosh it's really wet!
His teeth are green, yellow and mouldy, purple red and goldy
His legs are like eggs, all soft and runny.
When he runs it looks really funny.
Is this a man you could really HATE?
Feel sorry for me, he's my BLIND DATE!!

Victoria Canning (Age 12)

A Fishy Tale

Ginger the cat was hungry
And he had but one wish,
So he strolled down to the river
To catch himself a fish.

But Ginger fell into the water
And he couldn't swim,
He tried to call a lifeguard
But he didn't have his phone with him.

He sunk down to the bottom
Where he found a fishing boat,
He crawled inside a great big hole
And found a ring to help him float.

A friendly whale came passing by
And asked him "Shall I stop,"
He put the cat upon his back
And swam up to the top.

Ginger jumped out of the water
And shook from tail to head,
"That's the last time I go fishing
I'll go to the shop instead."

Stuart Clabby (Age 15)

My New Cat

I have a new cat
He is as naughty as can be
He's tabby and white
And we've named him Sauxy

He hits the dog
And beats up our cat
My mum shouts at him
And calls him a rat

I hope when he's bigger
He will be alright
But all he does now is...
Bite, fight, bite.

Lauri Coleman (Age 12)

Summer

Skies clear
Larks sing
Sun like a hot fire
People gather in town
Leaves nice and flat
Bees buzzing looking for honey
Grass is nice and short
Fruit is juicy
Summer is like a ball of fire

Jeral Cooper (Age 9)

Monster Poem

His eyes are as round as snooker balls
His ears are as hairy as a cat
Up his nose it is so hairy just like a furry mat
His teeth are as sharp as razor blades
His mouth is cooler than being in the shade
His tongue is as long as a rope
His breath smells like a castle moat
His arms are as brown as a big brown bear
His claws can strike faster than an S reg Porsche
His skin is as scaly as a snake
His legs are as thin as a garden rake
And his feet smell like a mouldy cake.

Paul Copping (Age 11)

A Visit To The Zoo

One day I woke up Mum said to me we will go to the zoo today.
So quickly get dressed it is lovely and sunny.
We saw the ostrich with a long neck
We saw the lion roaring in it's cage
We saw the tiger in a roaring rage
We saw the zebra with its stripes
We saw the giraffe trying to reach up
We saw the dingo with its baby pup
We saw the ape swinging around
We saw the mole who lives in a hole.

James Craven (Age 12)

Never Say Goodbye

As I sit in this smoking room, the night about to end.
I pass the time with strangers, but this bottle's my only friend.
Remember when we used to park out above the street out in the dark.
Remember how we used to talk about busting out, we'd break their hearts.

Together - forever - never say goodbye, never say goodbye.

You and me and our old friends, hoping it would never end.
Say goodbye, never say goodbye.
Holding on we've gotten free, holding on to...
Never say goodbye.

Remember days of missing school, racing cars and being cool.
With a six pack and the lads, we didn't need a place to go.
Remember at the Prom that night, you and me we had a fight.
But the band they played our favourite song and I held you in my arms so strong.
We danced so close, we danced so slow and I swore I'd never let you go

Together - forever - never say goodbye, never say goodbye.

You and me and our old friends, hoping it would never end.
Say goodbye, never say goodbye.
Holding on to...
Never say goodbye.

Andrew Clifford (Age 13)

Misery

Obsession grows in me each lonely day
And all this misery does me enrage
The love I cannot own leads me astray
Into this evil, melancholy cage

In lonely, sad, depression I engage
By chains of cruel sadness I am bound
I'm trapped, alone, with feelings wrought with rage
Wherever there is sadness I am found

This misery is looming all around
The anger trapped inside me makes me cry
Then on the stony walls of grief I pound
For all this sorrow makes me want to die

Now, lured here by the love which was my bait
I slowly sink into the pit of hate

Ele Crane (Age 14)

Helping Hands

Green the hands that hold the child,
Protecting until, delicate and soft it emerges
Pink and young and tender.

Red the hands that reach to the sun,
Hiding in their midst the beginning
Of helping hands to come.

Brown the hands that bid farewell,
Giving their life to the future
Leaving hope behind.

Jacqueline Casey (Age 12)

A Storm

It's stormy
This gale is deadly,
The bullets are sharp
They slap on the chipping glass.
I'm staring out of a warm homely place,
To where I will soon be living.
A cracking, and a crash caught my attention
As the back door ripped clean from the rooting hinges
I watched it hurtle, hurriedly down the road and beyond.

The fierce howling stopped
To unveil the havoc and the total destruction,
My house where I would be living,
Tiles, walls and doors lay there,
Lay still and silent in a heap.
I'm not moving now,
I've got nowhere to go.

Joe Casson (Age 13)

The Golden Eagle

The golden eagle in its forest,
It's sitting on a branch.
It swoops out of the tree,
Its powerful wings brushing in the sky.
I look up and see its body and golden feathers.
It swoops around the forest thinking it's King.
It flies and flies waiting for it's prey,
He sees a mouse and swoops down and gets the mouse.
It squeaks and squeaks trying to get away.
The big eagle eats it all in one.

Wayne Cullum (Age 9)

I Love Horses As You Will See

Loving, caring.
Out and about on a horse.
Very carefully putting it's rug on.
Every day, chores as you will know.

Having a horse is a lovely thing.
Out in the fields horses canter around.
Riding in a school, teaching the horse.
Shows require lots of preparation.
Entering a show takes a long time.
Showing at the last day is very nerve racking.

Emma Cocker (Age 12)

Who 'Art In Heaven

As I sat holding his hand,
So pale and lifeless
I thought of him as I hadn't before,
Seeing not just a skeleton before me.

As a man he was hard and selfish,
Quick in his ageing, but never growing dumb.
I as a child, would tease and taunt him,
Never letting him get his tempestuous ways.

But now as I sit,
In this snow white, death reeking room,
I think of how much he had taught me
With his baneful games.

Violence and war was his life,
Now part of mine:
"Drive with your right"
"In with your left." Boxing days gone by.

Now deep inside my armoured hatred,
Was the warm cosy fire that the
Family sat around, in winter's savage storms.
So strange, the way my feelings change
Towards my Father.

Jesamine Cook (Age 15)

Perhaps She Won't Notice

My bedroom is not tidy
Not tidy is my bedroom
I need to tidy it quickly
Mum's heading for the stairs
She's going one, two, three
She's on the landing fast
She's heading for my bedroom door
Good I've done it now
Oh no I haven't straightened the rug
She's in my bedroom now
Perhaps she won't notice
And let me out to play

Alexandra Clarkson (Age 7)

Untitled

I was just getting to the good part of my dream
When . . . I heard a noise and I opened my eyes,
I saw it was a miserable day.
Ice and hail, snow and rain
When will this weather end?
Then things didn't get any better
My school bus was late because of the snow.
There was no break because of the rain
And just got cross with the hail.

Christina Carmichael (Age 7)

My Family

My sister is called Tabytha
Tab for short
Raymond is my brother
A boring one at that
Phillip is my dad
Fixes everything
My mum is called Caroline
Cooks up nice teas
And that is my family
Plus me!
Plus the cat!
Plus the kitten!
NOW! That's my Family.

Frances Cunningham (Age 8)

My Little Dog

I have a dog called Spot
Who sometimes gets quite hot
He is a little pain
But goes out in the rain
He likes to play and run
But not much in the sun
He quite often gets cramp
When he's in the damp

Vicky Cassels (Age 12)

Snow

The snow flakes fall one by one on the ground
And you can play in it
Snow is cold
It falls down
It gets colder and colder
It is on the ground
It is on the green trees
It is on the grass
Snow is exciting

Faye Creighton (Age 7)

Summer Times

Summer,
Sizzling,
Late sun goes down,
Early rise
Making no sound.

Summer,
Scorching,
Pleasant dreams fill my head,
The sinking sun is
Now dead.

Summer,
Breezy,
As lavender-maroon fills the sky
Homeward bound
Is now in my eye.

Victoria J. Cann (Age 11)

Weather

Whether the weather be cold, or whether the weather be hot,
We cannot change the weather, whether we like it or not!

Sometimes rain beats down, sometimes it does snow,
Sometimes there is fog, and sometimes wind does blow.

Sometimes there is sleet, and sometimes it hails,
Sometimes there is frost and sometimes there are gales.

Sometimes there can be hurricanes and lightning in the sky,
Sometimes there are tornadoes and thunder rumbles high.

Sometimes there is mist and sometimes there is ice,
It can be freezing cold and it's not very nice.

Sometimes the weather is really good, there is a rainbow in the sky,
With white fluffy clouds and the sun is shining high.

But whether the weather be cold, or whether the weather be hot,
We cannot change the weather, whether we like it or not.

Jessica Crangles (Age 11)

Hospital

In my room on the ward,
Sometimes I get very bored.
The nurses come and check me up,
That's when they usually cheer me up.

My boredom then becomes relieved,
In the morning when Mrs Fisher looks for me.
She's the school teacher along with Mrs Hill,
They help me with my school work before my meal.

Here comes the trolley full of food,
I don't recommend it, it's not very good.
I send my mum up the shop,
This is much better but costs a lot.

Here comes my doctor Nicky Harris,
She has to be weighed but gets embarrassed.
We have a bet, I wonder who will win?
She has to lose weight and I've to put on.

Thomas Bunny, is who I've met as a friend,
I hope he gets on well until the end.
I've also met Rebecca who was ill,
She's gone home now but we see each other still.

Tracey Chorley (Age 13)

A New Life

I stare out the window.
I'm astonished to see that now
The dull tees stand ghostly.
With sunlight bursting through them
The spooky old church standing there.
I now understand the sadness of what I see.
I was now depressed
The sobbing of people in the misty old graveyard
With sorrowful flowers now withered.
Slowly
Quietly
Fade into the hard frosty ground
With colours disappearing into the darkness.

Seeming like years later
The first rays of sunlight
Spread over the ground
Making the frost sink back through the earth
The dull trees with frail fingers
Are now full with colour
And the graveyard is full of fresh spring air.

Rebecca Cook (Age 12)

My Dad

My Dad and I like the same things.
We both support Ipswich Town.
Watching horror movies and football
All night long.

My Dad and I do the same things.
Sleeping in on work days.
After football we have lots of onions
And tomato ketchup on our hot dogs.

There is one thing me and my Dad
Don't agree on.
My Dad doesn't like 5
And I listen to it all day long.

Bethany Chamberlin (Age 10)

Snow Drops

Slowly snow drops to the floor and carefully melts.
Some snow drifts down and melts in your hand,
When you look at it, it looks like cotton wool.
When you have it in your hair it feels all fluffy.
When it falls it looks like dirt coming from a cloud.
Some snow falls down on your roof,
When it falls diagonally it sticks to your window.

Rhia Creighton (Age 7)

I Survived!

I was marching home with a gun on my shoulder.
The town was much colder.
Some survived,
Some died.

As I came into town everybody cheered
But the beaten Germans jeered
Because we had won the war.

I saw lots of gore but the war is over.

Christopher Coleman (Age 10)

Waterfall

I see foam water coming down a waterfall
I see lots of rocks lined up beside the foamy water.
I see lots of water splashing at the bottom
I see sparkling water in a lagoon near by.
It is getting cooler everyone starts going home
Everyone sees a flicker of light
It is coming from the lagoon
Everyone rushes to the lagoon
To see what has happened to the water
A glowing fish is swimming in the water

Zoe Cundy (Age 9)

My Good Friend Bethany

Bethany and I are different because
She likes mash, fishfingers and beans.
I like steak and kidney pie.
She likes football, I like tennis.
I try to get up early, but Bethany always gets up late.
I like History, she loves English.
I love my rabbits, but Bethany really likes dogs.
I have blue eyes, Bethany has green eyes.
I try to be neat, but Bethany can't be bothered!
I like playing monopoly, Bethany likes drafts.
I am not too keen on music, Bethany really likes it.
I go to see her play football,
She sits and talks to me while I eat my steak and kidney pie.
We both like fish and chips and a good laugh!
It shows we are not different after all!

Zoe Cole (Age 10)

I Feel Like

I feel like a freezer when it is shivery and shiny
I feel like the sun when it is bright and cool
I feel like a teacher shouting and shouting
I feel like a school child being very quiet
I feel like a cube when it is snowing
I feel like an ice block when it is so icy
I feel like a hot oven burning and burning

Becky Cullum (Age 8)

Inside My Box

I will put in my box
A farm of a thousand animals all with a name
A fairy who can grant any wish
A television the size of a cinema and 10,000 sweets for me

I will put in my box
A flash Ferrari brighter than the brightest red,
The bluest baby dolphin and family that I can swim with forever
And the funniest joke in the world

I will put in my box
A lions roar
A dusty stable with an open door
A crocodiles tooth and a sparkle from the midnight stars

I will put in my box
A rainbow coloured canary,
And an elephants tusk

I will draw in my box
In the great open country
Then colour with my rainbow colours
Which is what is inside my box

Jennifer Collins (Age 10)

Christmas Is Here

Christmas is about life and joy,
I spend Christmas with Uncle Roy.
I like Christmas it's the best,
Better than a spelling test.

I sing carols with a choir,
I roast chestnuts in the fire.
I put some turkey in a box,
And gave it to a hungry fox.

I hang my stockings on the fireplace,
I left them there just in case.
I wrote a list, sent up the chimney
Christmas Day, presents for me.

Neil Claridge (Age 14)

Snowflakes

Snowflakes fall down and round and round.
When snow falls onto your head it melts.
Snow is white, snow is fluffy.
Snow comes down slowly, or it might come down fast.
When it falls to the ground it turns to a white sheet.
If it was really cold it might turn to ice.

Jenny Carter (Age 8)

My Family

"Clunk", "Crash"!
TV blares,
Brother and I sit there,
Glued to it - like two statues.
This is my family . . .

In the kitchen mother washes up,
Acts as a servant girl.
Dishes sparkle as she scrubs.
This is my family . . .

Hamster sleeps in it's soft bed,
Sleeping,
Sleeping like a sloth.
This is my family . . .

Printer working,
Dad is working hard,
As hard as five commuters.
This is my family . . .

Ross Cubbon (Age 10)

The Charge

Mines, barbed wire, streams of machine gun bullets,
This is what I am now charging at, my life in danger.
The shells start pouring over like giant hail stones falling from the sky.

As we march towards the trench, I see the lines of men in front of me falling, being slaughtered
by constant bullets like a wall of steel.

As I scramble up ditches the pounding starts, and the whole world around me seems to fall.
Lying flat on my face I knew that if I lifted my head I would become one of the thousands
slaughtered like cattle on this day.

When the raid is called off the few survivors that have survived the siege crawl back to the
trench in despair, thousands of losses for both sides.
As I look over the ground the damage is clear, man after man of hurt and dying men; As I stand
there staring at the masses I wonder why the generals didn't stop it before the losses mounted,
they don't class us as men just things that fight and die for their country.

Alan Clarke (Age 10)

Phew!

On a cold day
On a really cold day
On a really really cold day
On a really really icy cold day
There is nothing better
In the whole world than
Sitting next to a
Nice, yellow, red, warm,
Cosy, boiling fire m..m...m..!

Daniel Charlton (Age 7)

Check It Out

Check it out, check it out
BBD is on the mike MC.
I'll show you how to use it nicely
I'll show you how to use it perfectly
I'll show you how to use it sweetly
I don't care if the people knock on my door
I will say come in and help BBD on the mike MC
And if you think you are a bad boy
Come and sing on the mike MC

Daniel Christie (Age 8)

Big Boy

Big Boy is the best,
Big Boy is the best,
Sadie is his guest,
But Big Boy is the best.

He gallops through his field,
While Sadie plods along,
Sadie is his girlfriend,
But Big Boy is the best!

Marie Cornelius (Age 11)

Who Am I?

I live in a hole under the ground
My door is green and perfectly round
I like to sing songs, hear stories and rhymes
And every day I have dinner two times
I like to drink ale and my tummy is fat
My eating and drinking see to that
I dress in bright colours yellow and green
My feet are quite furry and shoes are not seen
I went on a journey with some dwarf friends of
mine
I was away from home for a very long time
While I was away, a funny old thing
I met a strange man and I found a ring!
I saw wizards and elves, orks and goblins
And I travelled the lands of the ancient kings
I met a great dragon, scaly and green
I burgled his treasure without being seen
When I got back my relatives I found
Selling my belongings and my house underground
I sent them away, but forgave them their sins
And oh, by the way, I'm Bilbo Baggins

Christopher Cleeve (Age 9)

Elephant Trees

Elephant trees grow in noses
The branches are all full of roses,
Elephant trees grow in your ears
They hold all your fearful fears.

Elephant trees grow in your mouth
They live right down in the sunny south,
Elephant trees grow in your eyes
They like to tell a lot of lies.

Elephant trees grow in your nails
They like to read the Daily Mail,
Elephant trees grow in your spots
They like to grow an awful lot.

Elephant trees grow in your mind,
Search so hard but you still won't find
An elephant tree that you can share,
It's in my imagination - so there!

Helen Cross (Age 10)

An Introduction To An Orchestra

First it's the flutes
With their quaint little toots
The trumpets start a booming fanfair
For the trombones strident notes to fill the air

Then it all falls quiet for a duet
Involving an oboe and a clarinet
The clarinet hums like a busy bee
The oboe ends the duet with glee

Then the drum plays a swing beat
The audience feel the vibes under their feet
Then there is the conductor who waves his stick
At the instrument of his pick

Tom Chalmers (Age 10)

The Mice

Mice are very nice
When they are eating rice
They dance to the Girls of Spice
While rolling on a dice

Charlotte Clay (Age 7)

The Magic Box

In my box I will put,

The clop-clop of horses hooves on a gravel path, the splashing of water in a swimming pool,
The lemon yellow and bright orange of the sun, the laughter of people watching a funny show,
Thousands of brightly coloured pencils, and the sound of the dog woofing at the postman

In my box I will see,

Horses running for miles and miles in grassy fields, the beautiful colours in the rainbow after a storm,
Paintings done by famous artists, and chefs making the best mashed potatoes

In my box I will,

Ride beautiful horses in races, draw pictures that look so real, you feel as if you're in them, and
Win races for hurdling, running and also throwing

In every corner there are,

Toys and sweets galore, every colour pencil you can think of, and fuzzy stuffed animals

My box is made of,

A light material, like a feather it can fly, and you can mold it into any shape you want

The lid of my box,

Is bright and colourful, it holds lime green ribbons attached to every side and
Right in the middle is a white horse

My box is painted,

Bright yellow, orange, red, lime green and turquoise

Keighley Clark (Age 9)

Don't Forget

Don't forget the people who came back to town,
Who went war,
And had sores on their knees,
But came back well
After the war.
Many people died,
And only some lived,
The poppy's grew,
And people wore them with pride.

Cheryl Clack (Age 11)

Shark Cake

My friend always talks about shark cake
and how he likes it.
He says "Me, me, me like shark cake,
Oh I do, I do, I do."
But we say "Who jumped into the River Thames?"
"Me did, Me did, Me did,
to get my shark for me shark cake!"

Lloyd Chalkley (Age 10)

The Tiger

I am
Tree bouncer
Stripy rug
Roaring explorer.
I mean no harm.

I know
Only the sound
Of whistling birds
The pulling and sighing of animals
Being taken away to the Zoo.
Soon it will be me.
I mean no harm.

Christopher Chapman (Age 9)

Love

Love is kind,
Love is gentle,
It tastes like apple pie,
You cannot feel it nor can you see it,
But it is still there,
We use love for our friends and families,
Love is the colour of a red, red rose glittering in the sun,
We all use love but in different ways,
Some more important than others,
If you think you have no love,
Then think again we all have
Love

Amanda Carpenter (Age 10)

Hello Autumn

Brown leaves falling everywhere,
Trees are really very bare,
Small animals hibernate,
All of we celebrate,
Bonfire night,
From the bright fire comes a big light.

Summer has gone,
Now we all sing a song,
Of the harvest time,
The weather isn't all that fine,
Now we have horrid rain,
Autumn comes again and again.

Winter is now very near,
It comes around every year,
Animals are crawling,
Lots of leaves are falling,
People throw eggs at my door,
When I shout they throw lots more,
Trick or treaters come and go,
Oh my God I don't know.

Samuel Clements (Age 10)

Fireworks

Fireworks are magic spears,
Hurtling to the skies.

Fireworks are explosions of
Bright flickering flames.

Fireworks are hot-dogs
And bangs and sparks.

Fireworks are sparklers,
Hotter than flames.

Fireworks are happy families,
Scattered around the bonfire.

Fireworks are fun,
But quite dangerous.

Fireworks are loud,
BANG! BANG! BANG!

Tom Clements (Age 9)

My Brother

My brother is so annoying,
I try to avoid his snoring,
I like my brother most of the time,
Although he's been accused of a crime!

My brother is very smelly!
His tummy rumbles like jelly,
My brother likes his mother,
But not me, not his big brother.

My brother is rather funny,
He may have loads of money,
My brother loves ice-cream,
But he doesn't get any, if he's mean!

He is my brother,
I love him whatever,
I suppose I could cope,
So long as I know, he loves me.

Robert Clemson (Age 10)

Nightmare In Hell

It was cold nasty wet
Spooky messages ran through my body
I saw some massive eye
Blood stained red staring at me
I walked back and was ripped to shreds
And saw my heart boil away in acid
I tried to scream but darkness took the scream away

Ross Cameron-Symes (Age 10)

Winter

Winter winter you're so sweet I love your
Whiteness so bright and clean.

I love it so I really do
I wish my friends were here in the zoo
Looking at the peculiar whiteness
And smelling the beautiful air

Alan Corkery (Age 9)

The Music Of The Spheres

The music of the spheres floats
Over frozen ponds and frozen lakes,
In high, strange, wavering notes,
Travelling softly like a mist of soft snowflakes.

Earth's music so hectic,
Full of unknown surprises,
It is so complicated and frantic,
His notes are trickling from dangerous corners.

Jupiter's voice booms loud and clear,
As it thunders through the skies like a fist.
The roars of a lion, the growl of a tiger,
The crash of a wave at high tide.

Uranus's tune is a garden of trees,
Flowering and blowing in the scented breeze.
Neptune's music bubbles around like the seven seas,
A silvery cloud full of rain, suspended particles of crystal
tears.

Then far on the horizon, Pluto's music soars
As clear as a full moon, suspended in the frosty night sky.
As the music of the spheres flows past,
The stars breathe out a huge musical sigh.

Abigail Colley (Age 10)

Summer

Birds skating in the sky
Sun like a microwave in the sky
Leaves falling down like the rain
Clouds like candyfloss

Shane Corbett (Age 9)

My Gran

My Gran wasn't the same as you and me
She rode around on a motorbike
She never paid her parking fee
Her hair and clothes they smelt like trout
She wasn't really was she

She played monopoly at the bar
She drank all beers from very far
She was always singing la, la, la,
Her friends were laughing ha, ha, ha
My Gran wasn't the same as you and me

She tried to hang a picture frame
The curtain's out of place again
I think she should live right down a drain
She didn't have a very big brain
My Gran wasn't the same as you and me

Lucy Creighton (Age 10 ¾)

If You Want To See A Tiger

If you want to see a tiger
You must go down to the Siberian Jungle
Where it is dark

I know a tiger
Who's living down there -
He's big and scary and always hungry
For fresh blood

Yes if you really want to see a tiger
You must go to the Siberian Jungle
Where it is dark

Go down very very carefully and say
Tiger dada
Tiger dada
Tiger dada da da da da

And he will carefully come out of the reeds
But don't hang around for tea
JUST SCRAM!!!!!

Sarah Caller (Age 8)

Red Is?

Red is the colour of my blood
That's going around my body
Red is the colour of a heart
That goes up and down
Red is the colour of a juicy apple
Red is the colour of a poppy
For Remembrance Day
Red is the colour of a cool
Man U shirt

Adam Chestnutt (Age 8½)

The Journey Of My Train

My train set goes round
And round and round

Some times I get bored
But sometimes I don't

My train set gets bigger and smaller
And bigger and smaller

Trains big and small go round
Go round and round on it

My train set big and small rattle behind them
As they go round

The train stops at the station
The journey ends at last on my train set

Joshua Clarkin (Age 8)

Cat, Mat, Rat, Person, Merson

There was a cat who sat on a mat
Waiting for his daily cream
Along came a rat who sat with the cat
Waiting for his daily cheese
"Hi" said the rat to the friendly cat
"I'm waiting for my daily cheese"
"Hi" said the cat to the friendly rat
"I'm waiting for my daily cream"
Off went the cat with the tiny rat,
"Let's find our daily food"
Along came the person called Mrs Merson
She said "Kill that rat!"
Ahh.....thought the cat
It's a rat he'll be my daily cream
.........Instead!

Laith Chelache (Age 10)

Pollution

Rough cotton clouds hurry,
As a sultry days fury,
Wipes out everything in its path.
A nefarious kingdom,
Unceremoniously desolating the fallen countryside,
As weeds flourish over topless fields,
And the earth's sludge-coloured day is streaked with blood red
Only left is the faint lamenting of twigs
And branches laying lifeless on the grass
Suddenly an unearthly silence overlooks the metallic galaxy
A silence so silent as if the end of World War Three

Benjamin Clapton (Age 11)

My Bike

I have a bike,
It's bigger than a pike,
It's not a trike,
I do like my bike.

My bike is chrome,
My saddle is foam,
I keep it at home,
In a big dome.

My bike is bright,
You can see it at night,
It's got a light,
It gives you a fright.

Tristan Cocks (Age 10)

Weather

It was a rainy day
I asked if I could go out to play
My mother did say it's a very rainy day

The next day it was sunny
I went on my bike
And my dad went on a hike

The next day it was windy
I played with my kite
My dad bought a car and it was white

It was autumn I played conkers
My dad went bonkers
Because I beat him at conkers

Garry Coffin (Age 10)

My Bird Is So absurd

My bird is so absurd
He likes to eat banana curd
Then after that he's even stranger
He pretends to be a desert ranger
Why my bird is so absurd?
I do not know
I took him to the vets
He said "I've never heard
Of such a bird"
That is very very so absurd

Aisha K. Coppack (Age 8)

Let Me Out!!!

I'm stuck in the trenches
I've been here two years
I've been shot twice
I am in tears
It's soggy and muddy
With water two foot deep
The only company I've got
Is yellow and goes tweet!
With food like slop and clothes like rags
I can't wait till the day I pack my bags

Samuel Chumbley (Age 10)

At School

School is good for you
Cool at School
Have a nice day at school
On Friday we do PE
On Monday we make some cakes
Look at the books every day

Jade Coy (Age 9)

My Daddy

Daddy is clever, I want him to live forever
He plays the play station with me
But not when he's having a cup of tea
He's cuddly and bubbly warm and snuggly
He buys me sweets and I stay up late
This makes my mum very irate
I love my daddy its plain too see
The reason is he's just like
ME!

Ben Coggins (Age 8)

Christmas Time

I woke one morning
It was christmas time
I looked at the presents
As a lot of them were mine

All different shapes
Both large and small
I tore open the paper
To see them all

A nintendo or computer
Spice girl or guitar
This is what I wished for
And I got this by far

I then had my dinner
As it was Christmas day
But all I wanted to do
Was to sit around and play

Lisa Curry (Age 11)

Bombing

Whirr! Whirr! screamed the haunting siren
Smash! our rusty old shelter had been destroyed
We all went running into the lounge and cuddled up
Crash! Tinkle! the brand new patio doors smashed.
Suddenly . . . . Caboom! half our roof was destroyed
We hid petrified in the larder where there was no window
Creek! Boom! The lounge ceiling had caved in!
Mum started crying hysterically and so did Rosemary and Tim.
I was more terrified than I had ever been in my life
The food shelves collapsed
Zoom! Zoom! The evil German planes flew swiftly overhead
All went quiet and then,
Boom! The room shook wildly
It sounded like next door had got it!
I was petrified, angry
Zwiir! Zwiir! went the all clear siren
We had made it - I cautiously stepped outside
The garage had been blown up
My lovely pets were dead
And . . . my best friend who lived next door
His shelter had been destroyed
He was dead.

Jonathan Cole (Age 10)

Untitled

Mrs Lock thinks I'm reading but I'm . . .
Lying in a hammock
Swimming in crystal clear oceans,
Joining the pirates
In fact I'm not at school at all

Mrs Lock thinks I'm reading but I'm . . .
Living in the rain forest
Abseiling down a cliff
Travelling round the world
In fact I'm not at school at all

Mrs Lock thinks I'm reading but I'm . . .
Meeting a tiger,
Wrestling with a lion,
Saving the whales
In fact I'm not at school at all.

Alexandra Carruthers (Age 10)

The Snowman

One showery night
The snow was falling fast
A poor snowman was standing
No scarf, no hat, he must be freezing
But when summer comes
The snowman gets hot
So he melts away in pieces

Ben Curnow (Age 8)

My Dad

My Dad is nice,
My Dad is kind,
My Dad is as nice as can be,
My Dad is good and he drives the car,
My Dad is big,
I love my Dad

Adam Carpenter (Age 10)

November

No abseiling at Kilve
No climbing
No cycling down the road
No crazy golf
No walking miles
No grass sleighing down the hill
No making sandcastles
No running on the beach
No sports day on the field
No vember!!

Nick Cox (Age 10)

The Doctor
(In the style of Chaucer)

There was a doctor who was quick to judge
The type of illness a patient had.
He'd write a prescription, just like that,
And jump to conclusions without a fact.
He wore a suit and a large bow tie
And had a chauffeur to help him fly,
Away in his car, a motorbike too,
They zoomed so quick they almost flew.

He'd leave the surgery really early
And never care to stop, if someone was hurt.
He'd skip his shifts, but keep his pay,
This lazy doctor, so quick to judge, who makes
Mistakes almost every day.

Chloë Cockett (Age 13)

Summer

The sun shone down on the people below,
The beach is such a fun place to go.
The days are long and we have fun,
Playing around in the heat of the sun.

My brothers and I make sandcastles and talk,
While mum and dad go out for a walk.
A lady sits sunning herself under a brolly,
Here comes mum and dad -
Oh great they've bought us a lolly.

Rosie Collins (Age 9)

The Spaling Tost

We cam innto clas toeday
And are techear wos siteing down
Than are techear begin too saie
Were haveng a spaling tost, No.1 - Town.

On chilled pot his haned u
So are sire choose him
He spilt it "T.O.N. oops!"
So with a shootgun, sire gave himme a trim.

Tha hedless boy fall to tha flour
And sire sad "NO, T.O.W.N."
Next he chilled Sam with a chansaw
And with a grinade cilled Ben.

I was by tha dour,
Aind kreept ot as tha bac talbe ecsplooded
the roum wes coovered in goor,
And tha 4 wals ware al blood red.

It's all troo, jost as i say,
And i will sweer to thet.

You must improve your spelling
And your Grammar, Signed: Miss Nat

Peter Chaplin (Age 12)

Foggy Morning Poem

One day it was dark and gloomy
Because it was foggy
And you can't see anything
Because everything seems white
You can't go on holiday or travel
It is sad.

Ashley Cowell (Age 8)

The Summer Wind

The Winter wind is stiff
The Autumn wind is tossed
The Spring wind is fresh

The wind I like best is the summer wind
The way it, soothes your face, with a lovely feel to it.
The way it ripples the water
So very tired
After a summer shower
It moves it away to a far away land
It rattles the green leaves
It's breezy too though
On the beach it
Slowly rocks the waves
At home it rocks me to sleep at night
When summer goes
The summer wind
Says goodbye

Brittany Chaplin (Age 9)

Spring

Woke up to spring,
Going through bluebell woods,
Heaped with flowers galore
Squirrels from their hibernation
Waking up to a wonderful season
The best one
Of the year.

William Coyle (Age 11)

The Spirits Of No Return

I felt a shadow fall on me, I felt alone.
I felt the world around me melt, I felt alone.

I could see the spirits of evil, I could hear them cry.
I could tell they were after me, I could hear them cry.

They came from beyond the grave, they came so near.
They came out of the darkness, they came so near.

I tried so hard to get away, I tried to run.
I tried to escape their evil grasp, I tried to run.

I was stopped by their ghostly powers, I was taken away by them.
I was told I could never return, I was taken away by them.

I wanted to go home, I wanted to leave.
I wanted to get out, I wanted to leave.
I felt a shadow fall on me . . . . .

Alice Theresa Cook (Age 14)

Thoughts Of A Teddy

Once I was the treasure of treasures,
But now I am just an old tacky bear.
When I was younger she looked after me,
But now she let's me rot in hell.
She throws me about.
What did I do to deserve this?
My eyes are pulled out,
My ears are ripped to shreads.
But please tell me what I did.
My legs are ripped,
I've got no hair.
What else could be bad?
I used to be the best of the best.
Why can't I be the best of the best again?

Samantha Cross (Age 11)

Green Aliens

Clock strikes midnight
A droning sound
The spaceship lands making a hole in the ground

Look outside
I'm chilled with fear
Little feet coming near

Wrinkled skin
Slimy feet
It doesn't help with the fall of sleet

Wake up
Phew! it was only a dream
But outside is a brightly lit beam

Richard Cooper (Age 10)

Man United v Inter Milan

Reds score a header
Against Inter Milan Dwight Yorke
Man U could go through

The crowd goes crazy
Jumping mad and screaming loud
United go on stronger

Someone scores
Doesn't stand push on United played
Thank you ref thank you!

Second leg in San-Sino
Inter Milan against Man United
What a game this is!

Before kick off loud noise!
This is to be a hard game,
Kick off starts with us reds

Ronaldo has chance
But can't finish it, chance gone
Ventola scores 1-0 up

United come back
Finished 1-1 reds have gone through

Warren Capell (Age 12)

01-01-00

The smoke billowed the fires raged
Roaring flames engulfed the once proud cities,
Terror and panic rampaged through the devastated streets,
Pouncing on the doomed souls.
Overlooking the two, death bides his time
Knowing, in the vast impenetrable darkness that is his being,
That he would get his chance soon.

A group of soldiers charge into view,
As another do the same.
Black versus White.
Good versus Evil.

As their bloodshot eyes meet, amongst the screams of the tortured and the dying.
Both know there is no more White, only Black.

A great majestic wave of burning destruction
Cascades down on them
No more White, only Black.

The smoke dispersed the fires smouldered
Twelve pitiful chimes sound the hour of night
A small watch clicks
The date revolves to 01-01-00

Yvonne Cunningham (Age 14)

What!

It was tall and dark....
I saw it in the rain
What?
Yes!
Paddling in the rain.
I think it had two feet
Two toes as well.
What?
Yes!
With a leopard skin too
A spiky back
Not forgetting the thin
Sharp black eyes
Eight long whiskers
What?
AND a long nose
What is it?
A cheaorstheysharottehip
What?

Shelley Clayton (Age 8)

My Rock

A history book
As old as the earth
So old it saw
The first dinosaur at birth

A smooth bumpy surface
Of browny-grey
It lived on the ocean bed
For many a day

Engraved on its surface
There are one, two and three,
Fossilised amonites
That I can see

I wonder where
This ancient stone has been
And what wonders
It has seen

Lynda Clark (Age 11)

The Earth Story

The earth has appeared in outer space
No people, no plants, no trees,
A wasteless plane across its face
For life it holds the keys

Everything is coming, growing wild
Humans - no trouble the earth is so fair
The planet is regretting its human child
They have no precious time for care!

People are destroying, killing the trees
Poisoning the animals, polluting the seas
The earth is destroyed now, it came to a cruel fate
The humans no longer - maybe it's not too late!

The planet is forming once again
Its rivers and hills are here
The plants are growing through the day
Now there is no fear

Humans and selfishness
Don't walk this earth
Its animals in peace
A brand new birth

Luke Clewlow (Age 11)

The Beginning Of The End

As us the humans are cocooned
In our polluted earth
Unaware of what is to come
But only sadness for some
For our sins we shall be punished
And down from the heavens
Comes a blinding strip of light
Seething with rage
Followed by stunning flashes of red and blue,
Only creating a worrying whistle
Then a frightening silence
Some thought it was a miracle
And others thought it was doom
But they were both right
With the click of the fingers
The world was gone
On the horizon four men stood
Looking over their doing
Only to turn and disappear
They were
The four horsemen of the apocalypse.

Gary Cleweley (Age 11)

India At Night

The roads, like long sticky strips of fudge,
The trains slither past.
Street lights bare their yellow teeth,
As old cars chug along.
Motorbikes snarl as taxis form an army of ants,
Pavements grumble awaiting their pray.
Shop doors close, newspapers blow by.
Buses speed by me their head lights stare at me.

Jessica Carter (Age 10)

The Noisy Classroom

Chatting children
Leaking sink
Angry helper
Snoozing hamster
Sleepy child
Rolling pencil
Over worked teacher
Over worked children
The noise sounds
Like an avalanche from the mountain tops
Mountains of noise fill the room
Until it's time to go

Anna Crampton (Age 9)

Happiness

Happiness is yellow just like the sun
It smells like fresh flowers
And tastes like a melon
It sounds like birds cheeping in trees
And feels like water trickling through your toes
But where it lives is the beat of your heart

Rachel Cattermoule (Age 11)

Summer's Day

S unny day means swimming and sand,
U sing a blue and yellow beach ball,
M ummy and me lay on the sand,
M inutes later we are walking around Devon's mall,
E ating cream cakes and chocolate buns,
R oger decides to coat himself in jam,
S ending food and buns everywhere.

D addy says let's go back to our chalet,
A nd then it comes to the end of the day,
Y esterday was great let's do it again.

Katie Churchill (Age 9)

Rage

It was a cold and windy day
Nobody was out, no one, not a soul
Then all of a sudden I heard a cry
I looked outside and saw a girl
She was crying, I went outside and asked
What was wrong? She replied I am black
They treat me wrong, I am fed up I am
Raged!

Adam Crockett (Age 13)

Snow Snow

Snow snow to the ground you flow
Soft as a teddy bear
You spread around everywhere
Covering everything with a blanket of white
Sparkling in the pale moonlight
How you make the river ice
Just like ice cream it's so nice
The snowballs that we throw at each other
In the winter weather
The cold wind that you put in my face
As I try and make a snowman full of grace.

Caylie Clayton (Age 10)

School

School is very boring
School is very fun
I'm always late for school you know
And always have to run

All through the corridor
All through the hall
All through the dinner room
And crashed into the wall

Now at last I am there
Looking for my books
Eventually I find them
And everyone looks

I go up to the teacher
And ask him what to do
He tells me it's mathematics
And says "what happened to you?"

Charlotte Casey-Haden (Age 10)

Mouse Trap

Cat asleep,
Not a peek.
Mouse awake,
China plate breaks!
Cat awake,
Mouse on the run,
Chasing round and round,
This looks like fun!
Mouse trap there,
Cat can't bear,
The sting and pain -
Just can't explain,
Fun on the run in Mouse Trap.

Chase around,
Leap and bound -
Mouse trap's found.
Day is done,
Had some fun,
On the run in . . .
MOUSE TRAP!

Emily Cox (Age 9)

My Bedroom

My bedroom is always untidy
So I have to tidy it up every Tuesday
My carpet is always slidy
The door is always white

The legs on my bed are shivering
In a scary dream
My floors eyes open,
The telephones are always crying

At night my bedroom goes to sleep
In the bright shining morning
My room is awake making noises
And my room is shouting aloud
Trying to make me get up

The walls close in on me
I see the windows shout
The curtains whistle loudly
I hear the teddies and dolls singing
All I hear at night is sounds
They scare me all the time

Kelly Cairns (Age 10)

Poppies

P is for poppies as red as war's blood,
O is for Officers soaken in mud,
P is for politics that started it all,
P is for patriots who believed in their call,
Y is for years the war lasted long.

D is for death in the field of the Somme,
A is for Armistice the end it had come,
Y is for young men who died by the gun.

Catherine Caller (Age 10)

He Must Be Here

The stars are twinkling in the sky,
And the moon is out there too,
I must see Santa out there
He must be somewhere,
He just has to be there,
I'm staying at the window
Wearing my dressing gown,
Yes now he is here,
I can go to sleep

Lee Cunnington (Age 8)

My Upper Half

My hair is like a load of spikes,
My eyelashes are like strings,
My eyes are like wet marbles,
My nose is like a sharks fin,
My mouth is like a cave,
My chin is like a pendulum blade,
My neck is like a tree trunk,
My arms are like branches
My fingers are like twigs.

Alec Ciechanowicz (Age 8)

Me!

I am made of average ability,
Normal size and average agility
I'm not that sporty but I am artistic,
Give me a pen and paper and I'll go ballistic!
I can get aggressive if you tease me too much,
I'm left handed with a creative touch
My body size is really quite slim,
I'm well balanced and confident within

Leon Cauchois (Age 12)

Time

Time is a hamster running round in its wheel,
Or a child's roundabout made out of steel.
Time is a trumpet blowing on the hour,
Or time is as white as a bag of flour.
If time ever ended what would we do?
If time ever ended would we go to?

Jo Cleverley (Age 13)

The Blue Blue Sea

The blue blue sea
Crashing against the rocks
Fish jumping in the water
Boats sailing in the water
As fast as waves go
Whales talking to each other
And singing too
It's gone over the sand
The deep blue sea
Jelly fish as jelly as can be
The sea is deep
Waves are now roaring
It's very cold
Dolphins getting hurt
By lots and lots of sailors
The blue blue sea
Sea weed stuck on the sand
The blue cold sea
That's what's in the sea ... sea ... sea

Megan Chatting (Age 9)

The Little Green Man

The little green blob of
Goo and muck
He likes to play in his
Ship flying around
Shooting other ships
Playing with his
Little green friends
Playing goo ball
With his friends
He gets in his ship
And flies home

Lloyd Cole (Age 9)

Stars

1,000, 2,000, 3,000 stars
Why are they there I ask myself

3,000 stars flickering in the air
With granny up there

Were there stars when Jesus was alive?
Were there stars eleven years ago?

Are they babies that still have to be born?
Or are they people that have died?

Are the fairies fluttering around?
One thing will always stay in my mind
And that is

What are stars?

Georgia Collisson (Age 11)

Untitled

There once was an old Greek who knew
That he made a terrible stew
He threw in some seeds
And came out with some weeds
And soon it began to brew

Sophie Croom (Age 9)

My Bedroom

My bedroom is a tip
Satellite and old dino bites
Action man and headless Ken
Are fighting again and again
Dinosaurs and hipersaurs
Chicken pox and mange
Are lurking under my bed
Where Charlie's Boneo lays

Richard Cooper (Age 10)

My Sister

Diddle daddle poof
My sister is called Ruth
Her hair is not nice
It is tangled up with rice
Her eyebrows are so long
You can make them curl with tongs
Her eyes are purple her teeth are green
She's the prettiest girl you've ever seen

Hannah Colley (Age 9)

Rabbit's New Home

I felt frightened
About what's going to happen to me

I felt lonely
Left out as if I was never there
I felt small,
Confused inside about the noise I've never heard before

I was in shock
It was noisy and dark
I froze in the box
I was stiff with fear, cramped not able to see daylight
Unknown voices above
As I am slowly noticed

Freedom appeared
New sounds
New smells
Exploring the new home

Emma Candy (Age 12)

Rivers

Rivers are blue
Rivers are small
I go down to see them
They are very nice
They are like swimming pools
I see the ducks going down
I feed the ducks bread
Some rivers can be big
One by one the snow flakes fall on the river
But it melted in the night
It was dark
And the moon shone on the river

Hannah Cook (Age 8)

I Should Like To

I should like to take home
The blazing rays of the sun
On a glorious spring evening,
Steal the beams of moonlight
On a frosty night,
Capture the amazing beauty
Of a million flying birds in the morning,
Grab the spirit of a dolphin
Swimming free like a lord
Of the sea,
Take the soul of a cheetah
Running to and fro,
Snatch the pride of a ferocious tiger
Whose claws are like daggers.

Ben Connell (Age 13)

Valentine Sonnet

I love the way you look, I look at you
Your hair so dark your eyes like stars they shine
If you were mine, my heart it would be true
It's you I want I pray you will be mine
I see you every day and long to say
Come out with me alone and let us be
My shyness cure, my reticence allay
Oh won't you see my heart and be with me?
Your lips so ruby red I'd like to kiss
But only friends we are up to this time.
When you're away, your company I miss
Oh please see me and be my valentine
Be mine, be mine, I'll never ask for more
My one true love the one that I adore

Fiona Cresswell (Age 13)

I Think it's Not fair

I think it's not fair
That we have to line up
When others just push
Don't you think that's unfair?

I think it's not fair
That we get so much homework
We have to go out and do other things
Don't you think that's unfair?

I think it's not fair
That we have to wear uniform,
When others were normal
Don't you think that's unfair?

I think it's not fair
That school is too long,
People in nursery get half a day
Don't you think that's unfair?

Michelle Canham (Age 11)

The Big Boy Rap

I'm a big boy now
I can plough the field.
I would milk the cow
But I don't know how.

I live in a house
With my pet mouse.
I eat cow pie
With mixed up rye.

I go to gym
To make myself thin.

I'm a big boy now
As I've just said.
But I still don't know how
To milk the cow.

Nicholas Dart (Age 7)

Pigeons Present Of Thanks

I am a big fat pigeon
I sit high on your house
I like to watch you livin'
I do but nothin' else
I sometimes sit on benches
With people in the park
I hop on wooden fences
And always leave my mark
I love to coo and call you
From high here in the sky
I target for your left shoe
But I miss and hit your eye
I know it's no way to thank you
For all the left out food
How else though can I show thanks
Except a deposit of a poo.

Aaron Cornwell (Age 11)

My Best Friend Vincent

Vincent is my best mate,
He's a fantastic friend, he's really great
He is short I am tall,
He likes to act really cool
He's the perfect goalie in every match
He's always got the perfect catch
We play together in the rain and the sun
We're always having lots of fun

Ashley Carey (Age 10)

Untitled

There was a kid from Frome
He had a big home
He liked to eat foam
Then he lost his home
That's the end of the
Little kid from Frome

Andrew James Cade (Age 11)

Mystery Music

The clashing of repeating triangles
Stale string violin
Streaming xylophone
Anxious ripples flowing guitar
Gentle beats from the drum
Medieval racket clarinets
Hoot clang soft flute
Hair raising saxophone
Tweating beating wood block
Flicking shakers
To a halt!
There is violence to the silence

Jennie Cavill (Age 9½)

It's Not Fair

It just isn't fair
When I come home from school
And want to go out, mum says no, homework first
Oh I glare, it's not fair

Went to see nan
Round her house, rang the bell
She's not well
Oh I care, it's not fair

Out on my bike
Saw that red sports car I like
Can't wait to take my driving test
Oh what flair? it's not fair

Martin Davies (Age 12)

The Second Junk Room

My room's the second junk room
It's filled with clutter and mess
But in this hopeless doom and gloom
I cleaned to my very best

Rummaging through old toys and games
Brushing off the thick grey dust
I found some objects with funny names
I laughed with embarrassed disgust

I finished the cleaning it took a week
This room much larger a vast expanse
But now ... quite plain with designer chic
Will I miss that junk my past romance?

Matthew Day (Age 13)

Webs

Spider's home
To catch flies
She wraps them up
To eat for her tea

Thomas Driscoll (Age 6)

Where Am I

I can see lots of yellow and white flowers
I can feel the air brushing against my arm
I can taste the sausages from the farm
I can smell the lovely fresh air
I can hear the pheasant in the big tree
I am in a field

Lizzy Davis (Age 7)

Winter

Look out, look out,
Jack Frost is about his way,
So look out,
He is coming.
Hurry, he is coming.
He can freeze you.
He has frozen himself.

Jamie Dyer (Age 6½)

It's Not fair

It's not fair
I sit on my own
Don't you think that's unfair?

It's not fair
They won't share
Don't you think that's unfair?

It's not fair
I can't use the phone
Don't you think that's unfair?

It's not fair
I wouldn't dare
Don't you think that's unfair?

It's not fair
They just drown
Don't you think that's unfair?

It's not fair
They don't care
Don't you think that's unfair?

Laura Davey (Age 12)

Why Me!

Why me! What have I done
To deserve such pain
Why me! What have I done
My body's gone insane.

I took a bit
Of power and freedom
It threw my problems away
It happened quite often
Not just to me
Until that day.

I felt a shot of despondency
This writhing guilt inside of me
I determined this was the day
To give the smack a kick away.

I disposed of the temptation
My life is recklessly determined
But I know I will get through it
If I keep determined
COLD TURKEY!

Fiona Darch (Age 13)

Children's Chant

Working class - Noisy class
Clever class - Best class
Oh fun giver - Oh fun taker
Oh fun class what have you
In store for bored children today

From our class
Children's chat
Talking about this and that
"Did you see the match?"
"Will you play catch?"

Working class - Noisy class
Clever class - Best class
Oh our class what have you
In store for bored children today

Lee Derek (Age 9)

Rusty Tank

A rusty tank came my way
Dribbling out gasses and fuels
I watched as it manoeuvred over contours high and low

A rusty tank came my way
Its front splattered with blood
An indestructible killing machine
Coughing and spluttering
And without hesitation
It leaped upon someone crushing his stomach
And scattering his brain like confetti

Our tank pulled up beside me
And fired a rocket
It hit the rusty tank
And in a flash it was over
The rusty tank was gone

Carlo Degregorio (Age 13)

Thoughts Of Big Bear

I hope and I pray as hard as I might
For someone to love and cuddle at night.
Will a boy or girl pick me . . .I really don't mind
Just as long as they love cuddles and are really kind.

A little boy, all excited, running to see.
Please, please, please . . .oh please pick me.
He has, I've been picked, somebody to love.
We cuddle and cuddle we fit like a glove.

As the years pass me by, the bald patches appear.
But I'm still loved as much as the very first year.
My owner has now passed me on to his son.
My wonderful life, lots of love, cuddles and fun.

Craig Deane (Age 12)

Sounds Of The Atmosphere

Wind whistling in the treetops.
Dead leaves being rustled by cars that pass by.
Lorries going along the road as they go.
People talking and laughing all the time.
An old un-oiled gate creaking all the time.

Alexander Dark (Age 8)

Picture Poems

I can see a great, big frosty mountain
I can feel and hear the daisy white snow crunch under my feet
I can taste the clear white snow in my mouth
I can touch the spiky xmas tree
I can smell the frosty air
It looks like Alaska

Hannah Delaney (Age 7)

The Boy In The Playground

The boy in the playground is not real,
People say "Him you can't feel",
He's as thin as a post,
And his head's made of toast,
The roasting hot boy in the playground.

The boy in the playground wears a strange hat,
People do say "He once was a cat"
As tall as a tree,
He's like a bee,
For the boy in the playground makes honey.

The boy in the playground is backing away,
People say "With him don't play".
He likes eating jars,
And he is from Mars,
For the boy in the playground's an alien!!!

Amy Davenport (Age 11)

Bullied

Standing there
Near the history block
A tall boy came and said
"You're too small to fight"
And he beat me up

Ricky Dawes (Age 12)

Untitled

I wish I was a little bug
With a hairy tummy
Then I'd climb into the honey pot
And get my tummy gummy

Ellie Done (Age 9)

Cracking Conkers

Swaying big trees, falling red leaves
Blowing trees with golden, red and green leaves
The trees swaying and the leaves crunching
Falling brown leaves blowing big trees
Trees swaying, leaves on the ground.

Spiky hard outside soft and smooth inside
Spiky green cases lying on the ground
The prickly, velvety snug cases hanging on the trees
Needle cases brown and spotty
Prickly green cases squashed on the ground.

Soft smooth conkers falling on the ground
Conkers shining sparkling brown
Gleaming conkers hanging on the trees
The sparkling conkers smooth and brown
Vainy conkers sleeping in their squidgy beds.

Smashing soft brown conkers flying through the air
Conkers is a smashing crashing game
Smashed conkers lying on the ground
Conkers swinging on the strings
Smashing shouting cracking swinging mines the winner

Sarah, Ruth, Jacalyn, William and Sean

Worms

Worms are soft
And slimy
They're not sharks
They can't bark
They're wriggly
And fiddly
And they're
Tiny too

Aidan Davey (Age 7)

Summer Time

Sunflowers grow pink
Roses grow incredible colours
New baby animals are born
Great fun

Gemma Devlin (Age 5)

They Die For You

The defenceless creature suffers in a cage,
Just because you wish to cheat age.
The animal suffers incredible pain,
Just because you are so vain.

For your cosmetics an animal dies,
Is it worth more beautiful eyes?
Monkeys wired up to machines
Because this season's colour's green.

Would you rather see a baby goat
Or do you want that new fur coat?
The animal testers don't think it's funny
All they care about is money.

Stephen Durant (Age 14)

My Heart Is Lost

I'm cold and alone and there's not much to do.
I don't know what day it is as I speak to you.
My wife died a year ago or so it seems to me.
The war was never meant to be
Yet I know
My best friend died just yesterday
He was all alone.
He was the only one I really knew.
What would you do?
There's not much you see
May God help me.
As I say to you this was not meant.
Why did God not take me?
Blood stains are everywhere.
Why does it have to be?
Why will he not take me?
Why does it have to be?

Helen Deigan (Age 14)

Farming

I live on a farm it's an excellent place

Live stock is good to play with
I love tractors
Keep your sheep safe somewhere
Eat beef I eat it I like it

Farming is satisfying
A farmer works with the soil
Running around the sheep, the dog is puffed out
Moo the cow says it's time for me to go
In to the milking parlour, in they all come
Never leave a gate open
Good farmers look after their farm

Ryan Daw (Age 11)

My Rabbit Rosie

My rabbit Rosie is rather naughty.
She got out one day and got out one night.
She can be a very naughty Rosie.
He has got into fights and always wins.
He has got this sort of look in his eye
Which tells you he is going to do something mischievous.
But I don't know what!
He or she you may ask, Rosie or Roger.
I don't know!
he acts like a boy, he shows off with
His big brown coat of fur.
His little ears and big feet remind me of
Something, but I'm not sure.
He's a dwarf Japanese rabbit you know.
But I love my rabbit however naughty it is.

Hannah Dawson (Age 11)

Millennium 2000

Space - not many people get to see it,
Space - any other life?
Space - a strange place.

Nobody understands it.
Stars moon and planets,
Can aliens be alive?
We don't know.

But some people believe,
There is life.
Out there somewhere,
There must be something
To tell us that we are not
Alone in space

We may find out
In the millennium,
Or after.

Kieran Duff (Age 11)

The Old Apple Tree

Muddy ground, soggy grass
Last years apples rotting.
Orangy brown trunk, cracked and rough.
Clinging roots, with loving hearted ivy.
Opening trunk into a shapely way.
Dark green moss like a hairy fleece in the fork.
Light green lichen, like flowers, opened on the branches,
New branches, a new colour, greyly smooth.
Branches wide stretched into an icy cold day.
New life but a dead tree.
A dead tree but a new life,
Branches wide stretched into an icy cold day,
New branches, a new colour, greyly smooth.
Light green lichen, like flowers, opened on the branches,
Dark green moss like a hairy fleece in the fork.
Opening trunk into a shapely way.
Clinging roots, with loving hearted ivy.
Orangy brown trunk, cracked and rough.
Last years apples rotting.
Muddy ground, soggy grass

Zoe Dee (Age 13)

Smokey

Big wheels turning,
The polished grand body,
Stands above all other engines,
Hissing.

Stephen Daines (Age 9)

Sometimes

Sometimes,
I feel like a fish,
Swimming in my bowl.
Quietly thinking
To myself,
How nice it would be,
To swim in the sea.

Gemma Deaton (Age 15)

A Foggy Morning

One foggy morning,
Dusky and dull.
It was shivery and spooky,
When it was gloomy.
I was yawning and scared,
When it was cold and misty.
When I went back inside
And looked out of the window,
It looked very steamy.
When I went out to play
It was really un-seeable.
One foggy morning it was
Chilly and icy, rainy and dusty.
It was dull and gloomy,
I really hate foggy mornings.

Sean Davies (Age 9)

Celebrate!

I can't believe it, it's not true
the millenium's coming for me and you.
However far you run away
the parties will follow you bright and gay.
There will be parties and prizes
with lots of surprises
win cuddly toys in all shapes and sizes.
There will be disco's and streamers
you have got to believe us
get up, get out,
don't be one of the dreamers.
There will be good food to eat
with sugary sweets,
cup cakes and candy
laid out on a sheet.
It's nearly here so join in the fun
the celebrations of the millenium!

Nic Day (Age 14)

Winter

Fluffy clouds of snow drifting dreamily.
Flakes float silently, melting gently.

White blankets of snowflakes cover gently shaking trees.
The trees calmly sway in the softly blowing breeze.

The snow covered rooftops glisten covered like icing on a cake,
With a magical sprinkling of icing sugar.

The pond lies silver covered in skate trails.
Asleep 'til Spring rises and Winter rests.

Lauren Dealey (Age 10)

Spring

Morning

When I wake up in the morning
I hear birds sing
It's such a nice thing
To hear the the birds sing
In Spring the flowers grow
And the flowers are so pretty
To see in Spring
The babies are born

Evening

In the evening the birds are still singing
And it's so lovely to hear the birds always sing
And it's so nice to see the birds in your garden
And in spring all the babies hatch out their shells
And it's nice to see the birds on your grass

Tiffany Dowie (Age 9)

Autumn Months

Falling leaves tumble from the trees
Scattering everywhere.
Colourful butterflies flit from flower to flower.
Harvest starts now.
Trees are changing clothes,
Trees are looking like skeletons.
When the wind blows, it's kite time at the beach.
Helicopters swift to the ground

Peter Daines (Age 7)

If I Were.......

If I were the sun,
I'd dance in the sky,
Amongst the clouds up high.
I'd heat up all the day,
As the young children play.
If I were the sun,
I'd make everybody smile
Because my gorgeous rays will reach every isle.

Jessica Day (Age 8)

Fire

A bright dancing flame
The dark and black smoke fire flames
Crackling flames of fire

Jared Drayton (Age 9)

Godzilla

We walked down the misty moor,
There were only a few troops.
ARRR!!!
We halted,
I sauntered on,
We approached a small dark wooden den.
I would have thought it was a small creature.
ARRR!!!
We aimed at the den.
FIRE!!!
At first nothing happened.
Then thunder struck.
CLASH!!!
It was huge.
I couldn't move.
The troops fired.
STOP!!!
CLASH!!!

Kian Darvishian (Age 9)

Detention

D etention sucks
E verybody hates detention
T oday or tomorrow somebody gets it
E verybody's had detention
N ever forget your books
T eachers are mean to us
I n a way not all of them are that bad
O nly a few are kind
N ever be bad or you will not have a head

Carl Davis (Age 11)

Driving

My car instructor Betty Lee
When lessons were over, said to me
"Stay here Bill Smith, I'll teach you things.
About reversing amongst other things
And after that let's reinforce
Your work on overtaking a horse."
I said "OK" and shut the door.
She'd never been so kind before,
She said "So you can get it right,
You'll have to hold the steering wheel quite tight."
I held it here I held it there,
By gum I held it everywhere.
She kindly taught me, after that,
About clutch control and this and that!!!
Oh! gosh the things she taught to me
My car instructor Betty Lee.

Graham Denney (Age 11)

The Conker's Life

Leaves falling from the tree
Leaves rustling in the wind
Crunch leaves rustle in the breeze
Colours like red, yellow and brown.

Cases smashing on the floor
Conkers cradled in their cases
Spiky green cases in the tree
Cases prickly like pins and needles

Conkers smooth when they are new
Conkers falling on the ground
Shiny conkers on the floor
Brown conkers on the floor

Strings swaying to and fro
Conkers breaking in air
Strings twisting conkers spinning
Children shouting conkers smashing

Gemma, Sophie, Thomas and Josie

Horse Chestnut

The leaves are soft on the tree
The leaves are like big green fans as they fall to the ground
Trees are swaying to and fro
Crispy leaves crunching on the ground

Shiny green cases fall to the floor
Spiky cases prickling fingers
After a few days cases turn brown
Old cases rubbery and brown

Shiny conkers shimmering in the sun
New conkers waiting to be found
Conkers old and shrivelled, not much use for fights
Newest conkers ready for battle

New conkers winning many fights
Conkers crack when they are hit
Used conkers shattering to the ground
Old conkers smashing into tiny bits

Luke, Megan, Aaron and Alison

Trapped

I was trapped in a house far away
In a little village called Neglajay.

Trapped in a cage was a pig
With all to eat but a sprig.

Up in the bathroom was a spider
Trapped in the plughole what a disaster.

Up in my room was my dog
He trapped his tail under a log.

Up in the attic was a bat
Trapped couldn't move under a hat.

Ben Darling (Age 14)

All About Me

Writing writing so exciting, not!
Football bowball so goodball
Tennis lennis so menace
Drawing morning so roaring
History spistory so mystery
PE not so keen
Maths books so looks
Home time lone time so bone time

James Darling (Age 9)

The Big Break

Big game, heart pumping
Kick off, running jumping
Tackling, passing sharply
Nervous, full of sweat

Half time rest at last
The time is fleeing past
Second half, winning supporters,
Clapping, cheering.

Ref pointing, blowing his whistle
Sending off with his yellow card
People shouting, pitch invasion
Running in the tunnel
Scared of getting hurt.

Ryan Dowie (Age 11)

Bypass

Planners are planning a bypass through the wood
Protesters are protesting
They are killing the earth by digging it up
They are polluting the ground
Trees falling, chainsaws buzzing
Protesters chaining themselves to trees
Lots of builders shouting
Look out below
Police come, protesters win, builders go home

Freddie Davis (Age 10)

January Trees

January trees are wet with moss
And are dull and droopy and misty and black
Their branches look like bones from a skeleton
Its twigs are like the spiky fingers of a wicked witch
Its trunk is dark and grey
With branches and twigs like the spokes on a bike
Or like the straw of a broom,
The twigs are like witches cats fur when it stands on end

Rebecca Dale (Age 8)

Life

On January 19th I came on this planet, I looked so cute they called me Janet.

On February 23rd I started to walk, a few days later I started to talk.

On March 22nd I started at the toddler hall, and I thought I was really tall.

On April 2nd I started big school, but there were some big boys who were really cruel.

On May 28th I went to Secondary school, now I started to be really cool!

On June 17th I got my first job, in a little shop down on the Cob.

On July 4th I took my driving test, I really thought I had done my best.

On August 20th I got married to Tim Pring and he gave me such a lovely ring.

On September 8th I had lots of kids, Lucy, Jim and baby Sid.

On October 3rd My only daughter had a baby boy, he looked so like his dad they named him Roy.

On November 9th I was an old Gran, and it was then they lifted the pension ban.

On December 30th my life was coming to an end, I was sent to hospital but didn't mend . . . .

Sarah Dyer and Gemma Doble

Conkers

Oh, the lovely conkers hang so high
I just can not believe my eyes.
The spikey shells lay on the ground
While shiny conkers bounce around.

Nathan Dennis (Age 6)

Summer

Summer is coming,
Summer is here,
Summer is for everyone
Far and near.

The birds are chirping
Here and there,
Birds are flying
Through the air.

People are bathing
Out in the sun,
Lying on lilos
Taking in the sun.

Suddenly the sun drifts down
People go inside,
People gaze at the moonlight
In the midnight sky.

Steven Dobbs (Age 12)

Picture Poems

Where am I?
I can smell the fresh flowers
I can touch the spiky trees
I can feel the fresh breeze
I can hear the deer running
Through the woods
I can taste the smell of the cars
I can see the flowers
Dancing in the wind

Oliver Downton (Age 8)

I Used To Eat Bananas Sir

I used to eat bananas, sir,
And take great delight
I used to eat bananas, sir,
And be in for a fight
I used to eat bananas, sir,
But now to my plight.
I can't eat bananas, sir,
Because now I know they bite.

William Darby (Age 14)

Football

Liverpool are the best,
They can beat all the rest,
There's a boy called Robbie Fowler,
And he only plays when the sun's like a flower,
The goalies try to stop the ball from going in the net,
If they don't win the teams will be in a debt,
The players are very bold,
When they play in the cold,
When the match is over half of the men go for a walk
And the other half go for a talk.

Tracey Dawe (Age 11)

The Magic Box

I will put in my box
Three barking dogs,
A Caribbean yellow sun,
The smell of baking bread.

I will put in my box
The cuddliest hamster,
The cutest chipmunk,
And the goldenest sand.

I will put in my box
A summer silk cloth swishing,
In the corners some scared rabbits,
And a wavy sea with dolphins.

The hinges are little furry heads,
And all around it will be stars,
I shall swim with the dolphins,
And cuddle my furry funny friends.

Harriet Delves (Age 10)

Autumn

I like walking through the leaves
And kicking in them
I like watching the leaves falling from the sky
Animals hibernate in the ground
And some animals come out and look for food
And go back to their home
And bury their food under the ground
They dig it up again and eat it at Winter

Luke Dunne (Age 6)

My Uncle Charlie

My Uncle and I
Are like each other
He is like me but not like my Mother
My Aunty said at night time he steals the cover.

My Uncle likes messing around
One time he asked me if I wanted a hound.
My Aunty said he is a little absurd
But when I was there he crawled round the room and purred.

He has one blue eye and one brown
And I know he has got a green dressing gown.
You'll never ask for a better Uncle
Than my Uncle Charlie.

Gemma Deakin (Age 10)

Land Of Dreams

Over the hills and across the stream
Lives a fairy who loves to dream.
She once found a house of sugar,
And went to live there with her mother.
But then one day she had a shock
She had lost the bird from her cuckoo clock.
And just as she began to cry,
A dragonfly came gliding by.
And said in a slow yet kind voice,
"Come with me to the land of dreams".
And she replied,
"Since you tell of the land of dreams will you take me there?"
So as they flew into the sky so blue,
They landed on a toffee mount.
The fairy bought a house in the clouds,
And stayed there for ever and ever.

Naomi Deller-Vaughan (Age 10)

The Sky

The sky is blue
Sometimes cloudy
It doesn't have a clue
When it starts to rain

In the night
The stars come out
And the moon is so bright
When it lights up the whole of the sky

When the morning sun comes out
Everything comes alive
Even the flowers start to sprout
And the sky will always be there

Megan Davies (Age 9)

The Swamp

Slurpy, squidgy, slimey swamp,
Why is your power so great?
Well you're not going to fool me,
You steaming, sticky swamp.
Why do you rule the world with
Your strange smell?
You powerful swamp.
I will not be controlled by your
Power.

Laura Denny (Age 10)

A Cloud

A cloud is a white swan,
Swimming in a tranquil lake.

It is a ball of cotton wool,
Floating in a radox bath.

It is a dollop of creamy mash,
Splatted on a blue plate.

It is a bar of Dove soap,
Resting on a china basin.

It is a white boat,
Sailing in the deep blue sea.

Edward Dolton (Age 11)

How Did It Start?

Take a trip back in time,
To the beginning of the line.
When this story was untold,
The one I am about to unfold.

Take a trip to the ages,
When dinosaurs did rule,
And take up the first few pages,
Of this book that's new.

Then came humans (that was grand)
We took over half the land.
We used it for so many things.
Like tarmacing for metal wings.

But every time we did this thus,
We lost a little part of us.
A small reminder of how it started.
With this memory we had parted.

But every time we want to remember.
Of how this world became a member.
Of the planets we see all night long,
We can't, the memory is gone.

Diane Dundon (Age 14)

The Half Acid Eaten Monster

I saw him
He was as tall as Blackpool tower,
It lived in a cave down on the beach,
It had one eye bulging out of its socket.
The other gone,
The blood from his body ran down his nails
He saw me
I ran . . .,
And I ran . . .,
He followed me,
I ran faster
And faster
He disappeared
Then before I knew he had managed to pull my hair out,
I snatched it from his overgrown nails,
And growled
He roared at me,
I threw my long hair at his half acid eaten body
Slime and gung oozed out of the acid eaten body
The face of the monster hit the floor

Andrew Daniells (Age 9)

Picture Poem

I can see the clear water
Reflecting off the hillside
I can feel the still water
I can hear the brown leaves running
I can taste the slimy fish
I can smell the fresh fish
That the fishing men have caught

Lewis Downton (Age 8)

Shadows

I see them at night
There I am full of fright
I like to bite my nails
When it gales
Scared all night I lie
In my bed I cry

Laura Dale (Age 10)

A Foggy Morning

One morning it was damp and dull.
It was really creepy out in the misty fog.
On the road it was really chilly,
The air was cold and really slippery,
Dark and icy and really wet
Because of the drips of rain,
All the cars were really icy.

Emma Davies (Age 9)

Horror

Horror is disgusting
Sometimes very gruesome
The sitting odour of his flesh

To drag you to his dingy hold
He will cook you in his dinner pot
With flesh and bones

Hairy hands
With finger nails curved round

He has his eyes at one side of his head
He has his ears on his gruesome face

He went on holiday
Oh no will he come back???!!!!

Lisa Dugard (Age 10)

All Around Us

I went out it was hot
The sun shone on my pots
The sky is blue
The trees are new
The grass is green
The butterflies are king

Heather Dewar (Age 6)

Ready To Face The World

Rude awakening, shrill alarm,
My blanket of sleep ripped apart,
The skoosh of tyres on wet tarmac,
Heralds another rainy day.

Half asleep, sticky eyes,
I still have vague memories of dreams,
The warm smell of toast floats upwards,
As the letters drop to the floor.

Open curtains, patchy sunlight,
I suddenly realise the time,
A quick struggle with clothes and I'm ready,
Ready to face the world.

Louise Doherty (Age 12)

The Lost Tomb

People sweat to find a tomb
As the water boy rushes back and forward
The boy cries "I've found something"
People stop and stare
Nobody knows
Heart quickens
Eyes widen
Sand flying through the air.
A voice whispers,
"I shall curse you"
Twelve steps before them,
Was there a door at the bottom of the steps?
People getting nearer and nearer
There before them a sealed stamp
The candle flickers, tempting moment
The bar is thrust against the door the plaster crumbles,
Hot air is released with the scent perfumes.

Aaron Delarue (Age 8)

The Rain

Drippy droppy the rain is coming
I wonder what it will be like
I wonder
When I danced in the puddles
I soaked my new dress
My mum was very cross
And sent me to bed

Danielle Dawkins (Age 7)

Play Time

Play Time is like a volcano erupting
With children sliding down
Play time is like a gust of wind
That blows the children away

Christian Dacres (Age 6)

Horses

What I like about horses
Is that they never talk back
What I don't like about horses
Is that you have to clean their tack

I love it when we gallop
I love it when we trot
It's OK when we walk
But canter always beats the lot

When I'm jumping Holly
It's always very light
But when at night I go to bed
I always feel all tight

Emily Darling (Age 9)

Elephants

Elephants big and small
They can even be very, very tall.
When I was in the bath with an elephant
All the water fell out.
When an elephant came home
He went to Elephant Dome.
One day an elephant rode my bike.
My bike broke and the
Wheels fell off.

Cian Davis (Age 7)

It Came From Beneath The Bed

Head of a dragon,
Sting of a bee,
Horn of unicorn,
Came close to me.

Out of a black hole,
Maybe in space,
Colour of beetles,
In maggots waste.

Four yellow eyes,
And an awful stink,
It was changing colour,
Now was bright pink.

Six blue legs,
And a sword in one paw,
It was sinking fast now,
Into the floor.

I thought it was here,
Here to stay,
But it's going going,
Gone away.

Rhiannon Dean (Age 9)

Monkeys And Us

Monkeys chimps, gorrilas and golden marmosets
All live together in harmony I bet
Unlike us
Think of those terrorist groups
Machining children and adults down like troops
Unlike them
Why can't we just live together
In harmony for ever and ever

Louise Davidson (Age 10)

The Magic Box

I will put in the box

The faint face of a fossilised fairy
Blood from a raspberry red Unicorn
The emerald green ear from an eccentric emperor.

I will put in the box

The tune from a golden flute,
A spark from the Olympic torch,
The silver crown from King Neptune's treasury.

I will put in the box

The tail from a violet tiger,
The snout from a grass green aardvark,
A star from the most remote galaxy.

My box is fashioned from blue bronze and gold iron,
With unknown planets on the lid and surprises in every corner,
It's hinges are Pheonix's claws.

I shall sail in my box,
In a boat as blue as the sea,
I shall sail on unknown seas
Then anchor on an undiscovered island.

James Dawkins (Age 9)

I Have A Cow

I have a cow her name is Daisy
In the morning she's very lazy
In the morning I drink milk
That tastes like silk

Sophie Dodman (Age 8)

The Hot Greek

There once was a Greek with a view
It was hot so he said "Phew"
He could walk to the beach
With a nice juicy peach
For shade he sat under a yew.

Aaron Dredge (Age 10)

What They Saw

I saw hurdles over 100 feet tall
I saw eyes bright as flame
I saw the sun in the dark of night,
But what they saw was terrifying
What was blood freezing
They saw DEATH itself.

They saw Satan
Satan himself
Trudging through those awful trenches,
Past the dead bodies
Ever to be scarred with the cut of war.

Danny Duggan (Age 11)

Hocus Pocus . . .

Spooky noises in the dark,
Don't go walking in the park,
For witches, wizards, goblins, goons
Go out dancing in the moon.

Pixies, fairies in the clouds,
Go out making little sounds,
To tell everyone to come along,
To join in the witches song.

Great spell books and special potions,
Fairy dust and magic lotions,
Dragons, cats, spells Oh No . . . .
Hocus Pocus here we go.

Natalia Diaz (Age 11)

Phew!

On a cold day
On a really cold day
On a really really cold day
On a really really shivering day
There is nothing better than playing
In the white crunchy cold
Watery icy freezing snow
Yipee!!

Amy Donegan (Age 6)

My Child

My child . . . .

People may kill you with their words,
Burn you with their hatefulness,
Shatter you with their coldness,
Blind you with their flames,
Deafen you with their silence,
So you'll flee from them,
Far away,
You don't look back,
Because you've always known:
Like air you'll rise above them,
So they are the ones left below

Maria Dundon (Age 14)

Guess Who?

Who wakes me up in the morning?
Who kisses me good night?
Who always lives with me and
Who makes sure I'm alright?
Who talks to me?
Who washes my clothes?
Who makes my breakfast?
Who loves me very very very much
My mummy she's my best friend.

Jessica Danaher (Age 7)

My Monkey

My monkey jumped out of a bomber
The powercut got bombed by a corner
As for the plane, well Mr Way
Was in the plane, "Crash"
Then came the monkey "Splat"
"Jam on toast then"

Andrew David Davies (Age 10)

The Night

Wolves are howling
Under the ghostly moon

Shadowy figures lurk in the house
While the wind whistles in the dark

The family sleeps and
The dog snores by the fire

Tom Dyer (Age 9)

The Game

I want to invent a game
I already have an aim
I want to include a ball,
I'll get one at a stall
Perhaps some skates as well
I wonder who to tell?
It's like basketball on wheels
That'll get some squeals!
I wonder who will play?
No-one, they've all run away

Charlotte Davies (Age 10½)

The Playground

Everyone says
Our playground
Is overcrowded
But I feel lonely

Matthew Dent (Age 10)

Mysterious Time

Stars blink like dew and gems,
Lying in my bed asleep,
Even though I'm dreaming,
I feel awake,
But am I really dreaming?
Everything feels real,
Irregular things dance around,
Shadows make abnormal sounds,
Black as pitch,
I dream of something
that does not exist,
Mysterious objects appear,
Items that I can not explain,
This is the Mysterious Time.

Emma Davidson (Age 9)

A Day At The Farm

Every summer we went to the farm,
We used to stay with my Nan and Grandad.

The green grass smelt fresh, we sat drinking coke,
I enjoyed feeding the rabbits cabbage,
Watching them as they nibbled and then chewed,
They always used to hop away from me,
My sister and I argued over them.

My Nan sat smiling as I played with chicks,
My Grandad sat resting, often asleep.

The baby goats sucked milk from the bottles,
My sister looked scared, as she fed them all.
The chicken's sharp claws got stuck in my hair,
I screamed out loud, as Nan took it off.

Thinking of the farm I also feel sad,
I wish we could still go and see the farm,
But my grandparents have died, so we can't.

We were only young, and we loved the farm.

Claire Egerton (Age 17)

Wild Life Hunting

I am a jungle leaper
Can see more than humans
I crouch so slowly like a baby crawling
I mean no harm I mean no harm

I have golden fur
I hide in long dry leaves
Can stop no man hunting
For the fur on me
They come with long black shimmering guns
Can't stop no man hunting
For the fur on me
It looks like death for me

Roby Dewan (Age 9)

Bravery

Bravery is dark blue
It smells tangy like vinegar
It tastes hot like pepper
It sounds like a loud trumpet
It feels like rock
It lives in YOU

Melissa Dakin (Age 10)

Christmas Is Coming

Sweets and treats
Are under your seats
Waiting for you
To come and eat.
Trees, trees,
Christmas trees,
Are waiting for you to come and please,
Please, please old wise trees,
Give me some chocolate,
Put it in my pocket,
I will go to bed,
Take it out of my pocket,
Put it in my locket and
I will fall fast asleep.

Melody Douglas (Age 9)

The Hairy Beast!

He was hairy,
I can't bare it,
He has rotten teeth,
That never really meet,
He has one eye,
That was not for a guy
With a hairy face too,
He had no ears,
No wonder he didn't hear,
One,
Two,
Three,
He lost his teeth and they fell in a cup of water,
He goes out with no doubt,
To scare away some children
            BANG!

Samantha Edmunds (Age 9)

There's Something In The Castle

There's something in the castle,
A Ghost huge and white,
He floats around the castle,
And scares us all at night.

There's something in the castle,
I've heard it howl and wail,
He moves things in the castle
And makes us all go pale!

Ashley Dening (Age 9)

Farms

Farms.
Shiny corn
On sunny days,
Waving in the wind
Sounding like the soft sea.

Richard Elliott (Age 7)

My Brother

My brother Lucas is smaller than me
I can lift him up but not easily
He grabs all my toys and has a chew
And ends up crying boo hoo!
He talks to himself and gurgles a lot,
What is he saying, I don't know what
I wish he could talk,
I wish he could walk.
Maybe when he's one
He will be more fun

Harry Drury (Age 7)

Night Fall At Goosie Fair

Come to Goosie Fair
To have fun at night fall.
Excellent music, lights, rides.
Flashing horns on the 15th November.
Try Tubby Turtle,
A winner every time!
Come to Goosie Fair at night fall.
Sticky lollies, candy floss.
Jungle slide, ski jump, fun packed rides,
All at Goosie Fair!
Have a go at darts adults,
Try to win a cuddly mouse.
Bumper cars,
Sky master revolution,
They're all there!
Go to Goosie Fair,
IT'S ALL THERE!!!!!

Vicky Exley (Age 7)

Food

It's sometimes solid, it's sometimes runny,
It sometimes tastes real yummy,
But sometimes it tastes funny,
But all of the time it's filling my tummy.

Sprouts and stuffing they taste yuck,
I wouldn't feed them muck.
Chips and pizza they taste nice,
But I try them with cream rice.

Along comes pudding nice and cold,
If you leave it will it grow mould?
Pudding it can be hot,
But you have to eat it on the spot.

In our school,
They try to feed us gruel,
But I bring my own lunch
And go munch, munch, munch.

Hannah Everett (Age 11)

Sounds Of Silence

Can you hear my red heart beating
When I'm on the stage
Can you hear me growing
When I go to bed

Can you hear me thinking
To do my times tables
Can you hear me listening
To know what I'm doing

Can you hear my brain
When I'm doing this poem
Can you hear my ears
Moving sometimes

Can you hear my legs moving
When I walk around
Can you hear me tasting
A lovely meal

Can you hear me moving
Around the playground
Can you hear me chewing my
tongue
When I'm doing my maths

Laura Evans (Age 10)

Sadness

Sadness is the unhappy colour of black
It is the taste of sewer water
It smells of a dead rat
And it looks like a wilted flower
It sounds like people crying
And it feels like wet cold mud

Nicholas Elliott (Age 10)

Happy Birthday

Happy Birthday - it's my birthday.
A special day to me.
Party day for my friends.
Party time for me.
Yo-yo for me - yo-yo for you.

Birthday for everyone.
I like what I got from my friends.
Run to the food.
Harry my friend bought me my best present.
So make a funny dance to make me laugh.
The best day to me.
You are my friends.

Amber Elbrow (Age 7)

Tiger

Slowly, I move my powerful legs,
Keeping close the the shadows of the jungle
The trees tower high blown softly by the breeze,
Like a soft weeping whisper
Chattering monkeys silence as I pass,
Hoping that I will spare their lives
My soft, snow white paws pad softly
On the damp rotted, leaves that carpet the ground
FIRE! burning bright, like the devil's lair, in a place unseen
My supple body moves in rhythm with the breeze
But someone isn't as silent as me
Prowling for a meal I turn, like cat on mouse,
Ready to pounce, no fears at heart
I see the human I turn again,
Flashing like a candle flickering out on a dark night
I see it first and then I hear it
Bang! A rising spindle of smoke
A pain on my side a thousand knives
Unseeing glassy eyes
The king is dead

Rosie Eden-Ellis (Age 10)

Fear!

Fear is like a scream of death down the chimney
Fear is like someone rustling in your dark room
Fear is like someone breathing on your neck but no-one's there
Fear is like you walking down the woods late at night
And you feel like someone's watching you
Fear is like hearing zombies climbing out of their graves ready to kill
Fear is like being stuck in a room of darkness with creaking floorboards
Fear is like being pushed down a cliff

Vicky Evans (Age 9)

All Around Us

I was looking out of my window
And I saw baby foxes and baby lambs
And trees are growing leaves
My dog had a puppy
And blossom was on the trees

Katie Eastwood (Age 6)

I Can Hear

I can hear
Wind blowing in the trees and
Rustling of the leaves
People whispering messages to each other
Birds singing a tune
High up in the trees
Feet patting on the playground floor

Lucy England (Age 7)

Coal

Coal, coal
Is all I can see
Coal, coal
It's crushing me

Coal, coal
Why is it so heavy
Coal, coal
I hope it's crushing Mr. Levy

Coal, coal
It's getting lighter
Coal, coal
It's getting brighter

Coal, coal
It's made my school black
Coal, coal
I don't care I don't have to go back

Richard Earnshaw (Age 15)

Happiness

The smell of happiness is sweet and sugary
And sends good feelings all the way down into my body.
The texture of bird songs are soft and smooth.
The echo of the colour red flashes around the room like an alarm siren.
The texture of silk is smooth, shiny and soft.
The smell of happiness is sweet and sugary like candy floss.
The sound of grass is soft swaying in the breeze.

Jacob Elder (Age 12)

The Garden Of Tears

T ears fill my eyes
H oly grass all around me
E yes red and sore

G reen land by my side
A nger in my mind
R age in my heart
D isappointed with my mother
E nd of my tears
N ote

O f
F orgiveness

T hen my mother
E legantly down the path
A rms around me
R ound me tightly
S pring flowers in her hair.

Marie Evans (Age 13)

Rain

Rain is soft
Rain is light
I can see rain
Coming in the night

Bryony Finch (Age 6)

Friendship

Whenever I am blue
Or I am sick with the flu,
Sam is there when I need her.

If I am sad
And I need a helping hand,
I can rely on Loni to help me.

And when I am down
There's no need to frown
Because Cherelle is there to make me happy.

So, in return,
I give my three best friends
A headache for their trouble!

Diane Edwards (Age 12)

Autumn Wind

Drifting through the air,
Floating here and there
Meandering through the trees,
Rustling leaves

Roaring now it blows
Screeching as it goes
So the sound increases
Never ceases

Furious whirlwinds push
Torn branches as they rush
Headlong in their flight
Through the night

Robert Eddy (Age 10)

A Night In Bombay

A spectacular sunset descends
Over the horizon,
Like an explosion of colour

Old rickety trains jam-packed
With passengers
Like pages in a book

People crowd the streets
Like a group of
Penguins

Dry dusty roads, like the
Rough tongue of a cat

Houses their tin roofs carelessly
Placed on the mud brick bungalows

Sarah Elliott (Age 10)

Wanted - A Pirate's Parrot

Wanted - a pirate's parrot,
Must have a loud and noisy squawk,
Sharp beak and long claws,
Must be clever and aggressive.
Read maps and find treasure

Wanted - a pirate's parrot,
Able to look after all the treasure,
Guard it and keep it safe,
Able to spy on all the enemies,
Seeing all and hearing all.

Wanted - a pirate's parrot,
Must never be sea sick,
And never be afraid of loud noises,
Be braver than the fiercest pirate,
And fond of pirate's rum and their songs.

Wanted - a pirate's parrot,
His bones must be like steel,
His feathers must be short,
He can use an eye patch
But see for a million miles.

Alan Evans (Age 10)

Love

Love, a deceptive multiple meaning word.
A casual saying a fulfilling sensation
Or a painful encounter.

Love can be like a cheap tabloid,
A pleasing and attractive front page.
But after the disappointing read,
The print is still dirtying your fingers.

Love can be like a metal chain,
Every other linkage the same person.
Can be a loose accessory,
Or a structural support holding it all together.

Love can be like a meaningless advert,
Filling time in the television world, and life.
It comes and goes as one, your memory has simply passed it by.

You can really mean love,
But love can be really mean to you!

Life is non-returnable,
So don't let these verses terminate love in your life.
But I warn you, love nearly always brings tragedy, ask Romeo.

Love, a deceptive multiple meaning word.

Bradley Fricker (Age 15)

My Mum

My mum and I are not alike
She is short and I am tall
My mum has reddish brown hair
I have black and brown hair

My mum has hazel eyes
I have blue eyes
My mum likes Robson and Jerome tapes
I like Bewitched and other tapes
I love my mum

Sarra Ellis (Age 9)

Madness

The colour of the orange, madness
It smells like a fire burning
Madness tastes like tangy sweets from the corner shop
The sound of sharks grinding their teeth
It feels like landing in a field of spikes
And it lives in the centre of your mind

Katie Jane Fairbairn (Age 9)

The Ruined Day

The L'Jour was tenebrous
As the soaring titanic teneberance
Towers over the glistening pond
The Prehistoric pillars hold this monster of a building together
The crystallised water is caressed by a young child
Whistling with the indulgent wind
The colossal wind sways with the bulrushes back and forth
Tenebrous clouds unfurl to let the heavens open
Sombre colours try to open the day,
But is helpless against the precipitation
What once was a beaming, glowing day
With a jewelled sky
Is now just a philantrophic, stygian cloud

Ashley Edwards (Age 10)

Autumn

The crispy leaves falling from the trees onto my head.
Crunchy leaves under my feet,
Orange and brown leaves on the ground.
Children laughing dressed up warm
Throwing the leaves at each other.
Glittering leaves in the bright Autumn sun.
The trees stand bare in the Autumn light.

Christopher Froud (Age 7)

I'm Foolish

I'm foolish, I'm childish
I get jealous easily
I moan and sulk
When I don't get my own way
I act stupidly to get your attention
I pretend I don't care
When I really do
I say things without thinking
And regret it for days afterwards
I never say sorry or admit I'm wrong
I conform to other people
To hide the way I feel
At times I'm stubborn
I lie about things to impress people
And make them like me

I do all this
BECAUSE I'M FOOLISH
BUT
ALTHOUGH I'M FOOLISH

I do have my good points

Stephen Fakes (Age 16)

Southend

Warm summer's day,
Ice cream in hand,
Walking on the beach, toes in the sand.

Squeaks of joy
From the young children playing,
Off to the amusements, their parents wish they weren't paying.

Now to the High Street
For some non-stop shopping,
Hunt for the bargains, no time for stopping.

Feel a wave of sadness
As you walk down the street,
The poor and the homeless, with no food to eat.

With bulging bags
And aching feet,
Head for Macdonald's for a bite to eat.

Time to go home,
All pile on the train,
What good timing, we just missed the rain!!

Laura Force (Age 15)

A Visit To The Dentist

D aily cleaning means brush your teeth every day
E ating an apple helps clean your teeth too
N ever eat sweets too often in a day the dentist always says, ahh
T ools the dentist uses strange and peculiar
I nside my mouth the dentist peers with a small mirror
S tickers you will get if you look after your teeth well
T he dentist says "bye bye come again soon"

Eleanor Fallow (Age 7 ½)

Seasons

Spring is the season when all flowers bloom,
Summer's the season when the bright sun booms,
Autumn's the season when all the flowers die,
Winter's the season when we wrap up inside,
These are the seasons for all of the years,
The world goes round and round as if on gears.

Kevin Eastwell-Knight (Age 10)

Winter's Day

Winter's Day
Here to stay
Cold and bleak
Freezing sheep.

Snow and rain,
It's a pain,
Thunder and lightning,
Very frightening.

Fields are frosty overnight,
Looks very pretty in morning
light,
Days are short, nights are long,
I'll feel much better when win-
ter's gone.

Mark Floyd (Age 10)

Hurt

There's an angel on this earth,
He doesn't know he's here.
But I can see him in my mind,
All his sins I'll fear.

I forgave him over and over,
And what did he do for me?
He took my pride and dignity
That I couldn't see.

He's an angel from hell not heaven
He's someone I'll never forget,
He took my heart and threw it
And that I hope he'll regret.

Aimee Foad (Age 14)

Monday Morning's Boring

I wake up in the morning
A look at my old clock
Then I think it's Monday
And go back to bed

Then my mum comes in
And tells me to get dressed
Then I have my breakfast
And by then I'm fed up

Then I set off to pick up Nick
And trudge along the road
Then it starts to rain
Because Monday morning's
BORING!

Jack Ford (Age 10)

Summer Dreams

Far away on a summer breeze, the bird soared
On a current of warm delight.
Dazzling white were the frosted tops of the peaks
The mighty pinnacles of rock
Where firs grew evergreen.

On a distant river of sharp crevassed ice,
A cloud of men like killer flies,
Ate and were merry; and scraped the life away
From the mountain range old as time,
Where I am in my dream.

Now the wind stirs the delicate painted wings,
Of a butterfly's perfect flight.
Down in the deep green valley, parachutes soared,
Lazily spiralling to earth
Where many choose to stay

But I will stay with my memories up here,
In this high heavenly paradise.
In the distance cabins gracefully glide up the peaks,
Glinting like mirrors in summer light
That in my mind is seen.

Chris Foster (Age 15)

This Is The Cat

This is the cat
Who sat on the mat
And she was fat
At 10 o'clock she watched the bat
And wore a hat
And chats to her toy rat
And pats her back
As she wears a plait
And lives in a flat

Jasmine Field (Age 7)

Healing Hearts

Attraction frozen only in my heart
Thus stopping, making terrible mistakes.
Continuous times that we were apart
My darkest hours keeping me awake.

This wonderful satisfaction of mine,
Always he's been persistent and so kind.
His touch or stares send tingles down my spine
Adoring all there is about his mind.

True this love is, but if it was to end
Now I know that possessing enough zeal
Will get me through to the soul I must tend.
Evidently my falling heart will heal.

In time admitting to love someone new,
He'll be tinted in a red rosy hue.

Elizabeth Ford (Age 14)

Valentine Sonnet

Without those eyes the world so strange would be
For me your eyes so bright do light the way.
Your perfect smile so live it dazzles me;
The smile I loved when we first met, that day.
Your skin so golden brown it seems to shine,
I shudder at your warm and gentle touch
And shiny hair so light, so soft so fine
With wild and fluffy curls I love so much.
Your tuneful voice sends shivers down my back.
To hear, you always stops me feeling low
Your ev'ry move makes me feel like I'll crack,
And, scatter ev'ry where that you will go.
You're made from dreams, too lovely to be true.
My endless love will always be for you.

Kaya Freeman (Age 14)

Splash

On a rainy day
On a really rainy day
Then putting on my wellies and
Splash
Jumping
Splashing
Playing
Laughing
In the puddles
YIPPEE!!

Jamie French (Age 6)

I'm A Clap Of Thunder

I'm a clap of thunder
A noisy thump
When I crash down
I make you jump!

Oliver Fell (Age 6)

All Around Us

The flowers are coming
The trees are budding
The rabbits are running
The foxes are cunning
The birds are mating
The lions are bating
It's happy that spring is here
Birds have wings
And they sing
But we all love this world we are in
Lions growl and tigers prowl
But they can all sniff us out

Gregory Foord (Age 7)

Captivity

I walk fast round the zoo, leaving the rest of the group behind,
Eager to go home, then my eyes meet yours.
You stare blankly at me, at first, with a glazed expression on your drooping face.
But then, just for a short moment, we regard each other,
We communicate in a way I can not explain,
Not a communication between human and beast,
Nor gorilla and girl, but as equals.
As one sympathetic friend, to another friend in a fix.
Quickly, we glance away.
No longer are my eyes attached to your mighty body,
But your "home", your surroundings, your prison,
I glance up at you once more, sitting on your branch.
You are already looking at me,
Oblivious to anyone else gathered round your enclosure.
I scurry off, head down, so many thoughts buzzing through my mind.
I go back round the zoo, slowly this time.
I look at all the animals, each and everyone in turn.
Just as I thought, they all look back at me,
With the same, sorrowful plea you did.
They are all lonely, they are all frustrated, they are all in captivity.

Rachel Finch (Age 12)

The Truth

Revenge is sweet, they say.
But it isn't
Love is blind, they say,
But it isn't
God listens to you, they say.
But he doesn't
I think they lie a lot.

Ben Farmer (Age 11)

Little Ball Of Snow

I'm a little ball of snow
Rolling down a hill
If I don't stop rolling
I'm going to be ill

Hannah Freeman (Age 6)

Spring

It was cold.
I went to bed at night.
But in the morning I had a big fright.
For it was Spring.
Oh! Lovely Spring.
With the sun shining in the breeze.
So it was good night Winter
And good morning Spring.

Rosie Faulkner (Age 7)

Elephants

Elephants are very big.
Elephants can live in a zoo.
They can make you jump.
You think it could even be a bump.

Elephants could be small.
They can even to go school.
When they get home
They can go to Play Dome.

Elephants are grey.
They like to eat hay.
I've never seen an elephant
Go on holiday.

Elephants pull down trees.
They can come in threes.

Elephants learn to use their trunk as a horn
When they are just born.

Christopher Fountain (Age 7)

The Science Lesson

We are holding a dangerous acid,
Everyone's rather happy,
The mood is far from placid,
And the teacher's getting snappy!

Kris starts messing with a mortar,
She's the landlords only daughter,
Alice hits Melissa with a burner,
Someone go, get Mr. Turner!

The pale blue acid has sprung a leak,
The school shall close for at least a week,
We have caused a lot of mess,
And got our teacher in a major stress!!

Emily Francis (Age 12)

Christmas In A Different Way

Look around,
Look around,
Snow is falling on the ground.
Little children having fun,
Whilst only one is on her own
Freezing snow falls down her face.
As she wanders through the snow
All goes quiet not even a peep
Look around
Look around
Where's she gone?
She's disappeared through a winter's long

Zoe Fisher (Age 11)

Nutty Aunts

N utty Aunty Nats
U tterly nutty is our Aunt Natalie
T otally completely off her nut
T ango dancing she'll kick butt
Y ou'll never guess her favourite passion
A unty loves to dress in fashion
U nlike you or me though
N utty Aunty loves to·go
T o a party dressed as Po!
S illy nutty Aunty Natty

Alex French (Age 13) and **Mark Hardiman** (Age 12)

Chocolate Egg

What does a chocolate egg symbolise
Love, care or heaps of lies?
Is it just because we like chocolate,
Or has it a special meaning?

It was the big stone
Of that man that was all alone
A man named Jesus
Who came to save his people.

God loved his creation
But he didn't have their co-operation
They lied, died
And didn't go to him.

He sent his only son
Jesus,
To die on the cross
And rise again.

So as your teeth sink in to that chocolate
It is no sin to remember
That man that died for you.

Heather Feldwick (Age 14)

Sport

I like sport,
Like basketball,
I like sport,
With a ball,
I like football,
Rugby too
I like sport
I HOPE YOU DO!

Michael Francis (Age 10)

In My Bedroom

In my bedroom
Is a chair
where I sit
There is only one
In my room
And this is it
I'm not lying down
And I'm not standing up
So this is the position
That I take up.

Sitting in my chair
Isn't up
and it isn't down
It isn't at school
And it isn't down the town
It's where I play my games
On the Nintendo 64
It isn't really anywhere
It's everywhere
And more.

Rhys Fitzgerald (Age 11)

A Fish

I am a fish
That is served on a dish.
Chips and peas make me pleased
And I am the bees knees.
I swim around in the deep blue see
Until a fisherman catches me.

Vicky Foster (Age 11)

Soldier

I'm a soldier in the war,
They said it will be great but it's quite a bore,
People going over the top, bang goes the guns, they get shot.
The generals order an attack,
They run into no-mans land and that was that.
All I could hear was bombs going off,
And screams of men as their limbs got torn off.
The war's a bloody thing, it's sad and full of pain,
The generals just think it's a game.

Matthew Foyle (Age 14)

Sweyne Park School

Sweyne Park is the best
Better than the rest
Tons of homework
Can be a pest
If you go to Sweyne Park
You should know if your
Naughty you gotta go
Sweyne Park is brilliant
It's got everything there
Fantastic gymnastics and
Brilliant clubs
IT rooms, Science rooms and
English rooms too.
The school is cool
It's got a brilliant pool
The teachers are great
There's no debate
If you don't go to Sweyne you must be mad
But I bet you're feeling pretty sad.

Gareth Fahey (Age 11)

The Autumn Wind

The summer wind is soft
Sweet or has a nice breeze

The winter wind is strong
And mischievous and
Sweeps the leaves along

The spring wind is fresh
And blooming and weak

The wind I love the best is autumn
Because the brown crispy leaves
Blow away and the bare
Trees stand like statues

Luke Fisher (Age 8)

November

No going outside
No playing on my bike
No going on holiday
No playing on the beach
No nice hot sun
No fun
No summer
NNN November!!!!

Hannah Foster (Age 8)

Fear

Fear is like being dragged away from your mum
Fear is like seeing your own bones being crunched.
Fear is like a demon taking you away to another land.
Fear is like the wind howling at you and you only
Fear is like being cursed with black magic
Fear is like creepy crawlies crawling up your back
Fear is like sweat and slime coming out your mouth
Fear is like being in a black and dull room
Fear is like being on your own in the street
Fear is like at night thinking someone's chasing you
Fear is like on your own but with no food or drink
Fear is like having a friend that turns against you

James Fisher (Age 9)

I Wonder Why?

Why are clouds so light and fluffy?
Why do parents get so huffy?

Why is ice-cream so very cold?
Why are people quite young and old?

Why are our woodlands so full of trees?
Why do children play on their knees?

Why do grandparents sit and sigh?
Why can butterflies only fly?

Why is the sea so deep and dark?
Why can't dogs talk but only bark?

Why are sweets so nice and yummy?
Why does food go to my tummy?

Why do I wonder, why do I,
Ask who invented apple pie?

Louise Finch (Age 13)

Winter

Ice like a diamond ring
Robins sing in the snow
Snow as white as sugar
Icing like snow
All sat by the fire in the warm
Snowmen talking to themselves
Snow softly blowing
Wind like a ball of fire
Winter is so delightful

Kellie Fowler (Age 8)

My Tiger

My Tiger in the night,
Wins every fight,
With his eyes glowing in the night,
With his whiskers white as snow,
His colour like sunset,
His ears pointed like mountain top,
And his teeth as gold,
His nose as pink as a pig,
And his black stripes as dark as pitch.

David Fewings (Age 10)

Dreams

There I stood on the edge,
Of the tall green wood,
It called to me, I walked in,
I needed to know what was there.

On one side was the babbling brooks,
On the other were beautiful trees,
But dead ahead, was blackness and deathly silence,
I had to know what was there.

Walking deeper and deeper,
Only blackness could be seen,
I turned, I spun, I looked around,
Something was there, something to give me a scare,
I could hear the breathing, closer and closer,
I ran and ran and then . . . . .

Stirring lightly from my bed,
As soft as roses red
I said it was only a dream,
And I softly went back to sleep,

To dream

Emma Frith (Age 14)

The Air Raid

The siren went
An air raid was coming
We ran in panic to the shelter shouting HELP!
CRASH! went all the bombs
The hot shelter wobbled over
We ran to the house
Then the all clear siren went
We were relieved.

Ross Fletcher (Age 9)

Michael

Michael likes to eat his cheese
Forgetting though to pay his fees,
Michael likes to suck his feet
Even during snow and sleet,
While he has a mouth of flesh
He covers himself with flower mesh.

He always murmurs "bibble bobble bobble bib"
And always seems to include a fib,
When his mother always calls
"Stop it! You silly, clumsy fools"
Of course he answers, "Bibble bobble bobble bib"
And uses it as a useless fib.

Steven Flynn (Age 10)

Survivor

In a battlefield of mud and blood
On a lonely mound it stands.

Like a skeletal creature,
Fingers clutching at the sky
A deadened, blackened
Twisted Torso, left alone to die.

It has been bombed and shot at,
Shelled and gassed,
Seen men killed, retreat,
And advance èn masse.

It has seen all the horror,
Seen all the grief,
Seen much bloodshed
Since it shed its last leaf.

Now it stands in the driving rain,
Amidst barbed wire and trench
Bodies lay in the mud around,
The wind carries the stench.

Branches broken, roots dried up,
The bark is cracked and old
But still it stands up on the mound
Indifferent to the cold.

James Feist (Age 14)

Scrummy Food

He loved his yummy scrummy food
But wasn't in a very good mood
He ate a hot dog
But found it was a log
And that was why he was in a bad mood
So never again with his food

Matthew Fitton (Age 11)

Stock Car Racing

Stock car racing is really fun,
But the noise is really loud,
The engine fumes go in the air
And suffocate the crowd.

Banger racing is the best
It puts the drivers to the test
The crashes are spectacular
Usually you end up with a mangled car

When the racing's over
And it's time for us to go
We stay for another half hour,
And watch the firework show.

Hannah Fell (Age 10 ½)

Rollercoasters

Thrills, chills, laughter, fun.
Screaming, shouting all way through.
Children, everybody, here they come.
Even adults, grandparents too.

Round the corner, down and up,
Scary, freaky, eyes of fear,
Sitting down or standing up,
You know the end is nowhere near.

Out of control, freaking out,
Never at a slow pace,
All you hear is a big long shout,
When is the end of this frantic race.

Aching body, dizzy head,
Still laughing, still cheering,
Getting ill, faces red,
Buzzing sounds, all your hearing.

It's all over, here's the end,
What a great, fantastic ride,
All I wanna know is when,
I can do it all again.

Maria Falbo (Age 11)

My Annoying Fish

I have a fish
He lives in a dish
One morning
I saw him yawning
At supper
I saw him drinking a cuppa
I was watching television
We saw him learning division
We were going to bed
I saw him chopping somebody's head
After that he was dead!

Jenny Flowers (Age 8)

Lucky

I love lucky,
Like us all.
Loves to play around all day,
Shiny coat
Glistening in the sun,
Chasing sticks through the woods.
Best dog in the world
Coming home to stay.

Alice Foggitt (Age 11)

I Want To Get Out Of This Place

I want to get out of this place.
It's like being in hell
No family to care for.
I want to get out of this place
It's like being in a blood shed
And there is nobody to talk to.
I wish I could shoot myself in the head.
I want to get out of this place
Nothing to eat except bully and biscuits
It is so cold I can't feel my fingers and my feet.
I wish I was at home tucked up in bed.
I want to get out of this place.

Emma Fisher (Age 14)

Inside The Egg

Darker than
night as warm
as the sun, as brave
as a robin, I am inside
this egg warm and cosy,
calm and quiet, smooth, shiny,
shell on the outside, which is protecting
me from danger. As I grow, I am getting
slightly larger, I am going to crack out of this
egg and grow up to be like my mother,
a beautiful chicken, I am getting
cramped inside this slippery
but smooth egg, until
one day soon I will
be getting a
chance to
break
out!!

Samantha Fountain (Age 10)

The Pond Of Shadows

A moonlit tree stood tall,
Towered above the pond of shadows.
Shadows of evil spirits and ghouls,
Descending after hunting hours.
Dead weeds and moist bank squelch
Under daring travellers feet.
Brown, dead leaves and creatures,
Gradually rot away into nothingness,
Occasional ripples in the misty, murky water,
Startle animals usually motionless,
As Autumn approaches,
Creatures begin to hibernate,
Shelter from the cold.
Leaves fall exposing the pond to icy airs,
Becoming a circle of dead leaves,
Only able to leave with sudden bursts of wind,
That pass through the lonely glade.

Georgina Freestone (Age 10)

Conker Poem

Leaves green, leaves brown all the colours of the rainbow
Long thin webbed leaves growing on the tall trees
Thin tree, fat leaves curling on the soft ground.
Big brown crunch leaves floating to the grassy ground.
Floating leaves shimmering in the Autumn breeze.

Cases spiky soft inside conkers warm from the wind outside.
Big spiky green shells hanging on the tall tree.
Soft as a bed inside, green spiky conker cases.
Hard green spiky conker cases.
Great big sharp cases.

New shiny conkers, dark brown on the ground.
Conkers shiny bright and brown.
Big shiny conkers, shining in the sun.
Shiny hard knocked cracked conkers.
Sparkling, round conkers, stand out in the sun.

Big shiny conkers exploding against each other
Big, little stringed conkers thrashing, bashing each other.
Shiny conkers on a string, hitting, smashing, winning!
Smashing, crashing bits of conkers all over the place.
Crack, crack, crackedy crack.

Hayley, Paul, Maxwell, Christopher and Harriet

Winter

It's winter and it's glistening like crystals,
As sharp as a splinter in a man's finger.
The squirrels are hibernating with nuts and snowy conkers
Which they keep in the winter to eat.
Sometimes it's so cold it freezes your toes to ice.

Emrys Gobey-Thomas (Age 6)

I Want To Go Skiing

I want to go skiing
I really want to go skiing
I want to go down the biggest slope
I want to feel the wind in my face
As I fly past trees

I went skiing
I really went skiing
But I didn't go down the biggest slope
I was frozen and sore and stiff
As I tried to get up from my knees

I want to go skiing
I really want to go skiing
I want to go down the biggest slope
I want to feel like I'm flying
I want to feel the wind in my face
As I fly past trees

James Forder (Age 9)

Christmas Day

Christmas Day,
Snow falling,
Turkey dinner,
Babies crawling,
Open presents
Say hurray
I'll stay here
And play all
Day!!

Feeling sad
Really bad
Just be glad
That I'm your
DAD!!

Leon Ford (Age 10)

The Kite

The
Kite spinning
Upside down
Round and round
And to the ground
The kite swirling
Crazily skimming the sky
Fly, fly up in to the sky and
CRASH
Back down to the

G
R
O
U
N
D

Thomas Foulcher (Age 10)

Children's Revenge

Oh! No! Mr. A Again
It is our turn to join his painful game
"Talking is a MUST NOT DO!"
"The result could be painful for you"
He is a coiled up spring ready to ping
Although he does everything for a reason
I would rather be tried for treason
His finger is a red hot poker
Sometimes he is a real joker.
"Watch out" I said "It is Mr. A"
"Go home" he said it is the end of the day.

Andrew Fox (Age 10)

In The Playground

Today
Children playing
Skipping feet
Playing football
Cut knees
Hurting feelings
Getting knocked over
Nasty bullying
Crying eyes
Little voices in the distance
Swapping all around
This all happened today
But tomorrow
It will happen all over again
Like children playing
Skipping feet . . . . . .

Robert Franklin (Age 9)

I Woke Up In The Morning

I woke up in the morning it was pouring with rain
I looked at my uniform it had a little stain
I walked down the stairs bumpety bump
I came to the second step and I went jump. . .

I opened the door creakety creak
I saw a little mouse and it went squeak!
I gulped down my breakfast lovely and sweet,
When I'd finished that I fell of my seat.

I opened the door the cold got my ear,
Then I just remembered I'd forgotten my gear
I hopped on the bus hoppety hop
I sat on the seat and the bus went stop
I got off the bus skippety skip
I saw a little dog and he was called pip.

I walked into school it was so cool,
But then I fell in the swimming pool!
I walked into school lovely and hard
Then I saw somebody dressed up as a guard

David Farrar (Age 8)

The Mess

Mum:

Clean up your room I'm not doing it for you
Get it done by half past two.
Make sure it's spick and span,
You'd better go and fetch the brush and dustpan.
You can make me happy, you can make me blue,
But either way you've got 'till half past two.

Child:

I'm doing it now, don't rush me,
Can't you change it to quarter past three.
The carpet is full of chocolate and ink,
The socks in the corner really stink.
My clothes are spread out on the floor,
I think that cleaning should be no more.
There is cheese in my bed,
At the bottom not the head.
The bin is full of rubbish, the cat has smelt the whiff,
Of the mould in my drawer from last May the fifth.
I know my room is messy and that I can not lie
That my room looks like a pig sty.
It's messy in the morning, it's messy in the eve,
So if my room is bothering you, just get out and leave.

Michaela Francis (Age 10)

The Wind

Hands of the wind pull and push
Branches and twigs, spoiling the hush
Of the haunted silent night

Whipping and whisking the silver leaves
As they dance and weave among the trees,
Elfin shadows against a waxy moon

Strangely yelping a frantic cry,
This angry visitor charges by
Cupping the sea and tossing out life

Calm and gentle the mid-summer breeze
Caresses the cheek of baby Louise,
This motherly touch that traces a smile

Bethany Fuller (Age 9)

Butterfly

I'm a little butterfly
Proud of my wings
They are very colourful
I fly all day
I have a three course dinner
Insects
Flies
Insects
Afterwards I fly it off
Now I'm fine
I go to sleep and close my wings
I wonder what tomorrow will bring

Matt Foster (Age 9)

Woodland Walk

Crows screeching and flapping vigorously,
Trying to fly away into the air
Rushing river flowing racing away,
Chasing like a cheetah.
Grass swaying in the gentle breeze,
Swaying away from me.
Wind blowing the rusty leaves far into the land.
Trees speaking to each other,
Whispering, laughing secretly.
The loneliness of the woodland.

Faye Fullalove (Age 9)

Season's Poem

Spring is a happy time to hear the birds chirping,
Spring is a happy time to hear the frogs burping,
I love Spring when I wake up in the morning
I hear the birds sing.
Summer brings the sun, summer's really fun,
Time to go on holiday and it's time to play.
Autumn's back again, oh what a pain,
When you have to clean up leaves
Winter is very cold, men have to wear hats because they are bald,
Everyone around the town is wearing a frown.

Lauren Farnworth (Age 8)

Arsenal Is My Life

When I was born a little Arsenal fan,
A bib I received till I was a man,
Dribble, dribble over my gorgeous bib,
Dinners finished it's time to hit the crib.

When I awoke some thirteen years later,
George Graham was the Arsenal manager,
A brand new signing called Ian Wright'y
Gave us a chance to fight for the title.

When Georgie left involved in some scandal,
I got information off my bro. Paul,
That our Arsenal were in some type of fix,
Because they weren't eating their weetabix.

Soon to come the Arsenal Newcastle game,
A Cup tie final would put them to shame,
Overmars, Bergkamp the Dutch saved the game,
The game was ours and the double again.

Next came the new season of Ninety nine,
The new signings would make the title mine,
Anelka, Vieira and Petit too,
Boring Arsenal? I think it's up to you.

Mark Griffiths (Age 16)

Sound Of Fireworks

The sound of fireworks is
A bang
A pop
A whoosh
A wheeee
A zagzi
A crackle
A boom

Sam, Thomas, Jenny, Charlene & Martha

Thoughts Of A Teddy-Bear

I lay here in the darkness,
Squashed by other things,
But once I was amazing,
Beautiful and clean.
Nobody even cares, that I was the best,
And now I am dying.
I loved all the care and attention I got,
That was great.
Now I wish I could see some light,
Maybe even get played with.
Once I had beautiful white fur
And a velvet No.1,
But now my fur is dirty,
Old and grey, I get dustier and dustier,
Every single day.
But when I was played with
They kept me clean,
Every day I remember my past like yesterday
But I still go on hoping you will play,
With me today, tomorrow and forever.

Katy Greenyer (Age 11)

Flowers

F lowers grow every day,
L ovely snowdrops come in February
O h what a lovely sight!
W et or dry they still will grow,
E arly in morning when rain might fall.
R oses grow taller and taller
S ome flowers are a great glory to you and me and everyone.

Jessica Gardner (Age 11)

Woods

Woods
dark woods
dark spooky woods
bats live in there
wolves and foxes live in there
the grass is all matted and tatted.

Emily Gadd (Age 7)

The Model

She turned to face her left, and the catwalk, effortlessly, she floated down the white steps,
A 'drug addict' stare clouding over her face.
She was on autopilot, glaring straight ahead as the lightning flashes pierced the dark around her.
Her dark hair was tight and shiny against her head, but shot out in long, sharp spikes at the back,
Black eyeliner was smeared down her cheeks and her eyebrows rose to her hairline.
Her bony shoulders extended into skeletal arms and icicle fingers,
The paper-thin white dress draped over her lack of a chest and sheered down to her wasp-like waist,
There it exploded into layers of frosty chiffon, a white waterfall cascading over her twiglets of legs,
Her feet were bare and the paleness of their skin was aggravated by the black ice runway.
She swung round to make her return journey, now focusing her stare on some of the flashing public eyes.
She reached the end of her flight and entered the dressing room, where vain peacocks preened.
They pulled, twisted and fluttered their designer feathers, fixated by their own reflections.
An overwhelming sense of inferiority crept into her head and she stole into the toilets.
She had brought her emergency bag which she now opened, and devoured the sugary contents.
She guzzled water from the fountain to mix her stomach load, then crashed into a cubicle,
And vomited.

Stephanie Gunner (Age14)

November 6th 1998

A firework fades, green glitters to the ground,
Yet fire remains, a smile and moistened eyes.
Lights shimmer, a sea of starlight surrounds;
In breathtaking grace, stars before us rise.
Your touch, your gaze raise the cool of the night,
And in your eyes beauty and calm glisten.
Alone, I feel you there, see you without sight -
Afraid, I hear your laugh, and listen.
Before there was nothing; just empty dreams,
An endless wait, a hole in which I hid
Unseen by all, not being what I seemed;
Self-pity forming waves in which I slid.
Now we sit, your smile, eyes and warmth enough,
Watching fireworks climb and glow, knowing love.

Geoffrey Gilbert (Age 17)

I Love My Tamagotchi

I love my Tamagotchi
My virtual reality pet
I feed it when its hungry
And change it when its wet
Sometimes it is not happy
And just wants me to play
He goes to sleep at night time
And stays awake all day
Just like me he has to learn
So off to school he goes
And me, I am the teacher
I taught him everything he knows
When he is ill I am the nurse
And give him an injection
I hope he soon gets better
And fights off his infection!

Jenny Gale (Age 7)

Buzzards

Brilliant brown buzzards
Soaring high, brown wings
Which have bright white tips on the ends
Golden feet and beak which is golder than gold
Acute tallons which sparkle in the sun
Its wingspan is far reaching and the way it sways in the sky
Gliding calmly in the heights of the clouds.
Hovering gracefully over tree tops
Swooping high and low, spying on a small brown field mouse
Silently the bird swoops in got it.
The bold brave bird eats its meal and gently flies off.

Sam Gratton (Age 10)

Snowman

Slippery shining ice, like a full moon,
Now it's nice cold winter.
One little boy in an orange coat,
Waiting for his mum.
Mummy comes and helps him build me.
And they get a carrot for my nose,
Now I'm finished yipee! yipee!

Emma Galley (Age 7)

The Frozen Lie

The early morning frost licks the dented church spire,
A lazy silence hangs around in the cold air,
The village hall clock echoes through the emptiness,
Fields of frozen foliage glisten in sunlight.

A lonely robin hops through the sparkling hedges,
Joining his red-breasted friends, desperately searching,
But even they are torn on this perfect morning,
Their heartache nothing compared to the villagers.

The night before had been far from peaceful, bombed,
The murdered still line the unmourning, frozen lanes,
The destruction of the night before, remembered,
The frozen morning begins their frozen, shattered lives.

Gemma Godfrey (Age 15)

Beginnings

It started with a look, a look of hope and honesty,
A swift but calm breeze and a blazing sun,
A shudder down her spine and a tingle inside,
A warm, gentle smile and a moonlight reflection.
The touch of his hand felt soft and comforting,
His love and affection were strong and powerful.
She could feel his words without any sound,
As his whisper reached her, she felt cold but special.
His body next to hers felt pure and perfect,
She knew this feeling inside was exquisite.
She knew now, any gamble would be right.
The risk of unhappiness was a fear far away.
She realised this was the start of the beginning.

Toni Greenway (Age 14)

My Family

Lizzy is like a little mouse
She squeaks when she goes around the house
Mummy is like a butterfly
She flits around as if she was in the sky
Daddy is like a great big bear
He growls and chases me up the stair
Me, well I like to be a pussy cat
And that is that!

Kathryn Sarah Giles (Age 7)

Colour Poems

Red is for blood that vampires have.
Red is for Manchester United that are the best.
Red is for Strawberry that is in the field.
Red is for traffic light
Red is for a heart that's in your chest
Boom! Boom! Boom! Boom!

Jessica Gibson (Age 7)

Me!

Me!
My hair is as long as a motorway
Me!
My skin is as white as snow
Me!
My friends are really great fun
Me!
My homework drives me mad
Me!
My school bag weighs me down
Me!
My saxophone is great fun
Me!
My bedroom could be tidier
Me!
My friends think I never get tired
But I do

Charlene Galea (Age 11)

Spring

Spring spreads
Through the gazing meadow
The flowers open their sleepy petals
The trees smile as their twigs turn the colour of varnished oak
The grass grows and stands tall and covers the mud.
The flowers spread open their coloured petals
The sun shines in the pupil of your eye
Up there is a bright blue sky that lands on the flower like an angel
The worms wriggle themselves through the soft soggy mud
The bush grows and covers the nettles
The leaves sway in the calm breeze
The birds play or sing a song like heaven
The bees fly around and collect their yellow pollen
All through the month the meadow dances in joy

Claudette Gumbs (Age 11)

Microphones

If there's anything in the world,
I would like to be,
It's Brittany Spears microphone,
So she can sing to me.

I know she sings to everyone,
When they come to hear her,
But front row seats cost fifteen quid,
And I would be much nearer.

Another thing that strikes me,
About being up that close,
Is I could smell her perfume
And see right up her nose.

I know microphones get dribbled on
But so what the hell?
It's the perks of the job when it's Brittany's mouth
And I'd get in free as well!

Christopher Gwilliam (Age 13)

David's Drum

When David's in a stress and runs into his mum,
he likes to go upstairs and PLAY HIS DRUM.

When David's doing craft and hits his thumb,
he likes to go upstairs and BANG HIS DRUM.

When it's Friday after school and his friends don't come,
he likes to go upstairs and BANG HIS DRUM.

When he's finished lunch and he's got a full tum,
he likes to go upstairs and BANG HIS DRUM.

When he's feeling lonely and he hasn't got a chum,
he likes to go upstairs and BANG HIS DRUM.

When he's forgotten his gloves and his fingers are numb,
he likes to go upstairs and BANG HIS DRUM.

So remember that . . . . .
he likes to go upstairs and BANG HIS DRUM!!!!

David Gordon (Age 12)

Football

Pass, save
Yah, mate pass here!
Quick-shoot-lob the keeper.
Very bad luck mate you hit the bar!
Half time!!!

Let's win
This match-get a
Goal - put the keeper in the
Net. We've scored were going to win!
Full time!!!

Daniel Greenman (Age 11)

All Around Us

It is spring
Hedgehogs from hibernation
Are back in creation
Lots of them around
Some still under ground

Charles Gorton (Age 7)

Birds

Look at them fly
Up in the sky
Singing
Flinging
Swerving
Curving
Playing
And saying
"I am super bird
Can I be heard?"
"They don't say a word!"

Jake Goodchild (Age 12)

Autumn

Shiny purple blackberries hanging on the prickly bush
Waiting to be picked.
Ladybirds tiptoeing across the soft, gentle leaves of the apple bush.
The shining sun blazes down on them.
Little squirrels scurrying around the forest floor.
The mossy woodland banks with the leaves fluttering down
Like feathers from the sky.

Verity Grigg (Age 7)

Untitled

Owls curl up in the day
And awake at night,
Hunt for their food
Like big white mice.
Their eyes are amber,
His claws are sharp as
A pin, as is his beak.
Owls sleep in barns
And big old oak trees.
Their feathers spread out
Like an Eagle.

Kirsty Griffiths (Age 11)

The Magic Box

I will put in my box

The teasing, secrets of the universe, magic of the greatest powers
Sparkling stars shining silently, a thousand grass green veils
The centre of a vampires heart, the arguing shouts of goblins

Snow from the highest mountain, sound from the soundless sea
Books of magic from sorcerous lands, elves from the highlands of Ida
Warriors to protect the secrets, monsters controlled by magic

Material unknown to mankind, demons which are not really there,
Yet will be, which are, Minotaurs from Crete

My box is made from iron forged from worlds far away
Its colour changes from gold to red to orange, with runes on the outside
And dark powers within, the key of destiny must open the lock

I shall live in my box living on sorcerous powers
Until I too am a sorcerer with powers unimaginable.

David Green (Age 10)

Field Of Friendship

Tweeting birds	Leaping rabbits
Sneaking foxes	Guarded dens
Trapping holes	Swaying grass
Naked shivering trees	Laying sticks
Flittering puddles	Tornado leaves
Horses galloping	Cows mucking
Sheep shivering	Dogs howling
Worms wobbling	Grasshoppers hopping
Centipedes stalling	Beetles digging
Limpets crawling	

That was the field of friendship

Joshua Gooday (Age 8)

Aliens

Aliens in my garden
Aliens in my house
Aliens in my bedroom
Please get them out

I see them in the day time
I see them in the night
I see them in my dreams
They give me a big fright

I sit in bed at night
Afraid to close my eyes
As all the Aliens are
Dancing around inside

Stacy Green (Age 10)

Autumn Time Again

Say goodbye see you later
To the summer
Until later
Now it's Autumn again
Misty murky darken day
Shall we not go out to play

Animals are hibernating
And we are now celebrating
The harvest feast of the year
Grown ups are drinking beer

Leaves are falling everywhere
Trees are growing bare
Colours orange red brown and more
Halloween is at my door
Ghouls and ghosts and many more
Trick or treaters are coming
I'm running
Autumn time again

Karl Gill (Age 10)

Phew!

On a cold day
On a really cold day
On a really really cold day
On a really really really cold day
There's nothing like a
Warm
Snuggling
Cosy wrapped up
Bed.

Helena Gray (Age 7)

Winter

The snow is white
The flowers are dying
I would not dare to go out.
I would not dare to
Walk to the shed and back.
The leaves are dying
The trees are bare
The water is frozen.

George Gates (Age 7)

The Monsters

In the shadows
The monsters creep
Silently up to your feet
Up your leg
They slyly crawl
Then they eat you
Bones and
ALL!

Wilhelmina Gibbs (Age 6)

Bloodshed

Poppies are as red as bloodshed.
We only know about the war from the diaries of the dead.
We know in our heart a way to feel sorry for the men,
Who fought for our peace.
My wife comes to my grave to weep,
I say it is not a nightmare in sleet.
I say my love is still there at your feet.
I say my love is still there at your feet.
A warm gust will warm you and say,
My love don't be sad today.
When the thunder thrills the enemy
It makes you feel so scared
I think what I put in my diary of the trenches we had to live in.
this was a secret until they killed and my diary was read.
My wife read about the end of me.
I was not there for Christmas,
Broken hearts all over the family.
Mother says fathers away overseas.

Holly Fiona Gyger (Age 10)

The Snowman

There stands the snowman
Solemnly, glumly,
With no expressions at all,
His covering a white blanket of snow.

His hat and scarf,
Tattered and torn,
Ragged and ripped,
Has been well worn.

The children who made him,
Are very proud you see,
They dance around him,
With jollity and glee.

Nearing the end,
Of this tiring day,
The snowman with tears,
Slowly melts away.

Ross Gehnich (Age 10)

The Pencils

Pencils in the sky
Rubbers at the bottom
Leaving their trails behind,
Lost but not forgotten

Elena Green (Age 5)

Body

I'm a silent footstep
Like a little bang
I'm a little hand
And sometimes I hang
I am a leg that can
Bend and run
And the body says
I'm like a
Gun

Peter Grundy (Age 6)

Spring

S spring has just begun
P primroses are coming out
R rabbits like the spring
I in spring the chickens have chicks
N new blossom on the trees
G growing flowers look pretty

Elizabeth Giles (Age 5)

Space

The space rocket, the space rocket,
Flies high in the sky,
The space rocket, the space rocket,
You might want to fly.

The satellite, the satellite,
They might want to have a fight,
The satellite, the satellite,
They do like to bite.

The great sun, the great sun,
You might want to have a bun,
The great sun, the great sun,
It likes to have fun.

The UFO the UFO
They always say go, go,
The UFO the UFO
They don't have a big toe.

Neil Armstrong, Neil Armstrong,
He lived in Hong Kong,
Neil Armstrong, Neil Armstrong
He hit the moon gong.

Ben Grundy (Age 10)

The Penguin

Black
and white
Yellow and Orange
Toddles, along, slow walker
Jumps and dives, swims
And catches   fish,
Dangerous   seals
Looking to   catch him,
All day . . . . hunting
For fish,   yellow fish,
Orange fish,   every colour
That he can wish   Yum Yum,
He chats while   hunts. Hatching
Babies coming   fast, trying to
Keep out the   way of
Seals chasing   them
Faster. Run   penguins
Run. Maybe   these
Seals only want to have
Some fun. Does anyone know?

Jason Martin Gibbins (Age 9)

My Newlyn Day

The winds coldness brushes agianst my face
Boats crawl away into the grey blanket of mist
The screeching and screaming of swooping birds
Rain drops fall onto the green and blue water like bombs
The engine of a boat is like a helicopter
Dead fish lay on the water's bed
Steam flies out of the boat's funnel
The long splutter of engines come from a small boat
The boats move gracefully along the harbour

Christopher Gall (Age 10)

Trapped Behind The Harbour Walls

Behind the harbour walls the boats are moored
Like captives,
In a big prison.
Trapped for the moment.
Protected by the harbour wall,
Only to come out at night,
When their master tells them to.
Finally when they return to the harbour,
They are captives once more.

Darren Gall (Age 10)

My Cousin Sammy

She is tall
I am small
I like to laugh like a hatter
She won't whatever the matter.

She likes cappuccino
I would rather have coke
She is sixteen and she sucks her finger
I am nine, I don't at all!

She wakes up late around nine
I wake up early around eight
I like to run about
She would rather walk.

But altogether somehow
We're the same and
We will always pretend we are sisters.

Gemma Garwood (Age 9)

The Sun

The sun hangs high in the bright blue sky,
She gleams on children on the sea wall,
On streets and meadows and the pier,
On birds awake in the limbs of the trees.

The meowing cat and the chirping budgie,
The screeching magpies high in the trees,
The horse that neighs in the warm paddock,
All adore being out in the sun.

People sunbathe to get a tan,
Flowers bloom in the summer sun,
Everyone wakes up to the blazing sun,
And go back to bed when the sun goes down.

But all of the times that belong to the night,
Snuggle up to bed to be out of her way,
And bats and badgers close their eyes,
Until dusk, the moon shall appear.

Stephanie Garrett (Age 11)

Phew!

On a cold day
On a really cold day
On a really really cold day
On a really really icy cold day
There is nothing better in the
Whole world than
Sitting next to
Yellow
Orange
Cosy
Warm
Red
Nice
Fire
Aahhh!

Mattie Gallagher (Age 6)

Foggy Morning Poem

It is very very foggy
It is very gloomy
I don't like it a bit
It is just like smoke
I think I want to push to push it away
I want to play in it
But it's too cloudy today
I hate it!

Nathan Griffiths (Age 9)

The Sparkling Night

When I see it with my eyes,
I wish, I wish, I wish,
I could be a part of it.
The sparkling sky.
The stars twinkled with all their
Might in the glowing sky.
The moon is so beautiful I want to
Bounce on it,
Although it has a . . . .
T I E!

Alexandra Green (Age 7)

A Day At Newlyn Harbour

The sky moves peacefully,
The sea, wavy and quiet.
The smell of small fish and oil,
Birds delicately bob up and down.

Boats moving slower, slower nearer,
A drift of cars on a pier.
A buzz of engines and a scrape of saws,
Oily smells in the grey harbour.

Nets are big; they catch fish for others,
Children's chitter chatter voices.
Workers struggle to work in the mist,
The pebbles in the water are so smooth and soft.

The seagulls swoop down trying to get food,
Ripples drift in the ocean by the boats slowly coming in

The day slowly goes on,
The sunset is set in the sky.
Finally the stars shine on the water like silver,
Flittering amongst the ripples,
Lost in their grave.

Bethany Grandy (Age 10)

Summer

Sky bluer than a blueberry,
People like a blob of colour,
Animals are like insects on four legs.
Flies are like blackjacks flying through the sky,
Clouds are like candyfloss flying in the air.

Kye Griffiths (Age 8)

Trip

The tramp from England went to Spain
All the time he was riding on a train
Through the ocean and through the land,
He went through all different countries including New Zealand.

He was a tall man with brown hair and glasses,
Bushy eyebrows and a big mouth to keep him warm
While he was in the ocean.

He went to New Zealand to see a kiwi.
But he ended up in Spain
He got quite wet because the train wasn't water proof
He had to go through lots of oceans including the Indian.

He went through the middle of New Zealand,
So he went back the way he came and ended up in Spain.

Lewis Goddard (Age 10)

Death Of A Wolf

The pack of black wolves roam the country,
The proud dominant male, leads
He keeps the males in order
The females are allowed to run anywhere they like,
With his pack, they hunt cattle,
He can overthrow a bull
Years pass, age catching up
The second in command, challenges
Teeth fly, the two wolves fight
He is defeated
He turns to being the lone wolf
He roams the country, alone.
Waking by the river, he puts a foot wrong
He's trapped,
A gun rose,
Fired,
Death comes.

Kai Gorringe-Stone (Age 10)

Summer's Sleep

I lay there at night
The stars all twinkly and bright.

The music in the distance
Is playing and playing just like an old record.

The darkness is fallen upon me
But it's hot and stuffy
After all it is a summer's sleep.

Adam Glover (Age 12)

The Bog

We were walking in the fog
And someone fell in the bog

We were walking in the fog
And someone fell over a log

We were walking in the fog
And someone was bitten by a dog

As you can see
This is an awful walk!!!!

Charles Graham (Age 8)

Grandma!!

So warm,
So cuddly
So safe,

Always there,
The warmth of her heart,
Beating softly in your ear,

No matter what you did,
She was never angry,
She just took care of you,

When she got ill,
When she needed looking after,
She just carried on,
As if it was a job,

When the summer term started,
She knew how to have fun,
Only this time,
When she tried,

The heart ache started,
Illness began,

Funeral Parlours
Were needed.

Kay Goodchild (Age 13)

Henry The Six Timer

Catherine of Aragon was as thick as a
dragon for marrying Henry VIII (Divorced)

Anne Boleyn she was nineteen she got her head
chopped off and then looked like a bean. (Beheaded)

Jane Seymour she was such a bore and
she died before she could say no more (Died)

Anne of Cleves she loved to see leaves but
she had to please your majesties (Divorced)

Catherine Howard was such a coward she
died before he could call her a bore (Beheaded)

Catherine Parr was trapped in a jar
but survived before she died (Survived)

Jenelle Green (Age 9)

Imagination

Is all the colours of the rainbow
It smells like 1000 flowers
It tastes like the sweetest jam in the world
It sounds like a lark which is singing
It feels like a cool and gentle breeze
It lives like stars round your mind

Rebecca Griffith (Age 9)

Premiership Poem

"I'm as fast as a motor bike at full blast" giggled Giggs gratefully.
"I'm as skilled as Van Gogh's paintings in a gallery" boasted Bergkamp brightly.
"I'm as clean as the crown jewels in London" grinned Ginola gracefully.
"I've got highlighted hair as a bright yellow reflector!" blurted out Beckham.
"I'm as hard as nails" pronounced Premier Prince Petit.

Oliver Geeves (Age 11) **and Ross Masters** (Age 11)

Monster Poem

He has hair like a worm
He has got eyes like marble
He has ears like Dumbo
He has got a mouth like a ditch
He has got teeth like knives
He has a tongue like a tree
He has got arms like tree trunks
He has got legs like a school
He has got feet like the ground.

Liam Graham (Age 11)

There's Something In The Garden Pond

There's something in the garden pond,
It only comes out at night.
It's so dreadfully ugly,
If you hear it gurgling
It's sure to give a fright!

Can you guess what it is?
It's green, speckled and hops about,
It croaks so loud without a doubt
You must know what it is?

Zoe Guzik (Age 8)

Girls

Some stink and some are sad,
When it comes to fashion they're really bad.

They're really temperamental and very rude,
When they get angry they stay in a mood.

But they're not all wimps, you have to admit!
When they get angry, man do they hit!

They prance around all night and day,
Doing what they want in their own merry way.

They stroll along then suddenly shout "Oh gosh!"
Then dash into a shop to spend all their dosh.

They look like pigs and are sly like rats,
They hang around shops like a pack of wild cats.

So as you can see girls are sad,
And if you like them you must be MAD!!

Edward Gosling (Age 11)

My Dad

My dad and myself, have loads of similarities
We love riding our bikes,
And eating Italian food,
We love making fresh pasta together,
We sometimes both get into a mood!

My dad and myself, love our two dogs,
And giving them a cuddle!
We will watch any programme together,
And would stay there forever!
We both love the Bee Gees,
And swim as far as we can out to the Italian seas.

My dad and myself, have loads of similarities,
But some things I love,
Soaps on TV
He hates them for me.
I love Arsenal!
But the team for him is Ipswich Town,
They are so low they're going down!
So I guess there are some things,
That my dad and I don't agree on.

Anna Guglielmi (Age 10)

Poem Of The Survivors

Thank you God for the brave ones,
All fit and healthy,
Ready to come home.
Care for them as they make their
Journeys back.
They risked their lives to save us.

Gareth Gillman (Age 11)

India Throughout The Day

Morning buses overflow like jugs filled to the brim.
A huge cascading coloured sash is draped around a woman's shoulders.
She has a symbol on her forehead,
Like a splurge of red paint.
Stunning buildings scrape the sky,
Tin roofs ungainly balance on mud bricks.
The dying sun screams to finish drying Bombay's wet clothes.
The evening traffic hums into the night.

Jasmin George (Age 10)

A Candle In The Dark

Life is all the blackness,
A candle in the night.
Burning brightly, white on black,
A great enchanting light.

Then suddenly a gust of wind
Came flying through the air.
The light had gone and death had come,
The candle wasn't there.

The lighter then came again,
A figure from the black.
The light was burning, bright as gold,
The candle's life was back.

James Graham (Age 11)

Red

Red the colour of school jumpers
It's the colour of a bomb when it goes off
The colour of a bonfire getting hot rapidly
The colour of a police lights woowh woowh.........
A Ferrari flashing past zoom zoom
Fireworks zooming up up up and away.
Like blood gushing out of your mouth when you die
Like a fresh red nose
The colour of lipstick on your lips
The colour of a heart for your valentine
As red as an apple when you take a big bite
Red the colour of danger in life.

Tyson Greenwood (Age 10)

There's Something In The Magic Wood

There's something in the magic wood,
A wand that glistens like a jewel,
As shiny as a silver coin,
Glinting like a diamond ring.

There's something in the magic wood,
I've seen it sparkle and shine.
All long, smooth and silky
Like a dragonfly.

There's something in the magic wood,
It's cast a thousand spells,
If you go down to the magic wood,
It's near the wishing well.

Natalie Gomm (Age 9)

Winter

Cold frosty snowing nights, skating with fun on the ice.
Ice cold frosty nights a dangerous time for skating.
Days are crisp and white under a blanket of snow.
To toboggan smoothly and swiftly.
People shopping quickly and merrily.
Cosy wrapped people, happily shop.
Trees are brown and still
They sparkle in the afternoon sun
Ducks sit beside the frozen pond
A robin hops from bush to tree
All is well with the world
The cold, white peaceful world of winter.

Lawrence Green (Age 9)

The Train

Get into the train,
Quick find me a seat,
When we're going,
We'll; have something to eat.
Look out the window,
You will see,
Cows in the fields,
Going under the trees,
Dark and scary,
The tunnel is black,
Out into the open,
The sun is so bright,
Up to the station and out of
the train,
Happy to be home again.

Milo Gamble (Age 12)

November!

No colourful trees
No buzzing bees
No light
No night
No silver moon
No golden sun
No fun
November.

Kerry Gower (Age 10)

Monster Trees

Conker trees, they are dull with dull colours.
Like brown and black, the dirty leaves,
Colours of brown, yellow and red, are disgusting.
If you walk past one the horrible rustling noise,
Gets on your nerves.
The rustling noise of the leaves,
Must be scary at night like someone's in a bush,
Coming to get you, or when the wind,
May make a conker come off,
And hit you on the head, it feels like someone's,
Hit you on the head with a hammer.
The annoying sound of little children
Screaming trying to get conkers, there goes,
The horrible whispering sounds of the leaves.
Again, whisper whisper.
Muddy brown conkers make me stay indoors.
Big, monstrous trees twenty feet, forty feet tall,
I wouldn't like to see one at night.
Old trees fifty years old or more,
For I do wait for Autumn to finish,
To get rid of these scabby trees.

Matthew Godwin (Age 10)

The Whirlwind

The howling wind rushing,
Gushing tearing everything down.
Houses devastated, children crying.
Glass smashing, trees snapping.
Thumping, jumping, shouting roaring.
The wind the wind.

Paul Gamble (Age 10)

My Cousin Lauren

My cousin Lauren is one year older than me.
She has brown eyes
I have blue eyes.
But I don't care.

My cousin Lauren loves to party
So do I
She has boy friends
So do I
But we don't care

My cousin Lauren is the playful type
When she comes to sleep
We fill the bottom of the stairs
With pillows blankets and cushions and
Slide down in a sleeping bag.

Kaleigh Greening (Age 9)

Christmas Time

Christmas time christmas time
Is my favourite time of year
Presents and sweets
At my favourite time of year
Christmas trees with lights
And big fat christmas puddings
Holly on the top.
There are people under mistletoe
Remembering Jesus in his bed
Now think of Santa
Climbing down the chimney
Leaving presents for children
If they have been good.

Abigail Gray (Age 8)

The Demon Headmaster

My teacher is called Mr. A
When he's in a nice mood I suppose he's OK
When he is happy he keeps at a level
But the rest of the time he is a devil
He is a strict angry male
When he shouts he makes me go pale
Sometimes I want to throw him away
And give him less monthly pay
He crams so much into my head
If I do any more I will surely be DEAD

Imogen Harrod (Age 9)

Countryside

I like the smell of the country
I love sounds of the water rushing
Past my ears smacking on rocks
That lay on the water surface

I can always hear creatures
Chirping and croaking all day
I love the smell of flowers
I like the weeping willows
That you can touch that reach out at you

Emma Goodship (Age 9)

Red Is

Red is the colour of blood, it runs around my body.
Red is the colour of a juicy apple.
Red is the colour of a post box that I put my letters in.
Red is the colour of my ears, they go red when I am tired.
Red is the colour of the post van, when the postman drives around.
Red is the colour of strawberries when it drips down my face.
Red is the colour of raspberries when I eat it.
Red is the colour of a ruby when it shines in my eyes.
Red is the colour of my lips when I eat strawberries.

Kimberley Greenslade (Age 8)

Rain

Pitter, patter, drip, drop I can hear the rain
It is raining in the dark
And I'm playing in the park
I like the sparkling water
I like to jump in the puddles
Sometimes I feel very gloomy
The tune goes splish splash splish
I am very cold and wet.
I like it when the lightning goes BANG
I like to wear my nice warm gloves

Naomi Gibbard (Age 6)

Tornadoes

Tornadoes are noisy, scary and fast.
Sucking up everything as they go past.
The angry winds uproot all the trees.
Sending them flying in a very strong breeze.
But
Now they have gone
And the village is calm.
Are all the chickens still at the farm?

Vincent Guest (Age 10)

Titanic

It hits the iceberg,
The water pours in the ship,
Slowly it's sinking.

The water is cold,
People drown in the water,
They die in the water.

Sinking, sinking sunk.
People die and people drown,
They cry for mercy.
Some are rescued some are not,
Soon all is quiet, they're dead.

Lucy Goodacre (Age 11)

A Freezing Cold Morning

I was in bed
I am not in the mood
For getting up
It's snowing outside
And hailing and raining outside
I want to stay in bed!
I am miserable
And I don't want to go to school
I am going to phone my teacher
I am going to school!

Hannah Giles (Age 7)

Feet

Feet are stinky like a footballers
Feet are tired like a marathon runners
Feet are dodgy like tennis players
Feet are strong like a rugby players
Feet are fast like a runners
Feet are slow like a babys
Feet are hot in the summer
Feet are cold in the winter
Feet are always great

Matthew Graham (Age 7)

In The Sea

Sharks biting
Dolphins jumping.
Whales chasing in the water
Seaweed sploshing
When the sound of fear
Comes nearer and nearer
Seagulls disappear.
Finally the night comes and the
Deep dark blue sea turns to black.
In the morning shiny,
Sparkling sea shells lit up
By the golden sun.

Bridie Gallagher (Age 8)

Remembrance

R is for red, poppies that grew wild
Every year on the fields where bodies were piled.
M is for mothers, whose hearts were broken,
Every one left with only a token.
M is for the millions of lives that were lost
Because of the fighting they paid the cost.
R is for remembering all those terrible years
And for soldiers who fought with hopes and fears.
N is for now we must never forget.
Collect your thoughts and honour the debt.
Eleventh minute, hour, day and month.

Florence Gallagher (Age 10)

Crime

Too much crime in the world
We've got to stop now before it builds
People crying screaming for help
The police? Pah! They're no help
As this world becomes a horrible
War, gun knife and hate
We've got to stop before it's too late

Kids out there on the street
Making a life just for the treat
We are begging you, please retreat.

Rebecca Gould (Age 13)

The Snow Snow Man

The snow snow man
Is a very jolly fellow
Oh a jolly fellow
He is a very nice
Snowman with
A big carrot nose

Andrew Horigan (Age 7)

The Unwelcoming Party

Finally the day's arrived,
For six whole weeks I've waited,
A mixture of feelings inside,
I am nervous, yet excited.
My hands shake with fear,
As I go, alone, through the unwelcoming gates.

All around me I can see them,
Tall, towering into the sky,
Like giants they wait,
Staring at me, ready to pounce.

What will it be like inside?
A black hole of no return?
As I walk alone,
To my destination,
My new second home
My new school.

Nicola Higginbotham (Age 15)

Christmas Eve

It's Christmas Eve,
You just can't sleep,
Your bed is warm,
And the snow is deep.

You try to stay awake at night,
But you're always asleep by midnight,
You wake up in the morning full of glee,
At all the presents under the tree.

Christopher Gordon (Age 10)

Cupid's Confusion
(Edited Version)

The Cupid fired his second shot
As I stood in your arms by the sea.
But by mistake went whizzing past
And instead of you hit me.

This Cupid he had 'L' plates
And didn't know where to begin.
The stupid Cupid did fire two arrows
And both of them missed him!

So there I was all loved up
And you just didn't care.
Why I'd cop both the arrows?
This love thing just isn't fair!

Things had not gone how I'd liked
And he was soon to go.
My emotions and confusing feelings
To him I could not show.

So now I put my pen to paper
To give you an idea.
But let me tell you before you go on
That words come nowhere near.

Gemma Howard (Age 16)

Lion On The Loose

Children in the hall,
Silent as a broom,
An urgent message calls
The teachers to the staff room.

Everyone is thinking,
And waits for a reply
No-one is blinking
But some people sigh.

"You must go to your class,"
Mrs Nichols said,
"Sensibly but fast"
Our class lead.

It isn't very funny
There's a lion loose,
It could easily catch a bunny
Or even a goose.

"No-one can go home
Unless you're with your mum.
You mustn't walk alone
But wait for her to come."

Lydia Hawkins (Age 10)

My Brother

I spy with my little eye
Something beginning with B
It doesn't fly,
In the sky,
Or swim in the sea,
It lies in a cot all day,
And is a brother to me.

Matthew Hurford (Age 15)

Winter

Above the snow,
In an igloo,
A hotel tower of ice,
There is frost water.
Ice cold.
It makes my fingers numb.
I play in it always.
Today I had a fun day.

Demi Hughes (Age 6)

Autumn

The leaves are turning to a red and a
brown
And then they all fall to the ground.
The squirrels are out at Cedars Park
And the evenings get very dark
It is fun to play in the colourful leaves
When they fall off the trees.

Gemma Harragan (Age 6)

Willow

The crumbling wrinkled tree stands perplexed and proud.
As solitary as an oyster.
The wispy branches hung low,
Like a shaggy dog ill and solemn.
The golden tipped leaves droop down towards the Earth,
Like tiny hands grasping for something desperately.
While down below the roots search monotonously for their water prey.

Josh Hall (Age 11)

The Squirrel

I like squirrels
They pick up nuts
They bury them underground
And when they are hungry
They dig them up again.

Jake Hackett (Age 6)

Notes On Jumping

There are pieces of light, fragments I see
falling from the edges of my eyes, but I can't
tell if they are splashing drops or pin-hard shatters.
My lids blink like a painstakingly slow machine made of paper.
I stand taller than the houses behind me, my coat a
Giant bulk, unsurpassable. I feel a wind whistle between my ribs.

Flat rectangles, all with cardboard corners and
the same figure in them, from different angles; smiling, scowling, sideways.
In this one quite pretty. With different people, associates, rivals, spies.
Below the cut-off bottom-edge torsos, busts, knees, my
Limbs unseen are scattered into space, fingers, digits, hands removed,
desecrated disintegrated to poison-sharp nothings like slitskin razors held
by air instead of flesh.

Each flake of every bees' nest is an impossibly taut muscle, is x-rayed out, Is
my skin, is a
Nuclear white explosion from the pitted core of the
sun's bitter light. My hair is a gutter of orange-gold.

Katy Haines (Age 17)

Winter

The crunchy sparkly leaves
On a frosty winter's day,
Spiders webs glittering like a
Jewel necklace all tangled up
The fantastic white pointed grass
As it shines like glittery jewels
The mist slowly, silently, slithering
Around in the air
The branches blowing
As if they are waving to me
The frosty beautiful
Patterns on my car
Oh, how I like winter!

Daniel Harvey (Age 7)

Tsunami

I am a dark blue sea,
Coming to get you
Run from the great monster.

Alex Heeley (Age 11)

The Stars

Thy artful stars are shining bright
In the very midst of night.
In the sky I can see
The constellations above me.

Gemini, Milky Way, Hercules, Galaxies.
The Eskimo Nebulae.
All loom above me in the sky.
I often sleep right through the day
But come out at night to watch and pray.

Thomas Hughes (Age 10)

Pegasus The Flying Horse

Pegasus the flying horse glided swiftly,
In the light of the moon,
To an elegant stop on the hill.
Its perfectly white coat twinkled like a star.
Pegasus's magical fluffy white wings,
Glistened in the rays of the moon.
Pegasus the flying horse flew without a sound
Into the sunrise.

Farran Harvey (Age 10)

Christmas Time

Now it is christmas and we all have parties.
We all build snowmen out in the snow.
We can hear the bells ringing then
We open our presents and go to church.
After we come home we have turkey
For dinner and a party for tea.
Then get more presents from Nan and Grandad
Aunties, Uncles, Cousins and friends.

Antony James Hewart (Age 8)

One Oyster Operating On Ostriches

One oyster operating on ostriches.
Two tatty ticks take toes to Timbuktu.
Three threatening throttlers throttle tinned tomatoes.
Four foot frolicking fiddletits fighting fainting foxes.
Five flipping fiddlers flip flippingly.
Six soggy socks snooply snip soiled socks.
Seven sad song spiders spin snake socks.
Eight edible Englishmen eat eighty eggs.
Nine knockout nimbletwits knit nits.
Ten tiddly toxic tooty fruits tan tummies.
Eleven elderly eggs eat elk.
Twelve twenty pences total trifles.
Thirteen thinking thinkers think thoughtfully.
Fourteen falling finders find their falling.
Fifteen fencing philberts fence frighteningly.
Sixteen spotted snakes spot spots.
Seventeen sickly soundbites sound sickly.
Eighteen endless eaters eat endlessly.
Nineteen noodles are naughty naughtily.
Twenty total tooties time tiddlers.

Julia Harris (Age 9)

Valentine Sonnet

A miracle, yes, that is what you are.
A ray of sunshine, pouring through the clouds,
And you could call me back from most afar.
I state my love for you so much aloud.
I do not know how I would be alive,
If separated from you I became.
My soul would find it hard, just to survive.
Yet you and I, I feel we are the same.
To me your love is every eve and morn.
Your face is beauty, music when you speak.
Your smile is each single, beautiful dawn.
You make me feel content, somehow complete.
Yet life itself will surely wear me down
When you don't see if I should laugh, or frown

Jill Hoskins (Age 13)

Daffodils! Daffodils!

Daffodils! Daffodils!
Like crystal gold.
The sun as bright as you.
Daffodils! Daffodils!
A spikey yellow glow
They light in the garden
They light down low.
The yellow of love
They pray in the sun
The life of a daffodil
Is such fun!

Genevieve Halpin (Age 6) **and Jasmin Hone** (Age 6)

Pitiful Town

The sweet sound of birds singing,
While farmers worked to earn a living,
From green all around and quiet roads,
Life was rich as a rose.
Population grew to meet the thousands,
Life was hard to make a living,
More people came to work the land,
Houses were built to meet demand,
Soon the village became a town,
With more and more people roaming around.

Merchants came to sell their goods,
And shops replaced the open woods,
Concrete soon replaced the grass,
Animals began to disappear just as fast.
The landscapes gone from green to grey,
With all the greenery swept away,
The village has gone from town to city,
The land has changed,
Oh what a pity.

Nicky Holloway (Age 14)

Watch Out

The howling wind gets louder and louder,
Waves crash and get a lot prouder,
Clouds are lurking over the street,
It sounds like a floorboard going creak, creak, creak.
Winds are howling day and night,
In the morning I hope it will be all right.
Babies screaming, mums moaning,
Waves are howling wind is groaning.
Is it going to get worse?
I hope there is no kind of curse.
So next time you go out for a stroll,
Watch out for the windy soul!

Charlotte Houghton (Age 10)

Friends

With your friends you can....
Go in a wood,
Eat chocolate pud,
Mess around at school,
Or go in the pool.

Also you could....
Smash up a table,
Or go in a stable,
Because friends are there to play,
And they never ever run away.

Phillip Hunt (Age 11)

Girls

Girls in books are lovely things,
But none of them skips or sings,
Girls aren't like that in my school,
Girls in my school are cool.

At lunchtime they don't skip or sing,
They don't like to do that thing,
Bulldog, charge, sumo are their games,
Hannah, Maria, Lindsay are their names.

They like Simpsons and South Park,
They do not woof or bark,
They also like Kenan and Kel,
They think work is total hell.

Horny girls like to kiss boys,
They don't like Barbie toys,
They also say, "We Rule",
They really are quite cool.

Can you see what I'm trying to say?
Girls are sweet. No way!
They are rude and rough,
Boys and girls are equally tough.

Nicholas Howell (Age 11)

Untitled

There was once a Greek who grew
Lovely potatoes for a stew
He took a bowl
And thought from the soul
This stew looks a bit too new

Ruth Horner (Age 10)

Mangled Monster

The stinky breath
The awful eyes
The bulging stomach
Makes him look hideous
He is fowl and disgusting
The ugly creature smells
Of rotten fish and old cat food

His skin is scaly bumpy and lumpy
He is green and green all over
The creature is mind boggling
Or even eye boggling
He is filthy and dirty

His blood is black and boiling hot
You couldn't get much worse
Apart from his teeth that are brown and holey
From eating people who pass near by
So be wary of the . . . . .mangled monster

Samantha Hammett (Age 10)

Guilt

Guilt is brown,
Tastes like a mushy apple,
Smells like sewers,
Sounds like the echoes of pleading, pleading, pleading
Looks like the wig that the magistrate wears,
And feels like a stone stuck in your throat.
Guilt is bad tempered
Guilt kills!

Jake Hemming (Age 10)

Firework Night

It's firework night
It's firework night
There goes a rocket
Fizzling out into the
Great dark sky
Banging, dazzling
Flickering on its way
People clapping and
The sky is lit up
Whoosh!!!
Up goes another
This one's magical
Bang!
It's like a shooting star.

Andrew Hudson (Age 11)

Dancing Piggie

Dancing Piggie
Ancing piggie
Ncing piggie
Cing piggie
Ing piggie
Ng piggie
G piggie

Piggie
Iggie
Ggie
Gie
Ie
E

Sabrina Howard (Age 9)

Night

A red sun sinks behind the mountain,
The moon comes out from behind a cloud,
The shadows sweep across the valleys,
The lights go out. Night.

A harsh wind blows across the mountain,
The moon is trapped behind a cloud,
The dark twists around the valleys,
An owl hoots. Night.

The red sun rises on the East side,
The happy birds can now begin to sing,
The dark creeps away beyond the mountain,
The night has gone. It's day!

Catherine Hartley (Age 9)

Family

Sisters!
Sisters are horrible, sisters are nice,
Sisters are fun, sisters hate mice.
Sisters are cool, sisters are annoying,
Sisters are always sisters to me.

Mums!
Mums are cool, mums always rule,
Mums get it wrong or get it right, mums always having a massive fight,
With anyone who gets in sight.

Dads!
Dads are here, dads are there,
Dads are almost everywhere.
Dads have their time, just like mums,
Who sit down and just suck their thumbs.
When I say dads are everywhere,
I mean just like mums, but over there,
You know where they always sit on Saturday night,
To see if there's a great big fight.
Of course most of the time there isn't,
But you will always find the odd one or two.
So that's my view of dads you see,
Oh by the way, the pubs a good one to check!

Claire Hellier (Age 12)

Rabbit

Henry is a furry friend
He nibbles in his hutch
He hops on the green grass
And eats too much!

Amy Hopson (Age 5)

Easter

E ach
A pril
S urprisingly what will I see?
T he Easter Bunny, an excited one
E ggs, lots of eggs, tasty treats. Easter
R abbit you're a sweet!

Lucy Henderson (Age 7)

Untitled

One gloomy night
My white fluffy blanket
Began to move
It gave me a fright
Scary and frightened
I froze to the spot
Then the ghost said
Boo to me

Jade Hounslow (Age 7)

Phew!

On a cold day
On a really cold day
On a really really cold day
On a really really icy cold day . . . .

There is nothing better in the whole world than
Sitting next to a
Yellow
Orange
Cosy
Warm
Nice
Spitting
Fire
        Ahhhh

Graeme Houston (Age 6)

Man U Vs Everton

Up David Beckham, up Andy Cole
Everton always dribble like a big, big mole!
Win 2 - 0, win 4 - 0
They should take a very good footie pill.
Man United won
When the F.A.'s done
I'll be cheering 'cos they won.
If they lost, I'll be flooding with rage,
I'll be mashing their opponents into compost.
When they're gone I'll go to bed
And dream about Man U winning.

Chris Herrett (Age 8)

Cold Months

Outside in the Autumn breeze,
I can hear the wind
brushing through the trees.
The sky like still waters
of a pink and golden lake.
The clouds like a herd
of frightened sheep break.

The summer crops
have now all disappeared.
Farm animals, their young
now fully reared.
I stand lonely and scared
in the driving rain,
as winter darkness shortens
the days once again.

Joe Herbert (Age 10)

A Harbour Scene

Cold wind makes drifting ripples
On the glistening silver sea.
The rusty decks of old fishing boats,
Are gathered with buoys like
Halloween pumpkins.

Huddled boats nudging each other,
And a skull and cross bones on a flag flaps.
A seagull bursts through bunched clouds
And glides through the cold air.

Oil and fish smells are rising to my throat,
The fish are flapping on the deck,
Struggling to get free.
Lobsters and crabs are lurking deep below.

Kelly Henderson (Age 10)

Fear

Fear is black like a night sky
It smells like burning rubber
It tastes sour
Fear sounds like trembling feet
It feels like sharp metal
It lives in the depths of your soul.

Aaron House (Age 10)

Shire

Shire, shire
Strong as an ox
Shire, shire
You weigh a ton.
You are so tall,
Taller than me,
You are as fat
As a hippo.
Long legs like,
A giant.
And gentle
As one too.

Daniel Howill (Age 10)

Diamante

War.
Crying, screaming,
Fighting, Kicking, shouting,
Hurt, sad, sharing, helping,
Caring, kind, speaking,
Friend, laughing.
Peace.

Kerri Holmes (Age 10)

War

Tanks, machine guns, destruction,
Gas, grenades, devastation.
Nuclear bombs, annihilation,
This is what war is about.

Our Air Force attacked,
Their Army counter attacks,
The whole Empire sacked,
This is what war is about.

Deep in the trenches, sinking in mud,
All around enemy bombs thud.
Screaming, explosions, covered in blood,
This is what war is about.

Surrounded by death,
The end of the earth,
He said with his dying breath
This is what war is about!
I don't want any part of it,
Where is the white flag.

Parmdeep Hothi (Age 13)

My Magic Box Poem

I will put in my box
A fish with wings
And a bird with fins
The wild winds of Scotland
And the sight of Loch Ness in summer

I will put in my box
A summer sun as bright as a star
And catching my very first fish
A wild howl of a wolf on a full moon
And sailing on a crystal clear lake

I will put in my box
All the magical spells of the world
And all the smells of the world
A snowflake landing on my hand
And leaves falling in Autumn

Michael Hartell (Age 10)

The Workhouse Master

Horrid, nasty, always cruel,
Feeds the boys on watery gruel.
They wake you early with a booming voice
You work thirteen hours without any choice.

One mistake and you will pay,
By not eating for at least one day.
And if that is not bad enough,
They'll beat you with a cane so you have to be tough.

They're tall and cocky, usually fat,
And they wear a sea-captain type of hat.
They have big buttons on their coat,
They keep an eye out and ALWAYS keep note.

Gemma Hanson (Age 10)

The Hedgehog

The hedgehog small and plump,
Wandering past the rotting tree stump,
Nervously looking at me,
Pausing,
Quiet as a mouse,
And then lays down some hay for his house.
Then carries on with his daily life while sniffing at the hay,
He's made a bed,
For the cold winter's day ahead.
Silently the hedgehog curls up,
With his spikes sticking out like sticks,
With great big ticks all over,
And then he wanders into the hay
And goes to sleep where he'll lie until May.

Ruth Hillier (Age 8)

Jack

Jack lived on a farm
With his Mum and Dad.
They also had a dog
Which was called Lad.
They had cows and pigs, ducks and sheep
And lots of animals they did keep.

Daniel Huckle (Age 5)

Anger

Anger is a raging purple
It tastes like red hot chilli's
It smells like choking wood smoke
Anger looks like a bull that's just seen red
It sounds like the seething waves
Crashing on a rock.
Anger feels like there's a fire inside me.

Catherine Hughes (Age 12)

Winter

As winter approaches,
The trail that he leaves,
Footsteps on the crisp white snow,
No colour in his face.
Jack Frost is his name,
His hair like frosted spiders' webs,
His teeth like icicles,
Sharp and jagged.
As he strolls along the cobbled road,
Turning everything to a vast cold state.
Freezing night air,
Long winters nights,
Short winters days.
He only comes but once a year,
Like a mysterious shadow putting darkness into every light.
But as winter draws to an end,
He settles into hibernation,
And the dew on the frosty lawn
Is all that he leaves behind.

Charlotte Hues (Age 14)

The Tiger

The tiger with its mighty roar
So loud it could wake the city up
Its really sharp claws
And its sharp teeth
That could break anything

Joseph Harrison (Age 7)

The Sun

When the sun was going down at night
And when the sun came up
It turned in to a sunflower
Everybody was very glad to see
The sun was turning into a sunflower

Lucy Harrison (Age 9)

Autumn

It's Autumn and I look out from the steamed window,
And look at the shallow icy pond,
With the ducks skidding fastly along
In the distance I hear a hollow sound,
Much like an energetic hound,
Being walked on this misty morning.

I put on my warm wellingtons,
And my cosy clothes,
And go for a walk
When I walk on the leaves they go
CRUNCH, CRUNCH, CRUNCH,
Then huddle in a small cramped bunch.

I look outside on this muggy day
And have to play indoors,
When I go into the cold great outdoors,
And I shiver in the horrid grey day

Sarah Harman (Age 10)

Moving

Boxes all around, it's as quiet as a mouse
Today is the day my family move house
Many thoughts crossing my mind.
Will the new place be as good
As the one I'm leaving behind?

Grandparents, aunties and uncles,
Teachers, neighbours and friends
Will the list of people I'll miss, ever end?

I've seen our new little house
I do actually like it a lot.
But it'll definitely never be
My comfy old home spot.

I've forgotten the times I've been unhappy and cried
Now I can only think of the people leaving my side
12 O'Clock, the day's begun
Time to say goodbye to everything and everyone.

Martha Henry (Age 11)

Fear

Fear is when it seems that the roof is about to cave in.
Fear is when the rain is continuously drumming on the window
Fear is when the lights flicker on and off.
Fear is when the phone rings and you pick it up and nobody is there.
Fear is when the wind blows over your face and the window is shut.

Richard Hartnell (Age 9)

Courage

Courage is blue like the sky in the morning
It smells like wonderful fruits
It tastes like pure melon
It sounds like beautiful music
It feels like strong steel
It lives in you

Jessica Harris (Age 9)

The Stars

The stars twinkle like diamonds,
They are as bright as the sun,
They shine like a torch,
When they go they are as dull as day.

The Wind

The wind howls like a wolf
As windy as a gale
The wind is like ice
Pushing you like a bobsleigh

The stars go . . . .
And the wind goes . . . .
And it's a boring old day
          AGAIN!!!!!!

Lauren Hitchcock (Age 9)

An Over Cast Day

Rain spitting and a little mist.
Boats move inches when waves touch.
Oily rainbow makes soft shapes on the water
Birds a whole community of them all in a group by the water.
Harbour walls grey and dull in its way,
Creatures in the depths below scutter to their homes,
Fish squirming around trying to find the surface of life,
Grey cloud forms rain from above,
The rope gently rots away into dust
It has to be replaced one day
In the wind a flag flaps ferociously
The shiver of a ripple drives into the evening sea.
A boat gently glides into the harbour,
Where it lays for the morning to come.

Leoni Hall (Age 10)

In My Box

In my box I will put . . . .

Three goals scored by Geoff Hurst.
The roar of a crowd from Wembley Stadium.
The thrashing of a big blue whales tail and the cry of a losing fan.

In my box I will put . . . .

A mouth watering slice of dark chocolate cake.
A ton of chocolate Easter eggs.
A million fruit pastilles, two million smarties.
The FA Cup, The Premier League Cup, and the European Cup.

My box is made from . . . .

Manchester United red hard metal.
It has nuclear missiles to protect it.
It has a jacuzzi and a swimming pool and a sauna too.

In my box I will put . . . .

Every living animal.
A rainbow that lasts for ever.
The warmest and sunniest days ever.

In my box I will . . . .

Play football, win every trophy and score hundreds of goals.
That is what I shall do with my box.

Philip Hall (Age 9)

My Brother

My brother and I are not alike
He likes cars
I like animals
He hates lettuce
I like lettuce
He has cream cheese sandwiches for tea
I prefer sausages and chips

My brother and I are not alike
He has blue eyes
I have hazel
He gets angry
I stay calm

My brother and I are alike
He has brown hair
So do I
He likes walking
I do too
So in some ways we are alike

Hannah Hammond (Age 10)

Christmas

C andle
H olly
R udolph
I nto
S now
T ree
M agical
A nd
S anta

Tom Hyams (Age 6)

The Seasons Of The Year

Spring is great
With birds flying high
Gracefully swooping
Into the sky.

Summer is brill
All hot and sunny
With no clouds to be seen
But the bright bright sun.

Autumn is nice
With leaves falling from trees
Resting on the grass
All brown and green.

Winter is fun
With snow all around
All white and cold
Floating to the ground.

Thomas Haslam (Age 10)

He's A Bully

If you dare go near him
He will kick you dead
If you see him on your bed
Be thankful you aren't dead
But when you are
Haunt him
One day he might be scared.

Justin Hendy (Age 10)

How The World Began

'Bang' was how the world began,
Earthquakes cracked
The newly formed surfaces,
Vast expanses of nothing but
Volcanoes.

'Bang' was how the world began,
Volcanoes ejected colossal amounts
Of scalding red-hot ash and lava,
Volcanic bombs and gas,
All these from its chamber below.

'Bang' was how the world began,
The only light was from the sun,
Filtering through dense gray clouds
Of ash and gas formed
By the volcanoes.

Lynette Hayhow (Age 13)

Autumn

Leaves are crunchy,
I like kicking the leaves.
Most leaves float.
In Autumn I like leaves,
But butterflies fly to hot
Countries like Africa.
It is very hot.
Do you know why?
Leaves are crunchy,
Animals hibernate,
Conkers cracking on the floor.
Leaves going crunch.
Children getting warm.
Leaves falling to the ground
Can be different colours.
Leaves are crunchy,
I like kicking leaves.

Christopher Hull (Age 5)

The Moon

Can you see the moon shining bright
One day he will come down on a spectacular night,
He will give us some cheese and some angel delight,
But one thing is for sure he is a wonderful sight

Amie Harry (Age 10)

November 5th

See the rockets
Shoot up high
Hear the catherine wheels
Screeching by

The flicking flames
Roar around
Making lots
And lots of sound

I see the cooks
Cooking the food
Ready for me
I am in the mood

The cooks, the adults
The children too
I'm just popping
To the loo

Isobel Hart (Age 10)

Monkeys, Monkeys

Monkeys, monkeys,
Swinging in the trees
Flying up above
With the bumble bees
Monkeys, monkeys
Swimming below
Drinking frothy cocoa
Monkeys, monkeys
Having lots of fun
Playing games
In the mid day sun

Elise Harding (Age 9)

My Cat

Cats I love
They're as sweet as a dove,
She wore my hat,
And slipped under a mat,
Ahh!!
I thought you were a rat,
You shouldn't scare me like that.
My cat put on a jumper,
Ran outside and jumped in a bumper,
She drove down the road,
And knocked over a toad.
I said you my cat are a fraud,
Quick get out those crime people,
Fred and Maud
That poor little toad,
To be buried in a churchyard,
Quickly open the goodbye card
My cat was arrested,
I started to cry,
I don't know why,
She was only a playful pussy,
Who wore a hat and went under a mat.

Lora Hawksley-Wood (Age 9½)

Autumn

People crunch the leaves on the ground.
Butterflies go to hot countries.
Animals hibernate and it gets colder and colder.
Conkers fall from the tree,
They bounce on the ground.
Leaves twirling scrunching
Squirrels collecting nuts,
While the hedgehogs go to sleep,
They curl up in the leaves.
Farmers take the animals in.`

Jacob Hall (Age 6)

Winter

A long spiny hand reaches out
Casting a slippery shadow across the land,
Once again this half earth is dark,
As the cold crisp grasp of winter engulfs us in his hand.
Many disappear, run and hide as the beast spreads his carpet
Like a rising tide,
Swooping and spreading. The ground is plain and crisp
As the creature begins his work,
With spiny spiders' web and glistening frost
The earth is dark but not all lost.

Theresa Hunt (Age 13)

Fame

The crowd yell out with happiness and joy,
Persistence of their zeal is heard below.
My subjects all and ever will destroy,
The tiny souls of followers of woe.

If I were missed at least I'd be free,
To hide away in corners dark and few.
So faint my life their eyes could never see,
Reflected only in the spring-time dew.

As I stand and face their most garish fire,
Obsession growing red and dangerous.
Disguised by their melancholy desire,
The flash of cameras bestowing a curse.

My life, like work, a film shall always be,
And when I die, you will remember me.

Laura Higginson (Age 14)

Polar Bear Poem

Polar bear, on the ice.
Polar bear, so very nice.
Polar cub, cuddly and white
Polar cub, what a wonderful sight!

Kurt Houghton (Age 5)

Family

My Mum
In her apron
Like a kangaroo

Dad asleep
Like a mouse in a shoe

My brother gets angry
He looks like a tiger

My uncle
As speedy
As a duck on ice

My aunt sells things
Just name your price

My granny is as brainy as a computer
But my great granny
Can't find anything to suit her

My sister chews gum like there's no next week

My cousin eats toffees so he cannot speak

Nick Hall (Age 10)

What I Like To Do

I like to go swimming and I like to read good books,
I also go to Brownies which is really really good.
I play the recorder and it's really fun,
I LOVE to do my art and also LOVE my country dancing.
I like to go on camping trips and like to go canoeing,
I like to watch TV and watch my favourite program.
I like to do a lot of things and this is half of them,
History is my favourite one out of all of the
LOT

Rachel Halcrow (Age 8)

The Intruder

There was an intruder,
Who walks through the reeds.

He doesn't have a gun,
But he's done his deeds.

He hides in the bushes,
And gently pushes, the leaves away,
And he's shocked to see a front fanged viper

Andrew Hammond (Age 7)

Frost

I went out
Snowlflakes on my car
Ice on my car
Scrape, scrape
It took a long time to clear
My coat was wet

Jamie Hanlon (Age 7)

A Ship

Ships are fast
Help people go across water
Iceberg Breakers
Piling cargo
Ships Cargo

James Hobson (Age 8)

Beauty And The Beast

There was a young girl, who lived with her dad
He liked to invent things and wasn't too bad
He took an invention to a fair
He got lost on the way and his horse got a scare
They came to a castle and went through the gates
The big beast said "It's humans I hate"
Beast locked him in a dungeon, then Beauty came along
She set her father free, then sang the Beast a song
They fell in love. (How sissy can you get?)
It was now Winter time, two months since they had met
The Beast had a fight, he really did die
Beauty said "I love you" and sparks began to fly
He seemed to be rising, coming back from the dead
And then he turned into a prince instead!

Gillian Hatherall (Age 9)

The Sea

As lions
Angry and ferocious
Roaring
Destroying
Killing
Gigantic, simple whales screaming
Waves crushing down
Swirling waters swallowing massive ships
Sharp as cheetahs
Speeding rapidly everywhere
Snapping crocodiles
Life trapped
Inside the sea.

Cheng He (Age 10)

I Remember

Beyond the distant stars
Faces of family emerge
Their voices echo through my head
And I remember times together
Happy times, sad times,
Good times, bad times,
I wish they were still here with me
But I can't change time back

Amy Headon (Age 9)

Easter

I buy fabulous toys
And it says "I am a boy"
Some lambs are born in Spring
They look so pretty
I go on holiday at good places
It's the end of Lent,
Chicks and lambs are born,
And you have a new life.

Sarah Hunt (Age 8)

Cats

Cats have tails cats have nails
Cats you tease cats have fleas
Cats eat cats peep
Cats climb cats rhyme
Cats catch rats cats sleep on mats
Cats with spots cats with dots
Cats meow cats row
Cats have paws cats have jaws
Cats cry cats sigh
          And that's a cat's life.

William Howe (Age 10)

The Sun Poem

The sun is shining so bright,
Shining with all its might,
But don't stay under too long,
Or else you will go red.
When you go in the water
Always put on sun cream
You might get a very stinging back.

The sun is shining so bright
With his eyes blazing hot
But when he goes down
He rests till morn.
The sun is blind
But when the sun is gone, the moon is up
But he doesn't mind.

The sun is shining
The moon disappears in a flash.
The sun is a ball of light
Shining with so much might.
The sun is wearing his shades
Behind his blazing eyes.

Lee Harris (Age 11)

Summertime

S corching sun shining down,
L onging for breeze in the town
O h! everyone out having so much fun,
W ater fights in the blazing sun.

D azzling sky not a cloud in sight,
O range sizzling sun, no wind to fly a kite.
W aterfalls splashing on the shinny rocks,
N ever want to turn back the clocks.

W e had a picnic in the shade,
A nd glad our best clothes didn't fade
I saw busy bees buzzing around,
T hey made such a bizarre sound.

F resh tickly grass on our feet,
O ther people sweltering on the street.
R ay of bright sun light the sky sends,

M osquitoes bite me and my friends,
E ven when the long weary day ends!

Emma Hicken (Age 10)

Fear Is Like

Fear is like rain forcing and banging against
Your bedroom window trying to grab your attention
Fear is like your telly clicking
Like skeletons bones rattling
Fear is like hearing a pack of wolves
Howling making a fierce shadow
Fear is like total silence with shadows
Of grave stones in a grave yard
Fear is like your curtain slithering about
And swifting in the wind
Fear is like a gruesome
Slimy ghost watching you
Fear is like standing on a cliff
And getting sucked in by the sea with sharks
Fear is like thunder crashing
In the night sky
Fear is like when you're near a forest
And owls are hooting
Fear is like a vampire
Sucking you under your bed

Laura Henden (Age 9)

Otters

Diving through the water gracefully
Gliding up and down
Cutting through the cold and mirky pool
Scrounging for food all the time
Playing, rolling around, curling up with each other
Biting each other
Smiling
Gliding through the water
Running to the holt
Watchful of predators
Getting all excited
Curling in balls and rolling around
Falling off the sides and landing in the water
Slipping down the slippery tracks
Leaping up into the air
Curling up and sleeping safe in camouflage

Ian Hunt (Age 10)

School

As soon as I step inside,
I know I'll not stay alive.
The teacher shoves us all in,
And makes us clean out her bin.
The big lock clicks and clatters,
And we all look like we've been battered.
After school mum asks,
How was your day at school?
She hit, she bit, she called Lee a nit,
She shoved us in,
And made us clean out her bin.
She opened the door,
We shouted no more.

Suzie Heale (Age 11)

When I Stole From A Shop

When I was little I stole from a shop,
Mum found out, it gave her a shock.
Well I didn't know we had to pay!
Mum said she was very ashamed.
I was only two, I didn't know the law,
Mum said it wasn't nice and she was sure!
So we took it back and said we were sorry,
I never stole again, honest,
But even now I'm 12 years old and I go into the shop,
They all look and stop,
I think they know about when I stole from their shop!

Becky Hopley (Age 12)

Snowflake

I'm a little snowflake
Short and stout
Here's my nose
So pull it out
And if you can't
Don't worry
Because I'm in a hurry

Sophie Howell (Age 6)

Parrot Poem

Parrot, parrot what do you see?
"I see a parrot tree"
Parrot, parrot what do you see?
"I see a lion chasing me"
Parrot, parrot what do you see?
"I see a bee flying with me"
"Do you think he will stay for tea?"

Matthew Houghton (Age 6)

I'm A Little Boy

I'm a little boy
When it's bright
The sun goes in
Out comes the rain
Splash splash splash
In the puddles

Matthew Higgins (Age 7)

In A Dark Musty Graveyard

Here I am in a dark musty graveyard,
Walking about, looking at graves,
Thinking about the people under them.
I see a church looming over me, casting darkness,
I see graves, dozens of them, still and lifeless.
Suddenly bats are screeching, and owls hooting.
A long moan fills the graveyard.
I feel scared, I try to run but fear glues me to the ground!

Suddenly the ground rumbles and the dead rise from their graves.
I feel my bones turn to jelly.
I hear the dead moaning, moaning for their souls,
Bats and owls hooting and screeching.
There comes a long deep moan, silencing the rest.
The dead are walking, forming a circle around me,
Coming nearer, nearer, they grasp me in their bony rotting hands,
They pull me down into the dark undergrowth,
Into a dark musty grave!

Matthew Hoyles (Age 11)

Ghosts

Ghosts
Are creepy
And cool, you see them
In horror movies on cinema walls you may
Hear your house start to creek and it
May give you the shivers or even the creeps
Some are good and
Some are bad
And some make you
Cold when you're
Having a bath
They tickle
You and make
You laugh
And some of them
Can make you
Feel daft have
You ever thought
Who the sock
Monster is maybe
It's a ghost so
BEWARE!

Jason Haddock (Age 11)

The Talking Tree

Christmas wouldn't be Christmas without a tree
Not to forget the dinner with carrots and peas
But why is there always a plain tree?
Why not have a talking Christmas tree?
Not to forget the snow
I bet you hate Christmas getting towed.
So why not get home to a talking Christmas tree.
Making a snowman in the snow is fun
So why not get home to the fire and a talking Christmas tree.
It's always good to have a talking tree ho ho ho.

Marc Hurrell (Age 8)

Sunday!

Sun was drawing in,
Sun was brightening.
Sun was soaring through the sky,
Sun was going by.
Sun was setting in the sky,
Sun was dying down.
SUNDAY!

Lucinda Heeks (Age 10)

What Am I?

I am the fire in the pit.
I am the gentle velvet kiss.
I am the plague of restless past.
I am the gift which never lasts.
I am the pearls inside your eyes.
I am the cause of your surprise.
I am the reason children weep.
I am the knife which cuts too deep.
I am the whispered secrets of love,
Carried on the wings of a dove.
I am the secret not heard before.
I am peace and I am war.

Katie Hehir (Age 13)

It Is Winter

It is winter
People have coats to wear
And Christmas is coming
We get toys from Father
Christmas
Then we open the paper
And play with the toys

Tristan Humphreys (Age 8)

Football

Football is my favourite game
But in cold weather it's a shame
I like playing when it's sunny
Being cold and wet isn't funny.
I like playing for Roche School
Playing football is totally cool!

Sam Higgs (Age 10)

Mum's Poem

Alice has got Science homework
Martha has got Maths,
Hannah's stuck on English work,
Laura has got SATS.

Alice is in trouble,
Laura's specs have smashed,
Hannah's told a porky-pie
Martha's knee is mashed!

Mummy helps with English,
She sorts out Martha's 'mash,'
She finds out what the trouble was
And what caused the smash.

That was all a week ago
Now it's all just swell,
The only problem is though...
...She's lost her keys as well!

Laura Hoskins (Age 11)

Our School Day

First lesson, Science, was a disaster
Half the class ended up in plaster.
Next lesson, English, wasn't so bad
Even though our teacher was going mad.
She gave us dirty looks
Because we'd forgotten our books.
Break time was an ugly sight
Most of the boys got into a fight.
Our Maths teacher was going spare
Because Emily Smith was combing her hair.
James made all the dinner ladies scream
He knocked over a table of food in the canteen.
We must all stay behind for an after school detention
Because in History we weren't paying attention.
Our last lesson, Art, was a colourful vision
Two of the paint monitors got into a collision.
As you can imagine there was paint everywhere
And Emily's crying because it got in her hair.
I hope you can see what an awful day we had
We are hoping tomorrow won't be as bad.

Kimberley Harlond (Age 11)

Yippee!!!!

On a rainy day
On a rainy rainy day
On a rainy rainy rainy day
There's nothing better than
Putting on my wellies and
Splashing
Sploshing
Splishing
Jumping
In the puddles
Yippee!!!

Oliver Hobbs (Age 7)

What Is Blue

Blue is cool
Blue is small
Blue is crunchy
Blue is a scrunchy
Blue is cold
Blue is my very best thing

Kate Harrison (Age 7)

Autumn

Crunch go the leaves
As they fall off the tree
The squirrels scrabbling,
Climb the tree to get some nuts
Leaves falling to the ground,
All brown and crunchy.
My feet make them go scrunchy crunch.
Those lovely golden brown leaves.
Mr Mouse has hidden in his hole
For the Winter nice and warm

Christopher Hoar (Age 6)

The Hidden Tomb

Excitement dashed through everyone,
Everyone cries,
"Dig! Dig!"
Sweat falling on the hot sand.
Finally someone hit a hard rock,
It was three thousand years old.
Everyone stopped, they held their breath.
Everyone began digging in the same place.
They walked down twelve steps
And came to an door.
They excitedly opened it.
All was silent,
They saw a case in the tomb....

Tom Hodgson (Age 8)

The Planets

Planets are big
All bigger than the earth
All except one - called Pluto
All planets have similars
All except one - called Pluto
Like Jupiter his is Venus because they're both gas
And Saturn is water like Neptune
And Mercury has two brothers Mars and the Earth
Why is Pluto always left out

Daniel Harwood (Age 10)

The Dark

A thick black cushion
Crushing our worthless souls,
A silk black shirt,
Capturing all the light
As a black panther
Parading in the sky.
The dark silk shirt
Creasing through evil
The silk shirt coiling,
Around our lives like a snake
Swirling through the moonless night.

Only one bit of light
The twinkling of a star.
A cold thrill of a pouncing panther,
Shivering down my spine
Murdering peoples minds.
Bat shrieks, owl hoots
Cries of horror.

Chantal Holbrook (Age 11)

Limerick

There was a boy called Tim
Who loved going to the gym
He sprained his arm,
Said it would come to no harm,
But by that time he was dead

Louis Henderson (Age 11)

Trees

In the day trees sway
In the night the leaves rustle
Birds make nests in the trees
People sit under trees for shade
When it rains the trees look like diamonds
Children use trees as goal posts.

Stephen Houghton (Age 8)

To My Valentine

V aliant is our love,
A ching my heart is,
L anding safe from above,
E nchanting is our kiss,
N aked are our souls,
T empting and tantalizing,
I mmortal are our goals,
N ow listen to the angels sing,
E verlasting we will be,
S adness will never come.

D aydreaming I have been,
A lways having fun,
Y ou are the one.

Helen Hunt (Age 12)

The Earth And Moon

Here on the round earth
There are people
Here on the blue earth
There is water
Here on the living earth
There are plants.

Here on the dull moon
There are no people
Here on the dusty moon
There is not water
Here on the dead moon
There are no plants.

Stephen Hamilton (Age 10)

My Doll

My doll makes me feel safe at night
My doll makes me feel happy
My doll is small
My doll wears real baby clothes
My doll has long black hair
My doll waits on my bed for me
My doll smells nice
My doll is nice
My doll is a real baby to me
My doll is always happy   .
My doll is the best in the World
My doll is my best friend.

Kayleigh Howes (Age 11)

Rain

Splash, dank crystal rain drops,
Pouring from the grey gloomy sky,
Dreary people hunched against the wind,
Paddling down the slushy streets,
The rain spat on the dingy windows,
Of the drenched towering office,
Murky, drizzle.
Sizzle, bright yellow beams,
Shining from the burning sun,
Smiling children,
Running down the sunsoaked flagstones,
The sun gleamed down on the glass windows,
Of the glittering office,
Dazzling, glowing sun.

Alice Hemming (Age 11)

The Manatee Lament

The gentle giant so softly swimming,
Through grasses, fresh weeds and a dazzling bay.
With zeal and effort to avoid hitting
The many obstacles that come her way.
Migrating now is her priority,
With calves in tow she so slowly escapes,
The cold waters far north she tries to flee,
All the freshwater springs, rivers and lakes.
She's covered in boat scars, covered in oil,
As a speed boat passes showing no care,
The creatures life now completely spoiled
As it scrapes her skin, gliding through the air.

As the Manatee dies, it makes you think,
These harmless creatures will soon be extinct.

Caroline Hatt (Age 14)

Monster

His eyes are as blue as the ocean
His eyes are as big as footballs
His ears are as big as Dumbo's ears
His nose is a s big as a playing field
His mouth is as big as Dartford Tunnel
His tongue is as bubbly as bubble bath
His breath is as stale as stale cheddar cheese
His teeth are as sharp as daggers
His claws are as long as a swimming pool
His arms are as long as a tree
His skin is as scaly as a fish
His feet are as mouldy as dead fish
His legs are like stumps of trees

Sophie Huggins (Age 11)

Love Letter

To my dearest love,
Were you really sent from above.
You have won my affection,
Now I may have your attention
I will make you feel better.
'Mum help me with a love letter'
'Well dear, put your emotions'
I will give my devotion
But, what if I don't feel this.
Should I seal it with a big kiss,
Or is it OVER?

Jana Loraine Hunt (Age 12)

The Mysterious Box

I will put in my box
A green rainbow
A flattened rhino
And dinosaurs toe
I will put in my box
A batchelors bone
An invisible box
And a witches home
I will put in my box
An alien's eye
My sister's brain
And a piece of pie

Oliver Harbour (Age 10)

Binkie

Bridle, saddle all the gear,
In the stable this time of year,
Nearly ready off we go,
Keep on going girl,
In the woods trit trot,
Easy girl slow down,

The ride is nearly over,
Heather, lumps of clover
End of ride is coming sooner.

Here we are at home,
Off comes the bridle saddle all the gear,
Rumble, rumble she is really hungry,
Steady on I'm coming,
Eat up.

Amy Heath (Age 10)

Mermaid

One
Two
Three
Open the door,
See a mermaid on the floor.
Hair as red as a garden rose,
Tail as pink as a persons nose,
Lips as red as a ripe strawberry,
Eyes as blue as a summer sky.
And then the mermaid will say
Bye
     Bye
          Bye
               Bye.

Hannah Harris (Age 9)

Day And Night

A burning fireball,
Blazing high up in the sky,
A golden bubble,
But, as night draws in,
The sun gives in to the moon,
A pale silver face,
With his distant lonely eyes,
His gentle smile shines,
As he sees his friends,
The stars,
A million jewels,
Shining, twinkling up high,
Like grains of sugar.

Alice Hunter (Age 12)

My Poem

My bedroom monster is peach,
My bed sucks me down into
The monsters dark lair.
My desk has never seen
Daylight, all it sees is
The nights twilight.
My black chair never moves
Stays there all the time,
TV high on the wall black as night.
Look at the door if you dare
Brown as a bear with sharp
Scary teeth, with silver hands
That never let go,
The white, white wardrobe
MONSTER
Never lets you in
Come into my bedroom
If you dare!

Kimberley Harris (Age 11)

The Merman

Hot sand bit into the silky unblemished skin
Of the Merman.
All chances of getting back to the sea were obliterated.
The tide was slipping out in the deeper area of the salty waters
And the stretch of beach which was once covered in water was like
A hot desert.
Wind gently ruffled the Merman's beautiful waves of
Ocean blue hair.
Beginning to feel the effects of being exposed to the dry air too long,
He tried to escape from this terrible torture,
Beating his tail on the blistering, scalding sand.
His seaweed green eyes showed fear and torment.
His weakening hands reached for his skillfully carved horn.
He could not grasp it hard enough.
He looked at his birthplace one more time,
Then, slowly closed his eyes.

Cari Hampson (Age 11)

The Bugs Maze

Bamboo canes tower over the maze of Bombay city.
Drunk flies hover in the peppercorn sea.
Through the maze, ant like people shuffle.
Striped beetles scuttle along wooden rulers.
The sting of the sun begins to fade.

Miar Harrison (Age 11)

World War One

This young man,
He's named Stan,
He went to fight in World War One.
With a tin hat, bullets and a gun,
Stan claims that he beat the Hun.

Ashley Holden & Emily Brazier (Age 11)

Thig The Pig

Thig is a pig fat and round
And eats a lot he is quite loud
Thig is green with pink spots
That's why he eats a lot.
Thig is soft and smooth but that's strange
Because he doesn't wash
He has funny round eyes
With squared glasses
Sometimes he bites people
Then they go "Ahh I want my mummy"
Silly thought thig the pig

Stacey Hunt (Age 8)

Ants

David met some tiny ants
David David wet his pants
The ants were fierce, the ants were cruel
I saw them playing a game of pool
The ants said, "David glad to meet you
Now I will try to eat you"
David David didn't worry
David didn't scream or scurry
He lifted his foot and squat them dead
He squat them right upon the head!

David Hine (Age 10)

Wanted A Pirate's Parrot

Wanted - a pirate's parrot.
Must be able to play football on deck,
And must have x-ray vision eyes.
Not afraid of gun blasts.
Not afraid to die.

Wanted - a pirate's parrot.
Able to balance on shoulder or post.
Has long sharp claws,
And willing to break all laws.
Expert at map reading.

Wanted - a pirate's parrot.
Must be good at sea.
Must be good and obedient.
Apply now for a job of a lifetime.

Kerry Hall (Age 11)

Bird Song

Melody truthful,
Twittering song,
Sweet sensation
Never truly gone.

Filling the sky
With it's faithful chant.
The birds of the west
Whose voices beauty cannot last.

Sweeter than flowers,
Sweeter than sky,
Stronger than drums,
Happier than laughter of children passing by.

The song of the birds
Whose voices sing
With merriment
Fit for a King.

Sung for us all that great bird call
Of joy and laughter forever.

Jessica Hamish-Wilson (Age 12)

Weather

I hate the rain,
It's the worst thing,
It makes you stay in.
My Mum loves the way
The raindrops sparkle
And when the trees sway
From side to side.
I like the way
The hailstones come thundering
Down on the car
Like marbles falling
From the sky.
It sounds like the glass
Will smash.
I like the way
The icicles fall from
The sky like stars.

Keith Hughes (Age 11)

Macbeth

Dogs blood dinosaur's droppings
Even the shoes from Mary Poppins
Cats brain and eyeballs too
It would be lovely in a little stew
A 100 legs of a centipede
That was chewing on a kind of weed
A toenail from a chimpanzee
Together they will be happy

Sarah Hancock (Age 10)

Fireworks

Fireworks are colourful,
The colours are powerful.

Fireworks are dangerous,
They could blow up in your face.

Fireworks are loud,
Sometimes they make a screeching noise.

Fireworks are bright,
Catherine wheels twirl at night.

James Hudson (Age 8)

When I Went To Space

When I went to space
I was in a race,
I saw ET
He was watching tv
When I went to space
I saw the moon,
At that time it was nearly noon
I saw Murth
He was looking down at earth

Julie Hancock (Age 8)

Christmas Day

Snow falling, Christmas day,
Turkey dinner after pray,
Present time say hooray,
Thank you God for this day.

Go on a sleigh ride at the park
Hear Santa's reindeer honk and bark,
Daddy said it's getting dark,
Hear the last of the reindeer honk and bark.

Nick Holder (Age 9)

Valentine Sonnet

Your eyes are sparkling big and blue, like sky,
Your hair is blonde and caught by beams of light.
Your smile is bold and bright. Our love won't die.
I love the way you look at me at night.
The fire is roaring with you next to me.
It's snowing outside, windy wet and cold.
We're cuddled up with some hot cups of tea.
When weather turns too cold it's you I had.
I dream of you whilst lying on my bed,
I imagine you with me by the sea.
Your eyes, your smile, all whizzing in my head,
I love you so much, show some love for me.
I love you always in rain or snow,
But do you love me? Will I ever know?

Kate Hardy (Age 14)

November

No colourful flowers
No bees
No playing tennis
No roller-blading
No sunbathing
No swimming in the sea
No waves splashing in my face
No horseriding
No light
No running in the grass
No legoland or Adventure parks
November

Amy Homewood (Age 10)

Disease

Disease is a virus that spreads,
It's a green slobbering goo,
Disease smells like a pair of rotten socks,
It sounds like a gentle breeze whistling
Through the air,
Disease tastes like a poisonous liquid,
It lives in the sewers below the city.

Matthew Hodges (Age 11)

My Teacher

A tall demon head teacher huddles behind me
With his deadly eyes to see me
I hear his deadly feet through the class
And see his blazing eyes through the glass,
When I am in trouble
I hear a deadly explosion,
He tells me to stop
I go pop

Jonathan Hartigan (Age 9)

My Cousin Kelly

My cousin Kelly is
Voice squeaking, eye winking,
Question asking, breath smelling,
Back chatting, mank supporting,
Rubbish joking, nose sniffing,
Video watching, money wasting,
Mess making, light leaving,
Tracksuit wearing, supper eating,
Awful singing, mum annoying,
Bottom burping, soap avoiding,
Constant talking, habbit forming,
Friend changing, Lewie hating,
Newspaper forgetting.
KELLY!!!!
(Apart from that she's all right!)

Nick Hook (Age 11)

A Foggy Morning

One misty morning fog covers everything
Damp, blurry, gloomily and very very white.
The air is frosty slippery and dusky,
Everything is quiet but very spooky.
Fog creepily crawls around you,
Everything is cloudy and steamy.
Unseeable, dark very very dim,
You can't see anything there.

Damp, dull, dusky and white,
Very, very misty all the time.
The ground is icy making it slippery,
When you're trying to get around.
It's very spooky when you don't make a noise
It's wet, icy cold but very creepy.

Katherine Heseltine (Age 8)

The Dream Of Winter

Spiky trees of magical winter
Staring, spirits,
Of a distant warm summer
The seas of forgotten souls
Whispering their lies
Like chariots of white horses
Galloping through the night.
Queens of frosted palaces
Watching over coldness
Like cries of weeping willows
Covered by the ice.
The coldness takes over,
An iceberg of threat
The people in horror
As winter rises in fret
Like peace in time locks
The great stories never told
All people start dreaming
While winter's growing old.

Simon Harris (Age 10)

My Morning Drapes

The tired tide creeps in silently
Stirring rusty boats from their slumber.
Cold air skims cheeks of shivering children.
Smears of confused oil in the smooth sea.
Black, flapping flags on top of the old boat,
Tangled and tied up ropes cover the deck.
Drops of cold rain bead in swaying water.
Developing small ripples.

Jade Hobson (Age 10)

Will She Do This Or That?

Will she do this?
Will she do that?
Will she wear the fireman's hat?
Will she pay?
What would she say?
I don't know,
Do you?
Does she eat?
Does she bleat?
Does she do anything?
What does she do?
Whatever she does, I like you!

Josie Hemming (Age 8)

Monster

Her ears are as hairy as a cat
Her breath as smelly as cow pat
Her mouth as big as a doorway
Her feet as big as Norway
Her nose shaped like a banana
Her teeth like fangs of a piranha

Her tongue as slimy as a slug
Her face is such an ugly mug
Her claws as sharp as razors
Her arms are the colours of our school blazers
Her skin is smelly and lumpy
Her legs are fat and bumpy

Nicola Hayes (Age 11)

Summer Sleep

The stars were twinkling in the sky
The moon was lighting the path outside
The trees rustling in the warm breeze
A dog was barking in the distance ahead

The summer night was so peaceful
I wish I could stay up for the rest of the night
But I could feel my eyes getting tired
The summer sleep had arrived

Gemma Hawkes (Age 11)

Headilla

My brother Headilla
loves to eat grass.
My brother Headilla
has a bed made of brass.
My brother Headilla
eats honey on crumpets.
My brother Headilla
plays 53 trumpets.
My brother Headilla
plays for the England team.
My brother Headilla
is like a sun beam.
My brother Headilla
eats rulers and cream.
My brother Headilla
if you see him, you'll scream!

Charlotte Higman (Age 10)

Guns

You may not have a gun
But I tell you they are fun
Take a day trip to the fair
Shoot the rabbit shoot the hare
Guns are all different shapes and sizes
Shoot the rabbit win the prizes
Load the bullets take good aim
Hit the target again and again
Blast the tins blast the clays
Have good fun for days and days
But take good care they're not a joke
Badly handled you could kill some folk!

James Hodgson (Age 11)

The World Of Jelly

The world of jelly
As bouncy as my granny's belly,
Let's jump on the world of jelly,
Wee! so bouncy I can,
See Aunty Lelly watching telly,
Uh oh! down I go,
Oh no! I can't stop,
Help somebody stop,
The yellow bouncy volcano,
Up I go again,
Help down I go,
Ahh!
I'm never going to
Bounce on the yellow jelly,
World again,
I'm glad it wasn't my
Granny's fat belly.

Amelia Hughes (Age 9)

Glistening Night

The stars are yellow,
The grass is like pebble,
And they all mix up together.
The tree tops are green peppers,
The tree stumps are grey bananas.
The chimney's are hot,
But we are still cold.
The hills are beauties,
With rivers like pinballs,
But at night it all disappears.
Water in the puddles,
Shining in the car head lights,
GLISTENING.

Naomi Isherwood (Age 6)

Santa's Coming

One Christmas Eve
I was asleep
I heard Santa's reindeer
On my sloping roof.
Once the rattling noise had gone
I heard him say ho ho ho.
Then I heard him shuffle down the chimney
With a bag of presents.
As he fell,
He burnt his bottom.
Because we forgot
To turn off the blaze

Hannah Hammonds (Age 8)

My Car

My car is a Volvo.
It is very fast,
It is green and red,
All I need is a roll cage and a metal mesh.

My car is talking to me vum vum,
It is blind,
I give it a bath,
I give it a drink.

Ben Hommell (Age 10)

My Teacher

My teacher is Mr A,
He comes to school every day.
My teacher he is a screacher,
Sometimes I think he is a preacher.
There can not be a day he does not yell,
Sometimes I think he comes from hell.
He wears the maddest socks you have ever seen,
They could be red or they could be green.
Sometimes he can be kind to us,
But most of the time he makes a fuss.
When he sends us homework home,
He is always in a cheerful tone.
When he points that wicked finger at us,
He sometimes stops making a fuss.
Mr Arnold, he is not our man,
If he cannot do it, everyone can!!!
COME HERE LITTLE!......

Emma Ireland (Age 10)

My Dad And I

My Dad and I
Are most alike.
He likes cars,
Just like me.
He also likes football,
Another thing I like.
The only thing seperating us,
Is our ages!!

My Dad and I
Aren't always alike.
He enjoys TV programmes,
When I like playing playstation games.
I like tennis,
He likes hockey.
So I guess we aren't always alike,
Are we?

Adam Jay Ivell (Age 9)

Leaving Stokes Bay

I love going to Stokes Bay
On a starry night.
I wish I could stay.
If only I could get another job,
Closer.

I would stay,
And still go fishing,
And talk to the fisherman.

On a clear night
All you can see
Are bivvies and tilly lamps
All down the beach.

It's beautiful.
I wish I didn't have to leave.

What if the sea is miles away?
I don't think I could cope.
What if life is noisy loud and fume filled?

I really don't want to leave.

I love it here.

Jake Jenkins (Age 14)

My Mum

My Mum is like a rose
Growing faster and faster into the sky.
She is a bowl of
Red, yellow and blue flowers.
She is a rainbow shining across the blue sky.
She is a robin
Singing in a tree.

Omar Sousa Ibrahim (Age 10)

The Animal Poem

The pony sat in the butter
The pig sat in the gutter
The cow sat in the churn
But that was just the poem

Anna Ilston (Age 9)

Macbeth's Fortune

To tell the future of Macbeth
We guarantee it ends in death.
To make all of the magic flow
Don't shave your arms
We need B.O.
Think of nasty evil thoughts
And as a bonus
Add your warts.
Now'tis time to cut your veins
Don't drip on your shirt
It stains.
Then throw in your bras and knickers
And don't forget your brand new Kickers.
They may be expensive
They may cost a lot
But they are more useful in our pot.
With this potion Mac will see
What an evil man he'll be.

Laura Jesty (Age 15)

The Baboon

There was a baboon,
He is a loon,
He likes cartoons,
He sleeps in a cocoon,
In his bedroom.

Ross Julian (Age 10)

A Sad Moment

A sad moment is when you
are left lost in a rainforest.
A sad moment is when you
are trapped in a cobwebbed castle.
A sad moment is when you
are left alone on a wet floor.
A sad moment is when you
are locked up in a small house.
A sad moment is when you
are chucked out of a friend's car.
A sad moment is when you
are left out of your friend's game.
A sad moment is when you
are moved around in a steel cage.
A sad moment is when you
are forced to go to a Country.

Benjamin Jayne-May (Age 7)

A Martian Sends A Postcard Home

Trees are huge with branches
Which are arms reaching out at night
Leaves are creatures that cling
On to the tree and cry.

A stream is like a ribbon
Twisting and turning,
Winding in all different directions.

Book is like a mechanical bird
With funny looking pictures on the front
And funny printed things.

A house looks like a loaf of bread
With breadcrumbs falling from it
Like a rocket being launched into space.

Cars look like lots of little bugs
That are moving in all different directions,
Fast and slow.

Zoe James (Age 12)

Daydream

I'm sitting looking into the sky.
Thinking of him,
He's my dream guy.
When he's around I feel as if I'm walking on air.
He makes my head go all tingly,
He says all the right words,
To make me feel all right.
His voice is so soothing,
His words are so kind.
He treats me like a best friend.
He's shy, but in a loving way.
That's why I like him,
He's my dream guy.

Eloise Jones (Age 12)

Thoughts Of A Zoid

I used to be the treasure of the toys,
Brand spanking new.
I used to be fought over,
By my masters friends.
But now my armour is dirty,
Not very shiny anymore.
My guns are out of bullets,
My motor out of power.
My legs have not moved for many years,
My feet have not come off the ground for years.
I am now just a lump of metal,
Standing there doing nothing.
My secret compartments are falling off,
Along with my aeroplanes and guns.
I used to be a knight in shining armour,
But now I'm rusted and busted.

Andrew Johnson (Age 11)

Running

When I start running
I put my shoes on
And tie them up.
Then I start running
I feel strong,
I feel fast,
I'm thinking about my tea.

Gavin James (Age 10)

Swimming

When I went swimming under the sea,
I saw little fishes swimming so happily,
And when I went snorkelling, guess what I saw?
A great big island, there was a treasure chest on it.
But first I saw a cave,
I thought I had better go in there first.
I swam up to it and guess what there was?
NO KEY!!

Carly Johnson (Age 9)

Coma

Here lying in this bed,
I may not possess control,
But I remember the day,
You said together, we could overcome anything.

I see you fret and feel your pain,
Don't be fooled by my sleeping state.
I can still hear you,
Though through only my heart can I tell you my secrets.

I cannot dance on this earth forever.
You have to let me pass.
Goodbyes make my journey harder,
So this is the only way I know to cause you less pain.

I ask you not to cry.
As although I can't see your tears,
I feel every splash they make,
On my tender soul that will be yours soon.

I leave you now.
You hold the key to all my hopes and dreams.
Keep them safe.
Together we will overcome my death.

Hannah Johnson (Age 14)

My Dog

It is a cold and frosty morning
And I don't want to get up out of bed.
I look out of my window
And see my puppy playing in the snow.
I think he is so sweet.

Bethan James (Age 8)

Too Much Racism

Too much racism around and about
Why should anyone be in doubt?
Even though they're black
Even though we're white
Why do we all have to fight?

Too much racism around and about
Why should anyone be in doubt?
They fight just like cats
We just fight like dogs
Even though we come from God.

Too much racism around and about
Why should anyone be in doubt?
Why can't we just get along?
Even though we have the same rights
Why can't we just stop the fights?

Victoria Johnstone (Age 13)

Sunset Dreams

The sun sweet berries of the Earth
are covered by sleeping clouds.
The sleepy songs of tired birds
settle everyone in the land.

Dreams, dreams the matter of life settle you
in your bed.

The endless dreaming all through the night
set your mind afloat.
The twilight world that you may feel upon you
the grass in the morning light is a deep green glow.

The rose crowned archway.
Where we wait for the fragrant hour of light.
Morning is nearly upon us
away slips our dreams until another
night.

Talia Johnson (Age 11)

Different Shades

I'm 'ere and I'm white,
You're there and you're black.
My mates think you're different,
But I think you aren't.
You're just like me but in a different shade.
Now I move closer since I feel this way,.
I've made new friends and their ok,
I was right we're all the same.
Why can't everybody be like me?
Liken blacks and whites just right.

Sarah Johnstone (Age 13)

Fairyland

Fairies, witches everywhere,
In the trees they hide.
Witches making magic spells.

Smells of thick fog and mist.
Pixies, fairies scuttling by.
Beautiful rainbows by the tens of dozens.

Witches brew by the gallons.
More witches than you can imagine.
This truly is a frightening sight,
With ghosts and goblins that haunt the night.

Victoria Jaynes (Age 10)

My Hamster

My hamster has little feet
That are rather neat
He likes to run around in his ball
Then bangs into the wall
When he plays with his toys
He makes a lot of noise
He has little ears
And lasts for a few years
I clean him out once a week
Because he has a leak
He buries himself in bed out of sight
If you wake him he'd have a fright
He runs round in his wheel till he gets dizzy
When he gets off he gets into a tizzy
He's brown and white
And comes out at night
He uses his hands to pick up his food
The stuffs it into his pouch which I think is rather rude.

Victoria Jones (Age 12)

There's Something In The Dungeon

There's something in the dungeon,
I don't know what it is.
As slimy as a slithering snake,
As dreadful as a dragon.

There's something in the dungeon,
I've seen it snap and snort,
All bumpy, boney and boisterous,
Like one slobbery snail.

There's something in the dungeon,
It's eaten lots of lunch,
If you go down the corridor
You'll see it crash and crunch.

There's something in the dungeon,
You see its mighty jaw,
Its gnashing and its gnaw,
There's something in the dungeon,
There is! There is!! There is!!!

Natasha James (Age 9)

Worry

Worry is gray.
It tastes like water at the bottom of the sea
With a shark growing closer,
And smells like a pond of blood.
Worry looks like a flame
And sounds like footsteps.
Worry feels like fear.

Roy Jones (Age 9)

The Snow Man

The snow man
The snow man
In the snow and the frost
Freezing to death
In the snow
Like a big lump of ice cream
In the snow

Jack James (Age 7)

Two Witches

There was a witch,
The witch had an itch,
The itch was so itchy
It gave her a twitch.

Another witch admired
The twitch,
So she started twitching
Though she had no itch.

Now both of them
Twitch,
So it's hard to tell which
Witch had the itch,
Which, witch has the twitch.

Rosie Jones (Age 8)

Super Ray

His name is Ray
He's kind in every way,
He's never in a strop,
He will take you to the shop,
If you fall over in the muck,
He'll take you home in his truck,
If you need help,
He won't let you yelp,
His name is Ray,
He will make you happy in every way,
He is here to save the day,
That's why we call him -
SUPER RAY!!!

Saul Jacobs (Age 11)

I Can

I can kiss my mum,
Hug my mum,
Play with my ball
And sleep

I can see,
Run up the hill
Go to the shops
And ride my bike.

Amy Johnson (Age 4)

Welcome To Corfu

May I welcome you to Corfu-the Emerald Isle
And tell you something that will make you smile.
Dramatic scenery, glorious beaches and the bluest of seas;
Friendly locals, whose hospitality will put you at ease.
But as you relax and start to unwind, there's a few odd things in Greece you'll find.

The tap water though safe to drink, is often a strange colour with a peculiar stink.
So I recommend that you purchase a regular supply,
Of bottled water-it's very cheap to buy.
The wastage pipes in Greece only two inches thin,
So please throw your loo paper straight in the bin.
Taking a shower can be quite a laugh, oh how you'll wish you had a bath.
No curtain and no hook on the wall. The water will flood out into the hall.
As you reach for the towel-you'll wonder if it's there, can it really be only 12 inches square!
You go into the kitchen the cupboards are bare, no kettle or teapot to be found anywhere.
No toaster or oven, just a couple of rings, no sink plug either- amongst other things.
But the restaurants are great and eating out's cheap and you only use your apartment to sleep.

You're beginning to wonder why on earth you did come?!
Because the Greek welcome is as warm as the sun.
Before long you realise it's a great place to be, with a lot more to offer than sun, sand and sea...

Ian Johnson (Age 14)

Hate

Hate is red
Hate tastes like mouldy carrots
Hate smells like metal
Hate looks like a raging fire
Hate sounds like a flickering flame
Hate feels like a mouldy apple

Darren Jones (Age 11)

November

No going on holiday
No sun
No playing on my bike
No flowers
No playing in the park
No insects
No swimming in the sea
No bees
No leaves on the tree

NOVEMBER

Vicky Kellaway (Age 9)

Macbeth

In the poisoned pot we throw,
Eye of evil toe of toad,
Lung of lizard snakes snot
I hope this evil spell,
Will last unless there is an evil cast,
'Cos if this spell does go wrong,
Then we will not exist for long.

Emma Jepson (Age 11)

Phew!

On a cold day,
On a really cold day,
On a really, really cold day,
On a really, really wet cold day....
There is nothing better in the whole world than
Bringing a colourful,
Multi coloured,
Shining,
Wet,
Damp,
Wooden,
Umbrella with you.

Alec Jeddere-Fisher (Age7)

A Foggy Morning

One foggy morning it was dark and cold.
The path was slippery, the car was icy,
It was a quiet foggy morning.
The ice was thick, this morning was horrible.
I was shivering with the cold.
The wind was blowing hard.
It was creepy outside, very, very creepy and cold.
The grass was frozen, the leaves were blowing.
Everywhere was white,
You couldn't see anything but white.

Stephanie Jones (Age 9)

Stream

Running down the mountains leaping like the foal,
Playful, active, bouncing happy cheery soul.
Rushing, galloping over rocks swallowing them whole,
Racing towards the home of the little fishes shoal,
Never growing old never growing slow,
Meeting others like his kind, on his journey he will go.

He has not a finger he has not a toe,
But he may be high and he may be low.
Dazzling, dancing raindrops, join his everlasting life,
Nothing in himself brings trouble or strife,
In the winter he feels as sharp as a knife.

But in the summer calm and bright,
He feels like warm summer evenings and nights,
But he's changing and no longer full of might,
Flies at his best at the first daylight,
Off he goes although now he's slow and peaceful,
His life is truly wonderful,
He's reached the sea and is now a grown horse,
A stallion beautiful and bold,
To join the white horses of the waves.

Millie Jenkinson (Age 11)

My Feet

My feet can run so fast,
And kick a ball a mile,
People are left so dizzy,
But not when I walk in single file.
I can walk straight and sideways too,
And walk around and around in circles.
I can curl my my toes and point them sharp,
But the best thing is I can jump and jump and jump and
CRASH BANG
WALLOP!

Ashley Jeggo (Age 8)

The Shark

Ferocious beast,
Slick character,
Coming towards you with death in it's eyes.
Strength of a bear,
Piercing teeth,
You hear the dying screams from the victims.
Haunting ghosts,
It all goes silent.
Suddenly you see nothing,
But red sea.....

Nathan James (Age 10)

On The Rigid Road

On the rigid road,
I ran over a toad,
When I told my Dad,
He said I was really bad.

When I told my bird,
He didn't say a word,
That's the way to be I said,
Then I noticed he was dead!

Then I told my Dad,
That I am really sad,
All he said was go away,
Or else you won't play football today.

Andrew Jones (Age 9)

Loneliness

Nobody to play with,
Nobody cares,
Nobody around.
I have no friends,
I'm dull and restless,
I'm sad and unhappy,
I'm unexcited and feel left out.
I am really feeling bad and miserable,
I'm tired and bored.
I don't know what to do,
I feel like running away.
I have no place to go,
I want to do something.

Benjamin James (Age 8)

School

School is so boring,
It happens every morning.
Kind teachers,
Mean teachers,
Teachers everywhere.

Some people feel like yawning,
While the teacher's talking,
Happy times,
Sad times.
The best time's HOME TIME!!

Hannah Johns (Age 10)

Animals Of The Zoo

I go into the zoo and I
Can hear the lion roaring.
I walk around the zoo and I
Can see the penguin feeding its
Young.

I go into the zoo and I
Hear the parrots squawking.
I walk around the zoo and I
Can see the hippos having a
Mud Bath.

I go into the zoo and I
Can hear the monkeys chattering.
I walk around the zoo and I
Can see the ostriches flapping
Around.

I go into the zoo and I
Can hear the elephants bellowing.

Oliver Johns (Age 10)

This Land I Love

No land is so cool when you are out of school
Blue skies and yellow lands.
The sand is soft the sea is wet.
People bathing in and out
Balls are flying, no-one crying, laughter smiles all about.

Ice cream of every flavour, fish and chips all at favour
Packed lunches, picnics, seagulls taking little bits
Bees and wasps buzzing around
Waiting for the can sound
If I go in the sea they won't catch me.

Shorts and T-Shirts, sandals and caps
No-one looks like a furry cat.

Costumes, trunks of every colour
Wet and dry in the summer.

Funfairs, rides amusement arcades
Everything including fun parades, stalls of artwork you can buy.
Toy shops selling sweets and toys
Toilets for the girls and boys.
Lots of people hear them shout all about this land I love
This is called the SEASIDE!!!

Vicky Johnstone (Age 12)

Phew!

On a hot day,
On a really hot day,
On a really, really hot day,
On a really, really sweltering hot day....
There is nothing better in the whole world than
Sitting in the sand,
Licking
A Lovely,
Nice,
Cold,
Ice Cream.

Elita Jackman (Age 6)

Wind

The wind blows swiftly,
The green grass goes swish - swash,
The beautiful flowers get damaged,
The big trees fall messily,
The washing goes here and there.

The wind thumps on the door at night,
The wind rocks the trees,
The wind howls like a wolf at midnight,
The wind clatters on the windows,
The wind makes spooky noises.

Jenna-Marie Jago (Age 11)

Force

Force means strength, power and intense
Force means effort and influence
Force means body troops and police
Force means in order to get something
Force means strain and over strain
Force means produce and a special effort
Force means effective force fully
Force means force of a persons hand
Force can be to force the issue
Force can be to force the pace
Don't be forced to do anything
Force is great if you use it right.

Martin Joyce (Age 12)

By The Sea

The blue waves lapping on the shore,
Nature's everlasting law.
Seagulls circling in the air,
Over silver sea and sunset fair.

The icy waters of a restless sea,
Try their best to capture me.
As the sun sinks in waters cold,
The story of the sea is finally told.

Peter Jefferys (Age 10)

War Isn't Glamorous

He glanced with eager eyes as they marched out of town,
Waving to his mother who looked so proud but sad,
Waving to his sweetheart with lust of love in his eyes,
But marching boldly they carried on,
Where he will never know what mistake he has done.

The lust of blood had overly been done in the line of death.
The groans and screams could be heard,
But the horror of reality came creeping.

The whistle came with a blast,
And they stumbled over the top.
With glistening bayonets and fear glittering in their eyes
They charged over the dead bodies.

The screaming steel pulled him down as a stab of agony hit him,
His clothes became blood-soaked as he realised he'd lost a limb,
He cried out to his family,
So near in his thoughts but yet so far.

The black blood became intense.
He gave out one last cry to his family
Then everything went a ghastly black.

Kerry Jakovljevic (Age 13)

Winter

It is a wintery day.
It is so icy today and
Snowflakes are fluttering.
But the thing I don't like is
That I can't ice skate on ice.
I slip over.

Emma Jakins (Age 7)

I Wonder Why

Walking along the street
Leaves crunching beneath my feet,
All yellow and dry,
I wonder why.

Wind whistling and blowing strong,
Removes more leaves, very wrong,
Wind makes me cry,
I wonder why.

Now raining still very cold,
Trees all bare looking bald,
The leaves all die,
I wonder why.

Leaves all wet, feet slide on the ground,
No more crunching, silence, no sound,
No leaves left high,
I wonder why.

Daniel Jackman (Age 11)

Pet Memories

Munch munch, crunch crunch,
That's my Moffy eating lunch,
Depending on me every day
For all his food and his hay.

Skip skip, hop hop,
That's my Moffy cute little Lop
In the garden tufty tail,
Up and down he will sail.

Soft soft, cuddle cuddle,
That's my Moffy in a huddle
Looking at me with his soft eyes,
In my arms Moffy lies.

Munch munch, crunch crunch,
Skip skip, hop hop,
Cuddle cuddle, soft soft.
My eyes may never see,
But in my heart you'll always be.

Nadine Jackman (Age 12)

Summer

Sun like a slowly moving golden ball
Suspended in the sky
People picnicking

Leaves rustling
Like a living hedgehog in the long autumn
Looking for somewhere to hibernate
Bees buzzing

Matthew Jordan (Age 9)

Space

New comets everywhere.
Some give me a scare!
Life on the moon could be true.
I don't know what to believe, do you?

Smells and noises are all strange,
But then again they always change.
Gravity is very little up here,
Sorry I must go, I'm feeling very queer.

Polly Jaynes (Age 10)

Once On A Rainy Day

Once on a rainy day
Where the kids are out to play,
Driving me nuts
And buying me nuts,
Oh please go away.

I'll tell you once, I'll tell you twice,
Just get away, please go away.
I'll fry you in a frying pan or
I'll toss you away.

I don't really mean that kids,
Come back or
I'll cry.

Ben Johnson (Age 10)

Thoughts Of My Action Man

Once I was treasure of treasures,
But now I am pushed aside,
I was best of the best,
Loved more than the rest,
And always by his side.

I was sleeping one day,
Until I was whisked away,
He said "Hello" to another boy,
And asked his Mum for a brand new toy,
I am tough and I am strong,
But I did not know for just how long,
Now I am old,
I am not treasured like gold,
Instead I am buried with the mould.

Scott Jacobs (Age 12)

Thoughts Of A Soldier

Once I was the treasure of treasures
Standing high and proud
With my great machine gun
Everyone wanted to play with me
I was a great soldier
Until they grew bored with me
They threw me into walls or something hard
They tore my legs off
And threw my army hat away
Nobody notices I'm gone
Who nobody loves
Rotting away
They just don't care
I'm never going to be loved again
All alone down here forever.

Carl Johnson (Age 12)

The Tiger

The young tiger,
Roaring for it's victory,
Over a young deer.

The fear of gunshots
Rings in his ears,
The fear of hunters,
Makes him aggressive.

Smooth and sleek
And as sharp as
A knife
He disappears
Through the undergrowth.

Yvonne Jeffery (Age 11)

Shopping

I was walking in a massive shop
And then I suddenly stopped
My mum had disappeared
This was very weird
I was in a frantic mood
When I was standing by smelly food
I was screaming like a worried dog
And I was jumping like an electric frog
It seemed like hours so then I screamed,
It was my lovely mum looking at me
YIPPEE......

Stevie Jacob (Age 10)

The Cat

I sneak around the house at night
When everyone is asleep
I jump on the beds
I purr in their ears
So they say to me
Up you come!!
They stroke me
I am happy again
That they have let me on the bed
When they wake up
I whizz downstairs
To wait for them.

Lucy Jenkinson (Age 9)

A World Of Chocolate!

It was winter in my house,
The Fuses needed replacing.
The Quality of the Street was covered in snow Flakes.
The wind Whispered through my ears
And froze my brain,
It got in a Twirl so I needed a Boost!

I went to the pond.
A Ripple appeared - a Humbug had come down.
There was a Crunching of snow,
A Lion appeared!
I did up my Buttons and flew away.
I sailed past Astros and Mars
And I went surfing on the Milky Way!
When I got home no one believed me
They thought I was on a rolo-ver!

Adam King (Age 11)

The Rodent's Morning

A dirt covered rat
Scrabbles in the morning dew
To find its breakfast

Samuel Kinchin-Smith (Age 11)

The Tigeroo

There was a squishy fish
Covered in skwidgy liquorice
The Tigeroo said
"That looks skrummy"
And bolted it into its greedy tummy

Lisa Keswick (Age 8)

Fireworks Fireworks

Dazzling fireworks like the roman candles,
Catherine wheels flaming bright

Dazzling rockets light up the sky,
With red, green and blue.

Dazzling rockets, whizzing through the sky at night,
Dazzling sparklers, sparkling like mad.

Dazzling dangerous fireworks,
Never put them in your pockets, they might go off.

Dazzling fireworks bing! bang! bong!
I would watch out whizzing and banging long! long! long!

James King (Age 8)

A Brilliant Christmas!

Christmas, Christmas you're getting near
I can't believe it will be my favourite, time of the year
Santa, Santa you bring sweets, treats and presents too.
I can't believe I'm not going to meet you.
I know I like you lots,
But sometimes I just can't undo your knots.
Sometimes I wonder how you get here,
Even when I forget Rudolf the red nose reindeer.
Lights, crackers and presents too,
I would like to dedicate Christmas to you.

Lewis Kennedy (Age 8)

My Teacher

He is kind nice maybe sweet
But when he is angry death with feet
His socks represent him in a way
For on his feet the devil will stay
He is a shadow in the class
For behind the glass
There is a volcano erupting all over the class
He is kind nice maybe sweet
But I still think he is a devil
In his Tazmanian feet

James Keys (Age 9)

Happy Christmas

Christmas
Christmas
Happy Christmas
Kissing under the mistletoe
Sitting under the tree
Is my present waiting for Christmas
Tied in a tight bow
When I come back from my friends house
I see the holly wreath
Open my front door when
When I reach the front room
Decorations dangling down to me.
I go to my room and I see mum
Putting decorations in my room
When I got in bed I felt something
It was a Christmas present
I felt like Santa had gone without me
Christmas
Christmas
Happy Christmas

Poppy Knight (Age 8)

The Exploding Box

I will put into my box
A thousand fireworks all firing into the fabulous air
I will put into my box
The deepest, bluest, clearest crystal clear sea
I will put into my box
The fastest bounding moving squiggling fish
I will put into my box
The creamiest richest smoothest chocolate
I will put into my box
The sounds of the funniest funfair in the world
My box is made from
The hardest shiniest smooth diamonds in the world
And the hinges are made from the webs of poisonous spiders
What I will do in my box
In my box I will play in the funniest fun fair arcade.

Michael Kimber (Age 9)

By The River Bank

In the river there's fish
Swimming in the dark edge of the water by the bank
Weeds swaying side to side
The water from the river is splatting and hitting the pebbles and rock
The sound of the river is a sweet and calm sound
You can see people fishing and walking
Bluebells and snowdrops are out
Drops of rain slide down them
Then they splash on the ground
Sprinkles of spray run
To my face from the dog who
Just jumped in
The river is a lovely place

Tess Kendrick (Age 10)

Up Down

Up in the sky
I can see the roofs,
Down on the ground
I can see all the birds
Up in the sky
I can see green fields,
Down on the ground
I can see lots of clouds
Up in the sky
I can see small cars
Down on the ground
I can see the planes,
But I like being down on the ground
Because I would rather have my feet
on the pavement!

Ellen Kennedy (Age 9)

Africa

As the heat from the sun beats down on the ground
The trees in the jungle make a soft sound,
Children running round and round,
      That's Africa!

People lying on the beach,
Teachers trying hard to teach,
Palm trees to the sky they reach,
      That's Africa!

Mothers carrying their babies on their backs,
Strong men carrying rice filled sacks,
Children drawing sand made tracks,
      That's Africa!

People dancing,
Children prancing,
Grown-ups on the beach romancing,
      That's Africa the place for me

Adun Kenogbon (Age 9)

Oyster Song

I am
Slow snapper
Sea sleeper
Singer of tunes
I harm no man

I know
Only the creeping
Of the angry crabs
The tangle and grab
Of the foot sucking anemones
At day and night
The sad oyster song
I harm no man

Lucas Kowe (Age 9)

My Family

I don't know where to start
My dad has no interest except his TV and Ferrari car
And sometimes his job with tar
My mum does nothing except sleep
And pile washing up in a heap
My brother is a little terror
Sometimes it's like he was born with an error
My gran does nothing but sit and knit
Or sometimes cook and go for a walk to keep fit
My grandad goes along with nearly anything
Even having a good old sing
Me myself I'm rather mad
I'm always happy except when I'm sad

Keira Jay Keveth (Age 11)

Isabella's Christening

Although I'm only eight, Isabella is my niece
We went to her Christening to wish her joy and peace.
Douglas is my brother who drives a big Mercedes.
There were lots of people there, most of them were ladies.
Off we all went to St. Mary's in the town,
Isabella looked a picture in her cream, silk gown.
The vicar poured water on Isabella's head,
"I now greet this child in the name of God" he said.
We got into the car to go to the celebration.
Daniel and I played on Doug's Playstation.
The guests gave their presents, the champagne corks went "pop"
The party took all afternoon and never seemed to stop.
Eventually it was time to leave, we had to go quite far.
I was happy but tired and fell asleep on the back seat of the car.

William Keen (Age 8)

Summer

The golden sun rises
In the morning
Animals awaken and now they're yawning
But there's one still that's still snoring.
There are birds like clouds in the breeze.
Golden leaves on the trees
Some falling and swaying
Down to the ground
To make a blanket
Now's the time
To say goodbye

Andrew King (Age 10)

Lost In the Shop

My confusing mum, she has left me alone,
Left me calling in this wild crazy zone.
I am having a panic,
Where should I look?
Under some bed clothes, on a mountain of books
I looked to my left
I looked to my right,
I looked absolutely everywhere.
I started to wail
And I wailed out loud
Everybody looked at me among the crowd
Then I saw mum a gleaming face
I ran towards her and picked up my pace
This was it, it was all over, here I come
Home sweet home.

Greg Kuhl (Age 10)

Class 3

Chitter chatter
Clang
Tick tock
Bang
The class is doing painting
What a silly thing
The teachers going crazy
She thinks we're all lazy

The splodge of merging paint
Lands on the floor
A dangling bit of paper towel
Hanging on the door

We finally manage to wipe it up
The carpet turning green
The teacher says I think you will
Have to keep it clean

Tristan Kiff (Age 11)

Cold And Bare

Wet, misty, cold and bare
There was no-one there
Only the sounds of clanging metal
The rubbish flies like torn off petals
The boats huddle
Metal in a muddle.
Welders weld the metal so disformed
The men they mourned
The weather, so mean and clawed
The monstrous machines so bold
What stories of old sea men can be told.

Darren Keast (Age 10)

Summer

The sky's as blue as the sea
Birds fly like feathers in wind
The sun is a golden ball
People like a blob of colour
Bees like a sharp pencil

Adam Knott (Age 8)

Where's Paul?

Paul oh Paul oh
Paul oh Paul
Where's Paul?
He's in the
Swimming pool!

Paul oh Paul oh
Paul oh Paul
Where's Paul
He's playing pool!

James Kenny (Age 8)

The Second World War

"Oh" sirens going off
I am definitely worried
So we all go to the shelter
When we got there we were scared
When we got there I had brought some pens, paper and a book
Just in case I go t bored
In the shelter we went to our room and it was very very squashed indeed
Gaps from the rain outside and it was cold
In the shelter it was smelly and hot

CRASH

There was a bomb in the woods
When the bombs go off the lead firing everywhere
I was crying and I was worried that we were going to get bombed.

Ross Knapp (Age 10)

School Days

School is fun and you can play
Cool outside because you can sit on the grass.
Have a nice lunch at school,
On Friday you have chips.
On Saturday you don't have to go to school,
Because it is the weekend.
Leave your crisps in your drawer at school.

Natasha Kellman (Age 8)

The Earth And The Moon

The Earth said to the moon
"You'd better clear
That muck up soon. "

So the moon decided
To call a cleaning goon.

But one dark night
The goon thought
I'd like a bite.

Of what he couldn't decide
So he fried the moon
And ate it soon ......

But the Earth woke up
And ate the goon.

And that's why we have new moons.

Anne Marie Kolthammer (Age 9)

My Dog

My dog is the best in the world.
He loves to play with everyone.
He sits up high when he needs the loo!
He always barks when he sees a bad guy.
When it's the end of the day
And it's getting dark,
He lays by the fire and
Dreams of playtime!

Leon Keung (Age 10)

Millennium

M y millennium will be special
I will dance from dusk till dawn
L eaving the past behind us
L ooney's become fun!
E ntering my first millennium
N ever ending fun!
N ever forgetting anyone
I will dance to my music
U sually I think it will never happen but
M aybe I will meet an alien!

Neil Kumar (Age 10)

Spiders

S potty spiders
P urple spiders
I ndigo spiders
D ark spiders
E fficient spiders
R ed spiders

Joseph Kirby (Age 9)

Fear

Fear is like a skeleton flexing it's murderous bones
Fear is like a skeleton rising from the dead
Fear is like looking at your grandma's grave
And you feel someone's coming up to you
Fear is like hearing the crackle of thunder in your bed
Fear is like hearing the howl of wolves in the forest
Fear is like hearing the whistle of the wind
Going through the gaps in your window
Fear is like feeling the wind running up your spine and it never stops
Fear is like watching Titanic and seeing Jack die

Jade Kent (Age 9)

Fear

Fear is like a skeleton flexing its murderous bones
Fear is like when you're lying in bed and someone's watching you
Fear is like when you're lying in bed and you can hear someone moving around
Fear is like when you've opened your window and your door is pulled to
And all of a sudden you climb back into bed and then you hear crackling of leaves
Against your bedroom window then all of a sudden the door blows shut!
Fear is like being dragged down a chimney top in a damp dusty spooky haunted place
Fear is like when you're on top of a mountain and then someone
Sneaks up behind you and pushes you and you fall and scream
And that is fear!

Sarah Kerr (Age 10)

The Big Game

The time had gone so fast,
It was the big game at last,
As the referee blew his whistle,
The ball was put down the wing,
So one of the players took a swing,
Suddenly it was a free kick,
The player placed the ball
So the opposite team made a wall,
He hit the ball with such pace,
It was only going in one place,
The keeper dived the wrong way,
Sadly he couldn't save the day

Ashley Kemp (Age 10)

Summer

The sky is as blue
As the wavy sea
Full of salt
The sky is as big
As a giant
Reaching out over the earth

Thomas King (Age 8)

Spring

Spring is nice
Spring makes daffodils grow
Spring is good
Spring makes everything grow
The colours are nice
Rain makes rainbows
Seven colours in the sky

Tom Lloyd (Age 6)

Favourite Things

I like the humour of watching
Cartoons on the telly
Or the feeling of delicious food
In my belly

I love the smell of bacon
Sizzling on the grill
It smells so yummy
It tastes brill

I also like
I'm sure that you'll agree
The icing on a cream cake
Baked by me

I like the feeling of
A nice warm bed at night
And the feeling of playing
With gungy paints, so bright

Scott Lewis (Age 11)

The Door

Go and open
The door
Maybe there is
A spooky forest
A haunted house
Or one eyed alien

Go and open
The door
Maybe there is
A space shuttle
An acid volcano
Or half alien and half man

Go and open
The door
Maybe there is
A strong tornado
A Tasmanian Devil
Or an alien town

James Koenig (Age 9)

Winter

Snow like white, sweet, cool sugar.
Ice like a diamond ring.
As fierce as a dragon.
Robins sing in all the snow
Cold like a freezer
Snow softly blowing in the wind
Winter's so cold and cool
But it is beautiful

Donna Kane (Age 8)

Liverpool Forever!

L, I, V, E, R, P double O, L Liverpool F.C.
Zip! Zap! Paddywack give us a goal!
The ball just rolled into the goal!

There goes Macca there goes Owen,
I just don't know what they're doing!
Miz! Maz! Paddywack give us a goal!
The ball just rolled into the goal!

The ref, very kind, just gave Dublin that dreaded card,
Ciz! Ciz! Paddywack give us a goal!
The ball just rolled into the goal!
(By the way, Liverpool won 3-0)!

Richard Lewis (Age 9)

Beginnings

The beginning of the end of the century,
How will it be?
All those questions unanswered,
We'll just have to wait and see.
The start of the century, how will it feel?
Is it just a dream, or is it for real?
All the talk on the news,
That everyone's seen,
If you look around, everyone's so keen.
All this new technology, and talk of the dome,
We only want what we call home.
The place that we all talk about with pride,
And the place that our ancestors
Fought for and died.
Will there be holidays, and trips to the moon?
It seems far away, but it's happening so soon.
With all these changes, how will we cope?
All I can say is
"We can all live in hope".

Jodie Leebody (Age 15)

The Cricket

In the long summer grass down by the river
Sat a little cricket in the pouring rain
As he got cold and started to shiver
He said to himself "I want to go to Spain"

Now how do I travel? It is so far away
By car, by boat or maybe by train
No - I want to get there in no more than a day
Of course, silly me, I must go by plane

He found his rucksack and started to pack
In went bucket and spade, T-shirt and hat
With barely a thought he rushed to the airport
Jumped on a plane
And guess where he landed
In Barcelona - Spain!

Alexandra Lindh-Fitt (Age 8)

Christmas Night

I put out some food
For Santa and Rudolf the red nosed reindeer
I went to bed
In the morning I got up and ran downstairs
Mum came down as well
I opened a present
Oh! a turkey, hooray! I cried.

Ben Littleton (Age 9)

Foggy Morning Poem

It was a cloudy day
I could not see well
And it is so misty
It is so dark
It is windy
Like the clouds come down
And you can see pictures in the sky

Samantha Lloyd (Age 9)

Tell Me Why

Doctor! Doctor!,
Tell me why?
Why is my neck
Five feet high?

OK, OK,
This is why,
You've been eating
Too much pie!

Spaceman! Spaceman!
Tell me why?
Why do rockets
Go so high?

I can not
Tell you yet.
I'm going on a
Jumbo Jet!

Peter Langton (Age 8)

Phew!

On a cold day
On a really cold day
On a really really cold day
On a really really freezing day
There is nothing better than
Playing in the
White
Smooth
Crunchy
Icy
Freezing cold snow

Owen Livett (Age 7)

Survivors

The war is gone,
The war is over,
It's time to begin the rest of our lives
In peace
No anger
Just lots of regret
Years have passed
And still the memories stay alive in our minds
The survivors are alone and confused
The war is not over in their heart,
It's alive and living
And will never depart

Gemma Lea (Age 10)

The Stalker

I see her, she doesn't see me.
She just walks, unaware of the danger,
Unaware of me.
She would have stayed home if she knew
What today had in store for her;
What I had in store for her.

For months I have watched her,
Her every move, her every breath.
She is mine and I study her closely.
Every inch of her body I know,
More than mine.
I have been in her house, her room, her bed,
But she is unaware of me.
I am her shadow.
I am always there;
Watching, planning, waiting.

I know her whole life.
When it began, when it will end.
If she won't accept me
She won't accept anyone.
I'll make sure.

Tom Lee (Age 15)

Our Planet

I look out my window at the big wide world
The clouds drift by held up in the air.
The sun is so bright, it shines from above
Our world is so precious, but not understood.

I came on this earth ten years ago
And in that time I have started to know
How to be good, how to be bad,
And what makes the planet a little bit sad.

The rubbish we throw by day and by night
All makes our planet a terrible sight.
We all must throw our rubbish away
To stop it from causing all this decay.

Our rubbish must go into bins that are green
So bright and clean and always seen.
The bin man calls to take them away
To be recycled and come back one day.

If our world is to stay in good condition
We must all stand up and sign a petition.
We must shout out loud to let people know
Our world had one chance and we must not let go.

Rachel Loveday (Age 10)

Love

Love is red
It smells as sweet as a rose
It tastes like food from heaven
It sounds like music
It feels as smooth as hair
It lives in the centre of your heart
It boils over when you meet the one you love

Edward Lockyer (Age 10)

Foggy Morning Poem

Fog gloomy fog,
We all hate fog,
Because it's dark, misty and wet
And smells like smoke flowing in the air
Who likes fog?
So do you like fog oh fog?

Roxanne Lewis (Age 8)

Friends

I like my friends,
Because they are kind to me.
The bestest best friends let you see
Their magazines and a Sindy doll.
And at the fair buy you a sausage roll.
But in the middle of the night
When it's raining and there is no light.
At times like these your friends aren't there
And shadows look, like a big brown bear.
And you can't wait for morning to come
To play with your friends
I really like my friends

Sarah-Jane Lancaster (Age 9)

Daffodils

Amber flowers sway in the bitter wind,
Trying to brighten up another sombre morning.

The smooth velvety texture of the blooming flowers,
Brings the early signs of spring.

Buttery coloured trumpets, surrounded by golden petals,
Are hidden behind long elegant leaves.

Soon they will die,
But we know they will bloom again,
Just as radiant as they are now.

Carla Lathey (Age 10)

My Cat

She sits all day with nothing much to do
The worries life brings don't enter her mind
If someone feeds her she doesn't care who
She has no problems or answers to find.

She watches people as they rush on past
She yawns, turns over and sleeps a bit more
She sees no point in doing it all fast
The occasional purr, sometimes a snore.

She sometimes goes out and catches a mouse.
A rat or bird if they get in her way.
But most of the time she stays in the house.
Her obsession is sleeping, night or day.

She'll sleep on the floor or on the door mat.
Anywhere will do for my lazy cat.

Amy Lord (Age 15)

My Favourite Dinosaur

My favourite dinosaur is the Thesaurus,
Made to help us and made for us

The Thesaurus is full of synonyms,
The words are spelt differently but have the same meanings

My favourite dinosaur is packed with pages,
But aren't dinosaurs from prehistoric ages?

Ben Lewis (Age 10)

A Best Friend

A little girl cries for her soul
Who will say play with me?
Won't you be that person
To come and say
That Saintly thing to me.

A little girl cries for her soul
While you play and I weep
What about each other?
We're thinking about ourselves
As you think of me
While I think of you
And we'll be happy in the end.

Helen Langdon (Age 8½)

It's Not Fair

It's not fair to have to
Do the hoovering
It's not fair to
Have to do the dusting
It's not fair to
Have to go to the shop
It's not fair to
Have to go to School
It's not fair when
We have to do our
Exams in Year 11

Leanne Leczynska (Age 11)

A Foggy Morning

One foggy morning it was damp and misty
If you go outside it's grey and gloomy
The floor outside is really slippery
It's a grey and gloomy morning

If you stand outside you will shiver and squeak
So I'm not going out today
It's really spooky and dusky and dim.

It's really blinding you can't see at all
And you shiver like mad
It's as windy as a hurricane and a helicopters blades
You will get blown off your feet!

It's not very nice because of the ice!

Ryan Leverington (Age 8)

War Poem

All smoke from gunshots
Faded away with the dead bodies of war,
We have our sorrow
Like everyone else
With grey dust under the heavens.
For war is a punishment.

Jordan Long (Age 9)

A Christmas Poem

Christmas comes once a year.
Christmas crackers banging all around.
Christmas trees are big and small.
Christmas is the birth of Jesus Christ.

Stacey Kilmister (Age 8)

A War Poem

I am hungry
No family to care for
Time to bury my friends
I want to go home
To see my mum and dad
My lips are purple
My hands and feet feel like ice
Nobody to talk to
I feel like I want to be shot in the head
I feel angry and upset
I want to go home and see my family

Amy Lamb (Age 14)

The Bully

Just because I'm different,
There's no-one else like me,
It ruins my life,
I have feelings too.

She slaps me,
She thinks I have no thoughts,
Teachers don't want to help me,
No-one cares.

I cry,
She laughs,
She says I'm pretending,
But I'm not.

No-one helps me,
No-one thinks how I feel,
Shall I tell you what makes me different?
I've got Downs Syndrome.

Ellen Lillywhite (Age 8)

The Beginning Of Time

He sat at his work bench,
Tinkering with his cogs,
Trying to make the perfect time piece.
Not moving until he succeeded.
Persisting through the hours.
At times he scorned it.
And at others he praised it.
Waiting to regulate the seconds.
Until he had it.
Gingerly he continued
Twilight came and then darkness.
When in the early hours of the morning
He cracked it.
The steady sound of:
Tick Tock, Tick Tock.
Could be heard through his house.
And so began an era
And a legacy
That has lasted generations
That era is time.

Adam Luckett (Age 12)

What Do You Eat?

Tiger, Tiger, what do you eat?
"I eat Wilderbeest"
Black Panther what do you eat?
"I eat Deer"
Mummy, mummy what can I eat?
"Eat Your Dinner!"

Thomas Lewis (Age 6)

Daddy

Daddy, baby, mummy
And me
Have I said
All my family?

Oliver Ludovino (Age 7)

Rain

We can play all day
We can play in the rain
We can splash in the puddles
And play with the rain drops
Rain is fun to play with

Adam Leaver (Age 6)

Starry Night

The sky is blue
The stars are light
They sparkle all the way
Through the night

The stars are like fairies dancing all night
The stars stay up all night long,
They're still awake and sparkling
When it's dawn

The stars sparkle through my window
They keep me awake all night long
Where they sparkle so bright
It saves me turning on the light

Danielle Lindsay (Age 12)

Secrets

Below the bottle green sea
Lie deep dark secrets
But small waves creep in gradually
They nibble slowly and softly at the hard sand

Drifting casually into the bottomless caves
Floating plate of misted glass
Tentacles of waving grass
A living pumping jelly

Sharp orange spikes sticking out
Suckers underneath waiting
Waiting just to suck you in
Looking, watching, waiting with deep, dark secrets to tell

Fae Lewis (Age 13)

Death Of A Maiden
(A Sonnet)

A silent, sparkling cold shows us our lives,
For seconds all is calm and not revealed.
The first are hit by ten thousand sharp knives,
Our deepest fate is painfully soon sealed.
The shouts echo around a lonely night,
The pain, the death, the tears, the last goodbye.
Our future tipped on end and us inside,
But me? My child? My life? My dream? Oh why?
A vision soused us in our helpless state,
He rears his head and leaves us with a sigh,
For all on life's long journey it's too late,
Their names are called and lost upon that lie.
Concealed in death and life and history,
The fate, Titanic, is buried at sea.

Hannah Llewellyn (Age 14)

Hurry Up You'll Be Late!

When I wake up in the morning
The wind is creeping
I am still waking
I get out of bed snoring and yawning
My mum starts roaring
When I get dressed I try to look my best
But my hair always looks a mess
I have my breakfast still feel half asleep
I trot upstairs and clean my teeth
Till they shine with delight
I run down stairs and spring
Out the door to the car
The car was rattling and rolling
Clattering and clanging
Yes I am at school at last
I wonder what the time is
"Oh No" I am late

Bryn Lloyd (Age 10)

This Is The Cat

This is the cat
Who wears a hat
Because his fur sticks up
This is the cat
Who chased a bat
And ate it all up
This is the cat
Who wears a plait
When his hair is wet
This is the cat
Who is the cat
Who is fat
Because he eats a lot

Kirsty Law (Age 7)

Night Time Animal

The prickles of his spikes
And the snuffling of his nose
And rolling up tight
It is all in the darkness of the night
I've been told

Hannah Lawrence (Age 9)

My Mum

She's like the colour of a red tulip
She smells like a rose
She tastes like a peach
She sounds like a violin
She feels like a nut dipped in chocolate
She lives in my heart

Joshua Loader (Age 9)

Snake

I am a big snake
Long and green
I hide in the trees
And I never get seen

My teeth are clean
And very sharp
I once bit a man
Who was playing a harp

He gave a scream
I said "What's wrong"
When I came back
I found he was gone

I had to go home
I knew I must
I saw the birds
Flying home at dusk

Thomas Lowman (Age 7)

What An Awful Day

Grey and gloomy day
Cold winds blowing
Woolly hats and warm coats
Wind and rain I am so wet

It's so dark to go out to play
Frost may be on its way
Wind and rain forcing against me
Blowing me back at every step

Leaves blowing from the trees
In a pile up to my knees
Jack frost on his way
The pile of leaves shall surely freeze

Danie Law (Age 10)

Tall Simon

Tall as the Eiffel Tower,
Skinny as a rake,
Likes a game of football,
He slithers like a snake.

He plays on his Nintendo,
There for hours and hours,
Never leaves the screen
Mum gets mad and growls.

He eats Twixs all the time,
Plays jokes on his mum,
He plays out until 9,
Playing with his gun.

Christopher Martin (Age 9)

The Mighty Slide

Children arrive in the morning,
And queue for the Mighty Slide,
The first to arrive is Denis Dunne,
He takes a little stuttering run,
Then Martin Bannister appears with his laces tied,
And follows Denis down the slide,
Others arrive,
The Fisher twins and Alice Price, a queue begins,
The slide grows longer front and back,
Like a giant speedy snails track.

And now the slide is really growing,
And the rhythm of the queue is flowing,
Some keep a place or wait for a friend,
Some dive down and reach the end,
There's shouting and shoving "Watch this" "Watch me"
"I'm floating", "I'm falling", "Oh Mother", "Wheeee",
If only they didn't have to go,
They would play on the Mighty Slide "Oh!"
It's time to go and everyone's sad,
Maybe the mighty slide is not so bad.

Kelly Lyons (Age 10)

Seaside

Seaside rocky full of of sand
Just a curve away from land
It stretches wide it stretches thin
It is a place to sink or swim
The sky is never ever grim
The water reaches up to your chin
Then you see the sharks fin
When you scream the sharks teeth gleam
It bites you once it bites you twice
You try to feed it lots of mice
You play Kerplunk
The shark gets drunk,
You leave the water you leave the sea
And retire to the cinnamon tree
Now this poem has to end
I have some money to spend.

John Lawrence (Age 11)

Spring

The bees start collecting pollen
The wasps start buzzing around
Baby lambs are born every day
And daffodils come out to laze around,
Roses and lillies do as well
And blossom starts to appear on trees.
Which looks like pink snow.

Alasdair Lamb (Age 10)

Football Is The Best

F ootballs are good at football pitch
O liver kicks the ball to the ball to the goal
O wen kicks the ball up in the sky
T hen the ball hit Daniels's head and the ball went in to the goal

B ecause the ball went in to the goal then
A rslaan scored a goal
L et's pick teams our teams
L et's start the game

Arslaan Lone (Age 8)

There's Something In The Greenhouse......

There's something in the greenhouse,
It's eating all the seeds,
It ate all my mum's tomatoes,
And some of the pesky weeds!

There's something in the greenhouse
It's eating all the glass,
It even ate the liner
And my mum's new grass!

There's something in the greenhouse,
It's some kind of wild snake,
My mum got scared when she saw it,
And hit it with a rake!

Joshua Long (Age 9)

Orange

Orange is a balloon
And a firework bang
Orange is a carrot
And a tin of bright paint
Orange is dripping syrup
And a plate of baked beans
Orange is the colour of Autumn leaves
And the light of a sunset
Orange is a tiger
And a parrot's feather

George Lavers (Age 8)

A Smile

It slowly spreads across your face
Like a slithering snake
When you're happy, when you're glad
But you can tell if it's a fake!

Once it's planted on your face,
It just won't go away,
In fact you could be stuck with it,
For the rest of the day!

But I'll warn you of one thing;
A certain kind of smile,
It's what you call a smirk,
And can be rather vile.

It's evil and it's wicked,
And does look rather smug,
So if you ever see one,
Please don't catch the bug!

So remember smiles are free,
They will lift your heart up high,
It doesn't matter who they're from,
Just never wave them goodbye!

Nina Luszowicz (Age 12)

Whale Time

See their glistening backs and sleek skins
Here come the whales
There's Jigsaw, Bubbles and Fins
They rush through the icy waters playing their childish games

They push to the surface of the water,
Their black backs shimmering in the sun,
And to think they could end up in houses of slaughter
Just for their blubber and sweet, tasty meat

They see something far down in their world below
And race to catch it before the others
A baby is left satisfied, he swims to and fro
Waiting for his mother to return from her chase

He calls to his mother quietly but not silently
But she doesn't respond for she's too far away
Now he's in a fright and splashes and kicks violently
He needn't have worried for we will protect him

Rebecca Langford (Age 12)

Trapped

I'm trapped in a cage
In my own body.
It's a large lead room
With no doors or windows
And no light.
That person in the room,
It's me.
It is my essence.
It is all my feelings boiled down
To something very small and very strong.
That person can cry and hate and laugh,
But that is me on the inside.
Sometimes it can escape,
And for a very short time
I will cry, or shout, or laugh
But normally I just stay quiet
And listen to that person
Screaming to get out.

Bronwen Lawton (Age 14)

Slocum Wins The Race

Hi! there I'm Slocum want a race
You what you couldn't beat me with your pace
Before you go you had better do up your lace
And when you go you had better get of my case

Sophia Lanley (Age 11)

Robert

R obert is a real rocking rocker
O bnoxious and original
B rave and best boy of Burnham
E xcellent and exquisite
R oaming real robber
T all and tricky

Robert Lacey (Age 12)

The Dismal Day

The day was dismal and I was bored,
But all of a sudden a knock at the door,
I opened the door and who did I see!
All my best friends had come calling for me.

We picked up a ball and went to the park,
And we stayed there playing until it was dark,
We all got home in time for tea,
Where my mum was waiting, just for me.

Christopher Lowry (Age 11)

A Baby Child

I'm a new beginning.
Well that's what I've heard.
I can hear a lot of things,
From inside my mother's womb.

I don't understand most things,
But I can hear what people are saying,
How exciting it is,
Getting ready for a new life.

I can hear many voices,
Happy, sad, crying, laughing.
Some familiar, some new,
Life must be fun.

I'm getting restless,
Kicking, stretching, floating, punching,
Life must be exciting,
In the outside world.

Something horrible is happening,
All the water's gone and I'm being pushed out,
I'd rather stay in her,
Than start a new beginning

Natalie Lewis (Age 13)

Phew!

On a cold day
On a really cold day
On a really really cold day
On a really really snowy day
There is nothing better than
Playing in the nice frosty cold weather

Daniel Langridge (Age 7)

The Weather

Strange leaves gradually falling
Slowly, twisting, turning leaves swiftly falling

Blustering winds, twisting, slowly,
Fast winds curling, twisting and tangling

Showering rain pouring slowly
Cloud bursting rain heavenly showering

Cold fog swirling dangerously
Thick cold fog swirling swiftly

Jennie Le Fevre (Age 9)

Lost In The Forest

In the terrifying forest
As wolves howled up at the moon
While the thunder cracked
Down upon the dark misty stone grey graves
As I walked through its ghostly graves
An owl swoops down
                        to catch
                        a rat
                        I
                        walked
                        off the
                        path
                        I trod on some crunchy leaves
                        a fox rushed past my feet
                        I turned
                        around
                        the path
                        was out
                        of view
                        I'm Lost!

Simon Lill (Age 11)

The Wonderful Rainbow

Red is for stop silent and still
Orange is for oranges lovely and round
Yellow is for the sun bright and hot in the mid-day sky
Green is for leaves scrunchy and silky
Blue is for the sky with planes whizzing through it
Indigo is for grapes all luscious and ripe
Violet is for violets tall and skinny as they carpet the ground
But my favourite colour is yellow
Because I love playing underneath the boiling sun

Jack Lee (Age 7)

Storm

A storm started and everybody was scared
Because the storm began to bang
And then they heard it was a big whirlpool
And thunder and lightning.
Then it all stopped then it started to rain
Every one was OK then everyone went to bed
Only the people that heard all of it went to the doctor
To see if they were alright and they were ok
But the little girl wasn't because she was out in it
And they found her dead in the garden
And they rang up some people who could take her body
To bury her when they pick a day for the funeral.

Carly Lloyd (Age 13)

Fireworks

Fireworks are wonderful to see,
They zoom up to the sky

Fireworks are loud
They make a wonderful sound

Fireworks are colourful
Green, red and white

Fireworks are like hundreds of little sparks
That have blown up into the sky

Kerrie Lacey (Age 8)

Bullies

Bullies hurt you and make you feel sad
They kick you all day long
They hurt your feelings very much
They call you names nasty ones
They make you feel like running away
They wait for you and hurt you
Don't listen to them,
Don't copy them,
Just stay away from bullies

Rebecca Lane (Age 7)

English

In we go,
She gives a task,
All the class give a gasp,
Then we get the books all blue,
So we hope our writing will be true,
We do our best in every way,
But sometimes our spelling goes astray,
When we go we all run,
Because the lesson wasn't fun

Thomas Lunn (Age 12)

School

School School School is cool
Then the day goes on
Then school isn't cool
Because the day is too long
If I had it my way
I would play all day
But lessons would get in the way
But I like school because it's cool
And that's that today

Scott David Lazenby (Age 11)

Animals

Dolphins swim through the sea
Chimpanzees scoff bananas for their tea
Elephants charge through the jungle
While lions stalk their prey

Giraffes heads in the sky
While all the birds fly
And all the tigers lay
As the zebras charge by

The multi-coloured parrots high in the trees
Watching all of the seven seas
Antelope graze in the grass so green
While the hyenas laugh at the scene

Rachel Lilley (Age 12)

My Senses Poem

With my eyes I can see people
With my ears I can hear rain
With my nose I can smell tomato soup
With my tongue I can taste fresh bread
With my hands I can feel mummy's skin

Abigail Lord (Age 4)

What's Inside

Is it a hamster with the tiniest appetite?
Is it a baby small and fat?
Is it a pair of trousers orange and long?
Is it a toy car that runs on the road?
Oh no it's my tooth that fell out today

Jenny Lloyd (Age 5)

Coming Back

My Grandad came back alive
From war
In 1945
He was brave and strong
And still very young
I was amazed when I heard the tale
He didn't scream
He didn't wail
When mum told me what it was about
He just sat there listening with a grin
He said
"I always knew we'd win"

Katie Lee (Age 11) and **Charlotte Tindal** (Age 10)

If I Could Fly

If I could fly I'd travel into space
And take a break from life's busy pace

If I could fly I'd travel to Mars
And spend the day eating chocolate bars

If I could fly I'd travel to Saturn
I'd have to learn languages
P'haps I could learn Laturn

If I could fly I'd travel to Uranus
I'd be too tired to walk back
So I hope there's a bus

If I could fly I'd travel to Neptune
But it would be cold
So I'd come back soon

Anita Mercy (Age 11)

The Muddleheaded Cat

Muddlehead cat sat by the fire
Darning his socks with picture wire
Upon his tail he wore his hat
What a muddleheaded cat!

Muddlehead cat went for a spin
Perched on his new rolling pin
Before he was through he was flat as a mat
What a muddleheaded cat!

Muddlehead cat crept up to bed
Wearing a saucepan on his head
This will stop nightmares and things like that
Said our poor muddleheaded cat.

Zoë Macleay (Age 7)

School Is Cool

School is cool
My friend loves ball
I like to do my sums
At dinnertime I eat my bread
And then I eat my plums

Maths is cool
It's fun to times
To problem solve and add
But when the teacher stops to talk
It really makes me mad

Science is cool
If you're not a fool
And don't just muck around
Experiments to find out more
To look at light and sound

English is cool
It's fun to write
To really work and try
But when it's time to tidy up
It nearly makes me cry

Nicholas Jeremy Jonathan Miller (Age 7)

The Bad Money Spider

I saw a money spider
Its legs are as fat as elephants' legs
Its eyes are as big as castles
It was as big as a giant
His breath is as loud as a motorbike
His favourite food is dolphin, zebra and snake
He slurps their blood and crunches their bones
And then he swallows them in one gulp

Charlotte Mixture (Age 7)

The Colourful Rainbow

Red is for leaves all crunchy on the ground
Orange is for carrots that you chop up and eat
Yellow is for lemons all juicy and sour
Green is for grass that you hide in and play
Blue is for sky that birds soar through
Indigo is for grapes all squidgy and round
Violet is for violets that have a beautiful colour leaf
But my favourite colour is silver because
I like counting the pretty silvery stars at night

Claire Musgrave (Age 7)

The Bear

This is the bear
Who went to the zoo
She saw a horse
Without a shoe

Jessica Murray (Age 6)

Snowflake

I'm a little snowflake
A little star shape
Just like a little cape
People like my little shape
Just like a little flake cake
I'm always white
I'm always right
I'm a little white kite

Katie Milburn (Age 7)

As Lonely As A Single Rose

As lonely as a single rose,
That's left alone to wither and wilt.
Lonely as a tear that flows,
That's shed because of so much guilt.
Once so beautiful, now so frail,
Fighting to the last, to no avail.
But what's this I see,
Another single rose?
Standing proud near my knee,
Sweet to my eye as to my nose.
Another flower takes its place,
A smile I feel across my face.
My loneliness lifts, I have a new rose,
A precious gift, my happiness grows.
We two side by side, both full of such pride.
This day I shall not forget, my friends the roses too.
Nothing to regret, it's all because of you.
The life of the rose gave me pleasure,
Memories of this I'll always treasure.

Cherelle Morgans (Age 12)

Christmas

I like Christmas time, it's the nicest time of the year,
All the family gather round the Christmas tree.
Carol singing, bells ringing,
Santa Claus is coming to town,
What a lovely time of year.

I like to help my mum
Putting up the decorations,
Switching on the fairy lights,
Writing out my Christmas cards,
Buying nice presents for my friends.
Christmas is the nicest time of year.

I love Christmas time.
Jesus Christ was born on Christmas morning.
Christmas is a lovely time of year.
I love the late night shopping
And all the Christmas fuss.
Christmas is a wonderful time of year.

Kerry Mathews (Age 7)

The Last Unicorn

Una was the last.
After her, they were all gone,
and she cried into the night.
The poor mythical creature
shed silver tears for hours.

Sionad Mackie (Age 7)

Autumn

Crunching, crunching the leaves go.
The conkers fall from the tree.
A breeze comes, the conkers roll
And people kick the conkers.
The bonfire smokes
You can smell the smoke.
Soon it's time for Goosey Fair

Hannah McGuire (Age 6)

All Around Us

When I went out
I saw some trees
Their leaves were blowing
All around me

I saw a little flower
That gave the sign of Spring

Douglas McAteer (Age 7)

Please Remember

The girl turned over as she slept
She dreamt of widows as they wept
Their faces full of pains and sorrows
Dreading endless empty tomorrows

They read a telegram which said
That one they loved now lay dead
Were told how bravely he had died
Showed courage but inside they cried

She slept again and to her mind
Came pictures of a different kind
She saw children born to people free
And so she sent the world a plea
Please never forget those men so true
Who gave their all for me and you

Fiona Mcleod (Age 14)

My Cat

My cat's not black he's tabby
He makes a lot of din
Every morning he is up and looking in the bin
My cat hunts at night
But soon I'll say goodbye
For he is going to die
So everyone will cry
We won't find a cat like him
Who eats stuff in the bin
I can't find a cat like him
So life's going to be grim

When cats die people cry
No-one likes the sight
But when humans die cats don't cry
They just mew goodbye

Christopher Morris (Age 10)

Handshake

Lying lost in a maze of hazy dreams,
Cushioned by throbbing ground,
Blanketed by rolling waves,
Shimmering, folding waves of heat,
The colours are mixed on the palette,
Stirring the images,
Playing with my eyes, distorting my mind.
Cool fingers of wind play with my hair and tickle my skin.
Cool heaven in such heat.
Grasp the icy hand that gently sweeps my body,
Refreshing my mind. Too slow.
The cool fingers drift away, wispy fragments dance,
Lightly stroking all in its path.
The heat returns,
Slow, fat, clumpy rolls, enveloping me,
Wrapping me in a suffocating blanket,
The icy hand waves farewell in the distance.
I wish for the clammy heat to unfurl its finger from around my body.
I'd rather be encased by the cold bony fingers of ice
Than the thick burning fingers of fire.

Phiona Maidment (Age 15)

The Wish Of A Maid

I wish I was a dancer,
I dream it night and day.
If there was a handsome prince
He'd whisk me away.

I wish I had a dance-floor
I really would work harder,
But as I've just become the maid
I only have the larder.

Mrs Smith the mistress
Won't even let me skip
Around the mop whilst cleaning.
She's afraid the bucket will tip.

I used to be 'The Lady'
With jewellery of gold.
But papa left no fortune,
So I'm shivering and cold.

I wish I was a dancer.

Alys Mumford (Age 10)

Red Is

Red is the colour of juicy strawberries running down my face
Red is a juicy apple in a fruit bowl
Red is the blood running around me
Red is my tongue liking the lovely strawberries
Red is the colour of a fire engine zooming across the street
Red is the colour of a fine red post-box that you put letters in
Red is the colour of your ears when you go out in the cold
Red is the colour of your red juicy lips
Red is the colour of a poppy on Remembrance Day

Sophie McAllister (Age 8)

Auntie

My auntie is a game.
She is Professor Plum in the library
Always leaving her mark.
Sometimes she is frustration hitting 'five'.
A pack of cards
You never know what hand you will get.
A game board of yellowing sunsets.

Sean Moody (Age 9)

The Tiger

The orange and black stripes
Run swiftly through the rushes
Ripping apart its prey
For its poor baby cubs
Soft as cotton wool
Roaring for its victory
Smell of fear
Fear of gun shots
Reckless and daring

Joshua Mills (Age 10)

My Garden

My bumble bee hive stands
Right under my wall
My cat called Olly
Plays with my ball

Abbie Martin (Age 9)

Have You Seen The Gigantic Green Troll?

Have you seen the gigantic green troll
That stamps and stumbles down the street?
He glares out from that gloomy hole,
Croaking and crashing at all that he meets.

Have you seen the gigantic green troll
With his slithery, slimy face?
His hands are hard and hairy
He greedily gobbles at a rapid pace,
And of the bulbous, bubbling body be wary,
As he staggers down the street!

Carl Moreton (Age 8)

A Foggy Morning

One day it was a foggy day
The fog was thick and really chilly
The road was slippery
Everyone was miserable
Every corner you will find a spook
It was dull and steamy and really dark
The fog is grey and white
It is wet and damp and a bit rainy
And it makes me shiver
The icy cars will hardly start
And soon it will be quiet
It is really dark out today
And really blurry too
So I wouldn't go out there, it's really creepy
It's really spooky and dusty in the house
And it is misty too

Ryan Merrigan (Age 8)

The Baby

A wet dribbler
A paper scribbler
A nappy wetter
A playdough setter
A floor crawler
A loud baller
A long dreamer
A horrible screamer

Ellie Medland (Age 10)

Limericks

There was a young boy from Devon
His age was just about seven
He had a big brother
He wished for another
And he came when he was eleven

Nicholas Marshall (Age 9)

Schools

School is a place we go every day,
School is a word we'd rather not say.
School is a place where children learn,
School is a place where teachers earn.

School is a place we'd rather not be,
School is a place we'd rather not see.
School is a place that we despise,
It makes us look stupid and makes us wear ties.

School is a place we eat food,
But the things they sell I think it's crude.
But even though I hate it I still go to school,
So when I grow older I won't be a fool.

David Moran (Age 11)

The Snow Leopard

The snow leopard its soft white fur
With dark black spots
And green sly eyes
Looking mean and sharp
Vampire's teeth
With its dark pink tongue
Ready to pounce
Crawling silently nearer
Step by step then
LEAP!
The prey is caught.

Bernadette Morris (Age 8)

Valentine Sonnet

Oh how am I to look away from you,
Your large pretty eyes have mesmerised
Your eyes are wonderful so deep and blue,
While I am asleep I am hypnotised.

And although I can see you through my eye,
The warmth from your body has somehow gone
Can love be found or maybe love's a lie,
Am I a jinx for everything goes wrong.

Maybe one day my dream will become true,
Shall I give up or will you notice me?
You're perfect, handsome, inside my mind too.
Any form of contact I will gladly receive.

Are you this perfect being I have seen?
Will you be the Valentine of my dream.

Lauren Macdonald (Age 14)

The Cat

My cat is as fat as a monster
He will creep out of the window at night
He will go into your bedroom and eat you up
You can smell his breath
It smells of rotten apples
If you go over to him and smell his breath you might die
So don't go over to him
I love my cat
He eats loads of cat food
I buy him loads of tins of it
His claws are very sharp
His legs are as thick as rope
He has glowing eyes
He will pull your hair

Jessica Murray (Age 8)

Guess Who?

Some are black, some are white, most of them come out at night.
Some are small, some are big, all of them I think can dig.
Some have red eyes, some have brown, I have never seen one frown.
Teeth are white and strong, never short, always long.
Some live in holes, like the moles.
Some stay at home, some like to roam.
They have four paws and razor sharp claws.
A coat of silk, they don't drink milk.
Ears are long, alert and ready, they stand very still and steady.
They can run like the wind when in a hurry, then stop dead to listen to the flurry.
Farmers would like to shoot them all and hang them on a trophy wall.
Some are wild, mine is funny.
Can you guess he's my
BUNNY.

Emma McPhail (Age 6)

My Brother And The Fight

My brother reckons he's so bright
So I started a huge great fight
Then I gave him a fright
By sending him on a flight
What a height
He hit the light
And now he's out of sight

Emma Margetts (Age 11)

Snowflakes

When the snowflakes come down
The church bells ring
And the children get up
When mums and dads are still in bed

Grant Mitchell (Age 7)

The Wind

The wind whispering in my ear
The wind meandering through trees
The wind stroking the grass
The wind swiftly flowing through back streets
The wind sliding under doors
The wind rattling windows wildly
The wind whipping away washing
The wind bellowing boisterously down chimneys
The wind creating chaos
The wind wrecking roofs with rage
The wind snapping telegraph poles
The wind demolishing farm land
The wind not caring of what it has destroyed.

Andrew Marten (Age 11)

What Is A Cloud?

A cloud is a piece of fluffy white cotton wool
Placed on a blue sheet
It is a white warm island
In the middle of the wavy sea
It is fluffy white snow
Falling from the sky
It is mashed potato
On a dark blue plate
It is Grandma's new hairdo
Resting on a light blue pillow
It is shiny white false teeth
In a glass of pale blue water

Elysia Madge (Age 10)

My Pony

Pony, pony dark as night
Sleeps inside a space so tight
When he's ready for a walk
He'll trot and canter all day long
Galloping here galloping there
Galloping everywhere

He's got a glint in his eye
Which looks so sly
He knows he can jump high as the sky
At home on the shelf are cups galore
And in every race he wins yet more
He knows he's the best
In north, east, south, west
Is he a boaster oh YES YES YES!

James Mills (Age 11)

Fishing

Peaceful calm day
Peaceful calm day
All fishermen gone away

The bait came in
I saw the fisherman's scheming grin
Fish went crazy
Swimming round and round
Thud, the bait hit the rocky ground
No no, I called in historic fury
I've seen what happens, disgusting and gory
But they couldn't, wouldn't hear me
Fish go for food
Snap one bite of bait
Realised it was a trap
But way too late
Man reeled it in
I saw the fisherman's scheming grin
I still have feelings
Though I'm just the sea
I wouldn't like that to happen to me!

Robert McArdle (Age 10)

Fred The Red

Red is the colour of Fred the Red
Fred is the mascot of Man. United
Every day he escorts them onto the pitch
Tricky as can be
He hugs the crowd and cheers them on
Excited as can be
Racing around the football pitch
Exhausted as can be
Dreading every day

Jamie Martin (Age 11)

Otters

Gliding softly
Silently they swim
Swiftly through the water
Chasing and playing with the fish.
Fish scatter
In all different directions.
The Otter has no chance
So
He swims
Back to his holt
And sleeps.

Peter McMillan (Age 9)

Adolescence

You don't know what to do,
So you do what you want.

You don't know what to think,
So you don't think at all.

You're wandering through life,
Confused by the crowd.

You think you've got nothing to offer,
So you decide to be proud.

You've lost all direction,
So you scream at the sky.

You've lost all incentive,
So you never try to try.

You're aching for a focus,
But you're losing your grip.

The world begins to tumble down,
You're sinking with the ship.

All words are condemning;
Is it too late now to pray?

It's easy to get lost in this world
When you never knew the way.

Rosalind Morgan (Age 14)

My Senses Poem

With my eyes I can see a robot
With my ears I can hear a tractor on the road
With my nose I can smell bacon cooking
With my tongue I can taste a drink of juice
With my hands I can feel my tennis racket

John Middlemass (Age 4)

Spider's Web

A crisp frozen spider's web
Is a prison for sunrays,
Drops of dew are sparkling diamonds
Glinting in the early morning sun.

It is a net for silver fishes
Dancing in the moonlight,
And the peace of the morning.

Rebecca Massey-Chase (Age 11)

Fishing On A Dark Night

It was a dark windy night
And two young men went fishing
Something was giving them a fright
The wind blowing in the bushes

They were scared of a monster
That was said to haunt the lake
They were scared out of their minds
No one else seemed bothered not even the drake

One night when they were fishing
A terrible sight they saw
The scary monster was coming past them
So they clambered over the wall

Getting very scared this time
They packed their stuff away
And went somewhere safe away from him
Then he went away

The next day they went back
To see the monster's spot
But they could not see any trace
Not even a dot

Rachael Matthams (Age 12)

The Band

The band started out
As a happy fluffy sheep
But then death came along
And took its life away

Stephen walked by
And took it back to camp
He had a great idea
Which he wanted to put to use

Stephen gathered the lads
And told them of his plan
They then cut open the woolly sheep
And robbed it of its bones

These bones were made
Into horns, flutes and rattles
Guitars, drums and xylophones
For Stephen's plan

The happy, fluffy sheep
Was now a band
As the end of one thing
Is always the beginning of another

James McIntosh (Age 11)

Guess Who?

Who eats my sweets when I'm asleep?
Who jumps in the bath as I clean the path?
Who broke the mop as I went to get some pop?
Who mopped the floor as I broke the kitchen door?
Who combed the dog as I threw a log?
Can you guess who?

Naomi Mann (Age 7)

The Leopard

The Leopard can run fast past a car
In a flash and bash into a car
Leopard ran fast far away in this day
Later he will stay to lay down in the day

Edward Manley (Age 7)

The Lion

There's a lion on the loose
He's near South Brent area.
Everyone's panicking
Radios going haywire
Everybody thinking the teachers are joking
Schoolchildren getting worried
A hundred sheep gone missing.
Lions are quite dangerous.
Is he dangerous or not
Oh no nothing to worry about
Nobody worrying now

Christopher McArthur (Age 10)

Elephant

Elephant huge, elephant small
Elephant drinks from the waterfall.
Elephant stamps, elephant runs
Elephant eats more and more.
Elephant banging, elephant crashing
Elephant tired.

Elephant huge, elephant small
Elephant runs from the gun noises
Suddenly bang the elephant dies with sudden shock.
The humans win again
And the elephant's dead.

Matthew Muldoon (Age 9)

Survival

Gleaming eyes of night peer through
The swirling mass of fog overhead
Tracks in the snow, direct and narrow
As a tightrope punctuate the perfect whiteness.

Hunger drives the sharp-faced creature to seek the cache
Hidden in anticipation of hardship ahead.
Frequently looking up, every sense alert, white tipped brush held high,
She scrapes and digs laboriously at the unyielding surface,
Breaking through to the forgotten soil of autumn,
She unearths a carcass, mercifully preserved by the cold.

Need lending her urgency she begins to devour the meagre flesh.

Suddenly she stiffens, every muscle tense.
A whisper of movement in the nearby wood,
The sharp crack of a twig,
A hated scent borne in on the faint breeze.
Muzzle tattooed rust coloured,
Jaws fastened tight-sprung around her trophy.

She turns and flees arrow-like
Into the welcoming undergrowth,
Its tangle closing in behind the sleek fleeing form.

Mark McKay (Age 14)

Otters

Slithering around beneath the cold murky water.
Splashing, playfully diving towards each other
And missing, chasing their silky tails.
Exhausted they scurry back to their warm dry holt
Snuggling up and resting.

Alistair Mares (Age 10)

25th Of December

I run down the stairs
I look under the tree
Why is there no present for me?
I saw a bit but that's not it
I forgot my glasses that was it
I ran down to the tree
I quickly put my glasses on
When they met my eye
I have a surprise
A big box
I open it quickly
It's a big cute thing
I suddenly realised that it was real
And she looked like this
A little face as cute as a monkey
Paws as fluffy as a teddybear's nose
A tummy like snow
What do you think my little pet is?
Maybe he is a bear or maybe a hare
I don't know do you know?

Ruth Maddever (Age 9)

Cats

Cat like milk
Cat like mouse
Everyday
Eat up cat
Milk and mouse
What you say
Meeow, Meeow, Meeow

Marria Masud (Age 9)

A Foggy Morning

One foggy morning it was wet and ugly,
It looked dim, dull, wet, and dusky.
When I looked outside it was rather creepy,
So I lay in bed bored and sleepy.
It was dusty, steamy and very miserable,
It looked damp, gloomy and almost unseeable!
It's really dark and horrible today,
Never am I going out there, no way, no way, no way!

It's really dark and misty,
But that's not the most I can say.
Because I don't want to stay in here,
Stuck in the house all day.
It's dark, cloudy, cold and misty,
It's horrible, blurry, gloomy and dusty.
It's the dullest, rainiest day we've had,
It's chilly, steamy, it's just so bad!

Paul Mosgoller (Age 9)

Purple Bouquet (Secret History)

I'm mending myself
And I'm sowing the seeds,
I'm digging a hole with my sin,
And an angel will come with a purple bouquet
And rescue me when I fall in.
I'm only a soul with no sense
And no deeds
To guide me through finding my care.
Though my angel has come and has whisked me away
He is shredding the shrouds of my hair.
Though it's a good love with depth and a means
It's re-opening wounds with its grin.
It has put me in chains, it's adoring away
The barriers holding me in.
I am forced to reveal
What I hate and despise
And have struggled to cover and shade,
When all that I crave is a purple bouquet
Tied with the ribbons I made.

Olivia Mace (Age 14)

Earth And Moon

Here on the round Earth it is full with trees, plants and people.
Here on the dull Moon there are no trees, plants and people.
Here on the colourful Earth there are buildings, towns countries and houses.
Here on the dusty Moon there are no buildings, towns, countries and houses.
Here on the bright Earth there are books, pens, pencils and erasers.
Here on the dry Moon there are no books, pens, pencils and erasers.

The Earth is full of fun things to do and play,
Here on the empty Moon it is full of nothing to do.

Claire Maunder (Age 10)

Sleepless Night

Dark shadows in the room
Cars on the streets after work
Baby's soft cry echoing
Through the hall
Dogs howling at the moon
Whispers
Of the teenagers outside
Party down the road
Full moon
Shaking from my water bed
Rattling from inside my cupboard
The scaring eyes on my china dolls
The light of the street lamps
Shining through the window

Claire Marshall (Age 11)

The Wind

The wind blows the grass
And brushes my hair
It calls to me and says
I can be fierce if I want
And gentle too
I blow the leaves off trees
To make a bed on the ground
But some days I'm quiet
And never a sound

Tom Morrison (Age 8)

The Rainbow Mystery

Red as bright as fire,
For you and me to admire,
Orange as fierce as the sun,
So very beautiful and cunning,
Yellow like a coloured leaf,
But never like a piece of meat,
Green as parsley and as grass,
Quite bigger than a whole class,
Blue as lovely as a clear sky,
As very different as a pie,
Violet like a flower bunch,
Just like a red glass of punch,
Indigo like a dark night,
With just the starlight.
You see why we like it well,
So every time it rings a bell,
But it doesn't come out very much,
But gold has been there to touch.

Catherine Minton (Age 8)

Loneliness

Sometimes I hate to be alone,
I just got no friends at all
Nobody around at all,
I just feel bored.

Sometimes I hate to be alone,
I just get really sad
I feel nobody cares,
I just feel bored.

Sometimes I hate to be alone,
I like doing something
I just feel like running away,
I just get bored.

Rhys Morgan (Age 9)

Dream Pony

Slow trot, fast gallop,
A fantasy at canter,
Silky mane and tail

On cold crispy grass,
He sails on, on and goes fast,
A large rocking horse

Palamino Mare,
With soft, pale snowy white hair
And kind hazel eyes.

Jo Matthews (Age 11)

My Family

Dad is crazy
And drives me round the bend
Due Sunday he'll have loads of stuff to mend

Mum is neat and tidy
Upstairs is a wreck
Mum hates our dog - Mum loves Star Trek

Sisters love to daze
It seems to be a craze
Soon she will be coming home
Together we all find the comb
Everyone look your best
Remember to tuck in your vest

Me I am fine
Yet in lots of rhymes
Soon I'll be a pro
Everyone will love in my show
Like me oh yes
Fight me oh no

David Monument (Age 10)

The Wind

The wind gently whistles
Over the tall woodland trees
It dances and sings
In the warm Spring breeze

The wind softly whispers
Around the hot, dry desert
It skips over the warm sand
Beneath the golden Summer sun

The wind is getting stronger now
It rushes the desolate forest
It whisks the leaves off the ground
And whooshes around in the Autumn rush

The wind is very fierce now
It pushes through the ice cold wood
It pulls the trees viciously
In the cold Winter days

Charlotte Miceli (Age 11)

Dancing In France

There was a young lady from France,
Who really enjoyed a good dance,
She'd dance 'till she'd drop,
And now she can't stop,
She's danced herself into a trance!

Kate Massey-Chase (Age 11)

Otters Sleep

Shaped like a ying-yang
They sleep snuggling nervously
Tangled up yet safe in their own company
Comforting each other
Sharing their warmth
In the security of their dry grassy couch
Safe from the howling wind outside

Calum Mould (Age 10)

Frightening Woods

I am in the woods, where's the right turning.
I knocked on the door,
Knock, knock, open the door,
I need to know the right turning.
I took a guess and went for left,
I walked through the spooky woods
With the birds howling and the trees swinging,
I saw a cave.
It was black.
With a sack at the entrance,
The bats were black with
Bright red eyes,
I thought I was telling a lie
But... but.... it was true.
I dare not go in there for the danger,
I heard a murmuring sound, I was terrified
Oooooww!

Daniel Moore (Age 10)

Silver

Softly, swiftly moves the stream,
See the moon make it gleam.
The silver birch in the garden's bare,
It's lost its leaves now people stare.
The reeds shiver in the grasp of an icy breeze,
Icicles hang jagged from the branches of my trees.
The flowers yawn and go to sleep,
The daisies bow their heads as if to weep.
The evening mist settles slowly all around,
Within, no creature makes a sound.
The night draws in and darkness grows.
The last light fades into a distant glow.
The sun goes down as if to say,
I'll see you again another day.

Stephanie Malin (Age 12)

The Dark

Slowly the jet black
Blanket takes over the sky
A city in complete darkness
The only seeking light
A full moon and
Twinkling stars above.
The blanket carries on
Through gardens and houses
Lanes and valleys
Covering everything in sight.
Owls are hooting
Foxes are hunting.
The blanket carries on
Then all at once
The blanket turns and
Starts to go.
The moon and stars have gone
No more owls hooting
Then the sun pops its head up
And day has finally come.

Kimberly Moyle (Age 10)

Spiders In The School

Please sir, listen clear,
I'm making a complaint,
It's those spiders again,
They're making me faint.

There's spiders at the window,
Spiders on the floor,
Spiders on the ceiling,
Spiders at the door.

Spiders are everywhere,
We've really gotta run,
Please sir, to the door
The spiders have come.

Yvette MacDonald (Age11)

The Twin's Parents' Evening

AAAAAH!!!
Parents' evening started today
I wonder what they will say
I wonder what I got in my tables test
Oh I hope I did my best
DAD WILL YELLL!!!
MUM WILL SCREAMM!!!
They threatened to throw us in the stream

I hope my report is good
I bet mine's bad
Mum is going to go mad
I didn't listen to the teacher
I forgot to clean the cups
Oh no! Here they come!

What will they say
Did I do well
So I did well then
I did well too
We're so glad it's finished
PHEW!!!

Sarah Moody (Age 11)

Waiting To Exhale

Every time I laugh he is there to laugh with me,
Every time I cry he is there to comfort me,
Every time I am questioned he is there to answer for me,
Every time I am alone he is there right beside me,
Every time I fall he is there to catch me,
Every time I breathe in he is there to exhale for me.

Leanne Mackerness (Age 14)

Winter

W hen autumn goes away
I cy winter comes out to play
N ight times are so cold
T rees are cut down to be sold
E veryone come down for tea
R oast chicken in my tummy

Shariful Mazumder (Age 10)

The King Of The World

The weather is strong, destroying the world,
An uncontrollable beast
With a puff of a breath a hurricane feeds
But soon it will be a feast
With a pound of a fist a city is dead
With a tear from an eye a flood will spread
When it catches a cold, so does the world
As snowflakes fall from the sky
An avalanche falls, a town is destroyed
And people are certain to die
It expresses its feelings with clouds in the air
Angry is black, happy is fair
It cruises the skies above the earth
Finding a place for a thunderstorm birth

Matthew McHugh (Age 13)

Fear

Fear is like a bedroom door opening and closing
And a ghostly figure coming in.
Fear is like a grandfather clock
Ticking in a shadowy hall.
Fear is like a sick animal howling in pain.
Fear is like a power cut
When your house is bathed in darkness.
Fear is like a graveyard
With all the people coming up from the grave.
Fear is like death closing round you.
Fear is being in the same room as a murder.
Fear is like when you know you're going to die.
Fear is like when you're shaking like a food mixer.
Fear is like when your skin is dropping off your bones.

Katie-Louise McCarthy (Age 10)

My Magical World

In my magical world
I'd have a worm or a snail
Where lions will lie down with the sheep
Where magic will happen in your sleep

In my magical world
Unicorns will gallop around
Where creatures like tiny dots
Make the most beautiful sounds

In my magical world
Theseus and the Minotaur will be friends
Where love and happiness never ends
Where war is a thing of the past

In my magical world
Pollution will be never more
And people will never be poor
This place of course is called paradise

Samuel Morton (Age 9)

Destruction

Danny the fox hid in his earth,
Even though there was no sign of danger,
Still he was in there as if he knew something was going to happen.
The trees stood there helplessly and
Rain began to fall and the trees were used as
Umbrellas by the animals who did not believe the fox. But then.
Came some men spraying Xs on the trees and
Then in a matter of seconds trees were being cut down
Incredibly fast and soon there were no trees.
Only the fox knew what was going to happen with
No help from his friends!

David Moffatt (Age 11)

Lost In The Shop

I was walking in a gigantic shop of evil shoppers
When I lost my confused mum
"MUM" I shouted
She had disappeared
She told me to hold the trolley
I ran scared screaming angrily in a forest of skirts
I was so short
I had legs like a fork
I saw my mum standing right there
She brought me a hare
We were a pair again
YIPPEE

Katie Maycock (Age 9)

A Sock

A smelly stinker
A nasty killer
A dirty Whaler
A rotten stink
A shoe lover
A foot wearer
A night retirer

Tom Morris (Age 10)

Fear

Fear is like death gliding toward you
And it's catching you wherever you go
Fear is like spooky ghost roaring at you as you go past it
Fear is wind lashing past you and dragging you
Up to hell leaving you melt into pieces.
Fear is sweat going down your spine
And it tickles your back and roaring at you
Fear is someone watching you
And you can see their shadow but they're invisible
And they're watching you every minute of the day
Fear is the door knob turning and someone
Is opening the door but there's no-one there
Fear is someone knocking on the door
But when you go to open it there isn't no-one there
But then someone is there and then it says BOO!

Amy Millin (Age 9)

Lonely Feelings Poem

I'm lonely I want to go out
It's raining so hard
And I'm so miserable
I've got no-one to play with
Oh please stop raining
I'm so unhappy
I feel so sorry for myself
All of my friends
I'm so lonely I want to go out
Lonely I want to see if
It had stopped raining
I stepped in a puddle
And I got so sad
Oh get me out of here
When I got out of here
I was cold and cross
I was upset so go away

Hannah McDermott (Age 8)

A Walk In the Woods

Bluebell shoots are growing
Great tree trunks are showing
Old brown leaves cling to their trees
Resisting the wind that's blowing.

Thorny bushes are pricking
As we go sliding and slipping
We'd stumbled up to Chiltern's top
And afterwards found a resting crop.

It was sunny and bright
Which was nice, right?
Bang in the middle of winter.

David Monks (Age 9)

157

Sectioning The Family

Sectioning the family....

Mum the machine and Dad the brick wall
My brother is a video
Grandad a computer and
My Nan an information book.

I'm sectioning my family....

Mum a sphere and Dad is a square
My brother is a triangle
My Grandad is a cylinder and
Nan is a square cube.

Sectioning the family....

Mum is a kangeroo and Dad is a lion
Brother a hyena
Grandad is an elephant
Nan is a wise old owl.

Sectioning the family....

Mum is a pear and Dad an orange
Brother's a satsuma
Grandad is a plum and
My Nan is an antique apple.

Craig May (Age 10)

Tree

So lonely,
Feeling sick with its green leaves,
Once a year has a phase,
Of madness, angriness, annoyance,
It shrugs off its red angriness,
And then grows with sickness,
Only needs a friend.

Tree so lonely,
Waving at you in the wind,
For help with its sickness,
Standing out storms,
By itself, tree so lonely,
Only needs a friend.

Tree so lonely,
Starts to end its mournful lifestyle,
Of sickness, angriness,
Starts to crumble,
Into a grey stick
All peaceful as it dies,
Tree was lonely
All it needed was a friend.

Nicholas Miller (Age 10)

Mr Fly

Hi I'm Mr Fly
Flying very high
Beware of fly traps
Because they're like sticky paper
The worst is the plant called Mad Morse.
Morse I think you're the worst!

Matthew Macleod (Age 9)

Mum

My mum is a sparkling silvery colour.
She smells like melted chocolate which makes me float to her,
She tastes like soft ice-cream,
My mum sounds like an enchanting flute,
She lives in my heart,
She feels like a soft fleece.

Laura McCarthy (Age 9)

Christmas Day

The snow is falling fast
The wind is blowing past
The air is freezing cold
It's Christmas we are told
Father Christmas is here
All our friends are near
The snow is leaving us
I've got to get on the school bus
In school we're making Christmas trees
Outside there is a very big breeze
Inside we are all nice and warm
All on this Christmas morn

Katie Mitchelmore (Age 11)

Trees

Trees are tall,
Trees are broad,
Trees keep living
Long and old,
They live a life of historic beauty,
Soaking in the forest's duty.
They live a life of coloured leaves,
That fall from the tops of those beautiful trees,
They live a life of twing and twine,
As the singing lark sings to the lonely pine.
The concise beauty of a tree,
Takes the words right out or me.

Chris Mourant (Age 10)

My Grandad

My Grandad was warm,
So loyal and down-to-earth.
Cruiser ship he was.
Agreeable, eager, pleasant,
Not forgetting respected.

Stood like a pillar,
Quiet but contributing.
Londoner he was.
He was in the war, you know.
Companionable and friendly.

Irreplaceable
With his little walking stick,
Still very active though.
I saw him on his soft bed
Where he finally lay dead.

His house has been sold
With the den in the garden
And his small jungle.
The stories my dad must tell,
I will never forget him.

Christopher Matthews (Age 9)

There Was An Old Man....

There was an old man in a tree,
Who was trying to scare off a fierce bee.
So the bee stung him in his mouth
And went off to the south
And the old man just stayed in the tree.

Nicholas Murfitt (Age 10)

No One Listens To Me

Sam it's time to go out!
Mum I've spilled paint on the settee
Come on Sam, time's getting on!
Mum it's soaking in
Sam we've got to go!
Mum there's going to be a stain
Sam we're going in five minutes
It's going to cost loads to get it out
Sam we've got to go
Mum it won't come out!
Sam we're going
Be careful with those paints
When are we going out?

Sebastian McBride (Age 12)

Rabbits

Rabbits are soft and
Eat a lot of carrots big
And cuddly all the way
Around bouncy and jumpy
All day long it's like my
Pillow tickly and skinny
Just like always he does

Tahlia Masood (Age 9)

Bubblegum Ballerina

Pretty pink tutu
Like a piece of bubblegum
As she points her toes

Like a graceful swan
She slides and sways on the floor
From a peaceful dream

Her pink ballet shoes
Bubblegum pink leotard
On her stretched body

Squeezy bubble gum
Forever moving – changing
Never staying still

Charlotte Mitchell (Age 11)

Under The Gun

Guns chattering
Men falling
Shells exploding
Ambulances roaring
Planes spluttering
Tanks eating
Cries of the wounded men
The sucking mud
Silence never comes

Olivia Moudy (Age 10)

Rebecca Can

Rebecca can do this
Rebecca can do that
Rebecca can wear a hat
And stroke a cat
Rebecca walks the dog
Rebecca can do this and that

Rebecca can do this
Rebecca can do that
Because Mummy lets her
Rebecca can do this when
She's at home
Because I teach her all the time
I know
My sister Rebecca

Chloe Mynott (Age 10)

The Thing

The thing is short and fat and hairy,
Round, long and very scary.

If you see him you will shout help!
And wish your mummy was about.

He lives in holes deep under ground and
Creeps around the forest without a sound.

So when you're walking in the woods at night,
Just make sure he doesn't give you a fright!

Katie Maun (Age 9)

Gobbledegook!!

When I'm naughty, all my mum says is
"WHAT A LOAD OF GOBBLEDEGOOK!"
"What does it mean?" I usually say,
"It means you're not cute
You have muddy boots
And you're afraid of newts."
Then I say.
"WHAT A LOAD OF GOBBLEDEGOOK!"

Today I learned a brand new thing
How to dance and how to sing.
Is this the brand new life
When I learn to use a knife,
Used on a plane,
Even in the rain ... wait ... oh?!
Then I say,
"WHAT A LOAD OF GOBBLEDEGOOK!"

Phillip Mead (Age 10)

In The Meadow

The sky is blue,
The sun is yellow,
The lush green grass of the open meadow.

Children playing football
And running around,
Or listening to the sounds about.

The adults yapping,
The dogs yelping,
The birds singing in the nearby tree.

I love the sky,
I love the sun,
I love the meadow and lots of fun.

Ashley Mills (Age 11)

Open The Door

Go and open the door
Maybe there is an amazing city
And a magic carpet that flies
Or a sandy beach
Go and open the door
Maybe there is a scary vampire
With fangs and a mummy
Or a haunted house.

Julie McEwan (Age 9)

My Feet

My feet are good for tapping
My feet are good for walking
My feet are good for dancing
My feet are good for jumping
My feet are good for skipping
My feet are good for stamping
My feet are good for climbing
My feet are good for tip-toeing
They are very useful!

Sian Major (Age 8)

Evie

Jenny had a pony,
Evie is her name.
Nuzzling my shoulder is a sign of love,
Nothing in the world can part us.
If I'm riding her it's great but
Falling off is not.
Either we will walk, trot or canter home,
Remembering the way we came.

Jenny Matthews (Age 10)

Senses (We Feel)

The feel of darkness is cold and hard as steel
The texture of sadness is as smooth as an iced puddle
The taste of fear is dry and choking
The smell of space is empty and lonely

The sound of grass is like a silent prayer
The smell of happiness is fruity and light like a summer breeze
The texture of birdsong is light and lilting
And the scent of smoothness is calming, gentle and warm

Ashleigh Morgan (Age 12)

The House That Wobbles

I squeeze through the side of the house
Not knowing where I am
I hear a noise, wobbling sounds,
I bounce down snakey stairs
To find a frying pan
Bouncing from floor to ceiling,
The sun comes up
The house melts and drips
I run out to a green sticky street.

Ben Moore (Age 10)

Me

Me!
My hair is golden like the sun
Me!
My eyes are blue like the sea
Me!
My skin is dark and tanned
Me!
My belly is like a bottomless pit
Me!
My legs are as dark as a digestive biscuit
Me!
My mouth is as big as a cave
Me!
My arms are like pencils always on the move
Me!
My nose is like a pyramid

Serena Mendies (Age 11)

Fear

Fear is like a leaky tap in the night
Fear is like lightening in the night
Fear is when you've just about gone to sleep and wake up
Fear is when you stay in a pigsty over night
Fear is a bang of gunpowder and you are searched
Fear is a dribble of sweat running down your back
Fear is when you hear the whooshing wind
Fear is being in a dungeon forever
Fear is when you are left to face the trouble.

Adam Meredith (Age 9)

The Summer Wind

The spring wind is bouncy.
The summer wind is refreshing.
The autumn wind comes and swirls round and round.
The winter wind is strong, icy and refreshing.
The summer wind is very hot.
It is a nice day to be on the beach.
The soothing wind blowing in your face.
The wind brushes the water.
The ripples of the sea is a soothing sight to see.
A beautiful view to see after the sunset comes out.

Holly Murphy (Age 8)

The Door

Go and open the door
Maybe there is a knife coming up to me
Or a spooky ghost growling
Maybe there is a skull

Go and open the door
Maybe there is a flying school
Or a forest of trees talking
Or a computer turning itself on and off

Natalie Murray (Age 9)

Fantasy Or Dream

Marble wall, bubble floor,
Fantasy all around me there may be more.
Is it a fantasy or is it a dream
Am I in a fantasy, fancy cake or cream?
Maybe I'm in a dream on the famous netball team.

Dreams are sweet,
They can be scary,
Fantasies are crazy,
And ever so neat.

Marble wall, bubble floor,
Who's that knocking at my door?
Is it a fantasy or is it a dream?
Would you stop eating my ice-cream.

Louise McFetridge (Age 11)

Health

The health of today
Ain't very good....
Oi you out there!
Too many people pollutin' the atmosphere
Nuthin guaranteed
In this crazy world!
Cars and lorries pollutin'
Nuclear weapons and reactors
All for human convenience.

Adam McKeown (Age 13)

Making Of Jealousy

Look at her just sitting there,
Long golden hair you can't help but stare,
Look at the boys just sitting there
Dribbling away, your worst nightmare.
Look at her deep, dark, blue centred eyes.

But what you can't see is a brain full of lies,
She's just a snake about to give a sting,
My heart is about to break,
Melting to nothing!

Natassha Murrell (Age 13)

Fear

Fear is like being locked in a dark cold room on your own
Fear is like being surrounded by ghosts and monsters and noises
Fear is like being in a graveyard feeling somebody watching you
Fear is like death gliding toward you then just black
Fear is like shadows dancing across your dark bedroom wall
That is fear

Andrew Murray (Age 10)

A Monster Poem

Its hair is a dry as sawdust
Its eyes are big and slimy
Its breath is cor blimey!
Its ears are as big as a car park
Its nose is like a cave big and dark

Its teeth are as sharp as spears
Its arms are as thick as tree stumps
Its skin is full of lumps and bumps
Its knees are wobbly like jelly
Its toes are really smelly!

John Mockler (Age 11)

Stormlion

A storm is a lion roaring through the streets
Running down the street
Howling in the night
Striking at the houses
Growling at its prey
Hungrily eating its food
Whining on the ground licking its prey

John Moulder (Age 10)

The Dark

A black blanket of velvet
Waving through the night-time sky,
A black hole filling the land,
A giant wave of evil
Creeping over, wrapping around.
Cubes of darkness rolling down the hills,
Dusk fighting for its place,
A full silk cover filling the atmosphere,
Slowly, slowly
The man of darkness is dead,
Dawn has crept its way in.

James McFarlane (Age 10)

Camel

The Arabian Camel it has three lumps
And when it walks it bumpity bumps
It has a natural water bottle
His camely colour is brown mottle

When he drinks he slurps
And when he eats he burps
And the camel's name is Kurt

Christopher Morris (Age 11)

Autumn Poem

As orange as traffic lights get ready to go,
As the orange of bricks that get covered in snow.
The orange of fruits, an orange flower,
Orange the leaves swept near a tower.
An orange sunflower that is bright,
An orange door that shines in the light.
Orange is bright, orange is dark,
Orange as the train leaves with a spark.

Richard Mason (Age 10)

Autumn

I love crunching in the leaves
The leaves fall off the trees
The animals hibernating
I get cold in the Autumn
Flowers die
The leaves go different colours in Autumn
The animals start to bury their food for the Winter

Robert Nicholls (Age 5)

Bedtime Excuses

Dad called to me
It's time for bed!
Dad -
I bumped my head!
Dad called to me
It's time for bed!
Dad -
I lost my Ted!
Dad called to me
It's time for bed
Dad -
Where's that book I read?
Dad called to me
It's time for bed
Dad -
Where's my bed?
Dad called to me
It's time for bed
Dad -
Alright I said.

Rowan Narborough (Age 8)

Drowning

Terrified screaming
Down - down - down
Oil - sea - salt
Kick - up and up
B U B B L E S
Light shining on the water
Calm water, ice
Ice cold
Shouting
People swimming
Life boats in the distance
Boxes clinging on
Hands stuck still
Extreme terror
Bodies - dead - floating
Imagining a coffin
Thinking about home
A warm bed - sleep
S L E E P
Sleep in peace!

Ian Nudd (Age 14)

The Power Of The Nazis

What Power forced good men,
To become ruthless killers?

What Power transformed useless slobs,
In to goose stepping automations?

What Power could determine,
Whether a race would live or die?

What Power had the potential,
To destroy entire nations?

What Power could be ruled,
By a devilish murderer?

What Power could only be beaten,
By its leader's insanity?

What Power?
What Power?
WHAT POWER!

William Nye (Age 15)

I'm A Ray Of Sunshine

I'm a ray of sunshine
Warm and bright
When I'm shining
I look light

I'm a ray of sunshine
Long and light
I can make you
Feel alright

Grant Marshall (Age 7)

Shops

Nike tops
Ellesse too
Dancing in catepillar boots

People watching
Shopping
All the
Eyes looking

Mikal Neal (Age 15)

Netball

The ball flies right into the net
And someone wins another bet
People watching all of the game
Trying to think of who to blame
Players catching no matter where
People cheering and shouting loud
Not a bit like a little crowd
Come on my girls it's time to play
We're gonna win the game today

Lisa Nicholls (Age 11)

Autumn

Animals hibernating, some are not
Crunch went the leaves,
And up popped the moles and work it all up.
Down everything went,
It was quiet again.
Squirrels are sleeping
But not for long.
Scuttling mice in their holes,
Out the rats come in the leaves and hide,
Hedgehogs with them and snuggle too.
Scuffing through leaves.
Floating ones too.
Sometimes in swimming pools
And the sea too.

Alec Neve (Age 5)

Phew!

On a cold day
On a really cold
On a really really cold day
On a really really icy cold day
There is nothing better in the whole world than
Playing on the
Slippery
Slidy
Soft ice
Yipee!!

Rosie Neill (Age 7)

Fear

Fear is like a ghost laughing in the hallway of a haunted ivy covered house
Fear is like being in a dark damp lonely room
Fear is like being on a desert island with ghosts and haunted houses
Fear is like in a cave and skeletons are coming to life
Fear is like a shiver running up and down your spine
Fear is like going to hell and turning into a newt
Fear is like living in a haunted house with bats, ghosts, vampires and witches
Fear is like being left alone when your friends and family have left you all by yourself
Fear is like having no friends and family
Fear is like a tarantula running up your back and biting you
Fear is like fainting and dying with no-one there to comfort you or help you
Fear is Hell!!

Kelly Neale (Age 10)

Spiders

Spiders,
Creep, crawl,
Black, beady eyes,
Long, thin, agile legs,
Lurk in dark shadowed corners,
Carefully watch my every move,
Busily make delicate silky sewn spider webs,
They see us when we don't see them,
But then it appears like a monster from its den!

Aimee Norman (Age 13)

Another Lesson

Come on now! Get started on your work
Oh no, I was just beginning to have fun.
Be quiet! .... Stop talking! .... Be quiet! ......
Can't she ever keep her mouth shut.
And don't answer back, sonny Jim!
She's a mind reader now!
Detention after school for you!
You'll be lucky!
And I'll be writing a letter home!
Oh, not another one!

Paul Nunn (Age 12)

The Snow

The snow blocks the drains
The snow is lovely too
Especially when you have a snowball fight
That's the best part of it

Richard Norman (Age 7)

Christmas

Christmas is good
Christmas is fun
What can we do without Christmas
The angel will sing
And the star will come
To bring the Christmas joy

Sarah Norman (Age 8)

Dogs

Bouncy playful dogs,
Dogs are cute and cuddly,
Fast, slow or medium,
That's the speed how,
Fast they go,
Dogs are smelly too,
Dogs are noisy,
They like their walkies too,
Dogs are eye catching,
Dogs are fat and thin,
When they bit you will know,
You can walk dogs can too,
You can run dogs can too.

Gillian Nelmes (Age 12)

My Performance Poem

My computer is a lot of fun
Not as nice as sitting in the sun
My Playstation is even better
You can't use that to write a letter
The television is the best
It's OK if you need a rest
The telephone can be exciting
I prefer to stick to writing
How about playing a CD
I would rather sing if it's up to me
Would you like to listen to my radio
I'm sorry friend I've got to go

David Newcombe (Age 8)

Heroes

They were heroes for our country
They could do anything for us
We must pay them back
And that is a must

They helped us in World War !
They helped us in World War 2
They helped us in the Gulf War,
And the Falklands too.

We used lots of bombs,
They had lots of guns.
We all had a lot of exercise,
That includes a little run.

It might be in different countries,
It might be placed anywhere.
But wherever it may be,
There would be blood everywhere.

It could be horrible,
Just anything from fun.
But there is one good thing about it,
We have always, always won

Lauren Nicholls (Age 12)

Martian Sends A Postcard Home

Dear Biboo,

Hair is like a long flowing river
That continuously needs cutting
Their colours could be clear or musty

A light bulb is a glow worm
That clicks on and off
But can run out

A river has boats and mountains
Floating along it
And it never comes to a halt

Coins are round shiny suns
That you earn

Crabs are oranges
With sticks coming out of them
With currants and claws

From Saberdie

Sophie Nash (Age 12)

Playing Cards

I love playing cards
Some are easy to play
Some are quite hard
I love the war hammers
I have never ever won
I had four banners
Saying have a go son
I only win against Dave
But only just be one
It's really good fun

Bobby Neville (Age 9)

Tell Me

Tell me, tell me, tell me why
Do pigs fly?
Tell me, tell me, tell me why
Do cows cry?
Tell me, tell me, tell me why
Do rabbits try?
PLEASE TELL ME!

Alex Newby (Age 9)

Funk

I am a pig
And
I am very big
And
Guess what I dig?
Funky music!!

Jack Nurse (Age 8)

Dreams

When you're asleep all warm in your bed
There's a land of dreams alive, alive from the dead
A dog coloured yellow, pink and blue
A cow that goes baa, a sheep that goes moo
Giants and witches and black cats that talk
And girls who are twenty who can't even walk
But in the depth of this wonderful fairyland
There is a nightmare city that's not at all grand
There are ghosts and witches and a man with an axe
And even a headless duck that still quacks
There's the green scaly dragon breathing hot flames of fire
And witches, wolves and goblins that never seem to tire
And when you wake up you don't remember a thing
About this land over the rainbow when sleep is your king

Naomi Nickerson (Age 10)

Aeroplane

Fiddling
In the air
Aggravating
Weeping
On an agency journey
Distinctive
Rapidly hurriedly
Muscular
Swiftly
Getting closer, closer
Screaming
Gliding
Gliding
Gliding
Suddenly
It has crashed
Has shattered

Claire Nicol (Age 11)

Girl Friendship

Emily likes Zoe
Zoe likes Becky
Becky likes Alice
Alice likes Liz
Liz likes Nicky
Nicky likes Holly

Holly likes Kirstie
Kirstie likes Laura
Laura likes Louise
Louise likes Sammy
Sammy likes Jodie
Jodie likes Emily

Elizabeth Oldershaw (Age 9)

My Magic Box

I will put in my box
The catching of cuddles
As we say goodnight
The scream of a bad dream

I will put in my box
The snapping of a crocodile
And the snap of a camera
The snipping of scissors as they reach paper

I will put in my box
The wobble of a tooth
From young children
And the bang of a door when someone is mad

I will put in my box
All the nappies and a scream
From a baby having cold cream

I will put in my box
The twinkle of the moon
And the dullness of the stars

Ayse Önal (Age 10)

The Heart Of The Ocean

You are my heart, you are my ocean, I love to see the sea and all its glory.
You are dangerous, you are wild, I don't care, you are my ocean.

How many times I stand and watch you, you crash, you whirl
You don't mean to, you are just the ocean.

As I stand and stare and watch you curiously, I wonder what you are doing.
The children are sitting on the rocks, peacefully, quietly, until your sea comes in.

It pulls them, it makes them cry, death is near, to the ocean.
I wonder why you do this, you hurt, you slay, you sometimes kill,

I wonder, wonder why.

As I walk away, you're sad, you're gloomy
Your eyes are wilting, just what else can I say?

Your heart is breaking there is nothing to live for
Just, O just for rage.

Why are you there? Why o why?
To stop us falling, to have fun, or just for torment?

Your mind is well but all I can say is
Good-bye, good-bye to the world.

The ocean is here and we are nearly gone.
For centuries and centuries the ocean will be here

Unless the world comes to an end.

Michelle Olliffe (Age 13)

Sunset

The sky darkens in the east,
Changing from blue to purple
As it is deprived of light.
In the west, the clouds glow
Red and orange,
Like the embers in a dying fire.
The sun, red and swollen,
Slips behind the green horizon,
Where the hills reach up to greet it.
And it is gone, to cast its light on some other land.

The embers die.
We are left with the ashes of dead clouds,
Scattered by winds
Over black plateaus of darkness,
Punctuated by stars.
The moon,
More subtle than her daytime sister,
Casts enough of her pale light
To create shadows in which nightmares can hide.
The people sleep, leaving the night to those who care for it.

Elizabeth O'Hara (Age 16)

All About Me

A Bubble

Wow!
I'm gently floating, floating.
Swirling round
See me!

See me glisten,
See my tender charm.
Down and around I bounce
I'm on the floor is this my end?

No! I'm floating up again,
Up, up. see me!
See my marbled coat
See me!

Now see me flicker
Silver skinned,
See me now,
See my silver glow.

I dip and glide in the air.
Oh no! I'm going!
I can't stop, not me!
No....

Kate Newcombe (Age 9)

The Monster Poem

It's hair is like some rusty old springs,
All tangled and in knots.
Its ears are as round as a funnel,
And its nose is like a tunnel.
Its eyes gleam at you like a pair of flood lights.
Its arms are as long as a snake and as rough as a carpet
Its skin feels like the grip of goal keepers gloves
Its legs are as hairy as a bearded old man
And its feet are like two diggers claws.

Liam O'Connor (Age 11)

Snow Flakes

Snow flakes fall in winter
Snow is nice to play in
Snow is cold and wet
Snow is white and fluffy
You can jump in it and
You can have snowball fights
You can make snowmen
But I wish it could snow every day

Ryan Osment (Age 8)

I Will Put In My Box

A little rain drop,
A swish of the sea,
And a little baby toy

I will put in my box
A zooming star
And a racing car
A mouldy carrot
Mashed potato cold

Maren Orth (Age 8)

Shakespeare

To fear or not to fear that is the question?
If I shut people out, no-one will know how I feel
If I lock myself in a quiet room, no-one will know where I am
If I seek out crying will people understand?
If I keep to myself maybe people will respect who I am
Till then I have no answer to give
Shakespeare is not the answer to everything!

Annette O'Ferrall (Age 15)

Dawning Of An New Age

I'm in the mood for losing my mind
It's not uncommon. I think you'll find
It's a frequent occurrence in people my age
To turn zombie like or fly into a rage.

It's a desperate urgency I feel
Inside of me. It's hard to deal
With the complexities of a mind,
Until these ages pass and then you find

It's too late. The clock will not
Turn back. Prepare to feel a lot
Of pain as your crimes are shown,
From the teenage years when your mind was blown.

Jennifer Oliver (Age 17)

Madness

Madness is red like a flickering flame
It smells like spitting bacon,
It tastes like fire hot curry,
And sounds like a lion's roar,
It feels like a burning stove
And lives in the flames of your worst nightmare

Rachael O'Brien (Age 11)

My Day Down The Loo

It was squishy with bits of toilet paper
It happened when I flushed the loo
As I fell down my parents laughed at me
If you were me I wouldn't fall down!

Scott O'Shea (Age 9)

Fredrick The Machine

Fredrick the machine
Can fetch things
Fredrick can pick up things too
He can hoover the stairs and
It carries you up the stairs
If it is raining you press a button
And a cover comes up and keeps you warm
It can talk and sometimes
You can become Fredrick's friends
It can tell the time
It cleans the place
He is cute, he has square eyes
He is colourful
Everyone wants to buy Fredrick

Kerry Osborn (Age 8)

A Misty Day At Newlyn Harbour

Grey skies and misty rain,
Clouds building up,
Rusty boats huddled together
Trying to keep warm.

Puddles amongst the cobbles,
Soak our shoes,
Seagulls screech and swoop,
Wind ripples the water.

Oil floats on the surface,
In rainbow colours,
A breeze rushing past our faces,
Making our hair fly about.

Jodie L. Outram (Age 10)

Summer

Skies like the beautiful big ocean
Birds like singing twit twoo
Sun like the sparkling sea
Bees like the buzzing bees
Green like green dipsy
Summer is like sugar

Jade Osborne (Age 8)

Just A Speck

A tea leaf in the Pacific teacup,
A speck of dirt in the dustbin of life.
That's all a learner driver ever is.

You have an excuse, you're still being taught.
People are meant to learn from their mistakes.
Tell that to other road users, I say.

Driving along, happy and contented
Then that dreaded sound, a fierce lions roar.
The driver behind is pumping the horn.

Patience, no! - I don't think they possess it.
But it's only pity I feel for them,
Those individuals with no self control.

Someone should tell them it's not life or death
Or that a few more minutes won't harm
Or that blasting the horn just wastes power.

A minute speck of sand on desert Earth,
That's all any road user ever is.
Because they were once learner drivers too.

Claire Peters (Age 17)

The Puddle

The puddle is shining undisturbed
Light does not pierce into its depths
Only skims off its calm, seemingly impregnable surface
The world beyond the puddle's shell is oblivious to us
A world connected to ours by a shimmering portal
A gateway to a wavy dimension.
As our world ripples the puddle,
The world beneath is thrown into a swirling chaos.
The gentle lapping above causes a whirlpool of destruction beneath
The dwellers of this world are slung up only to be reclaimed by their watery domain
They hang there wafting aimlessly before drifting down
To wait patiently for us to destroy their world again.

Andrew Parsons (Age 15)

Sand On The Beach . . . .

Sand on the beach
Sand everywhere
Sand in my shoes
Sand in my hair
Sand everywhere
So soft on your feet
And a bit soggy too
Much much better than going to the
Zoo!

Michelle Owen (Age 11)

Orange

Snakes and rats
Bees and bats
Parrots and hamsters
Ducks and spiders

These are the pets
At Badshot Lea
This is what you'll see

Orange Class (Age 6 and 7)

A Mouse

Good mouse
Bad mouse
White mouse
Brown mouse
Field mouse
House mouse
Spotty mouse
Big mouse
Small mouse
Any kind of mouse

Jordan Parker (Age 7)

School

Sometimes boring, sometimes fun,
Literacy hours for everyone,
Reading and writing not much fun.

It's assembly now and everyone gives a great big frown,
The teachers say sit down, sit down,
On the floor, first close the door.

Yeh it's play, it's play,
Up to the classroom,
On with the coat,
Out with the fruit,
And off we go.

Maths tests every day,
Mental arithmatic
I find fun,
But everything else is boring.

It's lunch, it's lunch,
Yum, yum, yum,
I think we have got a hot cross bun.

More work until
HOME TIME.

Alison Plumridge (Age 10)

Fireworks

Fireworks are bright and beautiful
You think they have stopped
But then there is BANG!

Fireworks are different colours,
Like red, green and blue

Fireworks are dangerous
But they are fun

You must be careful

Fireworks are big
But can be small

Fireworks are loud
And they dazzle

Sapphire Pierrepont (Age 8)

My Best Friend

My best friend and I are quite the same
I support Man United, he supports Man United
I like football and so does he
I am small, he is big
I like sweets, he likes sweets
I like the Simpsons, he likes the Simpsons
I'm a fast runner, he's a medium runner
I like the playstation and the computer and so does he
I have blonde hair, he's got brown hair
I like drinking Tango and so does he
We both like PE and Art
I like chess, he likes chess
Our favourite trainer make is Adidas
Our favourite type of books are Goosebumps
Our favourite colours are black and red
My favourite cartoon character is Daffy Duck
His is Mickey Mouse
And we both
HATE SCHOOL!

Jeremy Points (Age 9) and **Michael Buxton** (Age 10)

Forgotten Child

There is no-one in this orphanage,
Who asks me if I'm well,
No person in this orphanage,
This orphanage of hell.

There is no-one to pick me up,
If I have fallen down,
Instead they stare as I dust myself off,
And greet me with a frown.

Their only job is to keep me in order,
To stop me from going wild,
To them I am not unique,
I'm just another child.

One tiny mistake, and,
They fix me with a glare,
They haven't got the time for me,
No-one seems to care.

Lisa Prisk (Age 11)

Christmas

At Christmas time we have some fun
We make treats for everyone
We have meat smelling like our feet
At Christmas time we have mistletoe and wine
We eat lots of cake
And have a tummy ache
We have presents and things to make
And go for a walk down by the lake

Emily Phillis (Age 8)

The Wind

The wind rustling
All trees swaying
The leaves rustling
The people hollering

Robert Quick (Age 9)

Foggy Morning Poem

It's a foggy morning
Dark and miserable
You can't see
The beautiful world
And the flowers that God created
I do like the fog
It's spooky and gloomy

Stuart Parker (Age 8)

Father

Here right by your graveside I do stand now,
Do you hear me down there I hope you can.
Down looking at you, you were a great man,
All stillness and peace as we all down bow.
In a melancholy mood are we now,
Crying are people who new of the man.
Cowards you know just a shot then they ran,
To avenge your death I promise I vow.
Everyone's eyes glazed with crystal clear tears,
No one was better or ever so grand.
But what about Mother I have such big fears,
She walks around always her head in the sand.
But what of you father and all of these years,
You'll never be here again to give me a hand.

Joanne Palmer (Age 15)

Goodbye

You lied to me my friend,
You told me that your life would never end,
You said you'd be there when I was low,
You said you'd watch me grow.
You promised me you'd tell,
If the war went well,
Of stories sad and great,
You said that you would not be late.
Why not die when I was never born?
That way my heart would not be torn,
Why die now?
How? How? How?
All the answers I will never find,
    so for now,
        Goodbye my friend.

David James Puddle (Age 10)

The Empty Church

The church gates are tall and rusty
And the orchard is covered with weeds

The main door is all dirty and dusty
So bad that it would make you sneeze!

The church has been deserted for years,
Nobody comes to pray.

The graveyard remains with its weeps and tears,
But no souls ever come out to play.

The stained glass windows are all broken,
Done by vandals last Christmas day.

The organ has never been woken,
It's so old that it's forgotten how to play.

The sunday School rooms are quiet and empty,
Because all the children have gone away.

The bell tower stairs are all rotten,
And the bells have never been played.

The church has been forgotten forever
Because it's out of people's way.

Donna Pooley (Age 13)

All Around Us

All around us there is the sun shining
On new flowers, trees grow new leaves
Spring clothes in the shops
New flowers in the pots
Baby lambs, baby foals
That's what Spring brings.

Katherine Pendray (Age 6)

Blue

Blue
Blue, blue, blue as winter.
Blue, blue, blue as the sea.
Blue, blue, blue as the sky.
Blue, blue, blue as the blue-tits
In the sky.

Green
Green, green, green as the trees.
Green, green, green as the seas.
Green, green, green as the grass.
Green is my favourite
Colour!

Mica Pike (Age 7)

What Is...

What is the sun?
The sun is a star
Very, very far.

What is the moon?
The moon is as bent
As a spoon.

What is a cloud?
A cloud is a bag and
Makes the crops glad!

Susannah Pearce (Age 6)

Dolphins

Down at the seabed the dolphins play,
In their fun and exciting way.
Always leaping in the air,
While they share their love and care.

Down at the seabed the dolphins say,
In a kind of dolphin way,
Let's play until the end of day.

Down at the seabed there's lots of weed,
Where all the dolphins swim with speed.
Dolphins can be big or small,
But will always use a special call.

Dolphins are happy and kind,
With a big and intelligent mind.
So save the dolphins,
Save the dolphins
As their love you will find.

Emily Paul (Age 10)

A View From The Classroom Window

The brown skeleton trees on the green hill,
The stony playground for netball.
The red and green leaves falling off trees
Brown sloppy mud with people's footsteps.
Green leafy bushes waving in the air.

Chloe Parkin (Age 7)

A Day At Newlyn Harbour

Working people struggle
In wind and speckled rain.
As the mist hides from your eyes
Something in the hilltops.
Seagulls screech and swoop.

Boats rock from side to side
In the dead, murky ocean.
All clustered against the wall
Chains so heavy and dull.
The chatter of children.

A forgotten flag flaps
On a tall, rusty mast.
Oil collects in the misty air.

The sun sets in the sky.
The chatter of children fade away
Beyond, beyond ....

Jade Pryor (Age 10)

Autumn

On the start of a cold Autumn day,
Nobody goes out to play,
The wind rustles the tall trees,
The bright coloured flowers don't open for the bees.

The bright sun doesn't come out anymore
Not many people open their door,
Because of the freezing cold day,
People don't have much to say.

On the start of a dull Autumn day,
The prickly hedgehogs don't come out to stay,
Then when the day is dawning,
Everyone starts yawning.
Then the rusty leaves from the trees fall off,
We all get a horrible cold and start to cough,
Then we all rest our delicate heads,
And slip away into our comfy beds.

Geraldine Pennyfield (Age 10)

The Hunt

Strong ropes stretch then fall like flexing reins
Straining to hold the tethered boats at rest.
Their wooden flanks rub up against the harbour wall -
Their beams reach up as if they have surrendered ....
But still they buck and struggle to be free.
Sleepy fishermen carry wet nets onto their bound boats in the morning air.
Their prisoners are helpless until they loose the ropes
The masters start the panting engine and begin their hunt
Like riders on horse-back, the nets are now their hounds
The pack of hunters leave the stable

Jason Phipps (Age 10)

Frogs

A frog is green
And sometimes makes people scream!
A frog croaks
And nearly chokes
Upon the flies he has eaten.
He sits on a lily pad.
Gazing up at the sky
Wishing one day that he could fly.
A frog's life is not in the sky
But down on the ground
Safe and sound.
A frog is green
Not pink or blue
His skin's all green
And rather gooey.
That's a frog and I'm telling you!

Melissa Pretty (Age 11)

The Bad Cat

I am as tall as a skyscraper
I am as clever as a dictionary
I am as fat as an elephant
I am bigger than a hippopotamus
I am zooming like a hare
I am as sly as a fox

Jack Pullom (Age 8)

Snowflakes

Drifting it falls through the air
Running down the window
It's very cold
Finally it falls on the ground
Tiny snow flakes fall
It's good to play in
Nice to play in
Gentle it falls down

Kim Pearse (Age 8)

Classroom Noisiness

Hear the children chatting,
Feel the whispering sound,
The hamster is squealing,
People walking around,
The day has now ended,
There is not a sound.

Catherine Packham (Age 8)

Space Spinning Time

Space time, spinning faster
And faster making claps
Of thunder panicking
People horrible hurricanes
Flickers and flashes
Rays of sunlight
Computers on earth
Sending radars up into
Space

Joe Phillips (Age 9)

My Mysterious Box

I will put in my box.....

A cool dance by Billie the singer, the lime green misty colour of land,
The greatest power of a magician from a land called Kogamunga!!!

A deep purple wave from an imaginary sea, the centre of Venus and Mars,
And the taste of sugary, scrumptious, sweet strawberry laces.

Another 26 letters onto the end of the alphabet,
And the exciting squeals of delight from the funfair.

A flash bright red Ferrari, the most small Elf you have ever seen,
2,000 lands of paradise and heaven, and a little boy with an orange body.

The future, the past and the present, a fish with a rumbling belly,
And a bird walking on land and a tiger flying in the sky.

My box is made from rich maroon coloured velvet, tiger skin, ice, gold and silver,
It is decorated with an orangy carribean crush and a picture of a sunset.
The hinges are made from witches fingers, in the corners there are ghosts and ghostly noises.
The box can only be opened with the key of destiny!!

In my box I will dance for the animals and I will fly and explore magic lands.
My box is a mysterious box.

Charlotte Plant (Age 10)

Summer Sleep

Rock music blares from down the road,
The duvet feels heavy and damp.
The cat is fidgeting at the end of the bed,
The washing machine spins and spins.

A chorus of barks, come from outside,
A TV blaring downstairs
It's really annoying, incredibly boring,
But that, is summer sleep!

Kate Phillips (Age 12)

The Weatherman

Every night at six o'clock, he's there upon the tele,
Ready to advise us, if tomorrow we'll need wellies.
I'd like to be a weatherman and bring you all the news,
Of rainy days and sunny spells and happy seaside views.
I'd let you know if you need sun cream and a cool ice lolly,
Or whether you'd need your big rain mac and indeed your brolly!
I'd tell of mist and fog and sleet and very windy days,
And even when there would be snow, you're sure to be amazed.
So every night at six o'clock when he points at his map
Think how lucky we all are to have a weather chap!

Eleanor Peters (Age 8)

The Spider

Round as a pebble and goes back in it's home,
Comes back at night and scares you alone.
The spider saw a boy and the spider went pink,
To make the boys wink.
The spider races a man with an ugly face,
And the spider wins the running race.
The spider has a shower,
And uses talcum powder.
The spider goes home, gets into bed and turns out the light,
And says Goodnight.

Alice Paul (Age 8)

Animals All Shapes And Sizes

Some animals are rough,
As strong as an Ox,
As weak as a butterfly,
That flutters by,
As thin as an eel,
As thick as an rhinoceros,
That barges through,
The herds of animals,
As timid as a mouse,
As large as a blue whale,
That takes up the whole ocean,
This is the poem about animals all shapes and sizes.

Robert Prior (Age 9)

The Evacuee

How well I remember, feeling so sad
As I stood at the station with my Mum and Dad
We knew we were going but did not know why,
"Don't worry my darling the time will soon fly".

We got on the train all waving goodbye
Mum stood there trying I could see, not to cry.
A man waved a flag and then blew his whistle
In his navy blue coat, he looked so official.

The train then slowly pulled away, out of the railway station
Gathering speed along the track to an unknown destination
We were nearly there now and going on our way
I wondered where this place would be where we had come to stay.

I must have fallen fast asleep and woken with a jump,
As we pulled into a station, my heart began to thump.
I looked out the window wherever could we be?
We must be in Cornwall for I can smell the sea.

I'm living with nice people who are very good to me
But I'm praying to go home soon where I was meant to be!

Grant Pomeroy (Age 11)

A Man's Best Friend

My owner's best friend I am
But I'm not a cat pig or lamb
I am faithful, loyal and true
Always very happy to see you
When you leave me alone
I just play with my bone
I can run really fast
When my ball is cast
The one thing I really miss
Is being able to give you a kiss
Instead I can manage a lick
Along with a trick
If only I could talk
As well as I could walk
I could tell you how happy I am
I could tell you my name is Sam
I have so much to say
I have to store it all away
But miracles do come true
One day I'll be able to talk to you

Daniel Pester (Age 11)

Surrounded Table

This surrounded piece of mdf
Has a very cold metal leg
Some are big
Some are small
But this one is not big at all
It is perfectly straight
It would never break
It always stays on the ground
And very rarely makes a sound
It's best friend would be a chair
But they are not alive
So nobody cares

James Petre (Age 8)

Christmas Poem

C   is for christmas cards
H   is for holly
R   is for robin
I   is for ice
S   is for snow
T   is for christmas tree
M   is for mistletoe
A   is for angels
S   is for santa

Luke Plummer (Age 8)

Inside My Mind

Inside my mind,
The clocks tick.
The cogs spin
And I have an idea.

Inside my mind
The fog is thick.
The question is hard
And I can't answer it.

Ben Phelps (Age 10)

Christmas

C ame and went in a month, it's not fair!
H eavy snow falling fast, snowed in the house can't get out!
R udolph flying past seeing with his magic light
I n the shops every day, shopping till your dropping
S anta going, going, going, GONE! down and up the chimney
T rying to deliver all in one night! It can't get harder!
M agicly moving through the sky
A sking "can I have that?! "cool mum" trying to get more toys
S anta's coming, go to sleep, go to sleep zzzzzzz

John Parker (Age 9)

Who Is My Very Best Friend?

Who is my very best friend?
She is a helper
And she has blonde hair
Whose favourite colour is green.
Sometimes she might go to the Fair.
She's got a dog called Jess.
Who teaches me on Friday?
Who has brown eyes?
She's got black high heels.
It's Mrs Cable!

Rhiannon Perry (Age 6)

The Soldier

We are the British
We are the Brave
We were the young

Now there is no silence not through the night
No birds may be heard nor the cry of a child
May there ever see the known, where there may be silence

We are the British
We are the Brave
We will win

There is nothing that could describe
But no gun or fist may solve the pain suffered
But a shake between hands for peace solves thedeaths

We are the British
We are the Brave
We shall bring peace

The thing that keeps me going is not the joy or drink
But the red poppies that keep me going
But the war will not beat me
From the day I started to today, we both agree war is hell!

Ciaran Quinlan (Age 12)

Bear In The Zoo

There is a Bear
Who went to the Zoo
He saw a Parrot
And a Kangaroo.

George Passco (Age 6)

All Around Us

All around as
I looked out of my window
I saw blossom on the trees.
And I saw lots of leaves
And hedgehogs having babies.
And when I turn around my
Dog is having babies too.

Lawrence Payne (Age 6)

Waiting For The Whistles To Blow

It was World war One,
When it wasn't much fun.
When people went to fight
And used all their might.

Down in the trenches
Sitting on their benches
Waiting for the whistle to blow.
For the soldiers to go,
And fight for their lives
With swords and knives.

Thinking of my Mum while
Sitting here on my own,
Wondering what is happening at home.
Waiting for the whistles to blow.

Billy Pearson (Age 14)

Guess Who?

Who plays with his football?
Who brings my slippers down?
Who jumps up on me every day
When I come home from school?
Who eats my stew when he's meant
To be eating his own dinner?
Who follows me every day
Even when I go to bed?

Gemma Pemble (Age 7)

A Recipe For A Teacher . . .

Take some softness,
Whip it in with some quietness,
Build a person and shape with chalk.
Pour softness and quietness into the mould,
Make sure that no angryness or tell off bubbles rise.
Sprinkle with kindness and happiness everywhere,
Put on the flowery clothes,
Squirt with some perfume
And leave in a cosy, warm place,
Then you'll have our teacher!

(Please note: If any angry bubbles do get in, leave her to
rest, then start again!)

Natalie Pluck (Age 8)

Dreaming

Have you ever been to that place
Where every dream is a reality?
And the word 'wrong' does not exist.
A world where missiles bring messages of hope
And tanks and bombs are fun and laughter.
A place where the sun is always shining
Over a motionless blue sky
Patterned with singing birds
That circle a place which is a picture of perfectness
To every closed and dreaming eye.

Kimberley Peters (Age 15)

My Hamster

I have a Syrian hamster,
Who behaves like a little gangster,
Although I know he relies on me,
As his feeder and protector,
With his dark beady eyes, and razor sharp teeth,
He's as scary as Hannibal Lector.

One night I was eating chicken and sage,
When my hamster got into a massive great rage,
And knocked over his little cage,
He jumped out of his miniature door,
And scampered all over the floor!

His only weakness is his fear,
About this he sometimes sheds a tear,
Because whenever he sees a deer,
He thinks about jumping off a pier!

Although he can be fierce and mean,
If you give him a runner bean,
He will become rather keen,
And give a friendly little scream,
For a little bit more of that particular runner bean

Robert Paterson (Age 12)

A Winter's Day

I like the snow crunching under my feet
I like the wind blowing all the old leaves
I don't like the cold snow but I do like having a snow fight
I love skating on the ice
But I don't like it when the ice melts

Jamie Lee Phelps (Age 15)

I Care

I care about pollution
And the birds and the bees,
I care about pollution
And destroying the trees.
What can we do to stop it?
Can we change the Earth?
What can we do to stop it?
Give the world a re-birth.

I care about the animals,
The dogs and the cats,
I care about the animals,
And the little black bats.
What can we do to stop
The hurt and cruelty?
Just think how you would feel,
If it were you or me!

Natalie Poole (Age 14)

Beaches In Australia

Sometimes it can be wondrous,
Sometimes it can be dangerous.
Most the time it is fun and steep,
On certain beaches it really does reek
The shells are pink, orange and white,
And the horizon shines like a torch light.

I love exploring the old rock caves,
Sitting on top I can see the waves.
I can hear some people shouting and laughing.
They look like grandparents who have been rafting.

Under the water I suddenly see
A dark mark and it's heading for me.
I stand up to get a better view,
Everyone starts running for the loo.

The guards crying shark,
But I think it's all a lark.
It's only a baby whale,
That's got caught in a gale.

Leigh Pearse (Age 11)

Untitled

Tranquil air obscures the clerical grey sky
The ghostly breeze stuns me to silence
My eyes widen in painful surprise to see
The willow looking like a ghostly bridal veil
Soft mists and tawny skies arouse me
Yet the wind stays serene

Kristy Patrick (Age 11)

Beginnings

Before you, dreams
Ending the past,
Gilded hope:
Ill concealed, insidious
Names in the mist;
Never sought after,
If yet names still exist.
Now remembrance turned aside,
Goes beckoning before,
So lend me time.

Tia Psihogios (Age 16)

First World War

I am in the war.
They are fighting all day
People running
Around. He said it was cold
And wet windy.
It's dark, there are
Big trenches, he said
Bullets are flying
Around me
I am scared.

Dean Pepper (Age 14)

People

People big, people small,
Some people very tall.

People drive, people trot,
People always go in shops.

People fast, people slow,
People always on the go.

People run, people talk,
People always on the walk.

People shout, people chat,
People always stroke the cat.

People hit, people punch,
People always like to munch.

People laugh, people cry,
People always say goodbye.

People sing, people skip,
People like to have a kip.

People hate, people love
People like to carry a dove.

Luke Pomeroy (Age 10)

Earth Scape

Art is my pleasure, I indulge in drawing.
Drawing the shimmering sea, the silent foam upon the waves,
The gently rising, falling waves.
Intelligent dolphins playing upon the lazy rollers
And mighty whales singing eloquently beneath them.
I like to draw.

Art is my pleasure, I indulge in drawing.
Drawing the beautiful colours and diversities,
Of this wonderful and unique world.
This one community, beneath this one sun
Connected, together, this precious earth.
I like to draw.

But this world is being cruelly tortured
And the creatures cruelly scathed.
Soon there will be nothing left for me to draw.
This earth is swiftly dying,
Screaming, crying, painfully sighing.
I like to draw.

To draw.....
BREATH.

Samantha Pappin (Age 10)

School Days

We had a lonely first day
Scared and frightened
Together but alone
We sang an unknown song
And clapped our hands
We felt so small

But now we feel part of the school
Not scared not frightened
Together all the time
We sung that well known song
And clapped our hands
And now we feel so big

Steven Pantling (Age 11)

The Tale Of The Reluctant Reader

It's not always easy to find time to read,
But books are the key if you want to succeed.
A book can open up a whole new world,
Of fact and fiction like a flag unfurled,.
A world of fantasy you will find,
As images make their way into your mind.
As you read, your vocabulary's sure to swell,
And your English marks will improve as well!
The library at Thornden's the place to begin,
Mrs Stonham will tell you which new books are in.
So whether you enjoy a laugh or a cry,
DIVE INTO A BOOK NOW, give reading a try.

Stewart Peters (Age 11)

Message In A Bottle

Hello! whoever finds this message,
I have found an island,
I saw land
So I came ashore.
So here I remain
Going insane
On this island all on my own.

Rachel Phillips (Age 11)

Untitled

Old, rusty, metal
Chugging, navy coloured train
Hissing spitting, smoke.

Hannah Philp (Age 9)

Hate

Hate is as black as the night sky,
It smells like cold frosty air,
Hate tastes of cold, hard ice-cream,
It sounds like lightning cracking,
It feels like a pin pricking you,
Hate lives in the body of a devil.

Tamzin Plummer (Age 10)

A Martian Sends A Postcard Home

Dear Ollie,

Trees are bodies with many tentacles
They have little birds that slowly fly down to the ground

Flowers are very thin pieces of paper
Almost made by mankind
They have a long thin body and short fat arms

Bananas are moons but yellow
Their mask is pulled off
Then the moon disappears

Pens are snails that leave a trail behind them
They have small hats on top of their spiky heads

The sea is a big blue sheet
With ripples moving to and fro
They have many toys inside
That swim around run by batteries

Windows are a clear mind that can see well
At night the window goes black and the mind goes to sleep

Emma Pope (Age 13)

Summer

Glimmering Sun
Catches your eye
Silent sky
Clear as
Windows washed by
Water

Waving grass
Swaying around
Travelling
To a different world
Sweat dripping down

No school
For a while
Furiously hot
The leaves
Falling off trees

The summer has closed
So
Back . . . .
To . . . .

Josh Pickett (Age 10)

Doggy

There was once a young dog called Snappy
Who sometimes was rather happy
He stood on a rose
And stuffed it up his nose
So now he can't smell his Chappy

Mikhaila Tamai Pink (Age 9)

Snow Snow

Snow, snow downfall it gets cold
It looks white and looks like cotton wool
It drifts slowly and floats down to the
ground
The flakes are nice, the sun comes out
So you have to play in the snow
Before it melts

Kevin Pinkawa (Age 9)

Sitting On A Muddy Bank

Sitting on a muddy bank
Throughout the
Night and day
Daydreaming that
The biggest fish
Would come, not
Get away.
Sitting there hoping
That he would not
Catch a shark.
He was really wishing
That he would catch
A carp!

Emma Paveley (Age 8)

Fear

Fear is as black as night
It smells like stale bread
Fear tastes dry and stinging
It sounds like scratching on glass,
It feels like nails and pins pricking
on your skin,
Fear lives in you

James Panting (Age 9)

Puddles

I pull on my wellies, I pull on my mac
I've found a puddle, I've found a puddle,
SPLISH! SPLASH! SPLOSH!
There fly the muddy droplets of water
All over my clothes,
I'm all wet and muddy,
With a hot cup of cocoa and a biscuit
I'm cosy and warm now,
Tomorrow,
I'll be with the puddles again.

Eleanor Purnell (Age 9)

Ottery's Sounds

Splish splash, splish splash,
Hear the River Otter crash,
Flowing down the tumbling weir,
Slipping down the sides so sheer.

In the early morning light,
People hurry, time is tight!
Can you hear the whistles shrill?
Calling people to the mill.

Ding dong, ding dong
Hear the Church clock's chiming song
Ding dong the Church clock chimes,
Telling people of the times.

A single bell rings alone,
Telling all with solemn tone,
"Have you heard the news?" it said
"Bobby's Uncle Joe is dead!"

Again a peal of bells is heard,
Asking "have you heard the word?
My good friends, young Sue and Ted
Have today, just now, been wed!"

Elaine Pinkett (Age 12)

Similes

As scary as a leopard - as gentle as a dove
As hard as a stone - as floppy as a glove
As blind as a mole - as worn as a shoe
As cool as a cucumber - as warm as hot water
As thin as paper - as fat as a pig
As flat as a blackboard - as sharp as a pin

Robyn Poulson (Age 8)

Bubble Gum

Bubble gum, bubble gum
Sticks on your gum,
Bubble gum bubble gum.
Sticks on your mum.

It's a very sticky thing,
It makes your teeth go numb.
And if it's left upon a chair.
It sticks right on your bum.

Austyn Parkhurst (Age 12)

Watching Through The Window

Spring

Watching through the window,
On this bright clear spring day
I see lambs gamboling,
Snowdrops and daffodils sway
Spring is here today!

Summer

Spring turns to Summer,
Bees and butterflies flit past
Flowers, barbecues and picnics,
Fruit starts to grow at last,
Summer goes so fast!

Autumn

Harvest of vegetables soon,
I'm seeing lots of rain,
Leaves are falling rapidly,
Mud starts to collect in the lane,
School starts, what a shame!

Winter

Frost makes the view look magical,
For it is a winter scene now,
There's no leaves on the trees,
Next I'll be seeing snow,
From my magic, special window!

Tamsin Parsons (Age 11)

Colours

Colours come from the sky,
Wherever you look they are there,
They move across the world,
Roaming round like the Brown bear.

White is a colour that makes me think,
Of white albinos running feet in the ice cold snow,
And polar bears wandering like a lost soul.

Black is a miserable colour,
It reminds us of death and gothic things.

Pink makes me think of baby pink candy,
And the pink mouthwash at the dentist.

Blue is the colour of the sky,
Where birds fly so high.

Emily Pettiford (Age 12)

The Dark

Black snakes coiling around us,
A peaceful surrounding,
Until the dawn.

The nothingness,
Like giant bat wings,
Spreading across our sky.

Tearing through the stillness,
Slowly, creeping up behind us,
Hanging on to our villages,
Blocking out the familiar light.

Diving between valleys,
Like the bats,
Swooping down for their prey,
It takes over our sky.

It follows us,
This never ending tunnel,
Covers us in our sleep,
But in our wake,
It dies.

Terri Parsons (Age 11)

The Poem Of A Tragic Day

We ran to the shelter feeling scared and helpless.
I was carrying all my toys and belongings,
Opened the door and crept in silently.
Caroline and Pete were there.
EEK! EEK! went the clustery siren.

While I was waiting I felt alone,
Imagining poor men covered in blood.
When Mum shut the door I felt claustrophobic,
I was sweating, *CRASH*
CRASH gosh it made me jump.
BOOM! crash went the noisy bombs.
Most of the people were asleep.
The ground was shaking, bits were falling from the walls.

Thank goodness, the war was over.
I came out and looked around and
Saw my humble home had been knocked down.
My best friend had been horribly killed.
What a tragic day!

Charlie Preston (Age 10)

There Was A War

Go to war it's your duty lad
Who's for the game,
Enlist today! then at the sound of a drum out of their dens they come
As the naked earth is warm and spring the war is out there happening.
There my friend lies a ghoulish score of him left on the field for dead
The poignant misery of dawn begins to grow as war goes on
People dying as the wind is blowing like a song.
Then suddenly I shudder as I see a young man all weary but still
Stare unmoved as he stands he then falls down as if he were dead.

Anthony Pruvedenti (Age 13)

Sally Jones

Sally Jones is SCARY
Sally Jones with hands hairy,
Sally Jones, Sally Jones,
Through her skin you can see her bones.

She smells of smoke,
And wears rags,
She drinks coke
She is a hag.

I haven't seen her mum before,
I cannot bear to knock at the door, for
Sally Jones is SCARY
Sally Jones with hands hairy.

Holly Pitts (Age 9)

Inside The Dark Tunnel

Inside the dark tunnel
I hear ghostly moaning,
Yellow eyes stare at me,
I hear water dripping like blood.

The quiet pattering of feet scuttling like cockroaches
Bats in every corner
And giant monsters waiting for fresh meat
Leeches lurk in cracks in the wall

Aron Prowse (Age 10)

My Little Brothers

My little brothers were sent from hell,
To come and annoy me, let me tell.
They hit me and punch me and do what they like,
While I'm out fishing catching a pike.
I did a wrestling move on one of them,
Just to keep him away from my den.
I bought them each a new bike,
So now it's my turn to do what I like.

Daniel Pennack (Age 11)

Outside-In

Too many people,
Livin' in the streets.
Livin' under bridges
Nothin' to eat.

Too many people,
Livin' in crime.
Breakin' into houses,
Just to pass the time.

Too many people,
Beggin' in the park.
Sleepin' under blankets,
When it's gettin' dark.

Too many people,
Sleepin' in shop doors.
So many people,
Nothin' to live for.

Too many people,
Starvin' to death
Sooner or later,
There'll
Be
Nothin'
Left....

Sally Pearce (Age 13)

Tavistock

The bells ring from Tavistock church
Making loud noises and chiming
The church is big and the bells chime at night
They ring in the day sometimes too
They ring when somebody is getting married
And they sound happy

Peter Robson (Age 6)

A Wet Day At Newlyn Harbour

Rain splashing down like waves in the sea
Sky looking black with grey mist covering the hillside behind,
Clouds dull - like it's going to splatter with rain,
Wind making me shiver and the cars gushing past

Patterny sea with reflecting shadows,
Boats huddled in the corner, nudging each other.
A swirl of ropes like the rippling sea,
Seagulls twisting and twirling in the misty sky.

People chattering in the distance,
Children cluttering the harbour around the sea,
The sea drifting in silently and slowly,
A wet day at Newlyn Harbour.

Amanda Paul (Age 10)

Dreaming Of Dragons

As I travel to the land of my dreams
I look at this mysterious land
I see the purple silky scales of a flame flickering dragon
Defending its young from the dragon slayer

One final blow and the dragon would have died
But along came a dragon lover and stood beside her side
He saw his noble stallion run down the plains
Running from the dragons fearsome scorching flames

The slayer all on his own
The dragon wants revenge
In one more attack with all their might
They charge for the kill

The loyal shield against the horrific claw
The battle cry, the ferocious roar
Both foes fell down dead
There upon the river bed

As I leave the land of my dreams
I look back at the dragon's nest
I saw the dragon lover sit up with pride
To fight again tonight

William Pomfrey (Age 11)

Sneezing Hell

Walking down the street one day
I felt a little itch,
It was just in my nostril
When I began to twitch

It came out with a whoosh
It blew me on my knees,
It blew away a bush,
Yes it was a sneeze.

It made an old man jump,
It made a baby queezy,
He landed with a thump,
And then he said it's breezy.

It blew away a dog,
It blew away a house,
It blew away a frog,
It blew away a mouse.

It blew away a roof,
It blew away a stack of hay,
It blew away a photo booth,
This was turning out to be a real bad day.

Nick Phillips (Age 12)

Monday Morning

Dreams of roast dinner, strawberries and cream,
The happiest, yummiest heavenly scene.
I was snug, I was warm as I pictured my day,
Weekends are great as there's all day to play

Now what shall I do? Is what sprang to my head,
As I danced and sang and jumped out of bed.
My dreams fell to bits as the truth dawned on me,
Oh no! It is Monday, so little time's free.

Then HOMEWORK I thought, is it handed in?
There's English and maths, or is that in the bin?
The dreaded art head'll be in a bad mood,
I was never much good at those drawings of food!

I trudged into the playground, the usual scene!
Ski-rides for school bags, the usual scream!
I strolled into class, what a great surprise,
I'd won the poem competition, 200 points - first prize!

Nicola Patten (Age 10)

Ghosts And Spirits

Walking through the park,
But it's not light it's dark.
Looking around to see,
If anything is following me.
It frightens me to imagine,
What might happen,
The ghosts and spirits that may arise,
With me in the background screaming with surprise,
Since I was little, people have said,
That the ghosts and spirits will get me in bed.
But someone explained they were just sad.
You see when they were alive they didn't do their best,
But when the ghosts do, they can peacefully rest.

Zoe Pocock (Age 13)

The Ladybird

I am a lady in red
Peppered with black stains
I fly like a bird
Soaring, swooping then settling
In a graceful manner.
My wings are fitted beneath my glossy coat
So you couldn't tell
That I am a creature of land and sky
For I am the queen of the beetles in both.

Amandine Powell (Age 11)

My Chocolate Brother

When my brother is eating chocolate,
He gets it everywhere,
On his clothes, round his mouth, even in his hair!
Milky ways and mars bars,
Cadbury's Caramel,
Lion bars and Boost bars
Buy them by the carrousel,
Toffee Crisps, Dairy Milk,
Chocolate that feels as smooth as silk,
We love chocolate!

Becky Pardoe (Age 11)

The Sunset

Bright sunny turquoise,
A darker prussian blue,
All change to pale grey.

Pale grey to gold,
Gold to different oranges,
Then, orange to red.

Red tends to darken,
To burgundy and purple,
Purple turns to black.

Charlotte Powell (Age 11)

Bumble Bees

Bumble Bees fly around
Making a buzzing sound
Collecting pollen for their queen
Bees are yellow and black
With a stripy back
Visiting flowers
All day long

Amy Robbens (Age 9)

Power Yo-Yos

I like yo-yos
Yo-yos are the best
That's why I'm on a quest
To find a yo-yo that's the best
I think power yo-yos are
But my friend says
X Brains beat them by far
I'm going to buy a yo-yo
But not a wo yo
Because they are like pro yos

Christopher Ratcliffe (Age 8)

Summer

The summer's approaching,
The trees ahead,
All covered in blossoms
Hooray, hooray, hooray,
The summer's approaching

The summer's approaching
The creatures alive and free
Running around jumping around
Hooray, hooray, hooray,
The summer's approaching

But sadly the summer's died away
The trees have turned brown
The sun closes in
The flowers die away
The swaying rivers dry up
And we're in Autumn again

But joy doesn't leave us
Even though the sun closes in
And the animals go inside
Instead it starts all over again

Rhian Pearse (Age 10)

A Car

Red car
Blue car
Any colour car
Big car
Small car
Any size or shape
Long car
Short car
Sports car
Classic car
Any kind of cars

Andrew Rickman (Age 8)

My Brother

My brother and I are not alike
I ride around on my bike
He stays at home and watches TV
I am short, he is tall
I am happy, he is grumpy

My brother and I like different food
He likes vegetables I hate vegetables
He has pepper on his potato
I hate pepper on my potato

My brother and I
Like different sports
I like football he likes cricket
I like rugby he doesn't like rugby

My brother and I
Are not the same
But I play with him
He plays with me

Scott Pryke (Age 10)

People

Thin people, fat people
White people, black people
Short people, tall people
Normal and cool people
Many people can be seen
Some are even in between
Slow people, fast people
First people, last people
Mean people, clean people
Others are green people!

Zeke Rawlins (Age 11)

Winter

The leaves fall off
And then the trees are bare
Then the ice freezes the pond
I would not wish
To go outside tonight
Then snowmen can be made
Then they melt

Louanna Richards (Age 7)

Winter

Snowflakes are falling
Trees are bare
The pond is freezing
People are singing Christmas Carols
The postman is delivering cards
We put up our Christmas tree
We pull Christmas crackers
There is a party
Turkey and Christmas pudding
Presents are being opened

Alice Randall (Age 6)

A Martian Sends A Postcard Home

H2O is a liquid mirror that twists like a rope,
It jumps off cliffs and roars with pain but does not bleed.
A flight is a giant gliding bird that roars like a lion,
People are so scared of it that they give up their lives
And climb inside its giant belly.
On the landscape large boxes are scattered around,
They devour everything but lets it all out again
From the same opening as before,
After it has eaten, it lets smoke out of a pipe on its head.
Bugs run along black rivers that do not flow
When nature interferes it shines and bugs slip and crash.
A devil creature guards houses a screaming
Flickering flame that sends people running away and to it.

Rosanna Riches (Age 13)

Snowflakes

Snow, Snow, thick and white
Icy fingers in the drain
Snow, snow, snow
Snow, snow, snow
Snowy grass
Snowy houses as well
All frozen trees standing still
I see the children throwing snowballs

Edward Reid (Age 6)

Safe Places High

Poised on the shore I stood alone and cried
Somehow I had lost sight of all my dreams
I felt something inside of me had died
My future hopes had been washed down the stream

This feeling had become an obsession
When suddenly a star that was surreal
Came and lifted me of my deep depression
So light I felt with a heart full of zeal

Amazingly I felt that I could fly
I lifted off with wings so strong and sure
And found safe places high in new found sky
The air was fresh and clean, forever pure

No longer did I stand alone and weep
Never again would I descend that deep

Francesca Roberts (Age 14)

Starry Starry Night

The stars in the sky shining bright
As bright as diamonds glistening
The full moon is like a cradle
Rocking from side to side
Silver and gold running through the sky
Like paints in a paint pot
Star watching
Moon gazing

Jessica Riches (Age 11)

Indian Sunset

As the blazing rose-red sun disappears
Spooky silhouettes cover India.
Ant-like people scurry back to their anthills.
The towering pylons stand to
Attention like termite soldiers.
The trains, like millipedes, dangerously
Wobble along the metal track.
The waspish Sitars and spider-like taxis
Swerve to prevent crashing on
The tatty string of dust that is the road.
As dawn breaks, the first fingers of light
Push through the thick clouds
And another day crashes in......

Nicholas Rowe (Age 9)

Horrific Hockey

We were out there on the pitch,
With me in my shorts two sizes small,
As I forgot my kit.
I was racing down the middle,
When Sally came a whooshing up,
Knocked me on my face
And Jenny gave a giggle.
Cuts and bruises everywhere,
But still I must go on,
Racing down the pitch again
I didn't have a care.
I was going to score this time.
When the elastic in my shorts came loose!
They did have to be mine.
Everyone was laughing
But I was still determined to score a goal.
So with my shorts I came a panting
Running down towards the goal,
Everyone eyes a balling,
I reached the circle and there was a hole
I shot, I scored, oh no my shorts!

Kirsty Rouillard (Age 13)

Phew!

On a cold day
On a really cold day
On a really really cold day
On a really really stormy cold day
There is nothing better than
Eating some boiling chocolate,
Yummy, warm, hot
Nice bowl of soup
Mmmmm

Nicholas Raddon (Age 7)

They Go Crunch

When you step on them
They go crunch!
When you scrunch them
They go crunch!
When they get cold
They go crunch!
When they get really really cold
They go crunch! crunch!
When they get angry
They go crunch!
When it's raining
They go crunch!
When it's dark
They go crunch!
They are leaves in anger
DON'T HURT US!

Amy Roper (Age 8)

He Speaks No Words, Just Stares

After all the offensive things he said,
After all the embarrassment he put me through,
He still continues to haunt me.
I try my best to not let him see,
The weaker side of me,
I stand tall!
He's not going to make a fool of me!
Just because I'm a girl!

Once again I come top in the class,
But does he congratulate me?
No!
He turns to the boys with strong encouragement,
But do I get a look in?
No!
He speaks no words just stares,
Just because I'm a girl!

Why do people preach equality?
When they themselves can't live by it.
I shouldn't be treated like this!
Just because I'm a girl!

Julie Rumble (Age 14)

Pollution, Pollution!

Pollution, Pollution,
Is all around,
Sometimes up,
And sometimes down.

Covering sea, fields and land,
The source of pollution has been found.
It's from aerosols, factories and oil works,
They clot together and away it flirts.

Scientists tried to find the solution,
Who was really causing all the pollution?
Then a little boy called Dan announced,
"I know who's causing all the pollution, it's MAN!"

They all were shocked,
Was Dan right?
Scientists thought about it day and night,
Was man really the source of pollution?
Yes? No?
You come to a conclusion.

Jason Round (Age 10)

The Drink

The drink is cold
The drink is hot
The drink is lovely
But it is very nice
They're big
They're strong
They're grrreat!

Usman Ramzan (Age 8)

Mouse In The House

Mouse in the house all around
Creeping while everyone is sleeping
Down the hall
The stairs are so tall
Looking for some cheese

Samuel Robinson (Age 8)

Traffic Lights

Fire, sun, grass, go!
They all save lives,
They stop the crashing and
They help people get to their destiny.
Red for stop,
Yellow for get ready,
Green for go.
Traffic Lights.

Lee Rogers (Age 11)

Harvest Moon

Harvest moon so big and bright
A moon shines at night
Right in the sky a moon surrounded by stars
Very big and shining bright
Every night I think of the moon
Shining through my bedroom window
Tonight the moon is very tired
Midnight moon is out and about
On we go to the next night
Oh moon you had a long night lets take off for bed
Night night moon

Terry Reade (Age 11)

Helping My Mum In The Kitchen

Helping my mum in the kitchen
Making lots of cakes
Helping put the eggs in
Whoops I put a bit of shell in

Helping my mum in the kitchen
Dad will eat it anyway
Helping mum in the kitchen
I am eating the cakes
As I'm going along

Charley Rowley (Age 8)

Under The Bed

Under the bed
There is a sizzling
That sounds like a hamster to me
My little sister
Thinks it might be a dragon
Walking, ready to eat its prey

When it is really dark
In the middle of the night
I take my little sister
And look under the bed to see
A gigantic head and shiny white teeth
Two glowing eyes staring at me

We yell and shout
There's a dragon about
We head for the stairs
To escape from the dragon's lair

We hide behind the bookcase
And sleep in the cobwebs 'til morning
Then mum finds us
To get us ready for school

Jordan Redworth (Age 8)

Optimism

The colour of optimism is light blue
The taste of optimism is a jelly
The smell of optimism is fresh mown grass
The look of optimism is eyes open wide
The sound of optimism is a quiet class working
The feel of optimism is a dog licking your face

Edward Revill-Johnson (Age 12)

Autumn Mist

The crunchy brown leaves
Fly through the cold autumn mist.
The frosty fresh air
Floats over the tops of the houses.
The soft fluffy frost
Forms on the bright green grass.
Cold shivering dormice
Start hibernating
In the soft breeze of autumn dawn.
The cold dawn of a new autumn day arrives.
The sound of bleating sheep
Hangs in the mist.
Cattle come in as cold turns to freezing winds.
The day becomes night
And night......
Turns into another autumn day

Philip Rowtcliff (Age 9)

Candlelit Dreams

My love is like the morning sun, so bright.
Are you the one my heart desires so much
For you, my love grows stronger still alight.
My every thought depends on you, your touch.

And how my dreams take ghostly care of you.
Your softest touch doth bring me joy, so warm.
Your eyes doth fill me with the love, brand new
I hope these eyes don't change into a scorn.

Your smile doth fill me with such love brand new.
I hope your smile won't change into a scorn.
A scorn would tear my heart in pieces two.
A love like this, forever on 'til dawn.

Let me have your endless smile so bright.
A love like ours goes on throughout the night.

Samantha Rew (Age 13)

Winter

The frost makes the river frozen
It makes the children's hands freeze
The birds fly away
The people turn up their fires
The leaves all fall off
And the flowers die with cold

Kirsty Reed (Age 6)

Otters

"Come and stroke me"
Says the cute, young otter
With his big black nose, white whiskers,
Small eyes and rounded ears.

He wants fish, begging for fish.
"Give me some fish."

With his brown chocolate coat
With a caramel centre
He slips so quickly
Yet silently into the water.

But despite the outer cuteness
There is the inner viciousness of the hunter.

Frances Robinson (Age 10)

My Favourite Things

Toys, toys, toys,
That's my favourite sound,
Toys, toys, toys,
I have a lot which will astound.

I like my cat,
Who's plump and fat,
He acts like a doggy,
He's a real cool moggy.

My figures are cool,
Better than school,
I play with them at night,
Out of sight,
Under the covers,
Without those mothers.

I like the Christmas day,
In the month of December,
Because of the presents,
I always remember.

Jack Roberts (Age 11)

The Dragon From The Acid Water

Out of the acid water it comes
Leaving a trail of blood
It is the Dragon from Hell

The three headed monster from the deep
With a head as big as an elephant

The six-armed monster from the deep
With bronze feathers and teeth as big as a lion

A head as big as five tigers

One eye coming out of its socket
The other eye half eaten
One eye on his hand

It's the monster from the deep
And it's coming to get me......

Matthew Rolfe (Age 9)

Winter

Look out
Look out
Jack Frost is about
To freeze anything in his way

So look out
Jack Frost is about
To catch anything in his way
So look out

Luke Reed (Age 7)

I Can

I can climb a tree
Drink a cup of tea
Play with my tools
And jump on a trampoline

I can swing on a rope
Swim in the swimming pool
Hold a ball
And stand on a stool

Rupert Rolfe (Age 4)

Grim Reality

Charging under clear blue skies
Towards feeble German guns
Smeared with the gore of men he slew
Bold and brave, schoolboy fun
He will live forever, these epic days!

Charging under phantom skies
Towards monstrous anger of guns
Smeared with the gore of men he slew
Cold and numb, sick of sin
His brains oozed out, these epic days!

Jake Richards (Age 14)

How To Please Your Teacher ...... Perhaps

Make him go mad
That's the way to please your teacher
Don't do what you're told
Sing in school very loud
That's the way to please your teacher
Suck your toes
Pick your nose
Make him shout
That's the way to please your teacher
Kick him a hundred times
Break two lights
Smash the windows
Break the doors
That's the way to please your teacher
Annoyed and angry

Amanda Rowe (Age 10)

The Swamp

Stinky, stingy, seething swamp,
Why do you make people
Join you in the swamp
With your powerful embrace?
I can see what you're up to
And it's not going to happen to me.
I'm not joining your kingdom of death.
Sleeping, slimy, smelly swamp.

Chloe Russell (Age 11)

The Old Country Lane

As I walk down the lane
The wind blows on the window pane
The cows go moo
And the sheep go baa
People come by in their cars
The lane is so silent late at night
The people turn on their landing light

The little insects buzz about
"Goodnight" the little children shout
When the sunny morning comes
The little children suck their thumbs
When the animals are all awake
Time for people to have a morning cake
The process all starts again
The old country lane is quiet again
That is how I like it to stay
The country lane is far away

Cassie Richards (Age 10)

Mum

My mum talks for yonks about washing machines,
Telling me off for scratching,
Throwing my best toys in the bin without my permission,
Picking the fluff off my jersey,
Switching the cartoons off for news,
Talking about me when I am still in the room,
Then asking me all those times
What I want for supper, when she should know.

WHY CAN'T SHE DO SOMETHING FOR FUN???!!!

Like –
Abseilling from the bedroom window,
Damming up the gutters,
Holding her breath for however many minutes,
Painting the wall with her toes,
Digging up the lawn for moles.

WHY CAN'T SHE BE MORE LIKE ME???!!!

Elizabeth Reid (Age 11)

Flowers

Flowers smell lovely
Lovely flowers are growing
Oh lovely flowers
We can water flowers
Each day flowers can grow
Red flowers can grow with some water
So flowers can grow in the spring

Kate Rudman (Age 5)

Summer

Skies as blue as the sea
Birds tweet in the wind
People like a blob of colour
Sun so hot and gold
Leaves nice and green
Bees buzzing very loud
Grass swaying in the breeze

Daryl Rose (Age 8)

The Goalie's Glasses

The goalie wears glasses
They're big, black and round
And only cost a pound
He wears them everywhere he goes
Otherwise he can't
See beyond his nose

Geoffrey Ryall (Age 13)

Months Of The Year

January starts the year
People never ever cheer
February is so cold
It makes me feel so very old
March the spring has begun
The start of which is excellent fun
April all it does is rain
Oh is it not such a pain
May it's here it's Sats again
I feel like I'm gonna go insane
June the holidays are near
How much homework do we fear
July the sun has come out to play
If only it could continue to stay
August it's my sister's birthday
Her friends will be round to have a party
September it is back to school
Mum why subject me to this rule?

Elizabeth Robshaw (Age 11)

The Netball

The netball is orange and round
You can bounce it on the ground
You can shoot it at the post
Then you bend your knees and throw

The ball is round
Bouncing hard on the ground
It echoes loudly down the playground
The ball is running speedily to the post
To try to score the winning goal

You throw the ball into other hands
To get it up your end
Then you bend your knees and throw
YES we've scored the winning goal

Catherine Rendle (Age 11)

Changes

Sun

Shimmering sun
The day's begun
Carries on with sunshine shadows
Glistening yellow
Shining orange
That's how the day began

Wind

Wet wind gushes on my face
Slowing down to a gentle pace
Carries on with windy weather
No colour as it sees
Now slowing to a gentle breeze

Rain

Rushing rain ends the day
No children are out to play
Carries on with torrential flooding
Glistens silver
Sparkles blue
Don't think I'll be going out now, do you?

Lucy Reynolds (Age 10)

I'm Not Dead

I'm not dead
Just badly hurt.
I'm home. The war has stopped
My friends are dead
But I'm not.
I'm away from guns and stealth
Bombers that nuke the country.
I won't fight again.
I'll bury my gun and the only good thing is -
I'm not dead!

Hugh Richardson (Age 10)

An Indian City

Rays, like fingers of life beat down on the sun bleached city
Mosquitoes dart, menacing
The road is still, like a sleeping crocodile
The iridescent colour of saris swarms on the street
Skyscrapers stand proudly
The sun sets
Flooding the sky the colour of fire

Elanwy Rockey (Age 11)

The Beginning Of The End

This is the beginning of the end
The darkness is closing in, like a cloak of night.
I'm concealed, I'm convinced.
The dim glumness is tormenting me to despair.

My mouth is smothered,
My screaming muffled.
No one can help me now
The absurdity of the purpose,
Oh I wish I could start again.

I am desolate
I am intimidated
I am drifting into wretchedness,
My anguish towards my devious opponent
Is growing like a whirlwind of terror.

Now to my dismay the time has come...
To annihilate.

Jennifer Roberts (Age 12)

A Little Princess

There was once a little princess
Who was satisfied with everything she owned
This beautiful girl who was ever so kind
Believed in fairies that fluttered by
On visiting the fairy glen one day
She couldn't believe her eyes
The red and white mushrooms
That were laid upon the ground
Were hiding a wonderful spectacle
Of golden fairies, elves and gnomes
The princess sat quietly on her silver throne
All the crowds of fairies came fluttering by
And gave wonderful smiles

Hannah Rutledge (Age 7)

The Dragon In The Box

I saw a box
The box opened
Creak
A dragon came out
It blew fire
Boom
It cracked a tin
It got cross
It got angry
And it got mad
I had to run out quickly
The box creaked again
A puff of smoke .....
Everything disappeared

Dominique Rossiter (Age 6)

Yellow

Yellow is the colour of daffodils
Burning like a sun

Yellow is a hot colour
Shining in the sky

Yellow is a light colour
A butterfly flying around

Yellow is the colour of Easter
Chicks hopping around

Yellow is sweet just like honey
My favourite colour

Joanne Rickman (Age 10)

I'd Like To Play The Clarinet

I'd like to play the clarinet
I really think I'd try
I'd like to play the clarinet
Before it's time to die

They say you have
Three score years and ten
But that's not always true
I'd like to play the clarinet
Before I'm sixty-two!

Victoria Richardson (Age 9)

My Mummy

My mummy is like a colourful rainbow
Floating over the clear blue sky.
When you feel unhappy, she cheers you up,
She gives you a gigantic hug and a big kiss.
You don't know what colour she's going to be
When she picks me up from school.
After a tough day at work,
She's still the colour white!

Jessica Reddington (Age 10)

Greek Limerick

There once was a Greek who knew
He bred the most wonderful ewe
For she had golden milk
And her coat was like silk
So hooray for the brand new brew!

Rosanna Ridgers (Age 9)

A War Poem

They stood with their swords, shields and helmets
Looking proud and fearless,
Ready to fight and take the risk
Of dying for their countries,
Although one could see in their eyes the sadness
Of leaving their loving families behind.
It was silent and quiet until the fighting began.
As they fought with their enemies
It looked as if no-one would survive.
But lucky for some they did survive,
And went home to their loved ones

Bushra Razzaque (Age 11)

Bad Weather

Wild weather, rain slashing on
The windows,
Wind sweeping birds out of
The sky
Lightning flashing
Thunder crashing
Howling wind through
Torrential rain
Will this go on forever?
The sky so gloomy, dark
And mysterious.

Kerry Rogers (Age 12)

Animals Of India

As the lion like sun continues
Its ferocious growling,
The swaying snake weaves its way
Along its thin winding track.
Taxis like small beetles scuttle contentedly
On the lizard's ceaseless black tongue.
As night falls the shadowy temples
Look over their sun-bleached town.

Bethany Rowson (Age 10)

Death

Death is blood red
It smells like a hot spicy curry
Death tastes sour like a lemon
It sounds like one hundred dogs howling
Death feels like a cat's tongue
DEATH LIVES IN THE CENTRE OF THE EARTH

Tom Roberts (Age 9)

Children's Revenge

Mr. Arnold he is mean,
I cannot talk or I will be seen!
If I do something naughty my friends will tell,
Then he is a demon headmaster that's come down from hell!
His first name is actually Mike,
I must not be dumb or he will strike,
I must be careful when he comes over,
Or I will have to escape on a ferry from Dover!
When it is sunny, he likes to be funny.
He will gobble you up
With a second helping of Seven-up
He is everywhere,
So is his hair,
He gives us hard work
But in the darkness he shall lurk!
When you see him his eyes shall glow
And you know you're dead when be bends down low
He is like a dragon that's in a flare
He is hiding in the corner of his lair.

James Robertson (Age 10)

Bombay's Bugs

The sun is rising, like blazing fire from a dragon,
Cars start up like woodlice shuffling.
Signposts and pillars stand to attention like smart soldiers,
A boat chugs along like a water boatman with no engine.
Tin houses hunch together,
As ant like people get angrily pushed along in crowds.
Sand beetle mopeds scoot around corners,
On the winding road like a dusty cloth.
At the end of the day, the sun sets, like an explosion of colour,
And silhouettes fill the night, like cat-black ghosts.

Heather Roberts (Age 10)

The Trolls

Playing in the hot sunshine
On mid-summers green grass
The troll families are skipping
From dawn until dark

There are the trollkins called super-troll
And his little sister Kinn
Who takes dancing lessons
And learns how to sing

While the treasure trolls are wishing
By their faithful river can
The rest of them are building
Their own little dam

Allana Rider (Age 10)

Springtime

I can see the big mountains
And the multi-colours of the rainbow
I can feel the Houndstone Rock
Rough on my hands
I can hear the echo from the mountains
I can taste the fresh air blowing
I can smell the breeze floating in the air

Nicholas Redwood (Age 8)

A Foggy Morning

One foggy morning it was dark and gloomy,
Cold and icy, couldn't go out.
Creepy and spooky, didn't want to go outside
The windows were steamy and unseeable.
Cold and chilly I sat right by the fire,
Damp and wet it was too slippery.
Ugly and horrible, it was too scary,
Miserable and quiet, mum wasn't to be seen

I was shivering, did not know what to do,
Because it was so cold and icy.
Thick and dull, couldn't see a thing,
Dark and so dusty, blurry and unseeable
No-one to be seen.

Lloyd Randall (Age 9)

Christmas Night

The night stars twinkle
And the cold air is still
Jack Frost has come to sprinkle
Snow on my window sill

I can't wait to see
Christmas presents under the tree
And the happy shining
Faces of my family

But we must always remember
As friends smile and greet us
That the 25th of December
Marks the birth of baby Jesus

Charlotte Robertson (Age 8)

Have You Ever Seen

Have you ever seen
A monster dancing?
Have you ever seen
An alien invading?
Have you ever seen
A yellow monkey?
Have you ever seen
A red dog?
Have you ever seen
A golden lobster?
Have you ever seen
A walking snake?
Have you ever seen
A six clawed cat?

Have you ever?

Bradley Read (Age 9)

Fireworks

They ascend like glow-worms
That shine upon the night
Then sink to earth in turns
Of red, yellow and white

Like butterflies too wonderful to tell
Each colour shines out of blackness
And begins to fade as well
Like waterfalls in blackness

Only at night not in day
The fireworks seem to say
The message of great joy
Of the plan that failed to destroy
The King

Elena Rusalen (Age 8)

The Unfound Tomb

I've found it
Stairs leading to the tomb
The door stands untouched
They enter into the widening gloom
The flowers are still upright
The smell of perfume
The golden sarcophagus
Inside there lay a young prince
With the treasures of Eygpt
We'll take them
We're rich
But the curse is upon
Carter and his team

Harry Redin (Age 9)

Waterfall

Juggling fountains
Diving
Dipping
Taunting like a devil

Juggling fountains
Roaring
Ripping
Throwing like a heaving boulder

Juggling fountains
Swamping
Shovelling
Crazily manipulating

Juggling fountains
Flowing
Flooding
Descending......

Tom Reilly (Age 10)

Mum

My Mum's like a golden gem
She smells like a wonderful fragrance
My mum tastes like a soft, melting piece of chocolate
She sounds like a soft rabbit
My mum feels like a silky stream of cotton
She lives deep in my heart.

James Robertson (Age 9)

Limerick

There was an old lion in the zoo
Who watched re-runs of Doctor Who
When they turned the set off
He gave a long cough
And remarked that he liked Doctor Who!

Claire Routh (Age 10)

Flies

Flies are so annoying
They buzz around your head
If you try to gobble them up
They just fly away
They nest in your bed
And on a horse
And make it go neigh

Flies are so annoying
They go in your food
They go up your sleeve
And go in a pooh!
I just wish they would leave!

Luke Rosser (Age 9)

The Football

The football is kicked
Higher and higher it goes
Higher than the tallest tree grows
Zooming like an aeroplane
Through the bright blue sky.

Suddenly, it slows down
Lower and lower it goes
Lower than a blade of grass grows
Until it hits a bar
And everything goes a blur.

Arun Roy (Age 10)

A Stone Fight

I had a fright
And lost a bone
So I had a fight
And turned to stone
I saw the light
On the phone
In the middle of the night
I was on a throne
What a height
In a zone
I was tight
About the cone
Even though I might
Be alone

Matthew Rescorl (Age 10)

The Castle

It stands big and tall,
Majestic in the sun,
It's been around for centuries,
It's haunted by a nun.

It's been the home of Earls,
And visited by Kings,
It's full of fine paintings
And treasures and things.

The paintings I've just talked about,
Are big and tall and grand,
They show faces of good noblemen,
And scenes from all the land.

The long and winding gardens,
Are there for all to see,
The ducks swim on the river,
Surrounded by history.

Daniel Shilcof (Age 11)

A Poem

Dark and wet
Cold and windy
Sky, dull and grey.
Trucks going to trenches
Soldiers eager for the war
Sirens blaring out deafening me.
I am terrified.

James Samson (Age 13)

Loneliness

It's the time when no-one likes you
You feel angry, bored and alone
Nobody to play with
You think everyone treats you like sawdust
Everything hates you
Everyone says, "Ha! Get lost! Go away!"
You feel sad, hurt and unhappy
You feel miserable
They think you're disgraceful
Your lips fall down to a frown

Joshua Rousen (Age 8)

Misty Night

One misty night so far away
There was someone standing
It was a figure of grey
Stood upon the hillside
Perplexed, not moving at all

In morning light it was no man
But a rock upon the hillside
This mysterious man
Just a rock I sighed

Night again
The same man stood there
No rock this time
For sure a man
He stood upon the hill

But why?

Zoe Stagg (Age 11)

Christmas

On a dark and frosty, snowy night,
The wind was cold the stars were bright.
Father Christmas and reindeer fly
Right across the moonlit sky.
Sleigh full of treats and toys with bells,
Dolls with hair and crabs with shells.
In the morning children awake
And go down stairs to eat the cake.
Stockings full of sweets and toys,
Snowball fights with all the boys,
Trees with tinsel, presents with bows
Teddies with fingers, monkeys with toes
Then when it's time for bed they say,
"Come again and stay one day!"

Sarah Sharpley (Age 11)

Things I Heard

Birds tweeting, whistling, singing
Bees buzzing and fuzzing
Fan blowing and humming
Leaves rustling and hustling
People playing and chatting
Trees whispering and blowing
Mower cutting the grass
Gate squeaking loudly
Talking, loudly and quietly
Car driving, revving and bumping.

Luke Richards (Age 8)

Spring

Flowers blowing in the wind
Butterflies flying in the sunshine
And dreaming of all sorts of things
Daffodils growing everywhere
Spring is a very sunny time
I love spring!
Spring is a happy time
Everyone enjoys it
Spring brings all the small animals back to the forest
Cars are driving most of the days
They go in all sorts of different ways
Daisies are growing in people's gardens in all sorts of places
Even in some people's suitcases
Spring is a very happy time
I could sing it in a nursery rhyme
Please can spring be here every time?

Grace Smith (Age 6)

My Dreams

Chase my dreams, up and down,
Whirl and curl, spinning round.
Bright flashy colours, beaming streams
Colourful, amazing, are my dreams.

Fuzzy, I feel like a puppet on strings,
My dreams include some mysterious things.
Jump and spin as I race
Swirling at a tremendous pace.

Going deep into my dreams,
Colourful and bright as they gleam,
Wonderful, amazing, my dreams have shone
Going… going… going… gone!

Rachel Sleeman (Age 11)

Reindeer

Reindeer, reindeer
Did you say a manger?
Yes
But my room is a mess
It's Christmas, Santa's coming
When?
But he's in his den
Merry Christmas

Shannon Stevens (Age 7)

Spring

Spring is coming
Flowers are growing
Trees are growing
Easter bunnies

Jade Stone (Age 5)

Winter

When it is winter
The trees are bare.
The tree leaves fall down.
I like the snow because
You can play in it.
You can make a snowman.
And the grass is icy
You can go skating.

Lucy Smith (Age 7)

My Rock

The rock which I hold in my hands
Is a freckled and speckled, steely grey wonder.
It's been battered by rain,
Shattered by frost and blasted by wind.
The patterns glitter across its dappled surface.
Jagged crystals sparkle with history
That's been overloaded into this ancient weight.
This magical time warp
May have been
Trod on by the dinosaurs,
Thrown by the Aztecs and
Kicked by the Romans.
It may have been used by the Victorians,
Juggled by the Saxons,
Eventually held by me.
Think of all the years it's taken to form,
Think of all the people it's seen.
If only it could talk,
We'd have all the information
We'd ever need to know about history!

Alicia Snelling (Age 10)

Wasp

Wasp, wasp please go away
Please go away I beg!
You've nibbled at my plum
You've nibbled at my thumb,
Please go away I beg!

Wasp, wasp please go away
Please go away I beg!
You've nibbled at my toes
You've nibbled at my nose,
Please go away I beg!

Wasp, wasp please go away
Please go away I beg!
You've nibbled in my food
I'm getting in a mood
Please go away I beg!

Nicola Smith (Age 8)

My Magic Box

I will put in my box

The deepest ocean blue,
A picture frame to remember you.

The very exciting sound of cheers,
A box full of giant's tears.

The delicious taste of creamy chocolate,
Also a little money locket.

My box will be fashioned with tulips and roses,
Lots of little bunches like posies,
Emeralds and pearls
And inside baby curls,
A blue troll and a baby foal.

I will also have a little bed,
Coloured in a sunset red.

In my box I will swim and swim,
Until I reach my box's rim.

Then I shall have a cup of tea,
Gazing out at a dazzling sea.

Emma Shand (Age 9)

The Demon Headmaster

Please, please not me. It was she.
Do not take me to you dark room
Where you hear that crashing sound 'BOOM'!
It's Mr A who makes us pay.
He is tall and skinny
We suspect he drives a flaming mini.
He's the head who has risen from the dead,
He is strict and fierce with a voice that will pierce.
He is really angry,
For he is head of a brilliant school in Danbury.
He is mad about sport
But must have quite a bit of brie and port.
Mr Arnold has great expectation and prepares for full moderation,
He hates retaliation but he wants lots of concentration.
I do not think he likes me much – well that's just a hunch.
But he is never fair, answering back – we dare.
That is about it for Mr A who keeps us at bay,
But there is one more thing that gives me a ding and a ring,
He likes the girls more than the boys.

Maximilian Stechman (Age 9)

Who am I?

I am red
I am little
I am sharp
I have one screw
I have one hole in me
I am a sharpener

Stuart Sloan (Age 9)

Christmas

Christmas time comes again
Christmas time goes
Santa said ho ho ho
On the way to Mexico
Rudolph said I want to go
Santa said wait a mo
Christmas time will come once more
In December you can be sure

Rea Sargent (Age 8)

I Love To Go To The Seaside

I love to go to the seaside
It's the best thing yet
Going to the seaside
And getting all wet

I love to go to the seaside
Lying on the sand
Gazing at the clouds
And listening to the band

Rebecca Stafford (Age 10)

Goodbye Grandad

You blinked and a tear rolled down your cheek
You held your head in your hands and chose not to speak
The torment on your face showed the pain in your heart
I stayed by your side, not wanting to part
Your sorrowful eyes as you wept with despair
That isolated feeling when life's just not fair
A lump rose in my throat as I watched you think
A crystal clear teardrop as you feel your heart sink
You sat there deserted, as memories fly by
And silently you whisper your final goodbye.

Laura Shearer (Age 14)

Spring

Spring is cold, spring is warm,
New little lambs being born.
Flowers shoot up from the ground,
We are playing round and round.
Everyone is having fun,
Everybody enjoying the sun.

We are cartwheeling around and around,
We are jumping up and down.
I like the sun after it has been dark,
All of the trees were very stark.

Rebecca Sanders (Age 8)

The Magic Box

I will put in my magic box …
The slowest turtle
The brightest colours of the rainbow
And the fastest flash of lightning

I will put in my box …
The mouth watering taste of candyfloss
The exciting purr of the first ever cat
And a pure white snowflake

I will put in my box …
A crystal that glows in the dark
The first cry of a baby
And a melody played on the piano

My box is fashioned from the whitest cloud
On the lid of the box is a play script
Which has never been read
And my box has hinges made from witches nails.

I will act out the play script on my magic box lid
And draw the most exciting and imaginative picture
And step in …

Charlotte Strawa (Age 9)

How To Make A Teacher Mad

First of all
Bring a ball
Bounce it on the floor
And through the door

Secondly
Talk in the assembly hall
Sit by the wall
Fiddle with your book
And watch the cook

Thirdly
Sing too loud by the rack
And always sit at the back
Don't listen when told
Draw pictures of someone old

Finally
Fiddle with your hair
Ask to do something in a pair
Don't learn your spelling words
Sit and watch the birds

Jodie Southall (Age 10)

Sad Moment

A sad moment is when you have to miss your best friend's birthday party
A sad moment is when your best photo is smashed
A sad moment is when your pet has died
A sad moment is when you lost something
A sad moment is when you're moving out of your old house
A sad moment is when your nan or grampy has died
A sad moment is when your best friend has gone missing
A sad moment is when your mum or dad has lost their job
A sad moment is when you're trying to ring someone and it's engaged
A sad moment is when your electric has been turned off

Maxine Sampson (Age 8)

The Tall Tall Cut Down Tree

Tall, tall tree, cut down today
Landed on the truck
And broke the motorway
Motorbikes hit the truck
And the log flew off
It flew to the timber place
Where it was cut into timber
And made into furniture
And sold to you and me.

Nathan Shields (Age 8)

A Day In Bombay

At dawn, the sun is like daffodils,
As bright as electrical lights.
Taxis, like an army of ants search for food.
Scurrying along the dusty road of the city,
Sticky and sugary, like a thin piece of liquorice.
Houses close their eyes at night,
Only flickers come from their mouths.
Ferries, like dolphins, bobbing on top of the still, clear blue water.
Trains, their mouths open wide to see the skyscrapers,
Tall as giants roaming the city.
At dusk, the clocks chime… all is quiet.

Nick Simmons (Age 10)

If I Were A Pirate

If I were a pirate
I'd sail the seven seas
Fly my skull and cross bones flag
In my ship across the sea
I'd dig up all my gold and silver
Buried in the sand
Sail rough and windy seas
With my hook for a hand

Jade Smith (Age 9)

England

Glen Hoddle is talking about people with disability,
Which is a bit silly because he should be talking to his football team.

World cup Shearer and Scholes scored our first goals,
Owen was flying but then England were crying.

Euro 2000, will England be there?
Hopefully they won't despair.

Sweden two – England one,
Those Swedes stopped us singing our song.

Bulgaria nil – England nil, will we win a game,
Or will our results stay the same.

England three – Luxembourg nil, three points, three goals, brilliant three,
Finally we can be happy with glee.

France versus England, France beat Brazil with brilliant skill,
If England win what a thrill it would be.

Hoddle has got the sack, no more contact,
And he's never coming back.

Let's hope England can cope
Because they could begin to slope,
England's World Cup win made us sing,
Maybe England will win it again because they can win.

Alexander Skarbek (Age 10)

Colours!

Colours!
Bright Red
Purple, orange, blue
Colours of the rainbow
To brighten up the world

Metuka Stephens (Age 7)

Phew!

On a cold day
On a really cold day
On a really really cold day
On a really really freezing cold day
There is nothing better than sitting
Next to the warm, hot, red fire
Phew!

Kristian Stephens (Age 7)

Winter

There is a snowman in winter
The trees are standing bare
The snow is in the ponds
The air is icy cold
The people are putting on their gloves
They are wrapping round their scarves
The snow comes down from the sky

Isobel Smith (Age 6)

Spring

The hares are boxing each other,
Piglets squealing for their mother.
Daffodils are all over the place,
This is much better than space.

The chicks are like fluffy yellow balls peeping away,
The lambs are playing and eating hay.
Snowdrops hang down like a wind chime,
Yippee it's springtime!

Baby rabbits jumping about,
Oh look some little trout!
Outside it's really warm,
Tadpoles come out of their frog's spawn.

Jonathan Smith (Age 10)

Autumn

Leaves are falling off the trees
Animals hibernating
The leaves crunch, crunch
And they fall
The leaves flutter around and around
Leaves flutter, swirling, twirling
Onto the river and they go splash
Leaves changing in autumn
And they crunch and crackle
They start to come off the trees
The conkers bounce and bounce
And bounce and bounce and bounce

Philip Snell (Age 6)

A Tranquil Winter's Day

Jigsaws of frost
Frosty
Frozen
White snow falling
An invisible world
Just snow everywhere
Smooth
Shiny
What an astounding morning

Green polar light glowing
Glistening
Silky
Ice cold windows
Frost all over the spiders
What an astounding afternoon

A beautiful lambent shines
Out of the polished darkness
What an astounding night

Rachel Smith (Age 10)

The Fox

The fox scratched on the door
A lady came out
He crept in the house
He ate all the food
He went up the stairs
He turned on the taps
Put his feet in the sink

Zachary Skinner (Age 4)

My Pet Octopus

My pet octopus has legs as long as the Pacific Ocean
My pet octopus has breath as smelly as rotten apples
My pet octopus has eyes as red as fire
My pet octopus has skin as tough as a brick wall
My pet octopus is as fat as a hot air balloon
My pet octopus has a mouth as big as a blue whale
My pet octopus has skin as red as the sun
My pet octopus has a nose as big as a bedroom window
My pet octopus has suckers like a hoover
My pet octopus has a tongue as long as a school

James Scotford (Age 8)

The Raindrop

I'm a little raindrop
Going round and round
I can join the others
Floating on the ground

Sam Shead (Age 6)

Spring

Lambs leaping in the grass,
Leaves are green,
Sunshine is boiling hot.
Spring is nice new flowers
growing
Spring is beautiful blue sky.

Adam Smith (Age 6)

Snowballs

Snowballs are like
A snowman's head
I love snow because
You can make a snowman

Conor Smith (Age 7)

Things I Like

I like sausage and chips
I like dolls
I like everything but the boys

I like west island whites
I like black cats
I like all the animals on this lovely land

I like daffodils
I like red tulips
I like all the plants all over the land

I like my mum lots
I like my dad
They're the best thing on the land.

Danielle Sparrow (Age 8)

Phew!

On a cold day
On a really cold day
On a really, really cold day ......
There is nothing better in the whole world
Than sitting next to a boiling, smoky, orange
Red, hot, crackling, fire
Aahhh

Tom Smart (Age 6)

January Trees

A January tree is all wet and droopy
They look like someone doing a Mexican wave
It is all misty and cold
Like towers lost in a misty waterfall
The tree is bare with no leaves
It is spiky
Like witches' hands

Charlotte Smyth (Age 8)

Guess Who?

Who tells me they want their breakfast?
Who do I stroke?
Who plays with me?
Who do I give tea?
Who purrs?
My cats Ollie and Billy.

Christopher Stevens (Age 7)

Red

Red is a colour that everyone uses
Our jumpers, the Devil, our trousers, our buses;
From the red sky above to a red rocky cave,
The American Red Indians are strong and so brave.

The red squirrels of China have nuts to crave,
And the Chinese with red blankets have parties and rave;
A two headed monster with red arms and red legs,
With eyes that are bloodshot, and a red lumpy head.

So the point of this rhyme, of which it has none,
For red is a powerful colour, of some.

Jacob Smith (Age 10)

Earth And Moon

Here on the earth it is very polluted
Here on the earth there's lots of people
Here on the earth there's lots of plants
Here on the earth there's lots of buildings
Here on the earth there's cars and lorries
Here on the earth there's electricity and fire
Here on the earth there's lots of water for us to drink
And that's why not all planets and moons are the same.

Here on the moon there's nothing at all
There's only dust, craters, rocks and minerals
It's nothing like the earth because there's no plants
Creatures, lakes, cars, lorries or pollution
On the moon there are bigger mountains
But there's no snow on top of the mountains
On the moon there are plains called seas
And that's why not all moons and planets are the same.

George Steer (Age 10)

Winter's Welcome

Branches of bare trees
Like icy cold fingers
Glistening in the golden sun
Silver eyes watching me
Like staring souls in the light
Jack Frost clings
Like spiders on a web, onto cars and windows
Sticking to its prey
Frosty grass
Like stiff fingers on your hands

Michael Stanforth (Age 10)

My Hands

My hands are such clever things
I can write, push, pull and touch
All these things are easy and so important
Everyone can do them
Even God can do them all
And babies can do them

Jessica Sutton (Age 8)

My Pet Walrus

My pet walrus has tusks as sharp as penknives
My pet walrus has breath as smelly as rotten cheese
My pet walrus weighs as much as half an elephant
My pet walrus has skin as tough as rock
My pet walrus has eyes the size of large marbles

Joseph Sampson (Age 8)

Football Fool

There was a player from Liverpool
Who thought that he was really cool
One sunny day
In the middle of May
He slipped up and felt a right fool

Laura Schofield (Age 9)

Untitled

"I'm as mad as a millipede in a multi-storey car park!" moaned Michael miserably.
"I'm as perfect as an organised file!" pleasantly Peter pronounced.
"I'm sumptuous in every way there can be!" Stephanie superbly snapped.
"I breathe like lungs and beat like a heart!" Laura lovably lectured.
"I'm as wonky as Willy Wonka!" wailed William weeping.
"I'm as sunk as a sunken ship when writing poems!" Tyler tremendously bellowed.

Peter Swiggs (Age 10)

Winter

I see snowflakes falling
Slowly, slowly, twisting and turning as they go,
Cold, white and beautiful all around me,
Sparkling, clean and bright,
Falling playfully down.

Look at those decorations hanging on the wall.
Red, gold and beautiful.
Oh no! The paper-chain's ripped!
How annoying! Never mind.
Look at the presents under the tree.
Oh no not again!
The tree's falling down, quick hold it up!
CRASH!
How frustrating.

Crisp, silver, icy frost
Sparkling prettily and happily all around me.
Hopeful, cheerful, rosy-cheeked Carol singers
Singing beautifully and sweetly
Raising the Christmas hopes in everyone's hearts.

Hazel Smith (Age 9)

Chicks

A little chick hatched out of its egg.
Then it went to bed.
It saw a cow and said,
"Wow! Wow! You are a big, big, cow."
Then it saw a rabbit
"You are a big, big, rabbit. I know."
He saw his mummy and he had a hungry tummy
And that's how the chick got his mummy.

Toby Smith (Age 6)

Suns The Horse

A very proud, strong horse
Runs in the field
His name is Suns
He won two races
He took a hundred paces
His legs are so strong
Sometimes they go bong!
Sometimes men come to dig
He saw their pig
People say that there is gold
He ignores them
He thinks it's mould
He thinks his brother's silly
His name is Billy

Laura Sacre (Age 7)

I'm A Little Raindrop

I'm a little raindrop
I'm a little raindrop
Falling to the ground
I can make a puddle
Going round and round
And I go drop, drop, drop.

Lydia Skarbek (Age 6)

The Planets

Planets spinning round the Sun
Let me name them one by one.
Mercury is fierce and hot
A pleasant place to be it's not!
Venus has a gassy cover
To breath there would be lots of bother!
The red planet we call Mars
No river, water, lakes or bars!
Jupiter's a massive ball
The gravity would squash us all.
Saturn has its famous rings
They're very beautiful, mystical things.
Uranus is very far
Fifty years in a speeding car.
Neptune's a mysterious place
Of oxygen there's not a trace.
Pluto's very small and cold,
Our knowledge of it's not very old.
That just leaves our dear old Earth
Teeming with life for all it's worth.

Lewis Smith (Age 11)

Tavistock

Welcome to our town square,
You should come to it.
They sell everything there.
Fish and cheese,
Jeans and jumpers,
Sweets and chocolates,
Books and cards,
Umbrellas and wellies,
The shops are fun,
The sweets are yum.
I like the town, it's fun.

Rebecca Smith (Age 6)

Valentine Sonnet

I love you for a lovely, happy smile
You are so kindly, funny, bubbly, sweet
Which I see when I am at home a while
Oh my, it's obvious that you are neat
I think your eyes are gorgeous, milky blue
Your nose, a small button tipped down
A mop of hair, so blond of shiny hue
I have never seen a crease, not a frown
My dear, you are a muscle type of guy!
I feel your arms around me, feel so near
I look into your eyes I'm able to fly
Oh your only fault, you have no fear
My love for you is so unique my dear
So strong my love for you is, I've no fear.

Natalie Schramm (Age 13)

What If?

What if …
We didn't have to walk to school, but fly
Soar above trees and houses from upon high.
What if …
We didn't have Maths, English and Science
But we learned magic tricks and
How to turn ourselves into giants.
What if …
We didn't play outside in the playground
But spent our lunchtimes on top
Of a huge chocolate mound!
What if …
We didn't spend our life on earth
But in huge caverns beneath the surf.
What if …
Our dreams turned into things
We could touch and see
Imagine what a strange place
The world would turn out to be!

Amanda Skeels (Age 14)

Another Day

As soon as I step in the gate,
I know that it is too late,
I must put up with all the chatter.
I must go in and face the clatter.

It's one o'clock the bell rings,
It must be time for din dins,
I have to put up with it every day,
I know that it won't go away.

It's quarter to four I open the door,
I can't cope with it anymore,
But still I must go back tomorrow,
Now let's get rid of all that sorrow.

Claire Stevens (Age 10)

Autumn

Floating fluttering leaves
Gliding to the ground
Crunching crackling leaves
Hedgehogs rustling underneath
Conkers bouncing on the ground
Birds flocking
Flying to hotter countries
Animals thinking about hibernating
The air starts getting colder and frostier
Farmers start bringing in their crops for food

Jack Shepherd (Age 6)

My Nanny's Wacky

My Nanny's wacky
She lives in a haunted house
She had a pet scorpion
Who ate her pet mouse

My Nanny's wacky
She's crazy you know
She never has visitors
'Cause she won't let them go

My Nanny's wacky
She has straggly grey hair
She never brushes it
She just doesn't care

My Nanny's wacky
She wears a black coat
She had a black hat
That was eaten by her goat

My Nanny's wacky
She's different from the rest
She's one in a million
And I think she's the best

Elliot Sawyer (Age 8)

The Raid

Siren sounds
I panic and grab the nearest thing
Which happens to be my brother
Quick head for the shelter
Hurry says my mum in a panicky voice
Tiles come off the roof
And start crashing on the patio floor
We got outside
Bang! Boom! The house crumbles
Now we can see the planes
My brother starts to cry
Then the siren is to be heard
It's over but no one is happy

James Stevens (Age 10)

The Glittering Wonderland

Snow is like a white tiger
Pounding to the ground
Trees are like a glittering wonderland
Stars are falling from the sky
It's time to turn the fire on
To make the wind feel warm

Luke Stacey (Age 7)

When I Went Out

When I went out with my brother
I met an elephant

When I went out I met a bird
It sang to me

When I went out I saw a pig
It snorted at me

When I went out I met a gorilla
It growled at me

When I went out I met a giraffe
It looked at me

When I finally got to the shops
I met a person
He talked to me

Vikki Spiers (Age 8)

Spring

When winter relinquishes his grip on the world
And the first brave blades of grass
Poke their heads through snow covered fields
And flowers spring up on every hill
Dwarfed only by the blossoming trees
Meant not to hinder them but to tease them
When the nights are clear and the days are longer
And the air is filled with buzzing once more
When birds awake and start to sing
You shall know that spring is here.

Owen Spottiswoode (Age 13)

Spring

Blossoms look like dancing sheep
Potatoes growing in the deep
Lovely hot sun shining down on us
Lots of pansies and daffodils
And lots of lambs

Jonathan Scott (Age 6)

Space

On the small moon it is dusty
On the large earth it is clean
Moon is covered in strange coloured rocks
Earth is covered in bright grass patches
The gloomy moon is unexplored
The beautiful earth is well explored
The sky is light blue on earth
The sky is liquorice black on the moon
A gloomy moon
A bright earth
Moon's bumpy surface
Earth's desert land
Earth's ever changing weather
Moon's weather at a halt
Moon's everlasting days
Earth's short days
Earth's wonderful seasons
Moon's unknown seasons
The airless moon
The windy earth

Jennifer Shepherd (Age 10)

The Haunted House

One night I saw
A spooky house
With a spooky witch
With a pointed nose
And a vampire
Who had sharp teeth
Both had strong powers
To frighten people
The house was full
Of spiders and cobwebs
Which made the house very scary

Jordan Scott (Age 7)

The Thing

I am in my bed as I feel dread up the stairs
The thing I hear is coming up to me
I go under the bed as mum comes up with a cup of tea
I am on the floor then I hear a roar from the living room
But it is only the telly
I go to bed and I know now that I have a friend
And I call him Ted

Joshua Sherwood (Age 7)

School

School, school, boring school,
Meeting every day in the hall.
Maths, science, literacy hour,
All the teachers have a power.

Boring science making rain gauges,
Children making them all different ages.
Doing journeys Michael Palin
He never really thought of taking up sailing.

It's time for lunch, yum yum yum,
Maybe I'll have a current bun
Learn an instrument maybe brass
It's field play upon the grass.

Playtime is at half past ten
When I go out and drop my pen.
Then I go back in at eleven o'clock,
Then boring maths 'till twelve o'clock.

Home time is at three fifteen
When I go home and have a dream.
All we do is have a rest,
The teachers think it's for the best.

Stuart Seamark (Age 10)

A Ladybird

Ladybird, ladybird through the grass and flowers
Ladybird, ladybird through the leaves of trees
Ladybird, ladybird don't fly away,
Stay with me 'till the end of the day
How many spots have you got ladybird?
If you tell me, I will know how old you are
If you have five spots, you will be five
You can be red and yellow.

Rebecca Spooner (Age 8)

Nightmare Primary

Early morning rush
As we get on the bus
The bus pulls over
I see Mr Whitts' Rover
I walk into school
Mr Whitts says being late is against the rules
I try to explain
While he says don't be late again
The bell rings loudly
I try to get through the deep valley
I jumped up and hit my head on the beam
It was all a dream
Just like a wrongly stitched seam

Holly Skeet (Age 10)

The Cave Of Death

In the dark slimy cave of death,
A pool of stagnant water lay,
Lying on top of it a pair of old blood shot eyes.

In the gruesome cave of death,
A monster
With a half eaten eyeball hanging out of its socket.

It's coming towards me,
Nostrils belching,
Hands in front ready to catch me,
OH NO,
Too late,
The poems ending now,
I'm going to get ate.

Katie Stroud (Age 9)

A Tropical Winter's Beach

As I walk on the soft, white sand
I can hear no laughter, as if children were banned.
Coconuts fall on the floor
Piles of drift-wood on the shore
The palm trees sway in a light, gentle breeze
And a dog runs in and out of the clear blue sea.
It feels like humans are extinct
But as I walk I begin to think
That when winter is over and the summer is here
This beach will be packed with people playing near

Alex Sharp (Age 13)

Wildlife

Wildlife are lots
Cats, dogs,
Animals with spots
Frogs on rocks
Lizards as well
Plus snails in the dell

Homes are lots
Trees and bushes
Ferns and grass
Nests and sets
Fish in holes in the sand.

Hazel Smart (Age 10)

Fishing By Moonlight

Sitting by a lake in the moonlight
The cold wind swaying the trees
I can hear fish breaking the water's surface
Wind whistling and a gate creaking
My only light, a lantern by my side
And moonlight on the rippled water
I smell petrol from my lantern
And wood burning miles away
I feel calm and collected
Then my bite alarm sounds
And all my thoughts blow away

Christopher Swatridge (Age 12)

Food, Food, Food

Food glorious food
Oh food is good
Oh food is tasty
Do not touch my food

I like food
Sausages

Greens
Oh food is good
Oh food is tasty
Do not touch my food

Very tasty food is even better
Than fruit rummaging in my tummy
Yummy for my tummy

Greens
Oh food is good
Oh food is tasty
Do not touch my food

Terry Sommerville (Age 8)

Myself

I am Hollie
I am not a tree
I am me

My hair is fair
My eyes are hazel
My lips are pink

My name is Hollie
I have a dolly
And a friend called Molly

I like swimming
I play the piano
I listen to music

I am Hollie
I am not a tree
I am just me!

Hollie Southey (Age 8)

The Beginning Of The End

The woeful raven cries,
Echo in the skies,
The sharp crack of thunder,
Amidst all toil and blunder,
Land is lit with fire,
Fuelled by Hell's desire,
The oceans boil and roar
As Fury burns the shore,
He clasps our hopes and dreams,
And tears them at the seams,
He is the fruit of the tree,
That was planted by you and me,
And now he looks back and smiles,
And we see his evil wiles,
As, in turmoil he destroys the sky,
The beginning of the end is nigh.

Arup Sen (Age 15)

Snow

Snow white
Snowmen
Snowflakes
I need my scarf and wellies

Snowballs
Friends fight
Cold hands, cold head
I need my gloves and hat

William Smith (Age 6)

All Around Us

The sun is very hot
Flowers are growing in a pot
A new lamb is born on a lawn
The bring of spring
Has flowers and trees
There is a blue sky outside
Work should be done
You should see the view

Elizabeth Skinner (Age 6)

The Poor Little Pony

I see something standing under the oak tree
A little grey figure just looking at me
Tethered to the snow covered ground
As skinny as could be
I go in and it snuggles up to me
I wipe the snow off its face
Some deep black eyes and big nostrils
It must be a pony
How horrible people can be
Don't worry little pony
You can come home with me

Kelly Smith (Age 9)

Clouds

Thunderclouds with angry faces,
Soft, white clouds with fluffy bases.

Fields of vegetables. Plants which grow.
Stretching mountains of soft white snow.

Dull, dark and grey
Pretty white in May.

The fog drifts down,
Down and Down,
Fills all the spaces
And covers the town.

Emily Sams (Age 10)

Titanic

The ice in the sea,
Crashes against the iron.
Freezing cold water,
Cries of help in the cold sea,
Sinking, sinking down it goes,
Sinking, sinking sunk in the dark blue sea.
Screams and cries echo in the clear white waves,
Some are rescued, some are not,
Then all is quiet for the dead.

Felicity Sullivan (Age 12)

The Horse Chestnut Tree

The conker tree which bears the lush, spiky cases of the horse chestnut,
Is ready to drop the rock hard package of fun,
For the harsh, angry weather has weakened the stalk,
From which it hangs
On the conker tree.
Soggy, rustling leaves hide the conker tree's fruit.
I'm climbing the conker tree in which to retrieve,
More nut-hard conkers that still pricks me.
The conker tree sways in the angry, tempestuous wind,
Making the leaves rustle and the thick tree trunk groan,
Conker trees are fun!
Conkers that touch the hard, frosty ground,
But do not find themselves in young boys' pockets,
Bury themselves into the deep, muddy ground,
And grow into a new, young horse chestnut tree.

Emma Sturkey (Age 10)

Alone

One day I came home
I was all alone
Nothing to do
Nothing to see
As the wind whistled
Through the smashed window
It was totally dark
I could not see a thing
I bumped into the sofa
And all of the dust puffed out
My hunger got worse
Like bugs pulled my insides out
But then suddenly
I faded away
Into the darkness

Tim Stallard (Age 11)

Memories

Memories of special things will never die
But they may fade as if to disappear
Both good and bad will finally combine
But now all is gone that was once here

Men may be able to go to the moon
But no one's memories are immortal
Sorry memories blown into sand dunes
By the mind's subconscious portals

Sordid memories that are omitted
Come back to haunt even though forgotten
Callous mistakes being admitted
Taken to the grave to be forgotten

Memories of special things will never die
So I'll sit and remember with a sigh.

Hannah Spender (Age 14)

Me And My Football!

Other girls aren't so keen
I like the England football team
I dream of it in my sleep
While I'm counting sheep
I've got Alan Shearer bedcovers
He's not my little lover
But I think he is very clever
I like football
It's even better than darts and pool

Katie Spearman (Age 10)

Aliens

Aliens, Aliens!
Those one-eyed things
Those green-skinned things
You've gotta' stay away!
They even abduct
So keep on guard! Watch out now!
They could capture you!

They live on Mars,
And on Pluto
So don't go within a mile of them
I knew you wouldn't think about
Those awful one-eyed freaks!

There's one on Planet Zog,
That's a real meany!
He'll see you in five miles!
He'll suck you up into his ship
Then torture you after a while!

Jonathan Shearer (Age 10)

Men, Chocolate Or Chocolate Men

I can't decide what I like best,
Here are some and I'll leave the rest,
There's someone rich called Garry Rate,
But he can't beat milk chocolate.

I can't decide what I like best,
I don't like men with hairy chests,
Men with six packs (we're getting somewhere),
I still don't like men with hairy chests.

Men, chocolate or chocolate men,
I can't decide where or when,
There still is someone called Ben Ben,
But I think I'll stick with chocolate men.

Kayleigh Sargent (Age 10)

Moon

As I soar through the night
In my velvet gown
Draping along the clouds below
I am queen of darkness

My shimmering light is all that's guides
The tiny world below
To astronomers I am a floating rock
Pale and sad-faced

The glittering stars are all
That guides me on my tiring journey
Across the mysterious and magical skies
And through the endless space which surrounds me

Daniel Sly (Age 10)

The Shark

Hungry, fast and deadly,
He swims through the water steadily,
The silver grey beast of the seas,
Brings terror
To the fish that it sees.

Matthew Spencer-Small (Age 10)

My War Poem

My heart sank right to the floor
Because of the blood and gore
A man had been shot
And he fell to the floor.
Worst of all he was my husband
I will never look at a man again
'Cos I am in pain will I ever love again?

I will lock myself in a room
And suffer all the gloom alone
My dead husband is with me
Staring into the deep blue sky
Why did he have to die?
I hate the war and evacuation

I am very sad
For I have neither mum or dad
My husband has been buried
I take flowers to his grave at night
When will we be together again?
Tonight
Aaahh

Kerrie Savage (Age 11)

Limerick

There once was a lady from Kent
Who wanted to live in a tent
She slept on the ground
Didn't make any sound
That silly old lady from Kent

Gemma Sharpe (Age 8)

Spider

S cary shapes
P erishing fangs
I nteresting prey
D eadly poison
E erie looking
R ascals!

Christopher Smith (Age 9)

I'm Football Mad

I'm football mad
Like my fat dad
I support Leicester City
They're not very pretty
That's a bit of a pity
Heskey's my favourite player
And so's Tayer
Tayer is a layer and
I'm football mad

Ben Spooner (Age 9)

The Golden Arrow Whirlpool Disaster

The Golden Arrow wooden ship was sailing to Port St. Louis, Mauritius
We're sailing at fifty knots and we're fifty miles off the north coast of Australia.
The sea is calm until we heard and headed straight into the heart of a storm.
The sea is roaring and throwing waves at us
I'm trying to steer us out of it but the rudder broke off.
I now know that we're in danger of whirlpools.
Two hours after leaving Australia
We're all in lifeboats, we're floating in the middle of the ocean.

Jonathon Shelley (Age 10)

Beginning Of A Crush

The first fatal look has arrived
My eyes clamped on to him, like an eagle on its prey,
Every corner I turn he is there, controlling me,
Am I being greedy or just impatient?

People criticise me, sniggering in the corner
I don't care, I carry on my obsession
The anticipation is waiting to burst out of me,
Am I taking the risk too far?

As I walk home, I dawdle,
I hope to see his twinkling eyes staring right at me.
I have to stop myself from getting too enthusiastic
I crave him, but does he crave me?

Nikki Scott (Age 12)

One...Two...Three

One straight pointed ear peeped out of a chimney
Two scaly arms lifted its body out
Three gruesome heads slyly smiled
With four bloodstained lips
Five drops of blood dripped on to six round chins
Seven warty toes gleamed with brightness
Eight strands of lumpy hair
Fell off his three gruesome heads and landed on nine fingers
C R A S H
Suddenly the whole body fell apart
Into ten bits of flesh and bones

Emma Smith (Age 9)

I Hate Shopping

I dislike shopping
My ears start popping
When I walk around
It feels like I'm floating off the ground

We get to the check-outs
We get lots of brussel sprouts! (Yuck)
We pack the food into the bags up tight
Then we walk towards the bright sunlight

Jonathan Smith (Age 8)

Depression

I'm standing on a cliff all alone
Surrounded by a sea of darkness
There's no one to speak to
And nothing to be heard
I see my ghost walking alone
To the slow beat of a drum
While my hair blows with the wind
I'm alone once again
My cries to be ignored
That's something we have to live with

Jessica Southcott (Age 10)

I Am Katie

I won't describe myself as sugar, cherries and pie,
Because really and truly that is just not I.

I am Katie superstitious not weird,
I am Katie kind not feared.
I am Katie logical, intelligent,
I am Katie slightly elegant.
I am Katie creative, calm,
I am Katie I won't cause harm.
I am Katie really quite sensitive,
I am Katie I just like to live.
I am Katie extrovert with close friends,
I am Katie I believe there's a life when life ends.

My name is Katie, I believe beauty is only skin deep,
But although saying that I must have my beauty sleep.

Katie Solman (Age 13)

Thoughts Of A Rocking Horse

Once I was the treasure of treasures
Forwards and backwards I went
Taking people for on the spot rides
But now that fun is over
Dust tickling my nose
And bags rest over my neck
No one to love and care for me
Sadness comes from within
Up in the cold, lonely loft
Bats hanging upside down
Oh if only the old days would come back
I would be happy again

Kayleigh Smitten (Age 11)

The Seashore

The sand is white
And so bright

Rocks are so rough
But I am tough

The sea is blue
And the sky is too

The light of the sun is so hot
As if I am in a boiling pot

I looked at the beach
And I heard a seagull screech

Aaron Saunders (Age 8)

My Bedroom

On goes the twilight
Bye to the nightlight
Tomorrow I hope will bring sunlight

The drawers shut their mouths
While the cupboard shuts his eyes
AND THEN! Off goes the twilight until tomorrow night

While the twilight is off
The room is much dimmer
The bed sucks me under
"AHH! Oh bummer."

Then I awake and sunlight comes up,
I hope this won't happen again
But something will

Samantha Stapleton (Age 11)

And Life Begins Again

Spring is here at last
Things start to change
Lambs are being born
Chicks are popping up
Birds accompany each other in song

Heavyweight hares battle it out
Tulips dance in the wind
The hedgehog awakes from his winter slumber
Frogs croak to a musical number
And life begins again

Robert Sommerlad (Age 10)

The Dentist

I went to the dentist and she wasn't very nice
She had red hair and green head-lice
Her teeth were yellow and looked like jello
She tripped over and bonked her head
As she reached for her med
Her room was a tip
That's why she tripped
My little brother danced
And she began to prance
I reached for my hat and gave her a pat
I ran for my life it wasn't very nice

Alexander Scott (Age 8)

Pets

B ouncing
O n
N aughty
N ights
Y ellow teethed dogs

A lways
N oisy
D ancing

K icking
I rresistible
T earing
C aterpillars
H ouse

Rebecca Swanson (Age 14)

The Monster Poem

His eyes were as big as boats
His hands warm as coats
His teeth pierced when he was fierce
His breath was as smelly as old socks
When they have not been in the wash
His legs were stubby like his bubby
His claws were sore
When they were caught in the door
His feet hit the floor
When they slapped the door
And now he's completely blistered

Kiri Spencer (Age 12)

The Moon

A ready target
A bouncing balloon
A flying football
A cartoon smile
A lump of cheese
A silver hook
A juicy fruit
A burning ball
A flashing light
A flickery bulb

Joanne Summerhayes (Age 10)

Star Of The Week

Andrew asked for it
Beatrice blew it
Cathy caught it
David dived for it
Ethell entered for it
Francesca flew for it
Gary gagged for it
Harry hoped for it
Jonah jumped for it
Katy kicked for it
Lauren leaped for it
Misha munched for it
Natalie nattered for it
Peter piped for it
Richard ran for it
Sam sang for it
Tom tossed for it
Willy wanted it
Xena xonged for it
Zelda WON it

Michael Smalley (Age 10)

Janie The Chewing Gum Girl

Janie always chews her gum
She chews it everywhere
One day she blew a bubble
But it got stuck in my hair
Whenever she comes to my house
She sticks it on the dishes
But worst of all your never
She feeds it to the fishes
Once she blew a bubble
But burst it on her face
When her mother saw her
She was in disgrace
Later in her life
Her mouth felt like paste
Only because her gum
Was stuck in her brace.

Amy Smallwood (Age 11)

Haiku

On mountains I walk
In the winter I do ski
Summer months I walk

A small golden cocoon
A silver caterpillar
A new butterfly!

Summer sun, so hot
Take a long bathe in the sea
Feeling better now!

Rain pouring down it's
So cold, just freezing water
Falling from the sky.

Hannah Salmon (Age 13)

A Day In Bombay

As the glaring rays of the dandelion sun
Pierces India's beautiful landscape,
People are waking.
The train rattles its warning as it
Snakes along the twisted track,
Then it hisses to a halt,
As it arrives at the cramped station.
The waspish sitars angrily shove and buzz
Along the dusty crocodile back roads,
Mouse-like buses scurry to and fro
In the burning heat.
The rainbow coloured saris which ladies are wearing
Shimmers in the dazzling light.
The peach coloured sun is slowly sinking
Behind mountains, silhouetting temples and mosques.

Zoë Sycamore (Age 10)

River

Flowing fast, flowing slow
Down the mountains high
I drop a paper boat where the water's calm and clear
It's going down, it hits the rapids
It's going down the waterfall!
It's going down the waterfall!
Down it goes!
I clamber down the waterfall
It's
Gone!
Gone!
Gone!

Daniel Squire (Age 10)

Christmas Night

It is Christmas
When we have a lovely time
And we all open our presents
And we have a lovely
Christmas Day
With a lovely turkey tea
And a lovely pudding as well
It is Christmas Day for everyone tomorrow
So go to bed

Luke Southern (Age 9)

Surprises

Far away but yet among us
Lies a country all have seen
Cloudless skies and golden woodlands
Silver waters, meadows green
All the voices of the city
And the sounds of wild animals
Never reach that lovely country
Never spoil its happy life
All the roses will bloom forever
All the gold has no alloy
For the land of sweet surprises
Is the children's world of joy.

Gemma Sanders (Age 11)

The Enchanted Land

Wicked witches,
Wondering wizards -
Magic spells
And storming blizzards.

Howling winds
And whispering trees -
Weird sounds and mysterious echoes,
Floating on the chilling breeze.

Witche's cauldrons,
Cat of black -
Slimy frogs,
And snakes in a sack.

So the question is,
Will you go? – Will you dare?
And if you do,
Watch out and beware!

Charlotte Silveston (Age 10)

First World War

My Grandad once told me
About 1914,
How it was heard
How it was seen.

It was the first germ war,
The worst germ war
How it bashed,
How it crashed.

My Granny once said
How she lay in her bed,
Hearing the outside
Be bombed.

Now we have poppies
To remember those days,
Of how people fought
They deserve the praise.

Katy Spicer (Age 10)

The Otter

Sliding gracefully from the muddy bank
Seeking safety in the dark pool.
They silently dive head first
Into the murky cold water.

By the waterfall they play
Tumbling joyfully
Head over rudder
Rolling, playing, biting, happily – carefree

In the security of their holt
They snuggle, cheekily,
Cautiously listening for predators.

Amy Symonds (Age 10)

The Dark

Black snow dropping on you
When you least expect it
Quicker as winter creeps in
Street lamps raining
Its blanketing darkness
Eating its way through time
Preying on the weak
By freezing passers by
With blankets of coldness
But it dies
The sun kills it
In the early morning
Light

Luke Snell (Age 10)

Feelings

I feel a pain
Rushing through my vein

Holding your tum
Crying for your mum

Then you're holding your spinning head
The next minute you're DEAD!

Alyssa Smith (Age 11)

Ghosts

I was eating my toast
And an invisible ghost
Came to visit me
I crept up the stairs
And a shivering ghost
Was following me
I was shivering too!

Dannielle Smith (Age 8)

My Rock

The colourful waters of time
Plunging into history
Blood red puddles
Next to the bone of life

The rocky paths of light
Saw everything
From B.C. to A.D.
But no one noticed HIM.

Carly Stewart (Age 11)

My First Week At School

On my first day at school
I was very shy
I wished that I could fly

On my second day at school
We learnt to add
Some of us were very bad

On the third day at school
In the middle of play
I wet myself so I didn't stay

On my fourth day at school
I played with sand
And then played with rubber bands

On the last day at school
It's the end of the week
So we had a game of hide and seek

Laura Stone (Age 10)

Poor Animals

There are many animals in the world,
Hamsters, guinea pigs and squirrels,
Goats and sheep, cows and lambs,
Lots of people eat their meat,
Ears, legs and even feet.

The animals must be scared to death,
Who is going to lose their life?
Male animals may lose their wife,
I don't think people care,
Animals die every day, I don't think it's fair.

Cruelty to animals should be thrown away
And never be remembered for another day.

Michael Sinnott (Age 12)

Untitled

I know a colourful Toucan
Who lives life high in a tree.
He sends out a beat all summer
That will rock even you and me
He sings and dances around
While making a musical sound
With his feet a tapping
And his wings a flapping

I call him the boss above ground!

Bryher Simmons (Age 13)

Carnival

Lights, singing and dancing
Clapping and cheering
People dressed up and prancing.
Cold winter nights,
On the way home, fish and chips
With salt and vinegar
Tasty and ready for my lips,
Lights, singing and dancing.

Simon Shaw (Age 11)

My Family

My mummy is a bird
Which is quite absurd
My daddy is a laddy
He gets very happy
My sister is a twister
That rides round my room
She clears everything up
Like a very big broom
My brother is a pain
And he drives us all insane

Holly Sharpley (Age 8)

Death

Where do we go?
Do we start a new life?
If.... we do
Start a new life
Are we the same?
Are we spirits?
To heaven or hell
Where do we go, nobody knows
Will we see our family ever again?
When we are dead
Will we memorise the past?
If we're alive,
Are we dead?

But nobody knows about death
Does death come to everyone?

Laura Sear (Age 10)

Fuss

Fuss is the room
Fuss is in every room
Fuss is the world

Daniel Squires (Age 9)

It Would Be Weird

It would be weird
If pigs could fly
Or if an elephant baked a pie
It would be weird
If trees could talk
Or a recycling bin could walk
It would be weird
If grapes could sing
Or a banana ruled as king
It would be weird
If grass was red
Or if I could take off my head
It would be weird!

Alexander Sherwood (Age 9)

Bangladesh

Golden corn fields as harvest comes
Thank you Lord for our mums.

In Bangladesh when the flood comes
Thank you Lord for our plums.

Quick! quick! Your stalls are falling
Gather them up the Lord is calling.

Their crops are dying in the drifts.
Thank you Lord for the harvest gifts.

Gather your children and run away.
The autumn floods are coming today.

Thank you Lord for our rain.
Think of the children who are in pain.

Thank you Lord for the harvest that comes.
Think of the children without any mums.

Thank you for our English weather
Thank you for friends to share together

Rebecca Scott (Age 9)

Please

Please Mr Dunstone
Can I go out to play?
I'll do whatever you say
I really want a play.

Please Mr Merritt
Can I ring the bell?
I'll come and clean your desk out
I'll even clean the bell.

Please Mrs Cooke
Can we go out for P.E?
I'll scrub your trainers after
You can trust me.

Please Mrs Sperring
Can I please leave the hall?
I'll clean the plates from dinner
I'll even scrub the floor.

Claire Sheppard (Age 10)

Will We Cope?

The world was such a lovely place
Then came along the human race
We destroyed this
We cluttered up that
All for what a rubbish mat
Bareless trees
Poverty all around
Blazing suns
Burning and demolishing
We don't have a hope
How ever ...... will we cope?

Sarah Smart (Age 11)

Twist

Stars like eating strawberries
The sun likes eating buns
Aliens go round the twist
And the moon shoots his gun

Martin Sewell (Age 11)

I'm Bored

I wish I could go out
Mums shouting
Do something!
There's nothing to do
I could be ...
Digging for Treasure
Or
I could be ...
Ecstatic!!!
But I'm not
I'm stuck in here

Charley Stephens (Age 11)

Winter

All the birds go round the world
All the trees are bare
All the animals sleep
The sun goes down
The snowflakes twirl down
All the flowers die
The whole place is snow
The rivers freeze
The ducks are gone
Everyone lights their fires

Christopher Tucker (Age 6)

Spring

Spring is fun
Picking flowers
Running down hills
In and out of barns
Night is getting short
Get sunbathing in the sun

Amy Timberlake (Age 6)

S.W.A.L.K.

As I look at you, in the sun
Your eyes sparkle like the stars
Glowing like the moon.
Your hair swims through the air
Dodging the waves
You walk like a model walking down an aisle
You swim like a mermaid down in the sea.
I write letters to you sealed with a loving kiss.
S.W.A.L.K.

Kaleigh-Jane Treacher (Age 12)

Train

Steaming through
Under the dead bridges
Roaring…
Alive…
Crushing…
Screaming like a rocket launching
A long snake slithering
Ferociously
Fierce and fast
Angry
Creating the polluted air
Executing
The suffering track
Unstoppable
Angry
Invincible…

William Spencer (Age 10)

The Post Box

I never go past the post box
Because there's a monster in there
I wouldn't go near it if I was you
I went past the post box
And the monster said
BOO !

Charlotte Tomlinson (Age 7)

Bins, Bins, Bins

Bins, bins, bins, bins
What do they,
What do they say,
We don't need them anyway

Trash, trash, trash, trash
Why is it there,
We don't care,
It gives the place some colour.

Moan, moan, moan, moan
Granny go home,
I don't need a loan,
I'll just live on the streets.

Please, please, please, please
I need help,
Without a doubt,
Why don't you come and save me?

Jail, jail, jail, jail
What did I do
What did I say,
Please don't go away.

Sarah Tyrrell (Age 13)

I Like …..

I like football
I like sport
I like cars
Dodge Vipers all sorts.

I can't afford one
Not just yet
I haven't passed my driving test.

I drive my mum around the bend
I'm qualified for that my friend.

My dad he says
That's my boy
Leave that car, it's not a toy.

Today, tomorrow, sometime soon
I'll have that car, zoom, zoom, zoom.

Simon Turner (Age 10)

What's In My Box?

Is it a rabbit with long floppy ears?
Is it a plant with petals of pink?
Is it a teddy with long fuzzy hair?
Is it a book with pages of print?
Can you shake it?
Can you jump on it?
Oh no it's a slippery frog.

Rebecca Tremayne (Age 5)

I Can Hear The Rain

Pitter patter, drip drop
I can hear the rain
It's driving me crazy
It's driving me insane
I feel like sighing
I feel like crying
The rain is soft
I can hear it in my loft
When I sang a song
The rain went BANG
The floods are going swish
I can see the shiny fish
The rain now is dazzling, sparkling
And glistening

Rebecca Tandy (Age 7)

To My Valentine .....

We see the sun so slowly going down,
We watch the sun reflecting off the sea.
Your hair so soft, so smooth and golden brown,
I look at you, your gorgeous eyes at me.

All through the night we walk along the sand,
My heart, the hole, your love is here to mend.
We walk along the beach with hand in hand,
The everlasting night will never end.

Your face so soft it's like a calm day's sea,
Your eyes so blue they're like a summer's sky.
As you can see our love is meant to be,
I know you love me so please don't lie.

I love you lots and I know you love me,
Why don't you see how happy we could be.

Julie Tizzard (Age 14)

When Jesus Was Born

On Christmas we remember when Jesus was born
When angels blew their horn

On Christmas children have lots of fun
And tucked behind the clouds is the sun

On Christmas we put up our trees
And eat sweeties

We have lots of Christmas treats
And eat different meat

Santa is on his way
We will have presents on Christmas day

When you eat Christmas cake
You get a big tummy-ache!

Stephanie Tregenza (Age 8)

Netball

Hello! I come from Roche School
I'm one of the eleven that play netball
I've heard you need to be quite tall
And always try not to fall
And don't go off with a broken jaw
When it rains we play in the hall
That's when we really need to call
And shout for that bright orange ball

Elizabeth Trudgeon (Age 11)

My Monkey

My monkey
Sitting in a tree
Had a pet flea
Which drank tea
Upon his knee

Martin Trudgeon (Age 10)

Matthew

On Monday Matthew was glad
On Tuesday Matthew was sad
On Wednesday Matthew was mad
On Thursday Matthew was bad
But!
On Friday Matthew had
Enough .....
So he went to stay with his dad

Matthew Trunks (Age 12)

Death

Rough cotton clouds hurry through the gazing night.
Tenching car fumes poison the mid-winter's evening.
A shadow hides the vast city
Trying to wipe out everything in its path.
And at the end of a black and brackish pond
Surrounded by pine trees, whose dark foliage
Obscured by the light of day,
Stood a fearful figure
In coarse grey
Called the dragon man.
Instantaneously an unearthly silence sweeps
Across the metallic galaxy.
Mist enclosed the river,
Soft, white vapour drifted over the brown
Sludge covered Thames.
A silence so silent it was like the end of world war three.

Jonathan Townsend (Age 10)

Christmas Time

On Christmas Eve Santa has come with Rudolph
To help him out
With a panda for me
When I am in bed
I can see the stars twinkle and wrinkle
It's Christmas
We've got our pudding
But we made a mistake
Where's the food

Jonathan Taylor (Age 8)

The Horse

Gently breathing down the young girl's neck,
Brushing his head against hers,
Standing proudly,
Head held high,
Pricking his ears to the world;

Galloping across the buttercup field,
Kicking up dirt as he runs,
Never worrying about what's behind him,
Stronger than anything,
Free as a bird;

Tired out,
He takes a break,
Crops the grass
And breathes in the fresh air,
With no cares in the world;

Retired to the stable,
Fresh smell of straw,
Looking out into the wide world,
He bows his head
And drifts off to sleep.

Rosie Temple (Age 11)

All Around Us

I went out and I looked around
I saw the sun
The sun was hot
And it shone on my flowerpot
I see buttercups in my garden
Buds are growing in the trees in spring
There are new chicks and new foals

Charlotte Thomas (Age 6)

Dad

He is tall and thin
Like a beanpole,
His eyes sparkle
Like the blue sky
On a sunny day.
His mouth looks sad,
But he's not at all –
He's rather funny!
He likes to go fishing,
Read all the books.
Get his bag and his hat
To go off to work
Six days a week,
Always drinking coffee.

Sean Toomer (Age 11)

Shining Star

Shining star Oh shining star
Looking at the world from above
Shining star Oh shining star
Sitting like a pure white dove

Shining star Oh shining star
What do you see this night?
Shining star Oh shining star
I see a pure clear light

Shining star Oh shining star
The light I see tonight
Shining star Oh shining star
Must be the love of God
Shining very bright

Dearest Lord
Shining very bright
Dearest Lord
Bless the world tonight

Katie Thompson (Age 10)

My Birthday; A First Attempt At Poetry

My birthday was good
'Cause my baby brother was there;
I loved my birthday cake so much
There was a lot to share.

I shared it with my baby brother,
'Cause I love him so very much.
Emma and Oliver, all my friends,
Played in the garden with Caitlin.

Caitlin Taylor (Age 5)

The Waiter

In restaurant trying
To eat at noon
God sake waiter
Bring me my spoon
Dog went barking on
All day
I'd like my spoon
Today waiter
That's all I can say

Kelly Tyler (Age 12)

What We Are!

Our hair is spiky
Our hair is straight
Our eyes are green
Our eyes are blue
We all come from around the world
We may be fat
We may be thin
We may be big
We may be small

Joe Templeman (Age 7)

Thoughts

Life is so short, I hear you say,
But it's hard to survive day after day,
I'm so alone without a friend
I wish this short life of mine would end.

In years gone by while young and keen,
My family's love was pure and clean.

Then work, then bills, then final demands,
The money earned slipped through my hands.

Now I sit alone,
With just my thoughts, my family's gone
Love counts for nought.

If I died they wouldn't care,
My girlhood dreams are beyond repair.

Am I so bad as they all say,
Is that why they stay away.

Life is so short, I hear you say,
It's hard to survive day after day
I 'm so alone without a friend,
I wish this short life of mine would end.

Lisa Topley (Age 15)

The Man From The Climb

There was a man from the climb
Who did not care about time
He climbed to the top
He came down with a pop
His favourite fruit was lime

Kenny To (Age 9)

What Is Blue?

What is blue?
The lake is blue.

What is yellow?
The sun is yellow.

What is red?
A bit of the rainbow.

What is white?
A polar bear.

What is green?
The leaves are green.

What is orange?
Tiger's stripes.

Sarah Thomas (Age 7)

Snowball

Round - white - graceful
Soft - gentle - pretty
Creamy - bright - lovely
And they
Touch the ground

Jade Turner (Age 6¾)

The Weather Man

It's seven o'clock in the morning
I'm waking up at dawn,
The birds are singing in the trees,
There's dewdrops on the lawn.
I'm getting dressed at five past seven,
The windows are covered in frost,
I think I need to change my clock,
What? It says eleven!
The weather seems disgusting,
"Oh what a miserable day!" I think I shall have
My toast and marmalade in bed today!
I'm going outside at eight o'clock
But run back in to get my socks.
I put on my socks and gloves, my woolly overcoat too,
I pack my bag and got my lunch,
I say goodbye to my mum,
And dash outside to have some fun.
I am trudging through the snow, when it begins to hail,
I must find some shelter or I'll be blown back by a gale!

Liam Taylor-West (Age 8)

My Face

My eyes are like hard balls of rock
My forehead is like a lumpy ditch which is dry
My eyelashes are like prickles of a hedgehog
My hair is like a palm tree
My cheeks are like puffballs
My ears are like exploding volcanoes
My nose is like a mountain drift
My teeth are like sugar
And that is the end of my face!

Anna Tindall (Age 7)

My Dad

My dad and I are not alike
He is tall and he hasn't got any hair
I am short and I have lots of hair

My dad and I are not alike
He has tomato sauce on everything
And I don't

My dad and I are not alike
He likes to lay on the sofa and watch the snooker
I like to go and knock for my friends

Jack Tompkins (Age 9)

216

Crescendo

They congregate,
They intoxicate,
They debate .....

He orates, she repudiates,
He substantiates, she expostulates,
He remonstrates, she elucidates,
He denunciates, she elaborates;

They obstinate,
They intoxicate,
They altercate .....

She provocates, he imitates
She reprobates, he irritates;

They vociferate,
They intoxicate,
They deteriorate .....

He assassinates, she lacerates;

They annihilate,
They infuriate,
They disassociate .....

It reverberates.

Mark Thomas (Age 18)

My Easter Poem

Lambs are prancing like a ball of cotton wool
New born chicks are growing up
Everyone is eating eggs
Yummy and scrummy
It reminds me of a new life like Jesus in the stable

All the eggs with sweets in side
It makes me hungry

Gavin Turner (Age 8)

A Cloud

A cloud is a grey feather
Floating on a quiet lake
It is a creamy flannel
Shimmering in a deep sink
It is a smudge of white chalk
Lying on a blue shirt
It is a spoldge of white paint
Stuck onto a blue beemer
It is a grey patch
Stitched on a blue curtain

John Tanner (Age 10)

A Box Full Of Seasons

As white as snow, as clear as glass,
As hot as a dessert, as cold as ice,
As wet as rain, as soft as a cloud,
As dark as coal, as light as day.
All these things are included in one thing .....
A box full of seasons.

As green as an emerald, as hot as fire,
As foggy as soup, as cold as snow,
As wet as water, as soft as fur,
As dark as night, as light as the sun.
All these things make .....
A box full of seasons.

Clare Twomey (Age 9)

Boy Blurb

The boy is best at 9 years old
And doesn't stop in his bed mould.

He's not the kind to do a lot
And always hates his football, not.

We like computers
And like tutors.

We love blood
And so much mud.

James Trenchard (Age 9)

Meander

My life is full of never
Ending bumps and bends
And curves
Never will I stop meandering
To and fro I go in
Unending swerves
Running into the bank

Sarah Tyhurst (Age 10)

I Wish

Can you put a price on dying?
Fields of blood
And people crying.
Boys, only sixteen .....
Have so many dreams
Into the world, a baby boy
Who brings hope and joy,
Will he have to die?

David Trundley (Age 12)

Beginning Of World War VI 4002

Men have been captured,
Men have been tortured
They're held captive.
Robots built with determination
Laser built for deterioration.
Ready and active.
Making a judgement,
Emeralds as their eyes,
Saying, "None of us loses,
None of us dies."
Both the teams face,
Looking for annihilation,
The other robots that made man captive,
Says, "Time for extermination."
Bombs made nuclear,
Robots disappear,
Total demolition.
Massive great tanks,
All in different ranks,
Make total destruction.
"None of us loses, none of us dies."
All of them lost and all of them lied.

Thomas Twigg (Age 14)

What A Sister, I Don't Care

Knotted hair
A bear with no hair and
A bunny with no eyes

Tangled shoes
A dinosaur with the blues and
The frightful sight of her

A mouth full of gum and
Her eyes full of lashes of mascara

My sister can be a bull with no lead
When she's not allowed any money

Her mates are around all night
With anger to fight
While she's having some tea
Or some of me

But the secret you see
Between you and me
Is I love her with a guarantee!

Loni Thomson (Age 12)

Shadowy Night

Shadowy night
Shadowy night
Why does the night
Give me a fright?
Shadowy night
Shadowy night
Dad please turn
On the light.
No Dad
That's too bright.
Shadowy night
Shadowy night.

Edward Talbot (Age 9)

Birds

Birds float on the water
Birds eat bread
Birds flying in the sky
Three in a tree
Birds drink water
Owls hooting in the tree
Birds feeding their babies
Birds stood up
Birds frightened by the people

Daniel Tregear (Age 9)

Hurricane

Hurricane, hurricane
Growing bigger, bigger.
Blowing wildly,
Whirling through towns.

Trees overthrown
Bushes rustling
Leaves flying.
Forking lightning

Children crying
Slates flying.
Hurricane, hurricane
Dying, dying.

Martyn Thomas (Age 10)

Summer

Summer's here at last you see,
You can tell by the sounds of the bumblebee.
In and out the flowers they fly,
To collect the pollen to make a pie;
The collect the pollen to make some honey,
Then you can sell it to make some money.
When it's cold and they have gone away,
You'll have to wait for another day.
When summer has gone and the nights have drawn in,
You will not be able to hear them sing.
Winter is nearly here, and summer has gone.
And now you'll have to wait till next year.

Jessica Thomas (Age 11)

I Know An Alien

Did you know I know and alien?
I see him all the time,
I see him twenty-four hours a day,
Whether it's rain or shine.

My mum and dad they know him,
They know him very well,
For I am the alien,
And so is my brother as well.

Andrew Taylor (Age 11)

There's Something In The Cupboard

There's something in the cupboard,
A monster, huge, gigantic and green.
As scaly as a reptile
As thin as thin can be.
Let's hope he's been fed.

There's something in the cupboard,
It's making lots of noise.
It's banging and crashing,
It's eating all my toys.

There's something in the cupboard.
I think it scared the cat.
She's screeching and hissing,
She's hidden under the mat.

There's something in the cupboard,
I've seen it there before.
I'm getting very frightened,
IT'S COMING OUT THE DOOR.

Lauren Taylor (Age 9)

Dragons

Out of the acid water it comes
Leaving a trail of blood
It breathes hot fire
It breathes hot steam
Has one eye only
The other one vanished

Has very dark, black, sharp teeth
Red, green, humungous
Ever so dangerous
Carnivorous in every way
Devours its prey

Be aware of the sneaky, awesome creature
Who has sharp teeth
He may go on a rampage with you
He may drag you anywhere
So be aware of the sneaky, awesome creature!

Matthew Turp (Age 9)

Moment In Time

Kisses that once whispered words,
Now silent, never to be told.
Two hearts that were torn apart,
Fade away into the darkness.

Eyes of blue, touched my soul,
Untold secrets for you to hold.
Love became real for that moment in time
Bring back the past,
And you're forever mine.

Lauren Taylor (Age 15)

The Massacre

The Forlorn Hope is first to climb the breach,
With swords unsheathed and colours flying high.
Their name is surely true, for as they reach
The looming fort they know that they will die.
The deaf'ning cannons pit the soggy ground
And smash through walls and people just the same.
The men's ears strain to hear above the sound
Of shrieking soldiers shot like hunted game.
The battle ends, the living loot the dead.
They search for money, food or ranking stripes.
The bodies' graves are dug; few words are said
Whilst Colonels sit much shocked, smoking their pipes.
Wars never change, in trench or open field,
For honour's sake men fight and will not yield.

Victoria Turner (Age 13)

Why?

It's time to get up
What now?
Yes now
Why?
Because it's time for school
What now?
Yes now
Why?
Because it's eight o'clock
What now?
Yes now
Why?
NOT AGAIN!
Pardon?

Alex Toogood (Age 10)

Senses

If I didn't have my nose
I couldn't smell a rose
If I didn't have my eyes
I couldn't see the skies
I need my ears to hear
I need my tongue to taste
With my fingers
I need to touch then I .....
Can feel my face

Jeremy Tunstall (Age 9)

Book Myth

Breathing books
Dreamy pages
Flowering imagination
Escaping adventures
Shadowy mysteries
Blood thirsty murders
Swirling staircases
Dusty spines
Curling whispers of
Legendary authors
Filling the whirlpool of words
With wonder

Lucy Taylor (Age 9)

Thoughts Of My Old Doll

I once was a happy doll,
Now I'm all sad,
My owner treats me really bad.
She used to love and care for me,
And even sit me on her little knee,
But she grew an inch,
Then a bit more
And more and more,
Now she's two foot four,
She don't play with me anymore,
I used to have a lovely suit,
All beautiful and blue,
But it's just fallen apart,
Now all I own is one tiny boot.
I sit in the corner,
The little mice gnaw at me,
The spiders sit and snigger,
I just sit and cry
I only wish to die.

Katie Turner (Age 11)

The Air Raid

The screechy noisy
Siren went off
We all went
Running to the shelter
We heard a bug
BANG!
We were all scared
My sisters especially
After 4 hours
The all clear
Siren went off
We all went
Slowly to our houses
It looked awful
I felt relieved
After it all
Some of my friends
Had been blown up
I was sad

Benyameen Termezi (Age 10)

Winter

Fluffy snow slowly melting
A glittering blanket on the ground
The frosty silver lake glistening brightly
The tall spooky trees spookily shaking
Cold white snow gradually melts
White glittering ground
In the cold the freezing lake is glistening icily
The bare branches shivering in the moonlight

Lydia Vallance (Age 9)

Hidden

Excruciating pain, why won't it just go?
It had no invitation but gate-crashed its way into me
Reading my messages to heaven
As I silently cried out in it
I believed in you God
Why are you letting me go through this?
I fight so damn hard to conceal my hurting thoughts
From this cold-hearted hell
Beings want for themselves
In this capitalistic world
People always ready to prey
On an insecurity or weakness
To scar your soul,
I'm glad I know early
About the ways of the cruel human heart
Never to hand out my thoughts
Or leave myself open
Though sometimes I just want somebody
To hold me and tell me
That everything's going to be okay.

Lisa Thorne (Age 15)

Cheetahs

A cheetah prowling in the grass
Waiting for prey to come within its grasp.
Then pouncing out like a lightning strike,
Biting its head until it's dead.
Guzzling it down, watching then sits,
Spitting out the bones and keeping the bits.

Thomas Undery (Age 8)

We Are Children

We come from around the world.
We are black and white,
Our hair is long, short and curled.
Our hobbies are playing all day.
We don't like working
Oh no,no,no.
Some of us like football
And some of us don't.
Some of us like vegetables
And others like sweets.
We don't like being stopped
When we are playing.
We are such a good family.

Lee Underwood (Age 8)

220

Invasion Earth

Dead of night
Still can't sleep
Outside there came a sudden beep

I look outside
There's a U.F.O.
From it comes a laugh – Ho,Ho,Ho

Creep outside
At the dead of night
Give myself a dreadful fright

Creeping up
Closer as I go
To this massive U.F.O.

Trembling with fright
As I stare at the door
Opening, Opening, more and more

David Tufft (Age 10)

Basketball

A basketball is round
And orange
Bouncy and has lines
And full of air

Lewis Vickers (Age 8)

The Seasons

Spring is coming
It's on its way
It's getting closer
Every day

The birds are singing
Loud and clear
I feel that summer
Is almost here

As the children
Laugh and play
The air gets colder
Day by day

All the leaves
Start to go brown
Then Jack Frost
Litters the ground

Winter's presence
Is almost here
I feel it's been
A pretty good year

Elizabeth Tayler (Age 11)

War

I want to be in a world where,
There is no fighting or despair.
But during this very dreadful war,
I'd rather choke on an apple core.
Than see my people fall down and die,
Because of bombs falling from the sky.

My dad had to fight in this dreadful war,
Among all of that blood and gore.
Even though mum keeps us calm,
And tries to keep us out of harm.
Nobody really wants to fight,
Because we know it isn't right.

So people fighting around the world.
Put down your arms and look around,
At what we have done to the human race
And the orphan child who has a tear stained face.
Let's try to make a contract of peace
And give up our battles and war to cease.

Michael Wells (Age 11)

Boys

Babyish, irresponsible and they think they're
Very funny. But sometimes the only boy a
Girl can trust is her daddy.
Boys just have no time for girls and
Are always playing football.
But boys will be boys and
Girls will be girls.

Zoe Vince (Age 11)

The Snake

Slithery, slimy is a snake
Tongues pulling and hissing on the way
And red eyes looking at a mouse
Ready to eat it.

Katy Worth (Age 7)

The Butterfly Of Beauty And Its Plant

A young man once owned a butterfly farm,
He cared for and loved them with all his heart,
One day a kind old man paid him a visit, he meant no harm.
He wanted one quarter of the man's cherished butterflies
And in exchange he gave him a butterfly so rare.
That night the old man's gift began to glow,
The young man stood in wonderment and stared.
The other butterflies were attracted to the bright light.
One by one they came and joined, a change was taking place.
They were drawn to the brightness by some unknown power
And as he watched the magic unfolded creating an everlasting flower.

Stacey Ungless (Age 13)

Ocean

The sea rushes in
Breaking and foaming
It churns and sprays
Alert and moaning

The sun sets slowly
And the sky turns red
It lies above the horizon
Far ahead

The moon casts a shadow
On the sparkling gold
The sky clouds over
Menacing and cold

A silky sheet
Under the silver moon
Seagulls cry
And the morning comes soon

The sun rises
It's a brand new day
The water ripples
On the golden bay

Emma Vickery (Age 13)

A War Poem

Here in bases aircraft lie,
In position ready to fly,
Lyneham Hercules stand by,
With brave men prepared to die.

It might be their last prayer
But they will know,
Whatever happens .....
England will be proud.

Some men never experience a war
Like the Gulf war,
But now they know,
It's not all that nice.

They saw their friends dying,
Knowing they could do nothing,
The Hercules came back half empty,
For those who died,
Fought for Queen and Country
Their memories will lie forever.

James Varela (Age 11)

Body Parts

Hands can help
Legs make you run
Feet support your legs
Your mouth helps you eat
Eyes can make you see
Ears can make you hear
Our body is like a machine

Matthew Willis (Age 7)

Me, Myself, I

Jonathan Varcoe is my name, I'm a country boy I'd say,
I really wish I didn't have to go to school each day.
Sometimes when I am at school my mind drifts to the farm,
Mrs Murray shouts at me and takes me by the arm.
She takes me to Mr.Mitten, or to the office with Mrs Dale,
I have to sit in silence, I'm sure through school I'll sail!
Oh how I wish that I was sixteen and then my school days would be over.
I could work full-time on the farm and be as happy as a pig in clover.

Jonathan Varcoe (Age 11)

A Lovely Dinner

I ate a hammon
It tasted like salmon
It was very nice
So I ate another slice.

Then I had a turbil
It made me feel quite ill
And my belly got sore
So I didn't have any more

I wanted some more hammon
But we only had gammon
So I had to go without
But I really wanted to shout

Sean Vickers (Age 10)

What's In My Box?

Is it a cosy jumper?
Is it a bike?
Is it a little mouse?
Kick it. Stamp on it. Shake it.
No!
It's a scary spider.

Stephanie Wright (Age 6)

In Dreams

Dreams are images that flash
Before my sleepy eyes
Many nights I wake surprised
Dreams so vivid in my mind
I search for answers I can't find.

Images race around my mind
With nightmares of every kind
Good dreams bad dreams
Every night
You never know what you may sight
UFOs in the sky
Control the dreams before our eyes.

Lauren Wardley (Age 13)

Ode To My Toothbrush

Toothbrush oh toothbrush
My purple Colgate toothbrush.
Without you my teeth would be nothing,
Nothing I tell you.
I cherish your easy-grip handle
I value your odd shaped bristles.
Purple bristles, white bristles I treasure you both.
I love the way you massage my teeth..
Christmas is when you came to me.
Divine is what you are, you are.
When you're finished cleaning,
My teeth are always gleaming.
Toothbrush oh toothbrush you're mine.
Exquisite is what you are.
Day and night I appreciate you, admire you.
I'd never live without you toothbrush,
In fact I'll never let you go.

Ciara Whalley (Age 10)

Sports

Sports are really smart
I don't know where to start.
For girls there is netball,
To play, it's good to be tall.
Now you're wondering what the boys do,
They play football and basketball too.
There's tennis which is a good sport to play,
It's relaxing, you could play all day.
One of my hobby's was ballet,
My dad and brother likes rally.
Golf is also a good sport,
It's really easy to be taught.
It just leaves me with cricket,
You use a bat and a wicket.
I like sports, running is a blast,
But I'm telling you now,
I'm not that fast.

Greta Viertel (Age 10)

Guess Who?

Who tries to pop a ball?
Who tries to jump when they won't walk?
Who tries to start a fight near the night?
Who tries to chase the cat?
Who tries to rip up a hat?
Who tries to dig a hole?
Who chews a pole?
Well can't you guess?
My best friend is my dog, Zac.

Lewis White (Age 7)

Autumn

Animals digging up to hibernate
Leaves fly floating everywhere
In the sunny sky
Leaves crunch crackling
When people stand on them
Conkers falling off the trees
They come out of their shells
Their shells are green and spiky
The conkers are brown inside
On bonfire night there are fireworks
Some fireworks they're in the shape of flowers

Nathan Wonnacott (Age 6)

All Around Us

All around us in spring
There are things to be done
The sun is hot
The flowers are growing a lot
The leaves are green
The chicks are clean
Now this is spring
Let's go and sing
Baby foals being born
I love to see them

Samantha Ward (Age 6)

My Eyes

Your eyes are
different colours
Some eyes are different
Shapes and sizes
Some eyes cannot see
If they are blind
Some people have guide dogs
To lead them somewhere
If we did not have eyes
We could not see

Lisa Witherden (Age 8)

Untitled

Snow is a white ranger
The stars fall on the ground
Ice talks to you
The tigers bring us snow
Hats fly to you
Ice talks to you
The North Pole is coming to us
The tigers give you a snowball fight
The snowman flies to the North Pole
Where the snow ends

Alex Wood (Age 6)

My Foggy Morning By The Harbour

Sea patterned with oily wavy shadows
  The ocean calm and peaceful
  And gently rippling
  Slowly more water enters the harbour
Rusty boats bobbing about
  And swaying as if the wind were their master
  Boats disturbing the sea
  And making larger ripples
The sky cold and dusty
  Seagulls hover over the deep sea and swoop over our heads
  Rain spitting trickling down our faces
  All the children wet and bothered
Smells of fish and oil fumes
  Over the swooshing of the calm ocean
  It's hard to write the paper gets wet and our writing disappears
  My paper gets blotchy it's even harder to think
As the day moves on the time seems to go faster
  Unfortunately soon it's time to go home
  So faster we work
  Oh no it's time to go!

Gemma Waters (Age 10)

A Day In Bombay

As dawn breaks over the city of Bombay
Rickshaws striped like beetles dodging and waving through the
Never ending maze of streets.
A miniature aeroplane buzzing drunkenly around.
An old centipede bumping along an uneven ribbon of uneven dust.
A snake sways and wobbles along with its mouth open.
Pylon soldiers march off into the night.

Tom Wilkinson (Age 11)

Autumn

I crunch in the leaves
On the ground.
It's cold, it's cold.
Hedgehogs snuggling
And hibernating.
Conkers fall off the trees.
Falling they crack open,
We look for them,
They bounce on the ground.
Flowers die,
The farmers are busy.
The frost comes down and down.
Hedgehogs look for food.
Bonfire roasting hot,
Boiling hot, steaming hot.
Children playing in the field.

Emily Whittington (Age 6)

Wide Awake

I've watched a film
It's really scary,
It gives me the creeps
I'm wide awake
I can't help it
My mind has been running
The film is called
"Silence of the lambs"
I thought of counting sheep,
I'm still awake
Because I am scared
I listen for him
He is coming for me
I'm waiting
I'm awake

Philip Wilkopp (Age 11)

Winter

The snowman was happy
It is winter
The children love to laugh
They love to play
There must have been magic

Kieran Wenman (Age 6)

The Spider's Supper

I hope to catch some supper
But nothing has arrived
It's very late, I'm getting tired
Suddenly something comes
It gets away
I have to make it again

Joel Westlake (Age 10)

Halloween Time

Haunted houses everywhere
Apples ready for playing apple bobbing
Locks locking up ready for the fright
Lights going out people getting scared
Open up the clubs to party all night
Wicked witches spooking their spells
Every minute ticking away
Evil noises in the air tonight
Naughty goblins nicking people's grub
Twenty ghosts around the globe .....
I'm starting to get a fright!
Many people scared out of their skulls
Every year this happens and I'm glad it's only
ONCE!

Alister Wilmott (Age 10)

Calling

As I scan the bare parched ground below me,
The arid golden sphere of the sun makes it difficult to see,
My body craves fluid to drink until I burst,
To quench my ever growing thirst,
I run my lifeless fingers through the sharp, rough grains of sand,
Hoping. Praying for some tiny morsel of food to appear in my hand,
I tilt my lead filled head towards the sky,
In my mind I battle to keep going or at least try,
Then over the merging colours of the horizon gloomy shadows appear,
I strain my eyes and screw up my face and the image becomes clear,
It's a sturdy horse and a kind, gentle looking man,
He whispers to me softly "Clamber to your feet if you can."
He drags my limp, lifeless body onto his steady horse,
And rides us to a fresh water source,
With this total stranger I don't know how,
But I feel secure and safe now.

Sarah Wythe (Age 14)

There Was And Old Woman Called .....

There was an old woman called "Quickie!"
Who went home for a quick biccie,
She was such a snob, she was late for her job
So she sat like a slob
And she sucked on a 'hob-nob',
And now she's all gooey and sticky!

Colin Welsh (Age 12)

Powerless

Oh why am I feeling pain?
What have I done to deserve this?
I was just trying to be useful,
Why do I bother?

She always blames me,
But why?
I can't bear this,
I am supposed to be her friend.

My pain is the worst,
I feel like I'm screaming inside,
My whole body aches from it,
I need to let this pain out.

Why don't I stand up to her?
I suppose that is a silly question,
She's so powerful,
But why does it have to be me?

Beckie Wheadon (Age 12)

The Sun Was Only Sleeping

Do not say it's over
It's not, and never was.
Repeat the drone with us.
We'll fight the battle as before.
So take my hand, I'll lead the way
Into a sunset dead.
In similar verse, day by day,
Our lives are led by silver thread.
Come forth with me, wake land and sea.
The sun was only sleeping.
A dawn will come, our lives aren't done,
Though we feel sorrow creeping.
Conduct the sea and guide the breeze
In their musical tale.
The repeated drone – not as before,
Is just the guiding bass.
Don't say it's all right – you know it's not.
How boring that would be –
To have a rest from life's spitefulness.
Sweet life goes on ironically.

Rachel Whitworth (Age 14)

Carnival

Hey! Everybody the carnival's here,
The pubs are open only if you bring your beer,
People getting drunk
People having fights,
And lots of flashing lights.
Ambulances ne no ne no
Money throwing, ching, ching.
Generators roaring, spotlights in the dark night.
Hey! Everybody the carnival's over.

Ashley Webber (Age 11)

Jesus

He died on the cross
By a naughty little boss
And rose again next day
His name was Jesus

This man was clever
He could even heal lepers
So I like Easter
Hooray!

Paul Wakelam (Age 8)

The Monster Poem

Its eyes are big and bulgy
Its ears are long and thin
Its nose is flat and scabby
Its mouth is like a bin

Its tongue is like a fat pork
And its teeth
Are like forks

Its breath smells like B.O.
Its body moves so slow
Its claws are sharp as knives

Its arms is like its breath
Its skin looks bad as death

Its skin are shiny as pegs
Its feet are just like its legs

Albert Webster (Age 11)

The Phantom Of The Night

With a jump and a swoop, the phantom leaves,
A ghostly haunt in the midst of a church.
Like an Angel of Death, it glides o'er fields,
As night's dark embrace envelops the land.

The sun bids farewell, its rays start to wane,
As quarry emerges to feast on the earth,
Oblivious to danger, around and above,
A final and fatal mistake.

Hover, check, hover then dive,
Unevenly matched with no rival or foe,
The phantom succeeds, his reward small but good.
It glides to its haunt, ever silent and swift.

With a swoop and a jump, the phantom returns,
To a ghostly haunt in the midst of a church.
Like an Angel of Death it glides to its roost,
As day's warm embrace releases the land.

Andrew Warne (Age 13)

Springtime

Springtime!
Springtime!
The flowers are all out
And the hares are running about.

Chicks and tulips are here this very day
And they usually have nothing to say.

The blossom on the apple tree
Is as plain as plain as plain can be.

Through the rushes you can see
Ducks laying eggs just for me!

Now that spring is here
Everyone is full of good cheer.

The flowers are a wonderful sight
And the smell is a delight.

Amy Wakelam (Age 10)

Legs

I use them every day,
I like to run and play,
I like to go up stairs, down stairs,
And run in lots of races,
And go to different places,
At the end of the day,
My legs are tired and weary
So I go to bed and rest my legs
And before I know it there I lay
Ready to start a brand new day.

Kirsty Williams (Age 8)

The Nightmare

He's green and slimy
His claws are long
He is bloodthirsty for someone to
suck
His lungs are all red like blood
His eyes are gruesome green
He even eats his own flesh
Which is the colour of slimy slime
He grabbed me in his scaly hand
Everything went black

Lisa Whitbread (Age 9)

The Troll

There is a troll
Who lives in a hole
And his name is Porkypie
He is called Porkypie
'Cause he is so greedy
He is so greedy
Because he's needy
He is needy
Because he is greedy
I never got that bit!

Nicola Wilson (Age 9)

My Pride And Joy

If you was a dad it will be your joy.
To see you smile and have a child,
You will play all day long,
I don't care what it is as long a you're happy,
If it is a boy he will support West Ham,
If it is a girl she will play netball,

It will be your joy to be a mum,
Kirsten will have a lot of fun,
I don't care if you just have the one,
You will be glad to have the one,
It will be your pride and joy.

Kirsten White (Age 11)

A Bombay Night

As the mighty rays of the sun
Die down over India's gaping land,
The ant like people vanish into the silhouette
Of their ant hill;
To sleep against the darkened howling night.

As the blazing heat of the sun
Shines down again,
The city wakes ..... to see the towering structures
Scratching at the sky.

Arthur Williams (Age 10)

The Agony The Wind Can Make .....

'The Storm Cat' prowls the panicking waters,
Clawing, playing with the tumbling waves,
Turning, tumbling, crashing, cascading,
Thrashing wildly at the harbour walls.
Woman comforting children small,
Men waiting in agony for the terrifying waves
To calm down,
On the horizon,
Beyond the gloom of the raging sea,
A glimmer of light spread across the horizon,
Lighting up the grey quay.
The sun rose higher, higher,
The sky light pink, orange and purple.
Dolphins leaping in turquoise waters,
'Storm Cat' now but a tiny kitten at play,
Gently pawing the tiny shimmers on the water,
His green eyes lighting up, purring loudly,
As a friendly symbol of farewell.
Wagging his long tail,
Fading away into the brilliant horizon.

Rachel Weaver (Age 11)

Two Worlds

When I get home I go to my screen
And enter a virtual world
Of sites and bytes and disks and drives
And places I've never been
I chat to my friends on the internet
And always have lot of fun
I'm in the States and all over the place
Until I hear is your homework done?
I exit my world of virtual power
And go into my world of sweet and sour!

Simon Winter (Age 12)

Cornish Poem

Cliffs crashing
Sea waving and splashing
And soaking the earth like a flood.

Mines sliver
Mines are cold
Mines are slippery
As bright as gold.

Pasties are yummy
Pasties are crusty
Pasties are steamy
And hot

Cornish clotted cream
Is like a sandy rustle
In the sunlight.

Ben Warden (Age 10)

Seasons

In the spring new life blossoms
Flower buds open to show their beauty
Sun beams on cold shadowy places
Wildlife comes out from hibernation

The sun is shining radiantly, summer's here
Droughts emerge throughout the country
The soil is bone dry and thirsty
New grown flowers smile and spread happiness

Golden leaves rustle uncomfortably on the ground
Bare trees sway sadly in the breeze
Animals gather food to prepare for the winter
The wind howls sadly in mourning

The trees share their sorrow all freezing cold and lonely
The grass is frosty and stiff
Snow gracefully glides down
Winter slowly and bitterly drags on

Emma Weston (Age 11)

My Dad's A Referee

Every Sunday without fail,
He's out on the pitch in rain or hail
He looks so good in black and white,
Red card ready in case there's a fight!

The boys take their places and so does my dad,
But quick, lookout, there's a troublesome lad
The whistle goes to signal a foul,
Yellow card out – he's booking him now!

Still no score at the half time break,
Shooting goals is no piece of cake
Final score – 4-1 to the Reds
Dad's absolutely knackered – he's off home to his bed!

Lauren Wells (Age 10)

If I were .....

If I were a teacher,
I'd shout and scream,
If I were a teacher
I'd groan and moan,
If I were a teacher
I'd laze around all day,
I'd let them do what they want,
But I wouldn't let them out to play!
If I were a teacher
I'd sit and do nothing,
But since I'm a kid,
I'm really suffering!

Danny Washington (Age 8)

Horror

My cat wears a red hat
My dog wears a collar
My sister wears Barbie knickers
And I'm a little horror

Katherine Waldron (Age 10)

My Mate

My mate and I are quite alike.
He's short with brown hair and eyes
And likes riding his bike.
I'm tall, with brown hair and blue eyes
And like riding my bike.

My mate and I like the same sort of food.
He loves roast dinners
With gravy, veg and mash
And I don't mind the same.

My mate and I are good at sports.
It's football then basketball
Then tennis in the courts,
Netball and bowling and
Wrestling in the ring.

My mate's called Vincent
He's really great.
Although we have our differences,
Like I wake up early, he wakes up late.
We're the bestest best buddies all the same.

James West (Age 9)

War Poem

Of those who fought
Little survived
Those who died are resting

A lot of courage and bravery
Was used
Lots of mourning eyes
Hearts were breaking
As people heard the news

Four years they fought
For our country that still stands high
Not knowing when it was going to end
Scared and afraid they carried on

But now they rest with God
All their wounds healed
With all their friends they're happy
Waiting for us to join them

Hayley White (Age 12)

Summer

As hot as a heater,
Birds like brown feathers,
Yellow as a colouring pencil,
Tomatoes come ripe when the sun comes.

Paul Watkins (Age 7)

Untitled

Across my bedroom
Floor I saw my window
With rain tapping on the
Glass. I went down stairs.
I smelt bacon as soon as
I got down stairs, My mum
Was cooking bacon for breakfast.

Rebecca Williamson (Age 7)

Elephants

Elephants, elephants
I like elephants big and small.
They are very useful.
When you want an apple
They will get it for you.

Stephen Waylett (Age 6)

Wide Awake

Wide awake
Still can't sleep
Covers sticking to my feet
Doorbell rings
Kettle clicks
Taps drip, drip, drip, drip.

I can hear the television
And my grandad saying, "I think I've lost my vision!"
I hate my sister
She's asleep
Then why am I still counting sheep?

Laura Wharnsby (Age 12)

My Brother

My brother is so crazy
He likes to eat a daisy
I think he's really thick
And is as thin as a battered up stick

My brother likes his runs
And enjoys current buns
I think he's really funny
And he's got lots of money

My brother's name is Tim
And he's really dim
His girlfriend isn't nice
And she likes paradise

Mark Warden (Age 10)

Help!

Help! cried the homeless, help! help! help!
We need homes and quickly,
These people began to yelp.

Help! cried the Africans, who've caught
The famine fame.
Help! help! help!
This famine is hard to tame.

Help! cried the religious, who get persecuted,
We get killed and envied
By people who are stupid.

Help! cried a man, there's disasters in our world,
Hurricanes, fires and earthquakes
And people get killed.

We need some drastic action,
If this world is going to change.
But we can't deny, not you or I
That these happenings are strange.

Peter Wilson (Age 10)

Christmas!

Christmas is days of fun,
Buns and jellies, lots of tasty food.
Advent calendars with chocs and pictures.
Decorations brighten up the house,
A Christmas tree, branches spiky,
Tinsel and baubles are on the Christmas tree,
Also lights and little toys and sweets.
Then come the presents,
Arranged beneath the tree.
The children tear off the wrappers
While grownups open their's.
There are shouts of joy!
The children on Christmas Eve hang their stockings up.
Will Santa come?
In the morning the stockings are full.
Full of what?
PRESENTS!
Christmas is FUN!

Emily Winter (Age 8)

Mum

My mum is the sweet colour of pink,
The scent of a single rose,
And the taste of melting chocolate,
She is the sound of a bird flying softly by,
Her skin is as soft as cat's fur,
And to me she lives high up in the clouds.

Frances Watkins (Age 11)

The Alien

I once met an alien on Mars
Who said he came from distant stars
He could not sing
But ate everything
But sometimes had a problem
Digesting cars!

Martin Wilkins (Age 11)

Motorways

Motorway Motorway
Drive like mad
Up and down
Up and down
Broom broom!
Hum hum
Sing the motorway song

Lee Whitlocke (Age 9)

My Mate

My mate and I are quite alike
We both have a go at catching a pike
We both like riding our bikes
I won't yield on the football field
I'm in goal and James midfield

My mate and I are quite the same
Even though we don't have much fame
My poor mate James gets all the blame
And out of my head pops a flame

He always beats me at chess
He is just the best
My mate had a broken chair
So I moved it to be fair

Vincent Woollven (Age 10)

If You Want To See A Tiger

If you want to see a tiger you must go down to the Jerky Jungle.
I know a tiger who's living down there,
He's scary, sly, orange, small and loud!
Yes if you really want to see a tiger, you must be quiet look every second
To see if he's there and make sure to run!
Go down to the Jerky Jungle and say:
Tiger muma,
Tiger muma,
And then a bit louder   TIGER MUMA!
And he will pop out straight away.
And then run for your life!
But if the tiger follows you skip and then go side ways, left and right and
Eventually he will go away!

Charlotte Wyatt (Age 8)

In The Coldness Of Space

In the coldness of space, there you lie, the green planet.
Not green with copper rust
Or green with airborne dust
But green with life and grace.

Who would have thought
That it was covered with her
Combat and strife,
The vanquisher of life?

The greens, the browns
The lights, the sounds
All you must have heard
In the coldness of space.

Who would have thought
That it was covered in hunger
No food and no crops
Like flies life drops.

But you keep on lying patiently waiting
For more good times
A smile on your face
In the coldness of space.

Graeme Williams (Age 15)

A Winter Poem

Snow is like a
Polar bear glistening
In the sun

Frost has a touch
Of a feather floating
From the sky

Rain is like a
Pavement of water
Always floating down

Hail stones
As white as ever
Floating heavily down

Ice is cold and wet
Very slippery too
Always falling over
When I tread on you

Elizabeth Webb (Age 6)

Super Simile Poem

"I'm as fascinating as a glittering star." muttered Matthew mumbling
As he stared up at the star light sky.
"Well I'm as gentle as a drifting cloud!" chattered Charlie cheerfully.
"I'm as clever as a cheerful clown!" joked Jennifer juggling with their juggling balls.
"Im as hot as a freshly baked apple pie" piped Peter perfectly.
"My dive is as dazzling as a dolhin's flip!" Emma elegantly explained with a jump and a flip.
"I'm as black as night." whispered Willma wickedly!
"Super silly poems!" squealed shy Sarah!

Hannah Rowlings & Charlie Walker (Age 10)

There's Something In The Cupboard

There's something in the cupboard,
A monster big and blue,
As beastly as a bear,
As sticky as the strongest glue.

There's something in the cupboard,
I've seen it squash and squirt,
All filthy huge and hairy,
I know he'd really hurt!

There's something in the cupboard,
I really don't know what,
I'd like to know what it is,
But I think I'd rather not!

Stephen Witham (Age 8)

The Moon

The moon, a cold dead land.
No life, no air.
Just a freezing desert.
It shines on the river
Like a silver coin.
Lights up the night
For the wolf awakes.

Ross Waters (Age 9)

Newlyn Harbour

It was wet, cold and misty,
Boats disappear into the mist,
Seagulls twirling in the sky,
Then diving for fish and chips.
Ripples made by very strong winds,
Flags whipping in the low dull sky.
Nets and ropes tangled on boats.
Fish bubbling in the sea,
Lots of fish scattered on a box.
We come to the end of a day
At Newlyn harbour.

Charlie White (Age 10)

Footie Match

One day there was a footie match
The boys were queuing at the hatch
Suddenly the whistle blew
They had to leave their rabbit stew

They scampered out onto pitch
The goalie developed a sudden twitch
There was no time to stand and stare
The ball was flying everywhere

A foul for this a foul for that
Goalie went down with a splat!
The time went by no goals were scored
The fans were getting jolly bored

The whistle went it was the end
The fans came running round the bend
The hot dog van came into sight
The fans all needed a bit of a bite!

Laura Welch (Age 12)

India's Transport

Taxis, like lizards
Swerve in and out.
Buildings,
Their eyes watching.
Snakes,
Rattling on the train track.
Buses,
Like beetles carry people to the city.
Roads,
An everlasting, queue of vehicles – honking their horns.

Hannah Wickenden (Age 9)

Wolves

Wolves, wolves,
In your packs,
Eating sheep as little snacks.

When you come hunting,
Pigs start their grunting,
When you go by,
There's a sly look in your eye.

You hunt your prey,
At dusk of day,
Then you hit the sack,
With the rest of your pack.

Rebecca Woolacott (Age 10)

My Family

Georgi my sis at sweet sixteen,
Boys and horses she's very keen,
She talks to her bunny, it's really quite funny,
Specially when he tries to talk back.

My brother Ben, when he was ten,
Was smaller than me the size of a pea,
Now he's tall and very skinny,
He really looks like a total ninny.

My mum loves to sing when shopping,
But she makes nice cakes with creamy topping,
She has a short fuse and when it burns out,
You should hear her because she really does shout.

My dear dad's got a bit of a tum,
If I tease him about this he beats me till I'm numb,
My dad thinks he's a bit of a lad,
But my friends think he's rather sad.

Tom Wright (Age 11)

The Samanga

I am blue and red
With an orange head
And green and purple teeth

I have fearsome red eyes
With arms that can touch the skies
And bloodcurdling nails at my feet

I have blue fingers and toes
And a pink shiny nose
With green legs at the bottom of my body

Sarah Wilkinson (Age 10)

The Sun

The sun is hot and very yellow
You can have your swimming pool
Have a sunshade too
To stop you burning
Put on plenty of sun cream
You can have a barbecue too

Cory Williams (Age 7)

Patch And Homer

My cats Patch and Homer
My cats soft and sweet.
They hunt for mice and rats
And their claws are as sharp as pins.

Those playful cats are playing everywhere
As soft as they may be.
What would I do without them?
My cats are looking for me.

I love my cats whatever they do.
They are my teddy bears.
But I like them best when they're
Asleep and cuddled up in bed.

Emma Woodridge (Age 10)

Standing In A Graveyard

Standing in a graveyard.
As quiet as can be,
Graves are all around me,
Trees some with leaves,
Some without,
Leaves are on the ground,
There is only one sound,
That's me going crunch on leaves all around
There are sticks on the floor,
Headstones look like doors,
Welcoming us to the next world.

It is midday, the clock chimes twelve,
Suddenly a breeze goes past me,
Clouds get darker,
And it starts to rain,
In my leg I feel a pain,
I try to scream but,
My throat feels dry,
I can hear the rain going pitter patter,
And the wind whistling past my face.

Hayley Williams (Age 11)

Fauve's Bedroom

In her bedroom Fauve keeps....
Ten kittens made of mittens,
Nine adders that climbed up her bunk-bed ladders,
Eight cats that sat on mats,
Seven dogs made of clogs,
Six mice that threw a dice,
Five hives full of bees,
Four chickens reading Dickens,
Three claws poking out of doors,
Two kippers wearing slippers,
And....
One bear, so hugged he had no hair!

Fauve Williams (Age 10)

The Dolphin

The dolphin dashes through the sea
Like a sportscar
Its smooth, shiny skin glistens,
A newly polished sword
It jumps out of the water
Graceful as a gymnast
As clever as a computer
It cuts the water with its sleek body
Like a razor blade
Its eyes are bright lights

David Welch (Age 13)

Birds

Owls hoot
Birds sing in the sky
Birds fly
Birds tweet
Birds eating
Birds drinking
Birds stood up
Ducks dive
Three birds in a tree
Fourteen birds on a roof

Alex Williams (Age 9)

From The Depths Of My Cupboard

Come closer and I'll whisper,
Something in your naked ear,
And I'll tell you from the very start,
It fills my soul with fear,
It ruffles up the carpet.
It steals all our best shoes,
It takes things from my pocket,
Things I want to use,
I say, "Mum where are my slippers?
Mum where is my hat?"
She says, "In the cupboard darling."
And she knows I don't like that,
I know she hates to clean in there,
I know she hates the smell,
And if you come to our house,
You'll notice it as well,
I know there is a monster,
Beneath our ragged stairs,
I know it's in our cupboard,
But no-one seems to care.

Harriet Walker (Age 11)

Message In A Bottle

Hello! Who is it who finds this scrawny note,
Is it a millionaire with a sparkling yacht,
Or a fisherman with a broken down boat?
I'm stranded on an Island
Nine hundred miles from home,
I am in need of assistance,
And a mobile phone,
So whoever finds this note,
Please bring some hot food,
And a warm and comfortable boat.

Sam Waite (Age 11)

The Castle

There's a castle down the road
It's dark not scary,
Not as big as most but
Big enough for me.
At the front misty and scary.
But in the garden,
At the back
It's a fairytale land.
The trees are enormous and bloom
every year
The flowers smell like sugar.
The sun shines a wonderful
Bright yellow.
And the fruit off the bushes
Juicy and soft
I love the castle
It's my special place.

Danielle West (Age 11)

The Real Me

Strong that I am.
Short that I'm not
The physical side that I do not lack.

But I'm quite superstitious.
The things that I do well,
And the days that those things are on, I try to repeat
To try and do it well again.
I may not seem superstitious because I am popular, confident
And quite charismatic.
This is my social side of life.

The mental side of my life.
My brother thinks I am thick;
My parents think I am simple;
But they don't see my mental side of life.
I am clever when I think about it and artistic when I want to be.
Sometimes I am quite simple but I am not really thick.

Emotion is my weakness; You may not think it.
But I care about what happens to people and I am quite sensitive
But there is another side of me that is different,
I am volatile and just want to break free from behaving well.

Alistair Williams (Age 13)

What Is The Beach?

Hot and sandy
Children playing
People laughing

Swimming pools
Building castles
Making a moat

Having fun
Eating ice-creams
Chocolate, strawberry, vanilla

Sand everywhere
Between your toes
In your sandwiches

On the pier
Scary rides
Machines taking money

Tired and sweaty
Time to go home
To the caravan park

Elaine Wells (Age 11)

My Mum

My mum is a volcano
Fit to burst everywhere
She is an oven
Boiling hot
Baking lovely chips
She is snakes and ladders
Running up and down the house
With a hoover

Natasha Wiseman (Age 9)

Love

Yellow is a rose as well as a promise,
I am a girl longing for a prince
It is valentine, I have not one card yet
Please send me one or I will have no date.

Rachel Westrop (Age 11)

If I Could Be …..

If I could be thunder,
I would crash like one hundred symbols,
I would bang like one thousand drums,
I would shake like a powerful earthquake
And then wait for you to run!

Leanne Wells (Age 9)

Christmas

Crackers are bursting very loud
Mary having a baby
Happy and proud
Holly wreath on your door having fun
Angels gather around to see Jesus
Stars in the Sky
Sparkling very high
Present open escaping on the run
All the presents are having fun
Santa running by in his sleigh
Bethlehem is happy now
Because Mary had her baby Jesus
Jesus happy playing in the snow
Mary and Joseph go out to play with them

Fiona Webber (Age 8)

Playtime

Oh, what a save by Cooper boy,
But he's let it in, the other team jump for joy
Andrew's just got a yellow, now a red,
Blimey the ref's gonna be dead!
What a brill cross by Steve,
Johns slipped on a wet leaf.
What a volley by Gav, no, Dave,
Now the Law is jumping in rave.
Samuel's made a run alone,
He's lost track 'cause of an ice-cream cone.
Mark's boasting about his silky skill,
Broke teacher's specs got to pay the bill.
Tom's done an overhead kick,
He's running to the lavvy (gonna be sick).

Steven Worden (Age 10)

Mysterious Conker Tree

Hard conkers fall from the trees,
Bang smash, the sound of conkers colliding.
Shiny conkers in the sun,
Hang high above my head.
Spiky outer shell, but soft inside,
A sort of brownish red.
The amazing colours dazzle my eyes,
Quickly they tumble and land in a bundle
On the leafy floor.
The rough tree with its
High branches hold
Next year's wonderful seeds.

In the playground
My conker's a winner,
Strong and tough, hard and rigid,
The sound of smashing conkers.

Sometimes I wonder how it got its name
Horse Chestnut tree.
I wonder on, day after day.

Stephanie Wallis (Age 10)

Christmas

At Christmas it's all happy
All the decorations glowing in the dark
All the presents under the christmas tree
Father Christmas helpers loading the presents
The thing that I hate is trying to stay awake.

Daniel Wright (Age 8)

Leopard Dance

There was a little boy called Harry,
His sister was dying to marry.
So ugly was she, that he did see
Her boyfriend was a leopard dancing in harmony.

One day Leo the leopard married,
He married the sister of Harry's.
So on the honeymoon, the police did raid
The house where Harry's sister laid.

Bones on the sofa,
Bones on the floor,
Harry's sister was no more!

Melanie Westlake (Age 10)

Fear

Fear is like a spooky shadow creeping
Across your wall.

Fear is like the curtains rustling by your
Nice warm radiator.

Fear is like freezing wind blowing
On my face.

Fear is like the wind blown down
A vase of flowers.

Fear is like you standing on a cliff edge
And thunder and lightning striking
Right next to you.

Fear is like the hoot of an owl
In the pitch dark of night.

Daniel Wilson (Age 9)

Touring Cars

Touring cars are the best
Touring cars go east and west
Touring cars get so battered
Even though they get a little shattered
Touring cars go fast
When you see them they've gone past
The touring cars that are so slow
Never know where the other ones go.

Tom Watts (Age 8)

Five Years Old

In the house lived sweet Polly
She plays happily and she's like a calm sea
Then if I annoy her, you can see a storm
Brewing in her eyes.
Then she bursts!
Her eyes look like flashes of lightning which
Are very frightening.
She screams like a banshee through
The house.
Her fists come down like gigantic
Waves crashing on the shore.
If she doesn't get what she wants
Her tears turn to a monsoon.
Then she's given sweets and the storm
Subsides, and she's sunny once again.

Ben Ward (Age 10)

Listen

Listen,   to the wind, curling, swirling and gushing, through the dark, restless night
            next to the bubbling, gurgling river.

Listen,   to the hooves of horses thundering down
            the Lush, green grass of the racing track.

Listen,   to the elegant ladies chattering chirpily in cool summer dresses
            and long white gloves with hats perched jauntily on their heads.

Listen,   To the gentlemen laugh raucously as they place bets
            and smoke long, chubby cigars. Their hands clink nervously on their
            beer tankards slopping the light yellow
            liquid over the polished floor.

Listen,   to the methodical drumming of a train's wheels
            clattering along the steel rungs of the track.
            climbing a never-ending ladder, whistling
            a tune and smoking a giant cigar.

Listen,   to the silence, wrapping itself around the slumbering night,
            the restful river,
            the deserted rail track,
            the soulless bar and
            the desolate station.

Listen,   just listen …..shhhhh

Kirsty Watling (Age 11)

Orange

Orange is the fading sun telling us that
Autumn's begun
Orange is corn and wheat in the fields
Being cut for us to eat
Orange are squirrels, hedgehogs and leaves
Big brown conkers falling from the trees
Orange is bright like yellow and gold
But all of them fall to the ground
As they grow old

Dominic Warren (Age 10)

The Teabag

I'm a little teabag and stay at home all day,
And talk to other teabags in a teabag sort of way,
I like living in this box
I will never have to wash my face,
Or change my dirty socks
I would never have to do exams,
I needn't tidy rooms
Or sweep the floors or feed the cat,
Or wash the dirty spoons.

Christopher White (Age 11)

Who's By Me?

Who's by me?
Is it my friend?
Is it my brother?
Is it my sister?
Who's by me?

Is it my mum?
Is it my dad?
Is it my rats?
Is it my cat?
Who's by me?

Is it Moses?
Is it Simon Peter?
No!
Who's by me?

He made people well
Again,
Who is it?
It's ….. JESUS!

Jenna Welfare (Age 8)

When I Was Ill

When I was extremely ill in bed
The doctor came along and said

You are very, very, very ill
And each and every night to take a pill.

It felt like a monster in my throat
Half a horse and half a goat.

Then I felt tremendously sneezy
Working up to be very queasy.

After that I was really hot,
Then I came out in many a spot.

Next I caught the dreadful flu
And my skin turned black and blue.

My head was ringing like a bell
But all of a sudden I felt quite well.

My aches and pains have gone away
So now I'm going out to play.

Kit Wingfield (Age 8)

Sunrise

The ominous blackness of night is beginning to lift
And a bleak grey starts to take its place.
Soon, a hint of orange peeps up from under the distant horizon.
This orange becomes brighter and brighter
Until streaks of colour are painted all over the sky.
More and more of these beautiful rays appear
And the dew-covered grass of the awakening world is illuminated by this
Radiance
Now, the sleepy sun itself is creeping up into the sky
Adding to the amazing tapestry of light.
Birds sing their joyous songs
And dogs yap their praise to the spectacular, fiery sun.
Cockerels crow and milk bottles chink on doorsteps.
People stir from their peaceful slumbers
And ready themselves for the day ahead
And thus, once again, the breathtaking natural masterpiece of sunrise
Is born.

Alex Worthington (Age 12)

Dinosaur

Who's that knocking
At my door?
Can it be a dinosaur.

Dinosaurs are huge and grand
Leaving footprints
All over the land.

As big as any thing
They can be
I hope he isn't out for me.

I hope he isn't looking out
For juicy
Children lying about

Or nosing around to find a treat
Of pickled humans
Which are nice to eat.

I hope he hasn't come to stay
Oh dinosaur
Please go away.

Luke Webber (Age 9)

Graveyards On The Fields Of France

At first it seemed
It was meant to be,
The glory, the glamour, the fame,
But then we saw
The horror of war
By then it was too late.

We saw, what was the horror of war
Men dying from fire and flame,
Men slaughtered in droves, like lamb and sheep
The disease, the sorrow, the shame.

And now I lie in a pool of blood
Discarded like a broken doll,
I followed my orders
Not waiting to think
And how I paid the price.
For I am dead, for the sake of a yard
In the graveyards of the fields of France.

Damian Webb (Age 14)

The Bully

B uts in everything.

U nbearable to shout at you if there's a teacher.

L aughing at you for no reason at all.

L ying to you so you will get into trouble.

Y elling at you because he don't like you.

Victoria Whyman (Age 12)

The Computer

The computer groans at me when I turn him on,
His eyes flash when I load him up
He runs on electricity, it flows through his body,
He twinkles with power, feel him vibrate,
He's absolutely GREAT!

He's sometimes my friend,
But he drives me round the bend!

Willie Aspinall (Age 10) **Lucy Wait** (Age 11)

236

The Mysterious Dance

I'm walking silently across the lawn,
I'm walking silently until the dawn,
I'm running across the grainy sands,
I'm running to the strangest lands.

I'm shouting to the gods above,
I'm shouting to the one I love,
I'm talking to my wonderful friends,
I'm talking to the time that never ends.

Hear me now I've done my dance,
Let it work with just a chance.
The ground rumbled with a terrible roar,
Lights sprang out with magic galore,
I jumped back as scared as ever,
A lady came out with hair like heather,
I wish for this, I wish for that,
Then suddenly she turned into a bat,
A puff of smoke, a ring of cloud,
With big surprise I whirl around,
My wishes have come true with a leap and a bound.

Lauren Wills (Age 12)

Christmas Sonnet

The snow that lay upon the frozen ground,
With trees that bear no life but worn old bark,
Small rabbits bounce about the snowy mound,
December's chill with winds so cold and dark,

The robins call like joy and life entwined,
His fresh sweet sound rang through the crisp still air,
With mistletoe and kisses two combined,
Make Christmas time so special, green and bare,

Like satisfaction of a morning gay,
With Carols old and new to sing with me,
The joyous sounds of happiness each day,
Are shared alike throughout the world we see,

With Christmas time comes happiness for all,
When cold winds blow and drifts of snow do fall.

Laura Warren (Age 14)

The Olden Days

Across my bedroom floor
I saw my window with rain
Tapping against the glass
It is as cold as icicles
I have got to go in the cold
It is snowing outside
I have to go to work
In the farm with the animals

Haylee Walker (Age 8)

All Five Senses

My Eyes are like marbles
Our ears feel like circles around each other
Under the nose my tongue feels like a wet dog's nose
The nose looks like a button
Hands feel bumpy in places

All my five senses are fantastic
And I don't know how I would
Write this poem without them!

Kate Wright (Age 8)

The Silent Silhouette

As my cat sits upon the windowsill,
She stares up at the bright full moon,
It is calling to her,
She wants to go -
To be wild once more,
To feel the cool night air,
To play with the fallen leaves,
And to paw at the soft earth.
Her eyes are quick as she watches imaginary prey.
But as I stroke her back,
She awakes from her dreams,
She knows she cannot go.
So she turns, jumps down,
And curls up in front of the warm fire.

Susannah Wingent (Age 13)

The Golden Eagle

His beak is yellow and curved,
His feathers are shiny and golden,
His eyes are bright and looking,
He lives in a nest on the cliff top.
He can see everything.
He swoops down like a big black shadow
Looking for something to eat.
He sees a river with lots of salmon in
He uses his sharp claws to catch one.
Then he flies back to his nest on the rocks.
He shares the salmon with his chicks
And his mate.
Then he's off flying again.

Reuben Woolacott (Age 8)

Space Story

Woke up
Bright beams
All I wanted to do was scream.

Frozen stiff
From space?
What could be inside that place?

Door creaks open
Wow that's bright!
That definitely gave me a terrible fright!

Glance at the clock
Half past one!
I'm not having that much fun.

Close my eyes
Please go away!
Why don't you come back some other day?

Open my eyes
Please please please
Wow it's been covered with a pile of leaves!

Emma Wheat (Age 9)

Bobbly Belly

Bobboly Belly Babbaly Bubbuly Blobboly Blabbaly Blob
The Belly blew from Blobboly Blab to Blobboly Blabbaly Hill
Blobboly Belly from Blobboly Blibbily Blob
Said Blibbily Blobboly Blib
Belly bounced from Blabbaly Hill to Blonstonvil
I never liked Blobboly Belly from Blobboly Blabbaly Hill

Thomas Waefler (Age 10)

Forget-Me-Not

I saw your smile so warm, so sweet, so coy,
Your eyes were diamonds sparkling out to me,
Your laughter filled the room with sun and joy,
Your hair in waves of curls just like the sea.

You took my hand to dance the night away,
Our bodies touched you felt so safe and strong,
We danced like birds so smoothly glide all day.
Your kiss was like a dream so smooth and long.

I know I love you greater every day,
I'll love you till the day that I do die,
I hope you love me too, I wish you'd say
You love me, making sure it's not a lie.

Our love is like a flower that grows forever,
I know, my love that we will stay together.

Marie-Louise Watson (Age 13)

The Army Man

I feel sorry for my mates who died
I felt lonely, I felt sad in the War

But ......
Whoopee! I'm going home!

I want to get back
To help my dad
I have missed
Playing games with my family
I have missed
My sister's friendly face
She always helped me
When I was a little boy

Will they know me now?
I've grown
My voice is deeper
My hair is very short
I am in army clothes
Am I the same boy
Who went away?

I am a man now

Scott Ward (Age 10)

Greek Stew

There once was a young Greek who knew
How to make a wonderful stew
He sat down one night and had such a fright
For his stew was too hard to chew

Harriet Williams (Age 10)

About Me

I have got a dog that has not got any fluff
I've got a mate called Sam
I've got a dog that stinks when he does a guff
Who likes ham
I have got a mini
I've got a dad
And my mum does not wear a pini!
And he is never bad
My brother is skinny
And sometimes he is sad
My brother is so tiny
But sometimes he is glad
And he is always whiney
And my dad is a big lad

Darren Wade (Age 10)

Listen

Can you hear the beating of a swan's
Flapping wings as it meanders through
The white fluffy clouds?

Can you hear the panting of the ants
Breath after a hard days work?

Can you hear the footsteps of a dancing
Bee as his feet meet the veins of a
Fresh strong leaf?

Can you hear the tiny insects chuckling
Where to go in a game of hide and seek?

Can you hear the butterflies hum as
They jump about the blossoming bush?

Can you hear the clattering of a lion's teeth
Meeting after a nice tasty zebra?

Heidi Woodcock (Age 9)

Memories

My bedroom lends me memories
From all around my life
I've never liked to leave it
As it is all warm and wonderful
I've always liked to sleep in it
But never liked to cry in it
It is my favourite part of life

Eleanor Williams (Age 8)

Me

Me
My head is like a heart

Me
My hair is like smooth Sunny Delight

Me
My feet are like a chocolate bar

Me
My legs are like wooden sticks

Me
My fingers are like chopsticks

Me
My arms are like lots of sausages

Me
My chin is like a baby's bottom

Neil West (Age 11)

Storm

Attacking the amazed
Intoxicating intensity
Bewildering beast
Tearing from all trees
Gushing gusto
Stupendous speed
Whirling all over the compass
Curdling the curious
Devastating demon
Portraying power
Punishing all who oppose
Endless energy
Furious ferociousness
Demolishing houses
Jagged jaws
Kindling killing
Hunting the homeless

Peter Wilkinson (Age 10)

Tornado

The great gambling beast
Hunting danger
Rapidly chasing its destiny
Capturing
Grasping life's joy
Rebuffing everything
That stands in its way
Constantly sphering its eye
Repeating monstrous howls
A huge overpowering creature
Lurking around any unsuspecting corner.

Faye White (Age 10)

The Beginning Of The End?

The light flickered,
The immense cracks on the ceiling were revealed,
She looked around her bleak and mournful flat.
"Its time to leave."
Her murmurs echoed around the room.

As she wandered into the kitchen,
The petrifying sounds of sirens were acknowledged in her busy mind,
The police were drawing near.
Hysteria rose in the young girl's eyes,
As the cruel demons knocked on the door.

She picked up a knife,
Chilled by the night's atmosphere,
The weapon sparkled in the moonlight.
She swept the instrument across her wrist.

A flow of blood cascaded to the ground,
The room swirled around her,
She screamed in stunned silence,
As she plunged to the floor.

Lucy Webb (Age 14)

War's Hell

Wounded or gassed the men lay,
In the maze of trenches throughout that horrific day,
To them war was still just a game
But to Mr McDoom to kill was his aim.

Out of their dens the young soldiers appear
Equipped with rifle, tools kept near
Bang Bang Bang Bang!
Hunched as they fell the shotguns rang.

The barbed wire and tangle of trenches,
Just waiting for people to go to the benches
More people for the game,
And new general but same aim.

Going over the last hill,
No-one else to kill
At last no more of that smell,
War's Hell.

Vicky Webber (Age 14)

Caterpillar Caterpillar

Caterpillar caterpillar, what is your name?
Caterpillar answered, "My name is Jane."
Caterpillar caterpillar what have you here?
"I have a baby brother isn't it a dear?"

Bethany Welch (Age 8)

Stars

The bright shining stars in the dark
Dark sky at night
Are shining lightly down on us,
They give us light to help us see
And the moon does too
The moon and stars are up there
With the planets shining
Twenty-four hours a day
Day after day
Week after week
Year after year
Century after century
The stars are always up there

The big bright stars
Flying through the air
His legs pointing down at all
The other shining stars

Sarah White (Age 10)

Bub (A Bubble)

Magically born of a wand
Bub swiftly danced in his marble coat.
"I am a wonder!" cried Bub.
"The worst," called Bob.
Bub didn't care

Joyful as could be
But knowing death would come
Bub didn't care.

Bub became heavy,
Slowly dipped down.
Bub didn't care.

Blown by a wizard
Who caused his magic birth,
Bub started to fall
Once again
Bub didn't care.

His watery bones withered
"What am I?" whispered the bones
"What am I?"

Nicholas Ward (Age 10)

The Big Bird

I saw a big, big bird
They say it's called an aeroplane.
Whoosh, swish, gliding smoothly across
The clear blue sky.
How can they tell me that it's that weird name?
How can they say it's an aeroplane?
But even though they say it is
I still think it's a big, big bird.

Samuel Warne (Age 9

Cats

Cats spend their lives dozing
Stretched out in front of the log fire
Or legs folded away and tail tucked under
Or curled up like a doughnut
On the window ledge

Phillipa Waldron (Age 8)

All Around Us

Trees and flowers begin to grow
My Dad's growing a big marrow
Birds and animals begin to cheep
While the holiday train goes peep
Snowdrops, crocus and daffodils
Cats are sitting on window sills

Georgia Zervudachi (Age 6½)

Emotional Earth

Rain is an emotion.
Happy and playful,
Dancing to its own composition.

Wind is an emotion.
Restless and disagreeable,
Bored by trivial leaves.

Snow is an emotion.
Cold and envious,
Bitter with a long held grudge.

Sun is an emotion.
Loving and eager,
Warming the skies and the soil.

Hail is an emotion
Violent and angry,
Launching projectiles in a raging tantrum.

Amanda Weeks (Age 18)

There's A Monster Under My Bed

There's a monster under my bed!
There's a monster under my bed!
And if I go to sleep tonight it will come up
And bite off my head.
Ragghhh!
I went to sleep one night and awoke
With a terrible fright!
There's a monster under my bed!
There's a monster under my bed!
Ragghhh!

Jack Wellens (Age 9)

The Beginning Of The Day

The beginning of the day starts with sunrise,
When the Goddess sun climbs up the sky,
Spreading her beautiful rays.
The light shines on the jewels of the spiders web,
Mist removes her dangerous coat from the ground.
The milk cart rolls down the road
And makes for home.
It is then the people come out of their holes,
Ready to do their daily duties.
Once these are completed they return to their dens,
And it is then the beginning of the end commences.
Sun slowly climbs down leaving only Moon,
The Sergeant, and the stars, his soldiers,
To do their duty and guard the earth,
And wait for the Goddess to return.

Hannah Young (Age 14)

Football's Coming Home

Fowler and Owen are taking centre
Off they go at Anfield
Oh dear Owen has scored
Tottenham are one nil down
But Tottenham are on the attack
And Tottenham shoot hoo ow
Liverpool are hanging on to this one nil lead
Lots of red shirts running around
Still hanging on
Cheurons on the ball
Oh dear Owen has been fouled
Michael Owen is taking a penalty
It's a goal
Now Tottenham has got to score
Get in there, they shoot
Day Tottenham could still be in this match
Michael Thomas is ashamed of himself
End of match they say

Samuel Worden (Age 10)

The Haunted House

The school is an old place at night
It is creepy and lots of things happen in the giant school
It looks almost like a grave
At night it is haunted and sometimes the windows open
It is dark and spooky
The moon sets over the school
The school has steps that go like a slide
It has doors which have snakes on
And the doors are made out of slime
It has windows like spiders webs
And glass like leopard skin
It is a creepy place to go
If the doors open it will take out ghosts
Which have the most

Ben Yeo (Age 10)

Yellow

Dogs and cats
Fishes in tanks
Rabbits and birds
Budgies that chirp

These are the pets
At Badshot Lea
This is what you'll see

Yellow Class (Age 6 and 7)

BIOGRAPHIES
OF
POETS

ABBOTT, ROBERT JOHN: [b] 25/05/88 Luton; [home] Luton, Beds; [p] Martin and Fiona; [brothers] Barnaby, George and Trevor; [school] Crabtree Junior; [fav subject] Science; [hobbies] Skating, football; [pets] Tarantula;

ADAMS, LUKE: [b] 15/02/89 Reading; [home] Newbury, Berkshire; [p] Carol and Robin ; [brother] Jason; [sister] Kirsty; [school] St. Martin's CE Primary; [fav subject] Science and Creative Writing; [hobbies] Skating, swimming; [pets] Dog, cat and hamster; [ambition] To become a Fireman;

ADAMS, NICOLA: [b] 04/04/87 Essex; [home] Canvey, Essex; [p] Carol and Paul; [sister] Louise; [school] Cornelius Vermuyden; [fav subject] English; [hobbies] Dancing; [pets] Fish; [ambitions] To become an Actress or a Writer;

ALLEN, BEN: [b] 26/06/89, Chelmsford; [home] Danbury, Essex; [p] Mrs H Allen and Mr J Allen.; [sister] Charlotte; [school] Danbury Park; [fav subject] Art; [hobbies] Collecting anything to do with Beano; [pets] Dogs; [ambitions]; To become a Doctor or Science Teacher;

ALLEN, KATIE: [b] 05/10/90 Oxford; [home] Oxford; [p] Shirley and Garry; [brother] Sam; [school] Windmill First; [fav subject] History; [hobbies] Drawing and collecting Beanie Babies; [pets] Cat (Minty); [ambition] To become a Detective;

ALLEN, SAMANTHA JADE: [b] 01/01/84 Sasolburg, S. Africa; [home] Woolvington, Somerset; [p] Jacqueline Anne and Rowland John; [brothers] Benjamin Austin; [school] Haygrove; [fav subject] Art and English; [hobbies] Music (especially rock and metal), painting, drawing and poetry; [ambitions] To become a decent Politician or a Rock Drummer;

ANDERSON, LEE JOHN: [b] 19/07/87 Rochford; [home] Canvey Island, Essex; [p] Christopher and Joanne; [brother] Charlie; [sisters] Jade and Jody; [school] Cornelius Vermuyden; [fav subject] P.E.; [hobbies] Tennis and Boats; [pets] Dog, parrot, cat and gerbils; [ambitions] To become a better Poet and get a good job;

ANDREWS, NICHOLAS: [b] 12/01/88 Plymouth; [home] South Brent, Devon; [p] Ian and Jacqui; [brother] James; [school] South Brent Primary; [fav subject] Maths and Art; [hobbies] Football; [ambition] To play football for England in a World Cup;

ARMSTRONG, INEZ: [b] 05/09/91 Glasgow; [home] Chalfont St. Giles, Bucks; [brother] Alasdair; [sister] Imogen; [school] Chalfont St. Giles First; [fav subject] Art and swimming; [hobbies] Piano, guitar, reading and playing outside; [pets] My little brother!; [ambition] To be an Artist;

ASHFORD, SAMANTHA ROANNE: [b] 16/05/88 Winchester; [home] Eastleigh, Hants; [p] Joanne and David; [sisters] Amber and Chloe; [school] The Crescent Primary; [fav subject] Music; [hobbies] Swimming; [pets] Fish; [ambition] To become a Fashion Designer;

ASHMEAD, KIMBERLEY: [b] 12/04/90 Aylesbury; [home] Aylesbury, Bucks; [p] Becky and Simon; [brother] Jack; [school] William Harding Middle; [fav subject] History; [hobbies] Reading; [pets] Cat and hamster; [ambition] To do very well at school;

ATKINSON, KATE: [b] 06/07/90 Warrington; [home] Danbury, Essex; [p] Jan and Ian; [brother] Steven; [school] Danbury Park Primary [fav subject] English; [hobbies] Horse riding and swimming; [pets] Rabbit and guinea pig; [ambition] To be a Primary School Teacher;

AYERS, BECKY: [b] 09/10/87 Hereford; [home] Bicester, Oxon; [p] Peter and chris [brother] Mark; [school] Southwold; [fav subject] English; [hobbies] Karate and swimming; [pets] Dog called Rolo; [ambition] To be a Newspaper Reporter;

BABBAGE, MELANIE TERESA: [b] 04/11/89 Truro; [home] Breage, Helston, Cornwall; [p] Kenneth and Teresa: [brothers] William John: [school] Breage C of E. U.A. School; [fav subject] Art: [hobbies] Art, cooking, reading: [pets] Cats, rabbits; [ambitions] To become an Artist or Hairdresser;

BAKER, MARTIN WILLIAM: [b] 02/07/84 Winchester; [home] Romsey, Hampshire; [p] Stephen and Susan; [brothers] Christian and Adrian; [school] The Mountbatten School; [fav subject] Drama: [hobbies] Air Cadet (ATC); [ambition] Learn to fly:

BALL, DAVID: [b] 25/11/84 Newport, Isle of Wight; [home] West Wellow, Hants; [p] David and Theresa Ball; [brother] Graeme; [sister] Lesley; [school] The Mountbatten School; [fav subject] Geography; [hobbies] Cycling; [pets] Cat (Kitty); [ambitions] To become a member of the Legal profession;

BAMBER, CHRISTOPHER JAMES: [b] 23/06/87 Oxford; [home] Drayton, Banbury; [p] Christopher and Deborah; [brother] Philip; [sister] Claire; [school] The Warriner School; [fav subject] English; [hobbies] Sports, drawing and modelling; [ambition] To become a Marine Biologist;

BARKER, BENJAMIN: [b] 10/03/88 Truro; [home] Roche, Cornwall; [p] Michael and Mandy; [sister] Jamie; [school] Roche County Primary; [fav subject] Maths and Poetry; [hobbies] Grasstrack racing; [pets] 4 dogs, (Jake, Pebbles, Ronnie & Reggie); [ambitions] To become a Speedway Rider and Lorry Driver;

BARRETT, KATIE ELIZABETH: [b] 25/05/87 Southend; [home] Hullbridge, Essex; [p] Debbie & Neil; [brothers] Michael, Thomas; [sister] Danielle; [school] Sweyne Park; [fav subject] English; [hobbies] Horseriding, swimming; [pets] Dog (Timber), Horse (Chucky), cat and hamster; [ambition] To become a Journalist;

BARTER, EDMUND: [b] 17/02/90 Winchester; [home] Andover, Hants; [p] Kevin and Ann; [brother] Roland; [sister] Rowena; [school] Longparish; [fav subject] PE and Games; [hobbies] Playing football and watching TV; [pets] Goldfish;

BARTLETT, EMMA [b] 14/01/90 Ashford; [home] Pimperne, Dorset; [p] Jean and Tony; [sister] Clare; [school] Pimperne; [fav subject] Maths and writing; [hobbies] Cycle riding; [pets] Cat, rabbit, guinea pig, rat and hamster; [ambition] To become a Vet;

BASHAM, VICTORIA: [b] 28/05/89 Coventry; [home] Kingswood, Gloucester; [p] Elly and Hugh; [brother] Oliver; [school] Kingswood County Primary; [fav subject] English; [hobbies] Horse riding, music, netball, cross country; [pets] Cat (Vivienne) and dog (Basil); [ambitions] To become a Vet or a Novelist;

BATES, MATTHEW DAVID: [b] 21/11/88 Ashford, Middlesex; [home] Chard, Somerset; [p] Edward and Susan; [brothers] Michael and Christopher; [sister] Emma; [school] Buckland St. Mary; [fav subject] Maths; [hobbies] Fishing, football, hockey; [pets] Guinea pig, dog and hamster; [ambitions] To become a Policeman or Shop Owner;

BECKWITH, HARRIET LOUISE: [b] 29/10/90 Colchester; [home] Manningtree, Essex; [p] Paul and Nicola; [sister] Laura; [school] Lawford C of E Primary School; [fav subject] Art, History and PE; [hobbies] Dancing, walking, collecting pencil leads and beanie babies; [pets] Rabbit, guinea pigs and fish; [ambitions] To become an Author/animator or Archaeologist;

BEECROFT, SOPHIE ANNE: [b] 20/10/87 Taunton; [home] Otterford, Somerset; [p] Tina Gibbins and Brian Beecroft (Deceased); [brother] Lee; [sister] Laura; [school] Buckland St. Mary; [fav subject] English; [hobbies] Music; [pets] Dog (Megan); [ambition] To continue to be happy;

BEEDIE, LUCY: [b] 03/11/85 Rochford; [home] Canvey Island, Essex; [p] Sally and Richard; [sisters] Danielle, Fay and Jenny; [school] Cornelius Vermuyden; [fav subject] English and Art; [hobbies] Football, swimming; [pets] Dog (Toby) Rabbit (Daisy) Hamster (Stuffie) Guinea pigs (Nancy, Pansy, Mary and Joseph) Hedgehogs (Snoockems and Snuffles); [ambitions] To publish my own book and become a famous journalist;

BENNETT, PETER JOE: [b] 17/11/92 Plymouth; [home] Brentor, Tavistock, Devon; [p] Raymond and Nicola; [sisters] Zoë Elizabeth Jane and Katy Sylvia; [school] St. Rumon's; [fav subject] Creative Writing; [hobbies] Bird Watching, Drawing; [pets] Cat (Badger); [ambitions] To be a Naturalist and travel the world;

BERRINGTON, KATIE: [b] 03/04/91 Oxford; [home] Oxford, Oxfordshire; [p] Karen and Andy; [brother] Tom; [sisters] Emily and Amy; [school] Windmill First School; [fav subject] Science, Maths; [hobbies] Reading and Beanie Babies; [pets] A rabbit (Daisy) and a cat (Jayne); [ambition] To write a book;

BETTIS, CHARLENE LOUISE: [b] 05/01/89 Dagenham, Essex; [home] Ilfracombe, Devon; [p] Janice and Robert; [brother] James; [sister] Chelsea; [school] Ilfracombe C of E Junior School; [fav subject] Art; [hobbies] Playing piano, dancing and swiming; [pets] Hamster (Fluffy); [ambitions] To become a Pianist, Dancer or Singer;

BETTIS, JAMES ROBERT: [b] 01/10/91 Barnstaple; [home] Ilfracombe, Devon; [p]

Janice and Robert; [sisters] Charlene and Chelsea; [school] Ilfracombe County Infants; [fav subject] Art; [hobbies] Rock climbing, collecting bugs and insects; [pets] Rat (Gnasher); [ambition] Would like to become an Artist;

BETTS, CHRISTINA ELAINE: [b] 06/11/90 Oxford; [home] Shabbington, Bucks; [p] Roger and Gillian; [school] Long Crendon County; [fav subject] Art; [hobbies] Bike riding, kite flying and reading; [ambitions] To grow up a happy and kind person;

BIDDLECOMBE, SARAH: [b] 15/10/88 Leamington Spa, Warks. [home] Danbury, Essex; [p] Jenny and Ian; [brother] Adam; [sisters] Laura, Hannah; [school] Danbury Park County Primary School; [fav subject] Art, English and Drama; [hobbies] Drawing and writing; [pets] Hamster (Pickles); [ambitions] To become a Poet, Author, Artist or Pop Star;

BLADES, PHOEBE: [b] 31/05/88 Devon; [home] South Brent, Devon; [p] Sally and Roger; [sisters] Emily and Hetty; [school] South Brent Primary; [fav subject] Drama; [hobbies] Drama and reading; [pets] 2 cats; [ambitions] To become a famous Actress and win an Oscar;

BLOMFIELD, LAUREN: [b] 02/04/92 Watford; [home] Watford, Herts; [p] MaryDee Blomfield; [school] Parkgate Infants; [fav subject] P.E.; [hobbies] Bike riding; [pets] Snakes; [ambition] to become a Policewoman;

BOLLEN, MELISSA: [b] 16/11/87 Whipps Cross Hospital; [home] Buckhurst Hill, Essex; [p] Pam and Brian; [brother] Matthew; [school] Buckhurst Hill County Primary; [fav subject] English, art and maths; [hobbies] Reading, netball; [pets] Lacross, Rugby and shopping; [ambition] To become a Teacher;

BOND, MICHAEL: [b] 31/03/87 Canada; [home] Aylesbury, Bucks; [p] Robert and Elizabeth; [sister] Sarah; [school] St. Edwards R.C.; [fav subject] History; [hobbies] Warhammer models; [ambitions] To become a Pilot or Doctor;

BOSWELL, JAMES: [b] 26/07/86 Basingstoke; [home] North Baddesley, Hampsire; [p] Philip and Michelle; [sister] Christen; [school] Mountbatten; [hobbies] Swimming, rock climbing; [pets] Dog, rabbit, guinea pig and goldfish; [ambition] To become a Pilot;

BOUCHER, SAMANTHA: [b] 12/07/92 Gloucester; [p] Theresa and Peter; [sister] Kelly; [school] Robinswood Primary; [fav subject] Maths; [hobbies] Swimming and roller skating; [pets] Dog; [ambition] To become a Policewoman;

BRACE-DAY ZOË: [b] 17/07/87 England; [home] High Wych, Herts; [p] Carol and John; [brothers] Alan, Jay, Jamie; [sisters] Kelly and

Astra; [school] High Wych JMI; [fav subject] Art and Science; [hobbies] Swimming, tennis and violin; [pets] 5 dogs, 7 cats, 2 hamsters, rabbit and guinea pig; [ambition] To work in a Zoo;

BRACKPOOL, SARAH: [b] 08/09/84 Kingston, Surrey; [home] North Baddesley, Hants; [p] Christina and Phillip; [brother] Jonathan; [school] The Mountbatten School; [fav subject] English; [hobbies] Collecting Beanie Babies; [pets] 2 Siamese cats, 1 rabbit and 2 guinea pigs; [ambition] To swim with dolphins;

BRADLEY, ROSEANE: [b] 22/08/88 Chelmsford; [home] Chemsford, Essex; [p] Robert and France; [sister] Verity; [school] Perryfields Junior; [fav subject] English and PE; [hobbies] Reading/ and swimming;; [pets] Dog (Brutus) and hamster (Soda); [ambition] to be a Journalist;

BRIDLE, RACHEL: [b] 25/02/90 Brighton; [home] Eastleigh, Hampshire; [p] Barrie and Tracy; [sister] Amie; [school] Crescent Primary; [fav subject] History; [hobbies] Glass painting; [pets] Cat (Pebbles); [ambitions] To be an Author and to draw and to be happy!;

BRITTAIN, HOLLY: [b] 03/07/90 Treliske Hospital; [home] Breage, Cornwall; [p] Donna and Graham; [brother] Ben; [school] Breage C E VA School; [fav subject] English and Art; [hobbies] Learning to play the piano, ballet, gymnastics, cycling, reading, writing and poetry; [ambition] To be successful;

BROCON, ALEX: [b] 07/05/83 Plymouth; [home] Bude, Cornwall; [p] Ann and Steve; [sister] Hannah; [school] Budehaven Community School; [fav subject] English and geography; [hobbies] Rugby, fishing and swimming; [pets] Max;

BROMILOW, EDWARD: [b] 12/01/89 Exeter; [home] Exbourne, Devon; [p] Dr. John and Gilly; [sister] Kathryn; [school] Exbourne C of E Primary School; [fav subject] English; [hobbies] Playing chess and warhammer; [pets] Dog (Daisy) and cat (Tabitha); [ambitions] Design PC games, work at Games workshop;

BROUSSINE, CERI: [b] 28/12/88; [home] Kingswood, Gloucestershire; [p] Eric and Viola; [brother] Callum; [school] Kingswood County Primary; [fav subject] English; [hobbies] Cycling, swimming and collecting; [pets] Dog (Frodo) and corn snake (Sydney); [ambitions] to be a Vet or work with animals;

BROWN, CAROLINE JENNIFER: [b] 22/01/88 Plymouth; [home] South Brent, Devon; [p] Veronica and Peter; [sister] Michelle; [school] South Brent Primary School: [fav subject] I.T.; [hobbies] Cornet, badminton; [pets] Previously a cat; [ambition] to become an RSPCA rescue person;

BROWN, KIERA-MARIE: [b] 05/10/91

Portsmouth; [home] Waterlooville, Hampshire; [p] Anne-Marie; [school] Meadowlands Infant; [fav subject] Art; [hobbies] PE, writing and drawing; [pets] Cat; [ambition] To become a Vet;

BROWN, ROBERT: [b] 30/06/88 Welwyn Garden City; [home] Stapleford, Herts; [p] Andrew and Sharon; [brother] Daniel; [school] Stapleford JMI; [fav subject] Technology; [hobbies] Football, reading; [ambition] to be an Astronaut;

BROWN, SAMUEL: [b] 18/10/91 N.D.D.H.; [home] Ilfracombe, North Devon; [p] Lisa and Ray; [sisters] Leah, Elisha, Chantelle; [school] Ilfracombe Infants School; [fav subject] English; [hobbies] Football and swimming; [ambitions] Football player and to write stories;

BRUNSDON, CHLOË MELISSA: [b] 01/03/91 Reading; [home] Reading, Berkshire; [p] Melanie and Ian; [brother] Bradley; [sister] Melissa; [school] Katesgrove Primary; [fav subject] Maths and art; [hobbies] Ballet and modern dancing; [pets] Rabbit and goldfish; [ambition] To be famous;

BRYAN, GEORGIA ANNICE: 20/08/87 Exeter; [home] Exmouth, Devon; [p] Cynthia and Alan; [brother] Danny; [sisters] Alice and Aimee; [school] The Kings School O.S.M.; [fav subject] English, Tech.; [hobbies] Singing and shopping; [pets] 3 cats, cackateil and a fish; [ambitions] to become a Singer and live to be 100 years old;

BUNTON, EMMA-LOUISE: [b] 30/01/91 Swindon; [home] Cirencester, Glos.; [p] Andrew and Loraine; [brothers] Phillip and James; [school] Watermoor School; [fav subject] Maths and art; [hobbies] Play acting and swimming; [pets] 2 cats and 2 fish; [ambition] To become a Teacher;

BUFORD, KYLE: [b] 12/12/86 Gloucester; [home] Lydney, Glos; [p] Debi; [school] Whitecross; [fav subject] Maths and Science; [hobbies] Music, Playstation and volunteer on Steam Railway; [pets] Cat (Jake) and Hamster (Caramel); [ambition] To be a TV Presnter on children's television;

BURLEY, PHILIP: [b] 28/09/87 Truro; [home] St. Day, Cornwall; [p] Sally and Dave; [brothers] Stephen and Christopher; [school] St. Day and Carharrack Community School; [fav subject] History; [hobbies] Swimming, dancing, music; [pets] Bess (collie) and Honey (pony); [ambition] To be an Author;

BURLTON, TOM: [b] 30/03/90 Dorchester, Dorset; [home] Blandford, Dorset; [p] Dr. and Mrs. D. Burlton; [brothers] James, Ben and Sam; [sisters] Emma, (Rebecca - died in November 1998 aged 23); [school] Pimperne First School; [fav subject] Technology; [hobbies] Reading, cricket, chess, snooker, football, rugby and tennis; [ambition] To become a professional football player;

BURTON, PHILIP: [b] 20/01/89 Yeovil; [home] Milborne Port Nr. Sherborne, Dorset; [p] Jan and Adrian; [sister] Shelly; [school] Milborne Port County Primary; [fav subject] Maths; [hobbies] Rugby, swimming, cricket, football, chess and TV; [pets] Splash and Bubbles (cats) Cocky (bird); [ambitions] To play professional sport;

CAMPBELL, SERENA SKOV: [b] 15/12/88 Edinburgh; [home] Amersham, Bucks; [p] Kirsten and Ken; [brother] Samuel; [sister] Alexina; [school] Elangeni; [fav subject] Creative writing; [hobbies] dancing [pets] Rabbit (Cinders) and cat (Lucky); [ambition] To become a Pop Star;

CANDY, EMMA LOUISE: [b] 10/06/86 Salisbury; [home] Ebbesbourne Wake, Wilts; [p] Ian and Julie; [sister] Samantha; [school] King Alfreds; [fav subject] Science, design, art; [hobbies] Horse riding and swimming; [pets] Dogs, rabbits. cat. horses etc.; [ambition] To work with animals possibly;

CANHAM, MICHELLE: [b] 01/05/87 Basildon; [home] Canvey Island, Essex; [p] Donna and Alan; [brother] Tommy; [sister] Claire; [school] Cornelius Vermuyden; [fav subject] English; [hobbies] Sport - Majorettes; [pets] Fish, birds and a hamster; [ambition] To be an Infant School Teacher;

CARMICHAEL, CHRISTINA: [b] 06/07/91 London: [school] Windmill First School; [fav subject] Maths; [hobbies] Writing; [pets] Squirrel in garden; [ambitions] To become a Model, Actress or Teacher;

CARTER, JENNY: [b] 08/11/90 Yeovil; [home] Milborne Port, Somerset; [p] Richard and Sandy; [sisters] Sarah and Sophie; [school] Milborne Port County Primary; [fav subject] English and Art; [hobbies] Horse riding, reading, playing outside; [pets] Cat called Domino; [ambition] To become a Teacher;

CATTERMOUSE, RACHEL: [b] 06/10/87 Winchester; [home] Ashmansworth, Hampshire; [p] Nicholas and Judith; [sister] Claire; [school] St. Martins C.E. Aided Primary; [fav subject] Music; [hobbies] Flute and recorder (tenor); [pets] Dog (Polly) cat (Boots);

CAUCHIOS, LEON: [b] 06/06/86 Exeter; [home] Bradninch, Devon; [p] Jackie and Nigel; [brother] Jobo; [sister] Vicky; [school] Cullompton Community College; [fav subject] English, art and drama; [hobbies] Computer games, warhammer; [pets] Dog (Chas), cat (Sylvester), hamster (Wicket), guinea pig (Amy); [ambition] To become a Writer;

CHAPMAN, CHRISTOPHER: [b] 05/11/89 Reading; [home] Oxford, Oxfordshire; [p] Sharon and Lee Cole; [school] Windmill First School; [fav subject] Maths; [hobbies] Swimming and cricket;

CHARLTON, LUCY: [b] 03/04/92 Redhill; [home] Reigate, Surrey; [p] Martin and Carol; [brother] Matthew; [sister] Chloe; [school] Reigate Parish Church; [fav subject] Poetry; [hobbies] Ballet, modern dancing, swimming and brownies; [pets] Hamster named Bambi; [ambition] To become a Vet;

CHAY, CLARISSA STEPHANIE: [b] 02/04/93 Reigate; [home] Reigate, Surrey; [p] Geoff and Tania; [brothers] Darren, Kris and Philip; [sister] Abbie-Louise; [school] Reigate Parish Church School; [fav subject] Maths and IT; [hobbies] Bike riding and skipping; [pets] Furby; [ambition] To become a Vet;

CHELACHE, LAITH: [b] 01/03/88 Abu Dhabi, U.A.E.; [home] Harpenden, Herts; [p] Marilyn and Sameer; [sister] Hana; [school] Crabtree J.M. School; [fav subject] Technology; [hobbies] Computer games and tennis; [pets] Hamster (Anazoic) and guinea pig (Fluffy); [ambitions] To go to Antartica and to design computer games;

CHESTNUTT, ADAM: [b] 27/09/90 Dorset; [home] Yeovil, Somerset; [p] John and Wendy; [brother] David; [school] All Saints C.E.V.A. Primary; [fav subject] Maths; [hobbies] Football, playing on the computer; [ambition] To become a Policeman;

CHORLEY, TRACEY: [b] 25/07/85 [home] Bridgwater, Somerset; [sister] Emma; [school] East Bridgwater; [hobbies] Netball and any sport, plus watching Spurs; (The poem submitted was written whilst at Musgrove Park Hospital school during chemotherapy treatment for cancer);

CHURCHILL, KATIE MARIE: [b] 07/11/89 Winchester Hospital; [home] Bullington, Hants; [p] Carole and Andy; [brother] Thomas; [sisters] Amy and Kimberley; [school] Longparish (C of E) Primary; [fav subject] Maths and English; [hobbies] Bike riding, colouring; [ambitions] To do well at school and work with horses;

CLARKE, ALAN: [b] 20/05/88 Bury St. Edmunds; [home] Micheldever, Hampshire; [p] Judy and John; [brother] Ian; [school] Micheldever Primary School; [fav subject] Maths; [hobbies] Football, cricket and cooking; [ambitions] Inventor or professional cricketer;

CLARKE, ANDREW: [b] 29/10/87 Oxford; [home] Ducklington, Oxon.; [p] Paul and Linda; [sister] Emma; [school] Ducklington C.e. Primary; [fav subject] English; [hobbies] Tennis, table-tennis and fishing; [pets] "Squeak" the guinea pig; [ambition] to become a Pilot;

CLEEVE, CHRISTOPHER JOHN: [b] 18/02/89 St. Mary's Hospital; [home] Stubbington, Hampshire; [p] Stephen and Julie; [brother] Michael; [school] Crofton Anne Dale Junior; [fav subject] Mathematics; [hobbies] Football and scalextric; [pets] Cat

(Oliver); [ambitions] Live in a big house and earn a lot of money;

CLEWLEY, GARY: [b] 01/07/87 Aldershot; [home] Ash, Hants; [p] Tim and Glen; [brother] Dean; [school] Ash Manor; [fav subject] D.T. [hobbies] Computers, films and hockey; [pets] German Shephard)Roxy); [ambition] To become an RAF Pilot;

COCKETT, CHLOË [b] 19/03/86 Rochford; [home] Leigh-on-Sea, Essex; [p] Sue and Gary; [brother] Robert; [school] Sweyne Park; [fav subject] English; [hobbies] Reading, writing, sports and meeting with my friends; [ambition] To get lots of books published, the first before I am 20 and to become a Lawyer;

COGGINS, ARABELLA: [b] 06/06/93 Winchester; [home] Thruxton, Hants; [p] Samantha and Stephen; [brothers] Ben and Daniel; [school] Longparish; [fav subject] Maths; [hobbies] Ballet, gym and swimming; [pets] Cat and fish; [ambition] To become a Singer;

COGGINS, BEN: [b] 08/12/90 Winchester; [home] Thruxton, Hants; [p] Stephen and Samantha; [brother] Daniel; [sister] Arabella; [school] Longparish; [fav subject] Games; [hobbies] Playing and gymnastics; [pets] Cat and fish; [ambitions] Astronaut, Space expert;

COLE, LLOYD: [b] 19/07/89 Plymouth; [home] Liskeard, Cornwall; [p] Fiona and Martyn; [sister] Catherine; [school] St. Martins; [fav subject] English; [hobbies] Football and cricket; [pets] Cat (Lucy); [ambitions] To play football for Manchester United;

COLEMAN, LAURI ANNE: [b] 21/06/86 Southampton; [home] Shaftesbury, Dorset; [p] Sue and Steve; [sister] Sam; [school] King Alfreds Middle; [fav subject] English and geography; [hobbies] Swimmimg, drawing and music; [pets] 1 dog, 2 cats and 4 rabbits; [ambition] To travel the world;

COLLIGAN, ALICE: [12/06/91 Olney, Buckinghamshire; [home] Latchley, Cornwall; [p] Michele and Brian; [brother] Matthew age 4; [school] Culworthy Country Primary; [fav subject] English, in particular writing; [hobbies] Swimming, ballet and recorder; [pets] Tabby cat (Cherry); [ambition] To become an Author;

COLLINS, JENNIFER MARY: [b] 25/01/89 Chelmsford, Essex; [home] Beaconsfield, Bucks; [p] Julie and Keith; [brother] Alexander; [sister] Catherine; [school] Butlers Court Combined School; [fav subject] Maths and English; [hobbies] Flute, ballet, art and cycling; [pets] Rabbit; [ambitions] To become an Actress or Writer;

COLLINS, ROSIE: [b] 10/08/89 High Wycombe; [home] Amersham, Bucks; [p] Debbie and John; [brothers] Joe and Jacob; [school] Elangeni School; [fav subject] Art

and craft; [hobbies] All sports; [pets] Hamster (Poppy) and a goldfish; [ambition] To become a Vet;

CONNELL, BEN: [b] 12/04/85 Plymouth; [home] Southampton, Hampshire; [school] The Mountbatten School; [fav subject] Drama; [pets] 1 rabbit and 1 fish;

COOK, NICOLA: [b] 24/05/92 Watford; [home] Watford, Herts; [p] Tony and Gill; [sisters] Gemma and Lindsay; [school] Parkgate; [fav subject] Writing; [hobbies] Disco dancing; [pets] Cat named Jet;

COOK, REBECCA: [b] 15/09/86 Aldershot; [home] Aldershot, Hants; [p] Josie and Charles; [sisters] Sarah and Rachel; [school] Ash Manor; [fav subject] History and art; [hobbies] Swimming and horse riding; [pets] Snake and a hamster; [ambition] To become a Diver and dive with dolphins and whales;

COPPACK, AISHA K.: [b] 20/09/90 Chelmsford; [home] Roxwell, Essex; [p] Hina and Richard; [brother] Jack; [school] Roxwell C of E; [fav subject] Art; [hobbies] Computer games and recorder; [ambition] I would like to be an Author;

COY, JADE: [b] 28/11/89 Royal Berks Hospital; [home] Reading, Berks; [p] Amanda and Richard; [brother] Declan; [school] Katesgrove Primary; [fav subject] Mathematics; [hobbies] Football and swimming; [pets] Cats; [ambition] To be a Vet;

CRAVEN, JAMES: [b] 04/03/84 Essex; [home] Canvey Island, Essex; [p] Ann and Graeme; [sisters] Nicola and Samantha; [school] Cornelius Vermuyden; [fav subject] Sport; [hobbies] West Ham FC; [pets] Dog (Gizmo); [ambition] To be successful;

CRESSWELL, STEPHANIE: [b] 23 August Southampton; [home] North Baddesley, Hampshire; [p] Jo and Richard; [sisters] Natalie and Jennifer; [school] Mountbatten; [fav subject] Physical Education; [hobbies] Cycling and reading; [pets] Cat (Jasmine) [ambition] To go to America;

CULLUM, BECKY: [b] 15/05/90 Hampshire; [home] Basingstoke Hants; [p] Val and Phil; [brother] Thomas; [sister] Kristy; [school] Worting Junior School; [fav subject] Art; [hobbies] Irish dancing; [pets] Cat and fish; [ambition] To become an Animal trainer;

CUNNINGHAM, FRANCES CORA: [b] 17/04/90; [home] Mistley, Essex; [p] Philip and Caroline; [brother] Raymond; [sister] Tabytha; [school] Lanford C of E Primary; [fav subject] Art; [hobbies] Singing and dancing; [pets] 2 cats, 2 mice - Leah and Jasmine;

CURNOW, BEN: [b] 20/10/90 Truro;

[home] Gwinear, Cornwall; [p] Alison and Kelvin; [brother] Matthew; [school] Gwinear C.P.; [fav subject] Art; [hobbies] Swimming and fishing; [ambition] To be a Train Driver;

DACRES, CHRISTIAN: [b] 05/06/92 Watford; [home] Watford, Herts; [p] Emsley and Jacqueline; [brother] Alexander (9 years); [school] Parkgate Infants School; [fav subject] English; [hobbies] Collecting bottle tops and ballet; [ambitions] To be a famous Poet and a Ballet Dancer;

DALE, LAURA ELLEN: [b] 05/01/89 Tanton; [home] Taunton, Somerset; [p] Jim and Rachel; [brother] Jack; [sister] Eilish Anne; [school] St. Georges; [fav subject] English; [hobbies] Cycling, arts, crafts; [ambition] To write a book;

DALE, REBECCA: [b] 04/09/90 Harrow, Middlesex; [home] Croxley Green, Herts; [p] Julie and Peter; [sisters] Lauren and Alice; [school] Harvey Road School; [fav subject] Art; [hobbies] Gymnastics, dancing and swimming; [pets] 2 guinea pigs, Chocolate and Cream; [ambitions] To become a Nurse or Doctor;

DARLING, JAMES: [b] 28/02/89 Barnstaple; [home] Marwood, North Devon; [p] Sarah and Kevin; [brothers] Thomas, Michael and Henry; [sister] Cordelia; [school] Marwood C. Primary; [fav subject] Hand writing; [hobbies] Football and hockey; [pets] Guinea pig; [ambition] To join the R.A.F.;

DART, NICHOLAS: [b] 02/08/91 Portsmouth; [home] Coverack, Cornwall; [p] Deryl and Jeremy; [brother] Major Jonathan Dart; [sister] Philippa Woodruff; [school] Grade Ruan V.C. School; [fav subject] Science; [hobbies] Computer games, reading Dandy and Beano; [pets] Dog called Freud; [ambition] To go to another Country;

DAVIES, CHARLOTTE: [b] 26/07/88 Blackpool; [home] Roche,Cornwall; [p] Wendy and John; [brothers] Marcus and Martin; [sisters] Tracy, Lea-Anne and Stephanie; [school] Roche C.P. School; [fav subject] Art and English; [hobbies] Reading and recorder; [pets] Tropical fish; [ambition] To be a Musician;

DAVIES, MARTIN: [b] 26/03/87 Rochford; [home] Canvey Island, Essex; [p] Janice] [sister] Carrie; [school] Cornelius Vermuyden; [fav subject] History; [hobbies] Basketball and playstation; [pets] 2 cats (Meg and Kizzy); [ambition] To be a Chef and own a big red sports sar;

DAVIES, MEGAN BETH: [b] 16/01/90 Brighton; [home] Great Milton, Oxfordshire; [p] Roger and Vivien; [brother] William; [school] Great Milton C of E School; [fav subject] Maths; [hobbies] Poetry and drawing; [pets] Cat and hamster; [ambition] To become a Vet;

DAVIS, FREDDIE: [b] 09/11/88 Oxford; [home] Harwell, Oxford; [p] Fran and Lewie; [brother] Danny; [sisters] Kimberley and Charlotte; [school] Harwell CP School; [fav subject] Art and Maths; [hobbies] Basketball, moto-x and BMX cycling; [pets] Fish and stick insects; [ambitions] To be a Police Officer and a motorcycle road racer;

DAW, RYAN: [b] 24/10/87 Plymouth; [home] South Brent, Devon; [p] Lynne and Martin; [sister] Kerry; [school] South Brent Primary; [fav subject] Art and computers; [hobbies] Swimming and farming; [pets] Tropical fish and a dog; [ambition] To be the best I can;

DAWES, RICKY: [b] 14/04/87 London; [home] Woodhall Farm, Herts; [p] Mel (Mother) [brothers] Dean, Billy, Karl, Jamey, Chevy, Levi and Dion; [sisters] Tammy and Dinah; [school] Astley Cooper; [fav subject] Art; [hobbies] Ti-Ashe-Do; [pets] Rabbits, fish and a hamster; [ambition] To become a Fireman;

DEAN, RHIANNON: [b] 21/05/89 St. John's Hospital, Chelmsford; [home] Chelmsford, Essex; [p] Melanie and John; [brother] Robert; [school] Perryfields Junior; [fav subject] Art, Music and English; [hobbies] Netball, reading, and drawing; [pets] Hamster (Biscuit) and guinea pigs (Tofee & Rosie); [ambitions] To work with small children and to go to California;

DEANE, CRAIG: [b] 1987 Rochford; [home] Canvey Island, Essex; [p] Liz and Mark; [school] Cornelius Vermuyden; [fav subject] Art; [hobbies] Football, basket ball and rugby; [pets] Dog, bird, rat and a lizard; [ambitions] To go to Egypt and to be an Artist;

DEGREGORIO, CARLO: [b] 19/08/85 Bridgwater; [home] Bridgwater, Somerset; [p] Julie and Luigi; [brother] Enzo; [sister] Danielle; [school] Haygrove; [fav subject] Art; [hobbies] Drawing and playing on N64; [pets] Hamster (Matilda); [ambition] To work for the Ministry of Defence as a Naval Architect;

DELLER-VAUGHAN, NAOMI: [b] 26/10/88 Hitchin; [home] Pirton, Herts; [p] Ruth and Stephen, Pater (step dad); [sister] Rebekah; [school] Pirton J.M.I.; [fav subject] Creative writing and design tech; [hobbies] Reading, swimming, cycling and drawing; [pets] Chester - cat, Dusk - Lab and Moss - Springer; [ambitions] To become a Chef;

DEVLIN, GEMMA: [b] 12/06/93 Farnborough; [home] Farnborough, Hants; [p] Brendan and Michele; [brother] Sean; [sister] Rosie; [school] Farnborough Grange Infants; [fav subject] Reading; [hobbies] Rainbows and swimming; [pets] Cat (Charley) [ambition] To be a Vet;

DEWAN, ROBY: [b] 26/11/89 Luton, Beds; [home] Headington, Oxon; [p] Fokhrul I.; [brother] Rahat; [sister] Fahiza I.; [school]

Windmill First School; [fav subject] Poetry; [hobbies] Football and badminton; [pets] cat; [ambitions] Professional footballer or a Ddoctor;

DEWAR, HEATHER: [b] 17/09/92 Virginia; [home] Maidens, U.S.A.; [p] Bob and Linda; [sisters] Meg and Mckenzie; [school] Chalfont St. Giles 1st School; [fav subject] Maths; [hobbies] Gymnastic, outdoor games; [pets] Labrador;

DONEGAN, AMY: [b] 26/08/92 Brighton; [home] Marlow, Bucks; [p] Peter and Marie; [brothers] Alistair and Callum; [sister] Lizzie; [school] Marlow C of E First School; [fav subject] Maths; [hobbies] Swimming and reading; [pets] Oscar my puppy; [ambition] Learn how to ride horses;

DOUGLAS, MELODY JADE: [b] 14/09/89 Plymouth; [home] Ivybridge, Devon; [p] Neil and Sophie; [brothers] Adam Geoffrey and Harry Richard; [school] Stowford Primary; [fav subject] English; [hobbies] Loves gymnastics and is currently the Ivybridge Carnival Queen; [pets] Bubbles the budgie;

DRISCOLL, THOMAS: [b] 12/10/91 Frimley; [home] Wiveliscombe, Somerset; [p] Martin and Lin; [sisters] Abigail and Aimee; [school] Wiveliscombe County Primary; [fav subject] Maths; [hobbies] Beavers and riding my bike; [pets] 2 cats, 2 fish and 3 spiders; [ambition] To work with computers;

DRURY, HARRISON: [b] 25/07/91 Chichester; [home] Longparish, Hampshire; [p] Nick and Laura; [brother] Lucas; [school] Longparish; [fav subject] Sport and maths; [hobbies] Football; [pets] Hamster - Munch; [ambitions] To be a famous Footballer or a Stuntman;

DUFF, KIERAN: [b] 05/03/88 Luton & Dunstable Hospital; [home] Pirton, Herts; [p] Graham and Elizabeth; [brother] Luke; [school] Pirton School; [fav subject] Technology; [hobbies] Football, swimming, cricket and reading; [pets] 2 Gerbils (Gobi and Sylvester); [ambition] To be a great footballer;

DUGGAN, DANNY: [b] 14/06/87 Aylesbury; [home] Aylesbury, Bucks; [p] Ray and Richard; [school] St. Edwards R.C. School; [fav subject] Information Technology; [hobbies] Football, Playstation and reading; [ambition] To become a Football Commentator and write poetry;

DUNDON, MARIA: [b] 30/12/84 [home] Southampton. Hants; [school] Mountbatten School, Romsey;

EASTWELL-KNIGHT: [b] 12/12/88 Plymouth, Devon; [home] Bicester, Oxfordshire; [school] Brookside Primary; [fav subject] English;

EDEN-ELLIS, ROSIE: [b] 16/06/88 Camberley; [home] Camberley, Surrey; [p]

Linda (mother); [sister] Freya; [school] Connaught Junior; [fav subject] English; [hobbies] Drama and singing; [pets] Henrietta the cat; [ambition] To become an Actress;

EDDY, ROBERT: [b] 09/06/88 Truro; [home] Penzance, Cornwall; [p] Elizabeth Clegg and Howard Eddy; [brother] George; [school] St. Mary's R.C.; [fav subject] Maths; [hobbies] Cricket, table tennis; [pets] Two dogs, ferret and bird; [ambition] To become a professional Cricketer;

EDWARDS, ASHLEY: [b] 04/10/87 Oxford; [home] Ducklington, Oxfordshire; [p] Bev and Dean; [school] Ducklington; [fav subject] Tech.; [hobbies] Football, tennis and basket ball; [pets] Cat, rabbit and guinea pig;

ELDER, JAKE: [b] 05/12/86 Rochford, Essex; [home] Canvey Island, Essex; [p] Julie and Jim; [sister] Sophie; [school] Cornelius Vermuyden; [fav subject] Maths; [hobbies] Rugby, football, reading and IT; [pets] Dog (Chloe); [ambition] To be a Lawyer;

ELLIOTT, NICHOLAS: [b] 08/07/88 Guildford; [home] Lindford, Hampshire; [p] Jane and John; [brother] Christopher; [school] St. Peters; [fav subject] History and English; [hobbies] Computer and bikes;

EVANS, ALAN: [b] 30/04/88 Reading; [home] Reading, Berkshire; [p] Susan Herd; [school] Holy Brook; [fav subject] Maths; [hobbies] Swimming and cycling; [pets] Hamster;

EVANS, LAURA: [b] 03/12/87 Treliske; [home] Carharrack, Cornwall; [p] Dale and Andrea; [sister] Melanie; [school] St. Day; [fav subject] Art; [hobbies] Taekwon-do and netball; [pets] Two dogs and two fish; [ambition] Hairdresser;

EVERETT, HANNAH: [b] Whitehaven; [home] Milborne Port, Dorset; [p] Kevin and Sue; [sister] Beckie; [school] Milborne Port County Primary; [fav subject] P.E.; [hobbies] Swimming, running and football; [pets] Guinea pig, cat and a rabbit; {ambition} To sky dive and do a bungee jump;

EXLEY, VICKY: [b] 26/01/91 England; [home] Gunnislake, Cornwall; [p] Sue and Martin; [brothers] Matthew and Tim; [school] Gulworthy CP School; [fav subject] English , "Spellaway"; [hobbies] Drama and poetry; [pets] Speed the hamster and Dumpling the goldfish; [ambition] To become a Poet;

FARNWORTH, LAUREN JADE: [b] 24/12/90 St. Johns Hospital; [home] Chelmsford, Essex; [p] Russell and Tina; [brother] Michael; [school] Perryfield Junior; [fav subject] English and P.E.; [hobbies] Swimming and drawing; [ambition] To be a Vet;

FELL, HANNAH: [b] 15/07/88 Yeovil; [home] Milborne Port, Somerset [p] Andrew;

[brother] Oliver; [sister] Laura; [school] Milborne Port County Primary; [fav subject] English; [hobbies] Acting, dance and singing; [pets] Goldfish; [ambitions] To become an Actress, Dancer or Singer;

FELL, OLIVER: [b] 16/05/92 Yeovil; [home] Milborne Port, Somerset; [p] Andrew; [sisters] Hannah and Laura; [school] Milborne Port County Primary; [fav subject] Maths; [hobbies] Tennis and chess; [pets] Goldfish; [ambition] To be a Tennis Player;

FIELD, JASMINE JANET: [b] 05/09/91 Redhill; [home] Waltham Cross, Herts; [p] Susan and Stewart; [brother] William; [sister] Fern; [school] Waltham Holy Cross; [fav subject] Reading and swimming; [pets] Dog (Butch) 2 cats (Tiggie and Scattie); [ambitions] To be a Hairdresser or work with animals;

FINCH, LOUISE: [b] 19/12/85 Slough; [home] Coleford, Glos; [p] Lesa and Ray; [brothers] Mark, Karl and Aaron; [school] Dene Magna; [fav subject] Technology; [hobbies] Horse riding; [pets] 2 dogs; [ambitions] Own my own horse and become a Teacher;

FISHER, ZOE: [b] 12/10/87 Torbay; [home] Buckfastleigh, Devon; [p] Geoff and Angela; [brother] Christopher; [sister] Rebecca; [school] South Brent Primary; [fav subject] English; [hobbies] Badminton and swimming; [pets] Cats, rabbits and guinea pigs; [ambition] To see the Band (Steps) in concert;

FITZGERALD, RHYS: [b] Rochford; [home] Canvey Island, Essex; [sisters] Cara and Erica; [school] Cornelius Vermuyden; [fav subject] P.E.; [hobbies] Sport and computer games; [pets] Rabbit (Wemblie); [ambition] To be a professional sportsman;

FLYNN, STEVEN: [b] 18/05/88 Winchester; [home] Eastleigh, Hants; [p] Kevin and Elaine; [sister] Sophie; [school] The Crescent School; [fav subject] English; [hobbies] Sport, music and reading; [pets] Dog, cat, hamsters, birds and fish; [ambition] To become a famous Footballer;

FOAD, AIMEE: [b] 01/10/84 Princess Anne Hospital; [home] Southampton, Hants; [p] Kevin and Cindy; [sisters] Holly and Paris; [school] Mountbatten; [fav subject] Geography; [hobbies] Swimming and talking; [pets] Cat; [ambitions] To become a famous Fashion Designer and do a bungee jump;

FOORD, GREGORY: [b] 17/02/92 High Wycombe; [home] Chalfont St. Giles, Bucks; [p] Maria and Steve; [sister] Emma; [school] Chalfont St. Giles First; [fav subject] Science; [hobbies] Beavers, swimming, guitar and short tennis; [ambition] To become a Pilot;

FORCE, LAURA: [b] 03/10/83 Rochford Hospital; [home] Hullbridge, Essex; [p] Sue and Ray; [sisters] Sally and Katie; [school]

Sweyne Park; [fav subject] History; [hobbies] Dancing and reading; [pets] 1 dog and 3 cats; [ambition] To travel around America and Africa;

FORD, ELIZABETH ANN: [b] 13/12/83 Taunton; [home] Bridgwater, Somerset; [p] Maurice and Frances; [sister] Sarah Marie; [school] Haygrove; [fav subject] Art; [hobbies] Reading, shopping and playing music; [ambitions] To achieve good grades and to fulfil all my dreams;

FOSTER, CHRISTOPHER: [b] 30/11/83 Beverley, E. Yorks. [home] North Baddesley, Hants; [p] David and Julia; [brother] Andrew; [school] The Mountbatten School; [fav subject] Music; [hobbies] Clarinet, badminton and swimming; [pets] Fish and 2 gerbils; [ambitions] To have a song published and obtain a degree;

FOSTER, HANNAH: [b] 31/05/90 Yeovil; [home] Tintinhull, Somerset; [p] Caroline and Andy; [brother] Tom; [school] St. Margarets C.E.V.A.; [fav subject] Poetry; [hobbies] Horse riding [pets] Cat (May) goldfish (Sunny and Sandie); [ambition] To be a Jockey;

FOULCHER, THOMAS: [b] 12/07/88 Portsmouth; [home] Steep, Hampshire; [p] Linda and Kevin; [brother] Nicholas; [school] Steep Primary; [fav subject] Science; [hobbies] Scouts and flying kites; [pets] Guinea Pig; [ambition] To write more poetry;

FRANCIS, MICHAEL R.K.: [b] 17/05/88 Truro; [home] Roche, Cornwall; [p] Melroy and Jane; [school] Roche C.P.; [fav subject] Mathmatics; [hobbies] My ponies and football; [pets] Ponies and a dog; [ambition] To own a business;

FREEMAN, KAYA CHANI: [b] 02/12/84 Devon; [home] Braunton, Devon; [brother] Timmy; [sister] Naomi; [school] Braunton School; [fav subject] Art; [hobbies] Art, yoga and computer games; [pets] Dog (Sam); [ambitions] To go to as many music festivals as possible, try lots of new things and learn to play the guitar;

FROUD, CHRISTOPHER STUART: [b] 23/10/91 Guildford; [home] Gulworthy, Devon; [p] Carolyn and Roger; [school] St. Rumons Infant School; [fav subject] P.E.; [hobbies] Tennis and horse riding; [pets] Pony, cat and a hamster; [ambition] To be a Detective;

FULLER, BETHANY CLAIRE: [b] 12/08/89 High Wycombe; [home] Amersham, Bucks; [p] Marcus and Barbara; [sisters] Jessica and Rebecca; [school] Elangeni Middle School; [fav subject] Art and craft; [hobbies] Ballet, piano, flute and short tennis; [pets] Hamster (Poppy); [ambition] To work with animals;

GADD, EMILY: [b] 19/09/91; [home]

Tolland, Somerset; [p] Andrew and Serena; [brother] Adam; [sister] Kirsty; [school] Wiveliscombe Primary; [fav subject] Art, maths and writing; [hobbies] Horse riding and swimming; [pets] Rabbit (Meg) dog (Luigi); [ambition] To become a Vet;

GALEA, CHARLENE: [b] 26/04/87 London; [home] Rayleigh, Essex; [p] Ruth and Tony; [brothers] Terry, Marc and Craig; [sisters] Harriet and Michaela; [school] Sweyne Park; [fav subject] Drama; [hobbies] Art, reading and playing the saxophone; [pets] Cat; [ambition] To swim with Dolphins;

GALLEY, EMMA: [b] 19/04/91 Welwyn Garden City; [home] Croxley Green, Herts; [p] Pat and Andre; [brother] James; [school] Harvey Road; [fav subject] Art and drama; [hobbies] Bike riding, tennis and country dancing; [pets] 2 rabbits (Flopsy and Mopsy);

GARDNER, JESSICA ELIZABETH: [b] 06/12/87 Musgrove Park Hospital, Taunton; [home] Taunton, Somerset; [p] Stephen and Angela; [brother] Samuel; [sisters] Emma, Anna and Laura; [school] Trinity C.E.V.A. Primary; [fav subject] English; [hobbies] Netball and bowling; [pets] Dog (Rocky) 2 cats (Tom and Jerry); [ambitions] To become a P.E. Teacher or Nurse;

GOBEY-THOMAS, EMRYS: [b] 17/06/92 London; [home] Penwithick, Cornwall; [p] Everett and Clare; [sister] Maya; [school] Carclaze Infant School; [fav subject] Art; [hobbies] Bike riding and football; [pets] Cats (Pepper and Tea); [ambition] To be a Designer;

GODFREY, GEMMA: [b] 09/09/83 Boston, Lincs; [home] North Baddesley, Hants; [p] Stephen and Bev.; [sister] Amy; [school] The Mountbatten School; [fav subject] Religious Studies; [hobbies] Athletics, piano and badminton; [ambition] to be a successful Doctor;

GOODACRE, LUCY: [b] 25/06/87 Redditch, Worcs.; [home] Hempton, Oxon; [p] Judith and John; [school] Warriner School; [fav subject] French; [hobbies] Winnie-the-pooh and Titanic; [pets] Rabbit (Petrie); [ambition] To dance in shows and on stage;

GOODAY, JOSHUA: [b] 16/08/90 Maldon, Essex; [home] Danbury, Essex; [p] Richard and Cheryl; [brother] Samuel; [school] Danbury Park Primary; [fav subject] English; [hobbies] Swimming and writing; [pets] Dog; [ambition] To become a Zoo Keeper working with the animals;

GOODCHILD, KAY: [b] 28/11/85 London; [home] Hullbridge, Essex; [p] 'H' and Dianne; [brother] Jake; [sister] Clare; [school] The Sweyne Park School; [fav subject] Art and music; [hobbies] Walking and talking; [pets] Cat (Joint) [ambitions] To become a Lawyer and English Teacher;

GOODSHIP, EMMA: [b] 19/07/89 Lister Hospital, Stevenage; [home] Pirton, Herts; [p] David and Mary; [brother] Adam; [school] Pirton School; [fav subject] Reading, writing, baking and riding my bike; [pets] Used to have a rabbit called Honey; [ambitions] Undecided at present;

GORDON, DAVID: [b] 24/01/82 Guildford; [home] Feniton, Devon; [p] Robert and Penelope; [brother] Matthew; [sister] Madeleine; [school] Kings School; [fav subject] Art and sport; [hobbies] Drumming and playing the saxophone; [pets] Guinea pigs; [ambitions] To become a professional drummer in a Band and to climb Mount Snowdon;

GORRINGE-STONE, KAI: [b] 27/05/88 Devon; [home] South Brent, Devon; [p] Marianne Stone and David Gorringe; [school] South Brent Primary; [fav subject] Science; [hobbies] Judo, making things and nature; [ambition] To become a Vet and work with endangered species;

GOWER, KERRY LOUISE: [b] 20/07/88 Yeovil; [home] Yeovil, Somerset; [p] David and Alexandra; [school] St. Margarets; [fav subject] Art, science and maths; [hobbies] Swimming and athletics; [pets] Dog (Barney and a hamster; [ambitions] To be a Sports Coach or a Teacher;

GRAHAM, CHARLES THOMAS: [b] 29/03/90 Basingstoke; [home] Forton, Hants; [p] David and Brigitte; [sisters] Katharine, Alice and Jessica; [school] Longparish; [fav subject] Literacy; [hobbies] Football, dinosaurs and outdoors; [pets] Dogs, chickens, ducks and geese; [ambitions] Footballing and Archaeology;

GRATTON, SAM: [b] 31/12/87 NDD Hospital; [home] Barnstaple, N. Devon; [p] Peter; [brother] Christopher; [school] Ashleigh Primary; [fav subject] Design Technology; [hobbies] Sport, football and swimming;

GREEN, JENELLE-LEVI: [b] 23/07/89 Barnsley; [home] Taunton, Somerset; [p] Lorna and David; [sisters] Tara and Alanna; [school] St. Georges R.C. Primary; [fav subject] Science, English and P.E.; [hobbies] Netball and Gymnastics; [pets] Bubbles the rabbit; [ambition] To be on TV;

GREEN, STACY-JANE: [b] 21/07/88 Trelisk Hospital; [home] Truro, Cornwall; [p] Maureen and Kevin; [brother] Dean age 13; [sisters] Sophie and Sammy, Twins age 7; [school] Treyew C.P. School; [fav subject] Art; [hobbies] Football and netball; [pets] Dog (Misty) [ambition] To be a Chef;

GREENWAY, TONI: [b] 15/06/84 Guildford; [home] Ash, Hampshire; [p] Glenn and Lynda; [sisters] Hayley (17) and Lisa (12); [school] Ash Manor School; [fav subject] English and Maths; [hobbies] Reading, playing tennis and generally socialising; [ambitions] To do a parachute jump, ride in a helicopter, go to College and University and become a Primary School Teacher;

GRIFFITHS, MARK JAMES: [b] 28/05/82 Hemel Hempstead Herts.; [p] Jim and Sylvia; [brother] Paul; [sister] Jodie; [schoold] Astley Cooper; [fav subject] English literature; [hobbies] Sports, chess etc. [pets] My brother; [ambitions] To watch Arsenal do the double again;

GUGLIELMI, ANNA ROSE; [b] 19/09/88 Colchester; [home] Colchester, Essex; [p] Carlo and Lynda; [brothers] Thomas and Joseph; [school] Lawford C of E Primary; [fav subject] Drama and English; [hobbies] Dancing and clothes; [pets] Sawdust my hamster; [ambition] To become an Author;

GUZIK, ZOÉ: [b] 12/08/90 Aylesbury; [home] Aylesbury, Bucks; [p] Tom and Sara; [sister] Amy; [school] William Harding Middle School; [fav subject] Maths; [hobbies] Listening to music; [ambitions] To visit the Millenium Dome;

GWILLIAM, CHRISTOPHER: [b] 25/09/85 Gloucester; [home] Lydney, Gloucestershire; [p] Mr. and Mrs. Ian Brunsdon; [brothers] Adam and Oliver; [school] Whitecross in Lydney; [fav subject] English; [hobbies] Football; [pets] Rabbit called "Bunny"; [ambitions] Firefighter or Airforce Engineer;

GYGER, HOLLY: [b] 29/06/88 Exeter; [home] Plymtree, Devon; [p] amanda and Philip; [sisters] Isobel and Sophia; [school] Plymtree Church of England; [fav subject] Design and Technology; [hobbies] Roller blading and designing clothes; [pets] Cat; [ambitions] Go to University and become successful as a Clothes Designer;

HACKETT, JAKE: [b] 09/07/92 Harrow; [home] Watford, Herts; [p] Johanna and Nick; [brother] Sam; [school] Parkgate Infants; [fav subject] Writing poetry and stories; [hobbies] Playing football and drawing; [pets] Molly the dog; [ambitions] Fireman or Footballer;

HADDOCK, JASON: [b] 06/08/87 Royal Gloucestershire Hospital; [home] Lydney, Glos; [p] dRosemary and Andrew; [brother] Joshua; [sister] Sophie; [school] Whitecross school; [fav subject] Science; [hobbies] Swimming, cycling; [pets] A dog called "Sandie"; [ambitions] A career in the Army;

HALL, JOSH: [b] 22/10/87 London; [home] Witney, Oxon.; [p] Lucy and Simon; [brothers] Sam and Harry; [school] Ducklington; [fav subject] English; [hobbies] Football; [ambitions] Lawyer partnership with best friend Luke Goggins;

HALL, LEONI: [b] 24/07/88 Truro; [home] Penzance, Cornwall; [p] Sharon; [sister] Lowenna; [school] Heamoor C.P.; [fav subject] Art, maths and english; [hobbies] Ballet, flute and recorder; [pets] 2 guinea pigs, 4 rabbits and 7 fish; [ambitions] Police lady and do one really good piece of art;

HALL, NICHOLAS: [b] 06/05/88 Luton; [home] Harpenden, Herts; [p] Simon and Michele; [brothers] Daniel and James; [school] Crabtree Junior School; [fav subject] Maths; [hobbies] Football and kit making; [ambition] To become a Civil Engineer;

HALL, PHILIP W.: [b] 06/07/89 High Wycombe; [home] Beaconsfield, Bucks; [p] Philippa; [brother] Cameron; [school] Butlers Court School; [fav subject] Maths and english; [hobbies] Football and playing my play station; [ambition] To play professional football for Manchester United;

HALPIN, GENEVIEVE: [b] 10/08/92 Rochford; [home] Ashingdon, Essex; [p] Dominic and Denice; [brother] Christopher; [school] Holt Farm Infants; [fav subject] English; [hobbies] Drawing, animals and music; [pets] Dogs (Bertie & Jenny) and a cottontail rabbit; [ambition] To become a Vet;

HAMMETT, SAMANTHA: [b] 12/12/88 Chelmsford; [home] Chelmsford, Essex; [p] Jayne and Alistair; [brother] Matthew; [school]Perryfields Junior; [fav subject] Literacy, history and art; [hobbies] Poetry, karate and cookery; [pets] Dog called Taz; [ambition] To become a Vet;

HAMMONDS, HANNAH: [b] 09/05/90 Guildford; [home] Ivybridge, Devon; [p] Liza; [sister] Naomi; [school] Stowford Primary; [fav subject] Literacy hour; [hobbies] riding a bike; [pets] Two hamsters; [ambition] Story writer;

HANCOCK, JULIE: [b] 24/11/90; [home] Chelmsford, Essex; [p] David and Janet; [sister] Sarah; [school] Perryfields Junior; [fav subject] Art; [hobbies] Playing the piano and sport; [pets] 3 rabbits; [ambition] I would like to teach;

HANCOCK, SARAH: [b] 14/05/88; [home] Chelmsford, Essex; [p] David and Janet; [sister] Julie; [school] Perryfields Junior; [fav subject] PE and games; [hobbies] Playing the piano, sport; [pets] 3 rabbits; [ambition] To be a Hairstylist;

HARDING, JENNY: [b] 21/06/84 England; [home] Chesham, Buckinghamshire; [p] Bill and Barbara; [brother] John; [school] Dr. Challoner's High School; [fav subject] Chemistry; [hobbies] Sport - athletics, netball, horseriding and music; [pets] 2 cats Charlie and Amy; [ambitions] Going to Univesity and gaining a good degree;

HARRIS, SIMON: [b] 25/08/88 Barbados; [home] St. Day, Cornwall; [p] Allison and Steve; [brothers] Matthew and David; [sister] Emma; [school] St. Day C.P. School; [fav subject] Creative writing; [hobbies] Football, karate and reading; [pets] 3 cats; [ambitions] Royal Marine or R.A. F. pilot;

HARLOND, KIMBERLEY JADE: [b] 03/08/87 Honiton; [home] Ottery St. Mary, Devon; [p] Simon and Alison; [sister] Emily; [school] the King's School; [fav subject] French; [hobbies] Guides, playing the flute and church choir; [pets] 4 cats, 1 dog and 2 guinea pigs; [ambition] to travel the world and write about my experiences;

HARTELL, MICHAEL: [b] 14/12/87 Cheltenham; [home] Twyning, Glos.; [p] Geoff and Marlene; [brothers] Mark and Matthew; [sister] Melanie; [school] Twyning County Primary; [fav subject] English; [hobbies] Karate, fishing and reading; [pets] 2 dogs, fish and chickens; [ambition] To become a Doctor;

HARTNELL, RICHARD: [b] 26/03/89; [home] Cirencester, Gloucestershire; [brothers] Simon, Christopher and Andrew; [school] Watermoor C of E Primary School; [fav subject] Maths; [hobbies] Football, hockey, Cubs and playing percussion in local brass band;

HASLAM, THOMAS S.: [b] 12/02/88 Rotherham; [home] Chesterfield, Derbyshire; [p] Stephen and Jane; [sister] Olivia; [school] St. Josephe's Convent; [fav subject] Maths; [hobbies] Cricket and Scouts; [pets] 3 fish, one cat called 'Monty';

HATHERALL, GILLIAN: [b] 21/04/89 Cheltenham; [home] Twyning, Gloucestershire; [p] John and Jacqui; [sisters] Emma, Sally and Rosie; [school] Twyning C.P. School; [fav subject] English; [hobbies] Reading, writing, art and ballet; [ambition] To be an Author;

HAWKES, GEMMA: [b] 27/07/87 Rochford, Essex; [home] Canvey Island, Essex; [p] Paul and Jacqueline; [sisters] Alana, Meghan and Danica; [school] The Cornelius Vermuyden; [fav subject] Science and Maths; [hobbies] Going out and cooking; [pets] 2 dogs named Tess and Frankie; [ambition] To work in a large Bank;

HE, CHENG: [b] 17/04/88 Wuhan Huber; [home] Wuhan, China; [p] Father: Guang Yuan He and Mother: Kexiu Li; [school] Crabtree Junior School; [fav subject] Maths and football; [hobbies] Chess; [ambitions] To become Mathematician or Football player;

HEATH, AMY: [b] 28/04/88 Plymouth; [home] South Brent, Devon; [p] Carol and Conrad; [sister] Leonie; [school] South Brent Primary; [fav subject] IT and art; [hobbies] Listening to music; [pets] hamster; [ambitions] To become a Singer or an aActress;

HEEKS, LUCINDA: [b] 23/05/88 Gloucestershire; [home] Twyning, Tewkesbury, Gloucestershire; [p] Mary and David; [brother] Robert; [sister] Gemma;

[school] Twyning Primary; [fav subject] Maths; [hobbies] Horse riding, reading and music; [pets] Cats, pony, rabbit and goldfish; [ambitions] To become a Teacher and a famous Poet;

HELLIER, CLAIRE LOUISE RUTH: [b] 02/10/86 Exeter; [home] Ottery St. Mary, Devon; [p] John and Christine; [sisters] Georgina, Annie; [school] The Kings School; [fav subject] French and P.E.; [hobbies] Jazz dance; [pets] 2 Guinea Pigs; [ambitions] To become a Hairdresser or a Dancer;

HEMMING, ALICE LOUISE: [b] 09/01/88 Sydney, Australia; [home] Watton-at-Stone, Herts; [p] Diane and Mark; [brother] Joe; [school] Stapleford JMI; [fav subject] English; [hobbies] Acting, dancing, writing and reading; [ambitions] To become an Actress, Journalist or TV Presenter;

HENDERSON, LOUIS: [b] 23/09/87 Taunton; [home] Bridgwater, Somerset; [p] Debbie and Robert; [sisters] Hollie and Natalie; [school] Kingsmoor; [fav subject] D.T. [hobbies] Football; [pets] Dog; [ambitions] To be rich and famous;

HENDY, JUSTIN: [b] 16/06/88 Cornwall; [home] Ashton, Cornwall; [p] Enid and Derek; [sister] Maria; [school] Breage C of E V.A.; [fav subject] Art; [hobbies] Bike riding and reading; [pets] 2 dogs, 2 cats, 1 rabbit, 1 hamster and 3 birds; [ambition] To work with my Dad plumbing;

HERRINGTON, SCOTT: [b] 01/06/88 Bristol; [home] Farnham, Surrey; [p] Paul and Yvonne [brothers] Craig and Kristian; [school] Hale Primary; [fav subject] Art and history; [hobbies] Football, rugby and swimming; [ambition] To become a Clothes Designer for films;

HILLIER, RUTH: [b] 11/06/90 Dorchester; [home] Petrockstowe, Devon; [p] Ian and Carolyn; [brother] Adam; [sisters] Rebecca and Sarah; [school] Exbourne Primary; [fav subject] History and art; [hobbies] Reading, sport and art; [pets] 2 cats, 3 guinea pigs, 1 horse, 6 sheep and 3 goldfish; [ambitions] To become a Vet or an Athlete;

HITCHCOCK, LAUREN KIMBERLEY: [b] 24/03/89 Taunton; [home] Taunton, Somerset; [p] Melanie and Peter; [brothers] Daniel and Connor; [sister] Caitlin; [school] St. Georges R.C. [fav subject] Art; [hobbies] Flute, recorder and gymnastics; [pets] Rabbit (Otis) [ambitions] To become a Teacher, Author or Nurse;

HOAR, CHRISTOPHER: [b] 15/09/92 Plymouth; [home] Tavistock, Devon; [p] Pauline and David; [brother] Martin; [school] St. Rumons School; [fav subject] English; [hobbies] Football and swimming; [pets] Cat (Suki);

HOBSON, JAMES: [b] 21/11/90

Winchester; [home] Eastleigh, Hampshire; [p] Michael and Siân; [brothers] Edward, Charles and William; [school] Crescent Primary; [fav subject] Technology; [hobbies] Football, tennis and cubs; [pets] Cat (Meg);

HOLDEN, ASHLEY: [b] 17/02/88 Swindon; [home] Cirencester, Glos; [p] Rory and Julie; [sister] Trina; [school] Watermmor C of E; [fav subject] I.T. and English; [hobbies] Playing the flute; [pets] Dog and a cat; [ambition] To become a Teacher;

HONE, JASMIN FAE: [b] 29/07/92 Romford; [home] Rochford, Essex; [p] Philip and Deborah; [brother] Mason; [sister] Lauren; [school] Holt Farm Infants; [fav subject] Maths; [hobbies] Reading and cycling; [pets] Fish (Titch); [ambitions] To learn magic tricks and to go on Safari to Africa;

HOPLEY, BECKY: [b] 24/06/86 Southampton; [home] North Baddesley, Hampshire; [p] Michael and Margaret; [brother] Tomas; [school] The Mountbatten School; [fav subject] Drama, English and French; [hobbies] Horse riding and dancing; [pets] Siamese cat (Emily);

HORIGAN, ANDREW: [b] 03/02/91 Truro; [home] Gwinear, Cornwall; [p] Kim and Nicola; [sisters] Anna, Jane; [school] Gwinear C.P. School; [fav subject] Art; [hobbies] Computer and drawing; [pets] Rabbit (Whitefoot); [ambition] To become a Magician;

HOYLES, MATTHEW: [b] Rush Green Hospital; [home] Romford, Essex; [p] Tom and Wyn; [sister] Joanna; [school] Abbeylands; [fav subject] Maths; [hobbies] Football and computer games; [pets] Snake and fish; [ambitions] To become an Accountant, Solicitor or a Salvation Army Minister;

HUDSON, JAMES: [b] 16/12/89 Guildford; [home] Tarrant Hinton, Dorset; [p] Jeremy and Caroline; [brother] Charlie; [school] Pimperne 1st School; [fav subject] Technology; [hobbies] Computers and swimming; [pets] Dogs, guinea pig and rabbits; [ambitions] To become a Writer or a Policeman;

HURRELL, MARC: [b] 14/11/90 Truro; [home] Gwinear, Cornwall; [p] Jeanette and Andrew; [brother] Nathan; [school] Gwinear School; [fav subject] Art; [hobbies] Football and computers; [pets] Lamb (Snowdrop), chickens and geese; [ambition] To become a Builder;

IBRAHIM, OMAR: [b] 24/10/88 Funchal,Madeira; [home] Loughton, Essex; [p] Fatima and Said; [brothers] Michael and Ali; [school] Buckhurst Hill County Primary; [fav subject] Poetry and writing; [hobbies] Computers, bike riding and swimming; [ambition] To win swimming competitions;

IVELL, ADAM: [b] 30/08/89 Colchester; [home] Lawford, Essex; [p] Stella and Stephen; [brother] Joel; [sister] Rebekah; [school] Lawford C of E Primary; [fav subject] Art, design and technology; [hobbies] Cars, football, swimming and play station; [pets] Horses, dogs, cats, hamster, guinea pigs, rabbits, a rat and fish; [ambition] To be a TOCA Touring Car Driver;

JACKMAN, DANIEL: [b] 18/09/87 Barnstaple; [home] Barnstaple, N. Devon; [p] Dawn and Colin; [sisters] Georgia and Demi; [school] Ashleigh Road Primary; [fav subject] Maths and science; [hobbies] Riding my motorbike and fishing; [pets] Goldfish, hamster and budgie; [ambition] To become a professional Scrambler;

JACKMAN, ELITA: [b] 24/05/92 Maidenhead; [home] Marlow, Bucks; [p] Lorraine and Mark; [school] Marlow C of E 1st School; [fav subject] English; [hobbies] Dancing; [pets] Cat (Kitkat); [ambitions] To become a Teacher and to travel;

JACOBS, SCOTT: [b] 06/01/87 Rochford; [home] Canvey Island, Essex; [p] Margret and Keith; [brothers] Stuart and Spencer; [school] Cornelius Vermuyden; [fav subject] P.E.; [hobbies] Football, basketball, tennis and cricket; [pets] Dog (Max) cat (Sapphi) bird (Moey); [ambitions] To become a Vet or a Poet;

JAGO, JENNA-MARIE: [b] 14/12/87 N.D.D.M.U.; [home] Barnstaple, N. Devon; [p] Jeanette Ann; [brothers] Scott and Tyler-Jay; [sister] Kerrie; [school] Yeo Valley Primary; [fav subject] Art and English; [hobbies] Swimming; [pets] Goldfish; [ambitions] To become a Writer or a Policewoman;

JAMES, BETHAN: [b] 02/01/91 Oxford; [home] Headington, Oxford; [p] Heather and Brian Robertson; [sisters] Gemma, Lesley and Kathleen; [school] Barton Village First School; [fav subject] Maths; [hobbies] Swimming and drawing; [pets] Dog (Tyson) cat (Biff); [ambitions] To write more stories and poems;

JAMES, GAVIN: [b] 12/05/88 Truro; [home] Ashton, Cornwall; [p] Debbie and Michael; [sister] Hayley; [school] Breage; [fav subject] English; [hobbies] Football, cycling and roller blading; [pets] Dog and cat (Polly and Lucky); [ambitions] To become a Footballer or be in a Pop Group;

JAMES, NATHAN: [b] 20/05/88 London [home] Harpenden, Herts; [p] Mike and Anne; [sisters] Siân and Ffion; [school] Crabtree Junior; [fav subject] Maths; [hobbies] Football and roller blading; [pets] Dog, guinea pig and fish; [ambitions] To become a Footballer or a PC Consultant;

JEFFERY, YVONNE: [b] 24/11/87 Barnstaple; [home] Braunton, Devon; [p]

Evelyn and Michael; [brothers] Richard and Edward; [sister] Catherine; [school] Marwood; [fav subject] Art; [hobbies] Swimming and dancing; [pets] Cat (Casper) [ambitions] To become an Artist, a Poet, or a Pilot;

JEGGO, ASHLEY ALEXANDER: [b] 14/09/90 Aldershot; Hants; [home] Farnham, Surrey; [p] Martin and Samantha; [brothers] Ben and Rowan; [sister] Milan; [school] St. Peters; [fav subject] History and Maths; [hobbies] All sports and playing the trumpet; [pets] Rabbits (Bun.E.Rabbit and Blackie) guinea pigs (Wallace and Gromit); [ambition] To become an Author;

JENKINS, JAKE: [b] 16/03/85 Southampton; [home] Chilworth, Hampshire; [p] Liza; [brother] Ricky; [school] Mountbatten; [pets] Horse and a dog;

JOHNSON, AMY: [b] 21/07/94 Chace Farm Hospital; [home] Reed, Herts; [p] Jane Curtis and David Johnson; [brother] Lee; [school] Reed First School; [fav subject] English; [hobbies] Reading and drawing; [pets] Rabbit (Thumper) hamster (Snowy); [ambition] To become a Ballerina;

JOHNSON, ANDREW: [b] 28/07/87 Rochford, Essex; [home] Canvey Island, Essex; [p] Alan and Barbara; [sister] Sarah, Louise; [school] Cornelius Vermuyden; [fav subject] Science; [hobbies] Playing football, supporting Man. U. and model making; [pets] Cat (Jade); [ambitions] To become a Meteorologist or a Pilot;

JOHNSON, HANNAH SIÂN: [b] 13/07/84 Winchester; [home] Chandler's Ford, Hampshire; [school] Mountbatten School, Romsey; [fav subject] English; [hobbies] Horse riding;

JOHNSTONE, VICKY: [b] 17/11/86 Luton; [home] Winslow, Bucks; [p] Cathy and Brian; [brother] James; [sister] Grace; [school] Winslow Combined; [fav subject] English; [hobbies] Art, swimming, music (playing the flute and saxophone); [pets] 2 rabbits (Caranel and Snowball) 1 hamster (Sparkle); [ambition] To become a Nurse;

JONES, ELOISE: [b] 21/08/86 Gloucester; [home] Lydney, Glos; [p] Michele and Chris; [sister] Tanise; [school] Whitecross; [fav subject] Science and English; [hobbies] Swimming; [pets] Dog (Molly); [ambition] To be happy;

JONES, STEPHANIE: [b] 07/10/89 Newport; [home] Risca, Gwent; [p] Geraint and Beverley; [sisters] Katie and Georgia; [school] Risca Primary; [fav subject] English; [hobbies] Netball and Brownies; [pets] Rabbit and guinea pigs; [ambitions] To become a Nurse and to represent Wales at Netball;

JOYCE, MARTIN: [b] 21/06/86 Sutton Colefield; [home] Lydney, Glos.; [p] Martin Joyce and Vanessa Robinson; [brothers]

James, Philip and Jack; [school] Whitecross; [fav subject] Science; [hobbies] Football, rugby and fishing; [pets] Springer Spaniel (Patch) [ambition] To become a Navigator in the Navy;

JULIAN, ROSS A.: [b] 21/09/88 St. Austell; [home] Roche, Cornwall; [p] Paul and Julie; [sister] Katie; [school] Roche C.P.School; [fav subject] Mathmatics; [hobbies] Football, tennis and judo; [pets] Goldfish; [ambition] To become an Airline Pilot;

KEAST, DARREN ROBERT: [b] 07/04/88 Truro; [home] Heamoor, Cornwall; [p] Brian and Andrea; [school] Heamoor C.P. School; [fav subject] Science and Design Technology; [hobbies] Swimming (P.2 Club) and surfing; [pets] Cat (Elvis); [ambitions] To become a famous Comedian or a Policeman;

KEMP, ASHLEY: [b] 05/03/88 Truro; [home] Illogan, Cornwall; [p] Linda and Andrew; [brothers] Joshua and Samuel; [school] Treloweth C.P. School; [fav subject] Physical Education; [hobbies] Football and computer games; [pets] Dog (Heidi); [ambition] To become a professional Footballer;

KENNEDY, ELLEN: [b] 16/02/89; [home] Penryn, Cornwall; [p] Paula and Tim; [school] Penryn Junior; [fav subject] Maths and History; [hobbies] Netball and swimming; [ambition] To do well in Sport;

KENT, JADE MARIE: [b] 15/06/89 Cheltenham; [home] Cirencester, Glos.; [p] Jane and Paul Hurrell; [sister] Molly; [school] Watermoor; [fav subject] English and Art; [hobbies] Majorettes, swimming and reading; [ambitions] To become a Teacher, or a Policewoman, or an Olympic Swimmer;

KILMISTER, STACEY: [b] 30/01/90 Truro; [home] Reawla, Cornwall; [p] Zoe and Andy; [school] Gwinear; [fav subject] English; [hobbies] Swimming and playstation; [pets] Molly, Oliver, Fudge and Gizmo; [ambitions] To become a Vet or a Nurse;

KIMBER, MICHAEL: [b] 27/04/89 High Wycombe; [home] Beaconsfield, Bucks; [p] Anne and John; [brother] David; [school] Butler's Court; [fav subject] Maths; [hobbies] Roller blading and swimming; [pets] Cat and goldfish;

KING, JAMES: [b] 15/02/90 Dorchester, Dorset; [home] Pimperne, Dorset; [p] Philip and Glenda; [brother] Simon; [school] Pimperne First; [fav subject] Maths and Literacy; [hobbies] Riding my bike, cricket and football; [pets] Gerbils and fish; [ambition] To be an Air Traffic Controller;

KING, THOMAS ASHLEY: [b] 04/10/90 Reading; [home] Basingstoke, Hampshire; [p] Deborah and Paul; [brothers] Simon and John; [sister] Joanna; [school] Worting Juniors; [fav subject] Maths and English; [hobbies]

Football; [pets] 2 dogs; [ambition] To become an Accountant;

KOENIG, JAMES A. : [b] 11/10/89 Swindon; [home] Cirencester, Glos.; [p] Carole and Andrew; [brothers] Carl and Andrew; [sisters] Laura and Zoe; [school] Watermoor; [fav subject] History; [hobbies] Football and reading; [pets] Goldfish and a cat; [ambitions] To become a Pilot or something to do with the Armed Forces;

KOLTHAMMER, ANNE MARIE: [b] 03/11/89 London; [home] Lawford, Essex; [sister] Katie; [school] Lawford C of E Primary; [fav subject] English; [hobbies] Dancing and drawing; [pets] Rabbit and a cat; [ambition] To become a Vet.;

KOWE, LUCAS: [b] 15/12/89 Sydney, Australia; [home] Oxford, Oxon; [p] Ray and Anthea; [sister] Hannah; [school] Windmill First; [fav subject] Art; [hobbies] Design-lego, drawing and reading; [ambitions] To become an Archaeologist or an Author;

KUHL, GREG: [b] 06/12/88 Maldon, Essex; [home] Woodham Walter, Essex; [p] John and Ondri; [brother] Ryan; [school] Danbury Park; [fav subject] Art; [hobbies] Football, guitar and body boarding; [pets] Dog (Connie) [ambitions] To become a Cartoonist or an Osteopath;

LACEY, ROBERT: [b] 17/10/85 Heatherwood; [home] Cippenham, Berkshire; [p] June and Bob; [brother] Clive; [sisters] Adela, Vanessa, Nichole and Christine; [school] Burnham Upper; [fav subject] P.E.; [hobbies] Football and Scouts; [pets] Fish and birds; [ambitions] To be a Footballer, Racing Driver and Police Officer;

LAW, KIRSTY: [b] 19/11/91 Enfield; [home] Waltham Abbey, Essex; [p] Donna Adams and Paul Law; [sister] Zoe; [school] Waltham Holy Cross; [fav subject] Writing and Art; [hobbies] Brownies and swimming; [pets] Cat (Squeeky); [ambition] To become a Teacher and visit Disney World;

LAWRENCE, HANNAH: [b] 2/10/89 Maldon; [home] Danbury, Essex; [p] Michele and Graham; [school] Danbury Park; [fav subject] Poetry, Maths and Art; [hobbies] Swimming, Gym and Riding; [pets] 12 Guinea pigs, 1 rabbit, 5 Chickens and 2 geese; [ambition] To become a Police Dog Handler;

LAWRENCE, JOHN M.D.: [b] 01/07/87 Gloucester; [home] Lydney, Glos.; [p] R & J Lawrence; [brother] Shaun; [sisters] Rachel, Jane, Debra and Karen; [school] Whitecross; [fav subject] English; [hobbies] Dr. Who and rugby; [pets] 2 cats, dogs and fish; [ambitions] To become a Vicar, or some type of scientific work;

LAWTON, BRONWEN: [b] 05/01/85 SE London; [home] Reading, Berkshire; [p] David and Christine; [brother] Rhys; [school]

Chiltern Edge; [fav subject] English; [hobbies] Drama; [ambition] To learn how to work the VCR;

LECZYNSKA, LEANNE: [b] 27/05/87 Enfield; [home] Canvey Island, Essex; [p] Linda and Roger Hardy; [brother] Gavin Nicholls; [sister] Charlane Nicholls; [school] Cornelius Vermuyden; [fav subject] English; [hobbies] Horse riding and swimming; [pets] Cat (Tiddles); [ambitions] To become a Singer or a Model;

LEE, JACK: [b] 11/11/91 Oxford; [home] Aston, Oxfordshire; [p] Sally and Steve; [school] Aston and Cote CE Primary; [fav subject] History; [hobbies] Designing things and computers; [pets] 2 gerbils, 2 guinea pigs, a rabbit and goldfish; [ambitions] To become an Aircraft designer or Lego designer;

LEWIS, BEN: [b] 09/10/88 Taunton; [home] Taunton, Somerset; [p] Michael and Tracy; [brother] Christian; [sister] Sophie; [school] St. George's R.C. School; [fav subject] P.E. [hobbies] Football and music; [pets] Rabbit (Bonnie) ; [ambition] To become a professional Footballer;

LEWIS, NATALIE: [b] 31/10/85 Aldershot; [home] Aldershot, Hampshire; [p] Kevin and Chris; [sister] Charlotte; [school] Ash Manor; [fav subject] History; [hobbies] Swimming and tennis; [ambition] To become a History Teacher;

LEWIS, SCOTT: [b] 24/03/87 Plymouth; [home] Torpoint, Cornwall; [p] Martin and Christine; [brother] Craig; [sister] Sophie; [school] Torpoint Community School; [fav subject] English; [hobbies] Computers; [ambitions] To become a Lawyer or a Solicitor;

LILL, SIMON GRAHAM: [b] 24/02/88 Stafford; [home] High Wych, Herts; [p] Graham and Tina; [brothers] Dominic and Marcus; [school] High Wych J.M.I. [fav subject] Art; [hobbies] Swimming and rounders; [pets] Dog; [ambition] To become a Singer;

LILLEY, RACHEL JAYNE: [b] 13/03/86 Doncaster; [home] Lydney, Glos.; [p] Ian and Carole; [sister] Katy Louise; [school] Whitecross; [fav subject] Drama; [hobbies] Reading and writing; [pets] 2 guinea pigs and a hamster; [ambition] To become a Vet.;

LILLYWHITE, ELLEN: [b] 03/04/90 Winchester; [home] Eastleigh, Hampshire; [p] Lynne and Ross; [brother] Alfred; [sister] Esme; [school] The Crescent Primary; [fav subject] English; [hobbies] Reading and writing; [pets] Cat (Frankie) and 2 quails (Rusty and Tadge); [ambitions] To become an Author, Actor or Vet;

LINDSAY, DANIELLE: [b] 04/12/86 London; [home] Canvey, Essex; [p] Sue and Graham; [sister] Lucy; [school] Cornelius

Vermuyden; [fav subject] P.E., English and Computers; [hobbies] Swimming sports; [ambition] To become a famous Poet;

LLOYD, JENNY: [b] 22/06/93 Redhill; [home] Redhill, Surrey; [brother] Tom; [school] Reigate Parish; [hobbies] Ballet, drawing and reading; [pets] Rabbit (Basil);

LLOYD, SAMANTHA: [b] 24/10/89 Newport; [home] Risca, Gwent; [p] Angela and Peter; [brother] Jonathan; [school] Risca Primary; [fave subject] Art; [hobbies] Reading and writing;

LOADER, JOSHUA: [b] 24/05/89 Hereford; [home] Ledbury, Hereford; [p] Harry and Karen; [brother] Alex; [school] Bromsberrow; [fav subject] Design and Technology and Art; [hobbies] Football and fishing; [pets] 2 dogs, 2 ducks, 1 guinea pig; [ambition] To design cars;

LOCKYER, EDWARD: [b] 21/06/88; [home] Newbury, Berks.; [sister] Natalie; [fav subject] English Literature; [hobbies] Sport and climbing; [pets] Hamster and fish; [ambitions] To be an Artist, Writer and an Actor;

LONG, JORDAN: [b] 19/08/89 Truro; [home] Penryn, Cornwall; [p] Stephen and Nicole; [brothers] Austin and Nathan; [sister] Kerensa; [school] Penryn Junior; [fav subject] English; [hobbies] Rugby, athletics and drawing; [pets] 8 bantams and 4 ducks; [ambitions] To play scrum half for England and to be an RAF Pilot;

LORD, ABIGAIL EVE: [b] 02/10/94 Cambridge; [home] Royston, Herts; [p] Sally and Kevin; [brother] Joseph; [sister] Jessica; [school] Reed First School; [fav subject] Maths; [hobbies] Riding my bike;

LOWMAN, THOMAS: [b] 19/02/92 Winchester; [home] Alresford, Hampshire; [p] Mark and Ann; [brother] Daniel; [school] Sun Hill Infants; [fav subject] Science; [hobbies] Lego, reading and dinosaurs; [pets] Goldfish (Nemo and Flounder); [ambitions] To work with animals and see a real Dinosaur;

LUDOVINO, OLIVER: [b] 26/06/91 Reading; [home] Reading, Berkshire; [p] Judith and José; [sister] Rosanna; [school] Katesgrove Primary; [fav subject] Art and Maths; [hobbies] Cycling; [pets] Goldfish (Speedy and Captain Pugwash); [ambitions] To be an Archaeologist or a Cartoonist;

MACDONALD, YVETTE: [b] 16/12/87 Torpoint; [home] Polbathic, Cornwall; [p] Alison and Alexander; [sisters] Gemma and Selina; [school] Antony C.E.V.A.; [fav subject] Art and poetry; [hobbies] Painting and reading; [pets] Gerbil, dog, cats, ducks and chickens; [ambitions] To become a Diver and to help save the Tiger;

MACE, OLIVIA: [b] 17/05/84 Kettering;

[home] Taunton, Somerset; [p] Sara and James; [school] St. Augustines of Canterbury; [fav subject] English; [hobbies] Singing, reading and writing; [pets] Cat; [ambitions] To become a Psychiatrist and Novelist;

MACLEAY, ZOË FRANCIS: [b] 05/07/91 Harlow; [home] Harlow, Essex; [p] Keith and Catriona; [brother] Zachary; [sister] Gabriella; [school] St. Albans R.C Primary; [fav subject] English; [hobbies] Music, dancing, reading and writing; [pets] 3 goldfish; [ambition] To become an Author;

MANLEY, EDWARD: [b] 16/08/91 Aylesbury; [home] North Marston, Bucks; [p] Jonathan and Maisie; [school] North Marston C of E First School; [fav subject] Maths; [hobbies] Swimming and rugby; [ambition] To become a Vet.;

MARSHALL, GRANT: [b] 23/09/91 Yeovil; [home] Milborne Port, Dorset; [p] John and Irene; [school] Milborne Port C.P.; [fav subject] Maths; [hobbies] Drawing and snooker; [pets] Goldfish and a rabbit; [ambition] To join the Army;

MATHEWS, KERRY: [b] 24/10/91 Wales; [home] Chesterfield, Derbyshire; [p] Dr. and Mrs S.C. Mathews; [brothers] Keith and Keiron; [school] St. Joseph's Convent; [fav subject] English; [hobbies] Music, Irish dancing and tennis; [ambition] To become a Doctor of Medicine;

MATTHAMS, RACHAEL: [b] 03/01/86 Gloucester; [homes] Lydney, Glos; [p] Peter and Mandy; [sister] Stephanie; [school] Whitecross; [fav subject] Drama; [hobbies] Ice skating, swimming and music; [pets] Dog (Pepper);

MATTHEWS, CHRISTOPHER: [b] 19/08/88 Plymouth; [home] Trewidland, Cornwall; [p] Diane and Peter; [brothers] Joseph, James and Alex; [sister] Lucy; [school] Trewidland C.P.; [fav subject] Maths; [hobbies] Acting, singing, Scouts and tennis; [pets] 2 dogs and 2 cats; [ambition] To become an Actor;

MAUNDER, CLAIRE: [b] 26/12/87 [home] Tavistock, Devon; [brother] Chris; [school] Gulworthy C.P.; [fav subject] Maths and Art; [hobbies] Netball, art and swimming; [pets] Dog (Ben);

MAY, CRAIG: [b] 30/03/88 Welwyn Garden City; [home] Harpenden, Herts; [p] Penny and Brent; [brother] Scott; [school] Crabtree Junior; [fav subject] Maths and History; [hobbies] Playing on computers and football; [pets] Dog, hamster and fish; [ambition] To design and make computer software;

MAZUMDER, SHARIFUL HAQUE: [b] 05/09/88 [home] Amersham, Bucks; [p] Khushida and Shirajul; [sisters] Hasina, Rosina and Selina; [school] Elangeni Middle School; [fav subject] Maths; [hobbies] Sport;

[ambition] To become a Doctor;

McBRIDE, SEBASTIAN: [b] Plymouth; [home] Plymouth, Devon; [p] Tracy; [sister] Jasmin; [school] Hill Crest; [fav subject] I.T. [hobbies] Collecting Reptiles; [pets] Snake, dog and a parrot; [ambition] To do well at school;

McFARLANE, JAMES: 18/02/88 Truro; [home] North Country, Cornwall; [p] Robert and Julie; [sister] Nicola; [school] St. Day Primary; [fav subject] Art and Computers; [hobbies] Football; [pets] 2 dogs and tropical frogs; [ambition] To own my own business full of tropical fish and animals;

McINTOSH, JAMES: [b] 05/04/87 Canterbury, Kent; [home] Ash Vale, Hants; [p] Derek and Margaret; [brother] Ian; [school] Ash Manor; [fav subject] English; [hobbies] Football and computer games; [ambitions] To become a professional Footballer and an Author;

McKAY, MARK: [b] 20/05/84 Nottingham; [home] Southampton, Hampshire; [p] Gillian and Randell; [sister] Rebecca; [school] The Mountbatten School; [fav subject] Art; [hobbies] Clarinet and drawing;

McLEOD, FIONA: [b] 12/01/85 Southampton; [home] West Willow, Hants; [p] Ian and Patricia; [brother] Alistair; [sister] Emily; [school] The Mountbatten School; [fav subject] Geography; [hobbies] Riding, reading and sailing; [pets] Hamsters; [ambition] To learn the art of horse whispering;

McPHAIL, EMMA VICTORIA: [b] 03/03/92 Chesterfield; [home] Hardstoft, Derbyshire; [p] Margaret and Andrew; [school] St. Joseph's Convent; [fav subject] Maths; [hobbies] Horse riding and piano; [pets] Rabbit (Bouncy); [ambition] To become an Author;

MEAD, PHILLIP GRAEME: [b] 30/05/88 Winchester; [home] Eastleigh, Hampshire; [p] Julia and Colin; [sister] Becky; [school] Crescent Primary; [fav subject] English; [hobbies] Basketball, swimming and music; [ambitions] To become a basketball player or play a guitar in a Band;

MERRIGAN, RYAN: [b] 08/06/90 Newport; [home] Pontymister, Gwent; [p] Susan Merrigan; [brothers] Leon and Jamie Smith; [school] Risca Primary; [fav subject] English; [hobbies] Computers; [pets] Yorkshire Terrier (Bella); [ambition] Undecided;

MILLER, NICHOLAS: [b] 29/05/88 St. Albans; [home] Harpenden, Herts; [p] Tina and Trevor; [brothers] Christopher and Stephen; [school] Crabtree Junior; [fav subject] Science; [hobbies] Tennis and football; [pets] 2 guinea pigs, 1 hamster and a gerbil; [ambitions] To become a Zoo Keeper or an RSPCA Inspector;

MILLS, JOSHUA: [b] 17/02/88 Barnstaple; [home] Ashford, Devon; [p] Elizabeth and Andrew; [brothers] Ben, Aaron and Joel; [school] Marwood County Primary; [fav subject] Technology; [hobbies] Computers, basketball and painting war models; [pets] Dog, rabbits, guinea pig, geese, ducks and hens; [ambitions] To become a Rally Driver or Stuntman;

MITCHELL, GRANT: [b] 03/06/91 Yeovil; [home] Milborne Port, Somerset; [p] Terry and Gay; [brother] Tom; [school] Milborne Port County Primary; [fav subject] English; [hobbies] Football, swimming and cricket; [pets] 2 rabbits; [ambition] To play for Manchester United Football Club;

MITCHELMORE, KATIE: [b] 27/11/87 Plymouth; [home] South Brent, Devon; [p] Gary and Sue; [brother] Luke; [school] South Brent Primary; [fav subject] I.T.; [hobbies] Swimming and badminton; [pets] A mouse and 2 rabbits; [ambition] To work at an animal home;

MIXTURE, CHARLOTTE: [b] 10/06/91 Cheltenham; [home] Cirencester, Glos.; [brother] Benjamin; [school] Watermoor C of E; [fav subject] English and Maths; [hobbies] Horse riding, playing records, swimming and reading; [pets] Fish and hamsters; [ambitions] To become a Vet and to race a horse;

MOCKLER, JOHN MICHAEL: [b] 01/02/87 Rochford; [home] Canvey Island, Essex; [p] Brenda and Kevin; [sisters] Sarah, Rachael and Samantha; [school] Cornelius Vermuyden; [fav subject] Physical Education; [hobbies] Football, rugby and computer games; [pets] Dog (Poppy) [ambitions] To become a professional Footballer and a Millionaire;

MONUMENT, DAVID: [b] 24/10/88 Taunton; [home] Taunton, Somerset; [p] Bridget; [brother] Simon; [school] Trinity School; [fav subject] Maths; [hobbies] Reading; [pets] Cat (Inky); [ambition] To become an Author;

MOODY, SARAH: [b] 10/10/87 Frimley; [home] Bagshot, Surrey; [p] Marie and Robert; [brother] John; [sister] Clare; [school] Connaught School; [fav subject] Art; [hobbies] Dancing, acting, singing, netball, hockey, swimming and gymnastics; [pets] Guinea pig and a cat; [ambitions] To become an Actress or a Pop Star;

MOODY, SEAN: [b] 02/04/89 Harlow; [home] Loughton, Essex; [p] Joanne and Gary; [brothers] Jack and Charlie; [school] Buckhurst County Primary; [fav subject] History; [hobbies] Football, cricket, swimming and riding my bike; [pets] Cat; [ambition] To become a Professional Footballer;

MOORE, BEN: [b] 22/09/87 Essex; [home] Liskeard, Cornwall; [p] Penny and Robert;

[brother] Gregory; [school] St. Martins; [fav subject] Science; [hobbies] Computers and Quad riding; [pets] 2 dogs (Molly & Harry) 2 cats (Tess & Dillon); [ambition] To construct computers;

MORETON, CARL ADAM: [b] 30/03/90 Aylesbury; [home] Aylesbury, Bucks; [p] Dawn; [brothers] Jamie and Kieron; [sisters] Gemma and Emily; [school] William Harding Middle School; [fav subject] Science; [hobbies] Football; [pets] Fish, cats, dog and a hamster; [ambition] To become a professional Footballer;

MORGAN, ASHLEIGH LOUISE: [b] 02/10/86 Essex; [home] Canvey Island, Essex; [p] Tony and Debbie; [sister] Brittany Rose; [school] Cornelius Vermuyden; [fav subject] Music; [hobbies] Reading and playing music; [pets] Gerbil (Frisky); [ambition] To live to be 100 years old!

MORGAN, ROSALIND: [b] 18/12/83 London; [home] Pitstone, Bucks; [p] David and Johanna; [sisters] Judith and Eleanor; [school] Tring School; [fav subject] Art and English; [ambitions] To become an Artist, a Poet and to travel the world;

MORRIS, BERNADETTE: [b] 29/03/90 Okehampton; [home] Sampford Courtenay, Devon; [p] Anne and Patrick; [sisters] Clare and Olivia; [school] Exbourne C of E Primary; [fav subject] English; [hobbies] Table tennis, gym club and reading; [pets] 2 cats, 1 goldfish and a roach; [ambitions] To become a Writer or a Teacher;

MOUDY, OLIVIA: [b] 09/06/88 Barnstaple; [home] Guineaford, Devon; [p] Liz and Paul; [sister] Catriona; [school] Marwood; [fav subject] Science; [hobbies] Football and karate; [pets] 3 cats; [ambition] To become an Airline Pilot;

MURRELL, NATASSHA: [b] 15/01/86 Southampton; [home] Romsey, Hants; [p] David and Hazel; [brother] Joshua; [sister] Melissa; [school] Mountbatten; [fav subject] Drama; [hobbies] Swimming and dancing; [pets] 3 fish, 4 guinea pigs, a rabbit and a dog; [ambition] To become an Actress;

MUSGRAVE, CLAIRE: [b] 15/11/91 Oxford; [home] Aston, Oxon; [p] Keith and Debbie; [brother] Richard; [school] Aston & Cote Primary; [fav subject] Science; [hobbies] Reading and learning the recorder; [ambition] To become a Teacher;

MYNOTT, CHLOE: [b] 30/03/89; [home] Herts; [brother] Matthew; [sister] Rebecca; [fav subject] Art; [hobbies] Drawing; [pets] Dog, horses and chincillas; [ambition] To become a Teacher;

NICHOLLS, LAUREN: [b] 15/07/86 Edmonton; [home] Rayleigh, Essex; [p] Deborah; [brother] Jack; [school] Sweyne Park; [fav subject] History and Modern

Language; [hobbies] Reading and writing poetry; [pets] Rabbit (Sam) guinea pig (Jason); [ambitions] To become a Paediatric Doctor and to have a poem published;

O'BRIEN, RACHAEL: [b] 11/12/87 Reading; [home] Highclere, Berks; [p] John and Linda; [brother] Sean; [sister] Samantha; [school] St. Martins East Woodhay Primary; [fav subject] Science; [hobbies] Horse riding, football and reading; [pets] Lop eared rabbit (Flower); [ambitions] To become a Writer or a Three Day Eventer;

OLLIFFE, MICHELLE: [b] 14/10/85 Aylesbury; [home] Aylesbury, Bucks; [p] Marion; [brother] Darren; [school] John Colet School; [fav subject] English and P.E.; [hobbies] Titanic, sport and music; [ambitions] To become famous Writer (stories or poems) and to work at sea;

OSBORNE, JADE: [b] 27/04/90 N. Hampshire Hospital; [home] Basingstoke, Hampshire; [p] Frances and Mark; [sisters] Nicola, Emma and Paula; [school] Worting Juniors; [fav subject] Maths; [hobbies] Gymnastics and swimming; [pets] Dog (Jessie); [ambition] To become an Infant School Teacher;

OSHEA, SCOTT GEORGE: [b] 28/02/90 Winchester; [home] Eastleigh, Hampshire; [p] Kevin and Deborah; [brother] James; [sisters] Ellie, Jordan and Natasha; [school] The Crescent; [fav subject] Art and English; [hobbies] Football and cricket; [pets] Cat (Fudge); [ambition] To become a Writer;

PALMER, JOANNE: [b] 25/10/83 Taunton; [home] North Petherton, Somerset; [p] Joy and Colin; [brothers] Leigh and Kevin; [sister] Alice; [school] Haygrove; [fav subject] Drama; [hobbies] Listening to music and watching films; [ambition] To become a Primary School Teacher;

PANTING, JAMES: [b] 22/03/88 Newbury; [home] Woolton Hill, Berkshire; [p] Nigel and Gill; [brother] Matthew; [school] St. Martins East Woodhay Primary; [fav subject] Science; [hobbies] Keyboard and tennis; [ambition] To become a Vet.;

PARDOE, BECKY ELIZABETH: [b] 09/02/88 Maldon; [home] Danbury, Essex; [p] Gillian and Colin; [brother] Jack Nicholas; [sister] Jessica Ann; [school] Danbury Park C.P. School; [fav subject] Maths; [hobbies] Ballet, sewing and line dancing; [pets] Fish; [ambition] To become a famous musician;

PARKER, JOHN: [b] 22/11/89 Taunton, Somerset; [home] Reawla, Cornwall; [p] Paul and Ann; [brothers] David and Paul; [sister] Kayleigh; [school] Gwinear; [fav subject] Art; [hobbies] Football, meccano and reading; [pets] Dog, cat, hamster and chipmunks; [ambition] To become a Cartoonist;

PARKER, JORDAN: [b] 23/05/91

Winchester; [home] Eastleigh, Hampshire; [p] Michael and Jane; [brothers] Conor and Mitchell; [school] Crescent Primary; [fav subject] Maths and P.E.; [hobbies] Football; [ambition] To become a professional Footballer;

PASSCO, GEORGE: [b] 29/09/92 Bridgwater; [home] Bridgwater, Somerset; [p] Kevin and Kay; [brothers] Tom and Andrew; [sister] Christina; [school] St. Joseph's R.C. School; [fav subject] P.E. [hobbies] Football; [ambition] To become a Painter and Decorator;

PATTEN, NICOLA LOUISE: [b] 04/04/88 Reading; [home] Reading, Berkshire; [p] Jon and Karen; [sister] Amy; [school] Park Lane Primary; [fav subject] Art; [hobbies] Piano and drawing; [pets] Dog (Molly), rabbit (Snowy); [ambition] To write and illustrate childrens books;

PAVELEY, EMMA: [b] 27/11/90 Colchester; [home] Lawford, Essex; [p] Julie and Adam; [sisters] Caroline (7) and Zoe (3); [school] Lawford C of E Primary; [fav subject] P.E. and Art; [hobbies] Gymnastics and fishing; [pets] Gerbils (Fidget & Blackie); [ambitions] To be a gymnast or a lady footballer;

PETERS, ELEANOR: [b] 09/05/90 Southampton; [home] Chandlers Ford, Hampshire; [p] Sharon and Colin; [brother] Stewart; [school] Scantabout Primary; [fav subject] Art and English; [hobbies] Disco dancing, horse riding and golf; [pets] Cat (Crumbs); [ambitions] To write children's stories and poems;

PETERS, KIMBERLEY: [b] 22/11/83 London; [home] Slough, Berkshire; [p] Madeline and Jim; [brother] Gareth; [school] Burnham Upper School; [fav subject] Design Technology and English; [hobbies] Playing the trumpet; [ambitions] To continue writing poetry and to fly a Helicopter;

PETERS, STEWART: [b] 17/06/87 Southampton; [home] Chandlers Ford, Hampshire; [p] Sharon and Colin; [sister] Eleanor; [school] Thornden Secondary; [fav subject] P.E. and English; [hobbies] Football and hockey; [pets] Cat (Crumbs); [ambition] To be happy and enjoy my life;

PENNACK, DANIEL: [b] 30/07/87 London; [home] Chertsey, Surrey; [p] Rhona and Martin; [brothers] Adam, + Twins-Oliver & Jacob; [school] Abbeylands; [fav subject] Maths; [hobbies] Scouts; [pets] Gerbils; [ambition] To become a Lifeboat Coxwain;

PETTIFORD, EMILY: [b] 06/12/86 Gloucestershire; [home] Lydney, Glos.; [p] Jillian and Michael; [brothers] Jonathan and James; [school] Whitecross; [fav subject] English; [hobbies] Music, singing and reading; [pets] Cat and a hamster; [ambitions] To become a Vet, or to work with animals;

PHILLIPS, KATE: [b] 16/01/87 Rochford, Essex; [home] Canvey Island, Essex; [p] Geoff and Sharon; [brother] Tony; [school] Cornelius Vermuyden; [fav subject] English; [hobbies] Horse riding and reading; [pets] 2 cats (Leo and Brandy); [ambition] To become a Vet.;

PHILLIPS, NICHOLAS: [b] 15/08/86 Glos.; [home] Aylburton, Glos.; [p] Keith and Lorraine Purvis; [school] Whitecross; [fav subject] Science; [hobbies] Computer; [pets] 2 goldfish; [ambition] To be an Artist;

PHILLIS, EMILY: [b] 20/01/90 Truro; [home] Helston, Cornwall; [p] Ian and Rebecca; [brother] Sam; [school] Gwinear CP; [fav subject] English; [hobbies] Gym, reading and netball; [pets] 3 cats (Gertie, Matilda & Fergie); [ambitions] To become an Actress or Singer;

PICKETT, JOSH: [b] 10/05/99 St. Albans; [home] Harpenden, Herts; [p] Amanda and John ; [brothers] Luke and Chris; [sisters] Holly and Rose; [school] Crabtree; [fav subject] P.E.; [hobbies] Football; [pets] Hamster and fish; [ambition] To play for a Premier League Football Team;

PINK, MIKHAILA TAMAI: [b] 08/02/89 Taunton; [home] Bawdrip, Somerset; [p] John and Amanda; [school] Kingsmoor Primary; [fav subject] English; [hobbies] Clarinet, making things and bike riding; [pets] Hamster (Tui); [ambition] To become an Actress;

PINKETT, ELAINE JANET: [b] 07/11/86 Southampton; [home] Alfington, Devon; [p] Jack and Lesley; [brother] Derek; [sister] Joanne; [school] The Kings School; [fav subject] Art; [hobbies] Sewing and writing stories; [ambition] To become a Vet.;

PLANT, CHARLOTTE: [b] 10/02/89 Hillingdon; [home] Beaconsfield, Bucks.; [p] Martin and Michelle; [brother] Oliver; [school] Butlers Court County Combined; [fav subject] History; [hobbies] Dancing and singing; [pets] 2 Boxer dogs (Sam & Georgie); [ambition] To become an Actress;

PLUMRIDGE, ALISON LOUISE: [b] 29/09/88 Croydon [home] Milborne Port. Dorset; [p] Malcolm and Penelope; [brothers] Paul, Steven and Keith; [sister] Dawn; [school] Milborne Port C.P.School; [fav subject] Music; [hobbies] Singing and swimming; [ambitions] To become a Singer or an Actress;

POMEROY, GRANT NICHOLAS: [b] 10/06/87 Plymouth; [home] Torpoint, Cornwall; [p] Glenda and Nick; [sister] Laura; [school] Torpoint Community School; [fav subject] Physical Education; [hobbies] Football and Drama; [pets] Cat (Sooti) and a tortoise (Toby); [ambition] To become a professional Footballer;

POWELL, CHARLOTTE JANE: [b]

25/07/90 Banbury, Oxon; [home] Steeple Ashton, Oxon; [p] Nicholas and Lydia; [sister] Samantha; [school] The Warriner School; [fav subject] Science; [hobbies] Horse riding and bell ringing; [pets] 2 cats, 1 rabbit and 5 ducks; [ambition] To become a Vet, specialising in horses;

PRESTON, CHARLIE: [b] 29/11/88 Malden; [home] Danbury, Essex; [p] Louise and Alf; [brother] Lewis; [sister] Kimberlie; [school] Danbury Park C.P. School; [fav subject] Maths; [hobbies] Gymnastics and dancing; [pets] 2 cats (Bonny & Duchess); [ambitions] To become a Vet and to travel the world;

PRIOR, ROBERT: [b] 08/01/90 Berkshire; [home] Farnham, Surrey; [p] Teresa and Kevin; [brother] Alex; [sister] Hayley; [school] St. Peters; [fav subject] Maths and I.T.; [hobbies] Football and art; [pets] Dog, cat, owls, fish, budgies and cockatiels; [ambition] To become a Vet.;

PRISK, LISA: [b] 06/09/87 Truro; [home] St. Agnes, Cornwall; [p] Gary and Penny; [brother] Matthew; [school] St. Agnes CP; [fav subject] English; [hobbies] Flute, reading and writing poetry; [pets] Hamster; [ambitions] To become a successful Poet or Writer;

PULLOM, JACK: [b] 19/01/91 Swindon; [home] Cirencester; [p] John and Judith; [brothers] Ben, Simon and Jordan; [school] Watermoor; [fav subject] Maths; [hobbies] Magic tricks; [pets] Dog, 3 cats, 4 rabbits, 4 guinea pigs and 5 hamsters; [ambition] To become a Magician;

RANDALL, ALICE: [b] 20/08/92 Barnstaple; [home] Ilfracombe, N. Devon; [p] Alan and Jeanette; [school] Ilfracombe Infants; [fav subject] English; [hobbies] Tap and ballet dancing, sewing and reading; [pets] Boxer dog and a budgie; [ambition] To become a famous Author!

READE, TERRY MARTIN: [b] 21.04.87 Rochford; [home] Canvey, Essex; [p] Martin and Belinda; [brother] Jack; [school] Cornelius Vermuyden; [fav subject] P.E.; [hobbies] Rugby; [pets] Rabbit; [ambition] To play rugby for England;

REDIN, HARRY: [b] 27/02/90; [home] Loughton, Essex; [p] Gill and Mick; [brother] Jack; [school] Whitebridge Junior School; [fav subject] Art, writing poetry and stories; [hobbies] Playing football for the Belmont Team and playing golf; [pets] A black and white cat (Cookie); [ambition] To become an Artist;

REED, KIRSTY JADE: [b] 13/04/92 Barnstaple Hospital; [home] Ilfracombe, N. Devon; [p] Christopher and Tamara; [brothers] Dean and Robert; [school] Ilfracombe Infants; [fav subject] Writing poetry; [hobbies] Riding my bike and dancing;

[pets] Budgie (Dusty); [ambition] To become a Hairdresser;

REILLY, TOM: [b] 21/05/88 Birkenhead; [home] Harpenden, Herts; [p] Kirsten and Peter; [sister] Kate; [school] Crabtree Junior; [fav subject] P.E.; [hobbies] Football, chess, pets, trombone and warhammer 40,000; [pets] 2 guinea pigs (Sandy & Blanc); [ambitions] To become a superstar Footballer or a Marine Biologist;

REVILL-JOHNSON, EDWARD: [b] 23/01/88 Bath; [home] Crondall, Surrey; [p] Sarah and Anthony; [school] St. Peter's; [fav subject] English; [hobbies] Swimming, roller blading and table tennis; [pets] Siamese cat; [ambition] To become a Corporate Lawyer;

RICHARDS, LUKE: [b] 27/11/90 Truro; [home] Bodmin, Cornwall; [p] Paul and Caroline; [sister] Hannah; [school] St. Mary's; [hobbies] Cycling and football; [pets] Rabbit (Bluebell) and a hamster (Harry);

RICHARDSON, HUGH: [b] 30/05/88 Swindon; [home] Cirencester, Glos.; [p] Roy and Katie; [brother] Thomas; [school] Watermoor; [hobbies] Playing my guitar and football; [pets] Cat (Tigger) and gerbils (Joey & Chandler);

RICHES, ROSANNA: [b] 04/01/86 Gloucester; [home] The Pludds, Gloucestershire; [p] Philip and Paulette; [brother] David; [school] Dene Magna Community; [fav subject] Science; [hobbies] Playing Euphonium and Trumpet; [pets] 2 guines pigs, 2 fish and a cat; [ambitions] To become a Pop Star or a Poet;

RIDGERS, ROSANNA: [b] 08/07/89 Maidstone; [home] Birchwood, Somerset; [school] Buckland St. Mary; [hobbies] Riding; [pets] Pony (Partridge); [ambition] Would like to work with animals and write stories;

ROBERTS, JENNIFER: [b] 21/06/99 Aldershot; [home] Ash Vale, Hampshire; [p] Rosamunde and Kenneth; [sister] Laura; [school] Ash Manor; [fav subject] English; [hobbies] Horse riding, swimming and piano; [pets] Dog (Maddie), rabbit (Honey) and guinea pigs (Keogh & Bournville);

ROBERTS, TOM: [b] 03/08/89 Cheltenham; [home] Twyning, Glos.; [p] Andrew and Marie; [brother] Alex; [school] Twyning County Primary; [fav subject] Physical Education; [hobbies] Stamp collecting and mountain bikes; [pets] Sooty and Sweep; [ambition] To become a professional Mountain Bike Rider;

ROBERTSON, JAMES ASHLEY: [b] 14/03/89 Chelmsford; [home] Little Baddow, Essex; [p] Andrew and Georgina; [sister] Lucinda; [school] Danbury Park Primary; [hobbies] Football and fencing; [pets] Cat (Dennis); [ambition] To become an Astronaut;

ROBINSON, FRANCES: [b] 08/05/88 Barnstaple; [home] Dolton, Devon; [p] David and Celia; [brothers] Andrew and Rory; [school] Dolton Primary; [fav subject] Reading and Art; [hobbies] Ballet, riding, reading and animals; [pets] Hamster, rabbits and ducks; [ambition] To help children with head injuries;

ROBSON, PETER: [b] 01/08/92 Reading; [home] Mary Tavy, Devon; [p] Hilary and Andy; [sister] Jenny; [school] St. Rumon's; [fav subject] Maths; [hobbies] Football, swimming and bike riding; [ambitions] To work on a Farm and to visit Disneyland;

ROCKEY, ELANWY: [b] 20/10/87 Bristol; [home] Kingswood, Glos.; [p] Professor Patricia Broadfoot and Dr. David Rockey; [brothers] James and Laurence; [school] Kingswood Primary; [fav subject] English; [hobbies] Horse riding and music; [pets] 2 hamsters (Toffee & Bounty); [ambition] To write a book;

ROGERS, KERRY: [b] 17/12/86 Southampton; [home] North Baddesley, Hampshire; [p] Kevin and Kay; [brother] Karl; [sister] Karmen; [school] Mountbatten; [fav subject] P.E.; [hobbies] All sports; [pets] Dog (Ben0 and guinea pigs; [ambition] To play football for Southampton Ladies;

ROSSER, LUKE: [b] 10/12/89 Taunton; [home] Taunton, Somerset; [brother] Paul; [sister] Eva; [school] St. George's Primary; [fav subject] Maths, Biology and animals; [hobbies] Chess and running; [ambition] To become a Vet.;

ROSSITER, DOMINIQUE JANE: [b] 16/08/92 Bath; [home] Yeovil, Somerset; [p] Justine; [school] Pen Mill Infants; [fav subject] Writing Stories and English; [hobbies] Reading and playing with Barbie; [pets] Black Tomcat (Squidge); [ambition] To work in McDonalds!;

ROUND, JASON: [b] 14/02/88 Truro; [home] Penzance, Cornwall; [p] Edna and Peter; [brother] James; [school] St. Mary's R.C. School; [fav subject] English; [hobbies] Football, swimming and rugby; [pets] Cat; [ambition] To become an Actor;

ROWLEY, CHARLEY JANE: [b] 26/12/89 Harlow; [home] Pye Corner, Essex; [p] Andrew and Jane; [school] High Wych JMI; [fav subject] Art; [hobbies] Bike riding and swimming; [pets] 2 cats (Tiger & Fluffy); [ambition] To become a Teacher;

RUSSELL, CHLOÉ: [b] 05/03/88 Chelmsford; [home] Chelmsford, Essex; [p] Clare and John; [brother] James; [sister] Cara; [school] Perryfields Junior; [fav subject] English and P.E.; [hobbies] Piano, athletics and netball; [pets] Cat (Smudge) dog (Megan); [ambitions] To write a book and become famous;

RUTLEDGE, HANNAH: [b] 21/03/91 Oldham; [home] Bourton on the Water, Glos. [p] Jane and John; [sister] Katie; [school] Bourton on the Water County Primary; [fav subject] Maths; [hobbies] Swimming and Piano; [ambition] To go to University:

RYALL, GEOFFREY ALEXANDER: [b] 12/09/85 Yeovil; [home] Shaftesbury, Dorset; [p] Fay Smith and Malcolm Ryall; [school] King Alfreds CE Middle School; [fav subject] Maths and science; [hobbies] Making things and finding out how things work; [pets] Cat (Leo); [ambitions] Mechanical or Electrical Engineering, plus Carpentry and one day build my own house;

SAMPSON, JOSEPH: [b] 24/02/91; [home] Cirencester, Glos.; [school] Watermoor; [fav subject] Art and Science; [hobbies] Football and bowling; [pets] Rabbit; [ambition] To be a Conservationist;

SAMPSON, MAXINE ERICA: [b] 17/12/90 Swindon; [home] Cirencester, Glos.; [p] Jacqui and Andy; [brother] Symon; [school] Watermoor C of E; [fav subject] Maths and Poetry; [hobbies] Outdoor Sports; [pets] Love birds; [ambition] To become an Author;

SEAMARK, STUART: [b] 17/08/88 Yeovil; [home] Milborne Port, Somerset; [p] Helen and Trevor; [brother] Craig; [school] Milborne Port County Primary; [fav subject] English; [hobbies] Listening to music, tennis, rounders and Scouts; [pets] Hamster and a stick insect; [ambition] To become a Chef;

SEWELL, MARTIN: [b] 03/10/87 High Wycombe; [home] Chinnor, Oxfordshire; [p] John and Maureen; [sister] Claire Louise; [school] Aston Rowant C of E; [fav subject] Maths and P.E.; [hobbies] Football and cricket; [pets] Goldfish; [ambition] To play for Manchester United;

SHEAD, SAM: [b] 30/05/92; [brothers] Tom and Jack; [school] Milborne Port C.P.; [fav subject] Maths; [hobbies] Horse riding; [pets] Hamster; [ambition] To become a Vet.;

SHEPPARD, CLAIRE: [b] 24/03/88 Kent; [home] Antony, Cornwall; [p] Jackie and Nick; [brother] Alex; [school] Antony CEVA; [fav subject] Design and Technology; [hobbies] Swimming; [pets] Rabbit and a Pony;

SHERWOOD, ALEXANDER: [b] 30/10/89 Tunbridge Wells; [home] Lawford, Essex; [p] Janet and Kevin; [brother] Joshua; [school] Lawford C of E Primary; [fav subject] Art and craft; [hobbies] Archery, sailing and drawing; [pets] Hamster (Pippin); [ambition] To become a Designer;

SHERWOOD, JOSHUA: [b] 13/05/91 Colchester; [home] Lawford, Essex; [p] Janet and Kevin; [brother] Alexander; [school] Lawford C of E Primary; [fav subject] Maths; [hobbies] Painting, sailing and archery; [pets]

I love my hamster, but he has disappeared; [ambitions] To become a Sailor or Pilot;

SHIELDS, NATHAN: [b] 05/09/90; [home] St. Hilary, Cornwall; [brother] Liam; [school] Gwinear School; [fav subject] History; [hobbies] Cycling; [pets] Dog (Molly);

SILVESTON, CHARLOTTE: [b] 03/07/88 Stevenage; [home] Holwell, Herts; [p] Martin and Barbara; [brother] Benjamin; [school] Pirton JMI; [fav subject] Science; [hobbies] Cycling, swimming and reading; [pets] Rabbit, fish and a guinea pig; [ambition] To go back to Guernsey and live there again;

SIMMONS, NICK: [b] 15/04/88 Bristol; [home] Kingswood, Glos.; [p] Karen and Richard; [brothers] Gary and Jamie; [school] Kingswood County Primary; [fav subject] Maths; [hobbies] Football, hockey and cricket; [ambition] To play football for England;

SKINNER, ELIZABETH: [b] 21/07/92 Jersey; [home] Beaconsfield, Bucks; [p] Heather; [school] Chalfont St. Giles 1st School; [pets] Cat (Jasper) Guinea Pig (Cloudy);

SLOAN, STUART: [b] 24/09/89 Yeovil; [home] Montacute, Somerset; [p] Stephen and Diana; [brother] Martin; [sister] Lorna; [school] All Saints; [fav subject] Maths; [hobbies] Model electric railways; [pets] Dog (Harry); [ambition] To become a Train Driver;

SLY, DANIEL ANDRE: [b] 18/11/88 Ascot; [home] Bagshot, Surrey; [p] Fatima and Kevin; [brother] Christopher; [school] Connaught County Junior School; [fav subject] English; [hobbies] Football and skating; [ambition] To become a Barrister;

SMITH, DANNIELLE: [b] 13/09/90 Colchester; Essex; [p] A.K.M. Smith; [brother] Graham Smith; [sister] Nicola Chadwick; [school] Whipton Barton First; [fav subject] Art; [hobbies] Dancing; [pets] Cat (Rosie);

SMITH, HAZEL JANE : [b] 30/08/89 High Wycombe; [home] Amersham, Bucks; [p] Ian and Mandy; [brothers] Grant (11) James (7); [sister] Coral (5); [school] Elangeni Middle School; [fav subject] Art and Craft; [hobbies] Making Puppets; [pets] 2 Guinea pigs (Domino & Caramel); [ambitions] To become a Vet and to work with monkeys in a Zoo;

SMITH, JACOB: [b] 27/06/88 London; [home] Eastleigh, Hampshire; [p] Helena and Stephen; [sister] Eliza; [school] Crescent Primary; [fav subject] Astrology and Science; [hobbies] Roller blading; [pets] Cat (Delilah) [ambitions] To become a Graphic Designer and to travel the world;

SMITH, LUCY: [b] 07/09/91 Barnstaple, N. Devon; [home] Ilfracombe, N. Devon; [p] Ann and Bryan; [brother] Matthew; [school] Ilfracombe Infants; [fav subject] Art;

[hobbies] Swimming, dancing and tennis; [pets] Hamster (Rocky); [ambition] To become a Teacher;

SMITH, RACHEL ELIZABETH: [b] 25/05/88 Oxford; [home] Ducklington, Oxfordshire; [p] Kathryn and Stephen; [brothers] Matthew (16) Gareth (13); [school] Ducklington C of E; [fav subject] Art; [hobbies] Swimming; [pets] Cat (Dillon); [ambition] To work with animals;

SMYTH, CHARLOTTE: [b] 13/12/90 Watford; [home] Rickmansworth, Herts; [p] Peter and Sara; [sister] Harriet; [school] Harvey Road Primary; [fav subject] Art; [hobbies] Horse riding, tennis and swimming; [[pets] 2 Dogs, a rabbit and a hamster; [ambition] To become a Vet.;

SOMMERVILLE, TERRY: [b] 11/06/90 Watford; [home] Puckington, Somerset;[p] Angie and Steve; [school] St. Marys & St. Peters; [fav subject] Maths; [hobbies] Gymnastics, football and computers; [pets] Finches, fish and terrapins; [ambitions] To become a Computer Programmer or a Professional Gymnast;

SPENCER, WILLIAM: [b] 05/06/88 St. Albans; [home] Harpenden, Herts; [p] Anne and Tim; [brother] Alexander; [sister] Emily; [school] Crabtree Junior; [fav subject] Physical Education; [hobbies] Sport and reading; [pets] Cat (Domino); [ambition] To become a Professional Cricketer;

SPIERS, VIKKI: [b] 05/09/90 Oxford; [home] Headington, Oxfordshire; [p] Anita and Tim; [brother] Matthew; [school] Windmill First; [fav subject] Maths; [hobbies] Swimming and reading; [pets] Cat (Sooty), Dogs (Sam & Charlie); [ambitions] To become a Vet, Nurse or Writer;

STAFFORD, REBECCA CATHERINE: [b] 28/01/88 Yeovil; [home] Montacute, Somerset; [p] Tim and Angie; [brother] Jack; [sister] Megan; [school] All Saints Primary; [fav subject] History; [hobbies] Horse riding, music and reading; [pets] 2 Guinea pigs (Fudge & Pinky); [ambition] To become a Veterinary Nurse;

STAPLETON, SAMANTHA: [b] 15/10/87 Barnstaple; [home] Barnstaple N. Devon; [p] Chris and Alan; [brother] Nevin; [sister] Michelle; [school] Yeo Valley Primary; [fav subject] Art and P.E.; [hobbies] Line dancing, and cross stitch; 2 dogs (Bramble & Fern) and 2 love birds (Rosie & Jim); [ambition] To work with Elephants;

STEER, GEORGE: [b] 02/06/88 Hele Farm; [home] Gulworthy, Devon; [p] John and Rosemary; [brothers] Richard and Harry; [sister] Joy; [school] Gulworthy C.P.; [fav subject] Natural History; [hobbies] Football and wildlife; [pets] Cat (Tommy); [ambition] To be a Quail Farmer;

STEPHENS, CHARLEY: [b] 05/12/87 St. Austell; [home] Roche, Cornwall; [p] Margaret and Patrick; [school] Roche C.P.; [fav subject] Art; [hobbies] Judo; [ambitions] To become a Surgeon or a Beautician;

STONE, JADE BIANCA: [b] 01/11/93 Aylesbury; [home] Dinton, Bucks; [p] Sharon and Vic; [school] Long Crendon Combined; [fav subject] Reading; [hobbies] Horse riding; [pets] Bulldog and 3 goldfish; [ambition] To own my own Pony to ride every day and share with my Cousin Jessica;

STONE, LAURA: [b] 09/11/88 Leicester; [home] Taunton, Somerset; [p] Stephen & Kathleen; [sisters] Sarah, Clare and Emma; [school] St. Georges Primary; [fav subject] Art; [hobbies] Swimming, netball and cycling; [pets] Guinea pig and a cat; [ambition] To become a Policewoman;

STRAWA, CHARLOTTE: [b] 16/06/89 ; [home] Beaconsfield; [p] Lindsay and Phillip; [brother] Jack; [sister] Catherine; [school] Butlers Court Primary; [fav subject] P.E., Art and English; [hobbies] Piano, sports, dancing and music; [pets] 2 Cats (Felix & Phoebie) and a hamster (Chunks); [ambition] To be famous;

STURKEY, EMMA: [b] 01/09/88 N. Devon; [home] Barnstaple, N. Devon; [p] Amanda and Grant; [sister] Jessica; [school] Ashleigh C of E Primary; [fav subject] Literacy; [hobbies] Horse riding; [pets] Dog (Toby) and a hamster (Fudge); [ambition] To become a top Rider;

SWATRIDGE, CHRISTOPHER: [b] 15/09/86 Salisbury; [home] North Baddesley, Hants; [p] Nigel and Sharon; [brother] Alexander (8); [sister] Carly (10); [school] The Mountbatten School; [fav subject] P.E. and Drama; [hobbies] Fishing, golf and football; [pets] Did have hamsters, but now just a cat; [ambition] To become a Vet.;

SWIGGS, PETER: [b] 12/11/87 Truro; [home] St. Austell, Cornwell; [p] Zena and Paul; [sister] Danielle; [school] Pondhu C.P.; [fav subject] Maths; [hobbies] Playstation; [pets] Cat (Timmy); [ambitions] To become an RSPCA Inspector or the Armed Forces;

SYMONDS, AMY GRACE: [b] 25/01/89 Barnstaple; [home] Dolton, N. Devon; [p] Kim and John; [sister] Sarah Kate; [school] Dolton Primary; [fav subject] Science; [hobbies] Swimming and computers; [pets] Dog, cats, fish and a hamster; [ambition] To become a Doctor;

TAPPIN, BEN: [b] 31/10/89 Southampton; [home] Ivybridge, Devon; [p] Janet Hooper and Alan Tappin; [school] Stowford Primary; [fav subject] Geography; [hobbies] Football, swimming and drawing; [pets] 2 Guinea pigs and pond fish; [ambitions] To be a Vet or a Footballer;

TAYLOR, ANDREW: [b] 17/07/87 Rochford; [home] Rayleigh, Essex; [school] Sweyne Park; [fav subject] Music; [hobbies] Football, swimming and guitar; [pets] Large black poodle; [ambition] To become the next Michael Owen;

TAYLOR, JONATHAN REDE: [b] 10/01/90 Plymouth; [home] Plymouth, Devon; [p] John and Gill; [school] Stowford Primary; [fav subject] Science; [hobbies] Experiments, cycling and playing on the computer; [pets] Hamster; [ambitions] To become a Scientist or an Inventor;

TAYLOR, LUCY: [b] 28/10/89 Chelmsford; [home] Wickham Bishops, Essex; [p] Robert and Elaine; [brother] Gregory; [school] Danbury Park CP; [fav subject] Literacy; [hobbies] Reading, art and craft; [pets] Hamster, cat and fish; [ambitions] To become an Actress, Author or Illustrator;

TEMPLE, ROSEMARY LOUISE: [b] 10/04/87 Rochford; [home] Hullbridge, Essex; [p] Amanda and Stephen; [sister] Hannah; [school] Sweyne Park Senior School; [fav subject] English; [hobbies] Horse riding and music; [pets] Fish, 15 birds, 2 guinea pigs and a rabbit; [ambitions] To become a Vet and to succeed in horse riding;

TEMPLEMAN, JOE: [b] 27/06/91 Chelmsford; [home] Chelmsford, Essex; [p] Gary and Tracey; [brother] Sam (2½); [sister] Keeley (9½); [school] Perryfields Infant; [fav subject] English (spelling); [hobbies] Football, swimming and karate; [pets] Rabbit (Bugs); [ambition] To play football for West Ham;

TERMEZI, BEN: [hobbies] Computer and Sports; [pets] Cat and a rabbit;

TOMLINSON, CHARLOTTE MEGAN: [b] 01/09/91 Truro; [home] Yeovil, Somerset; [p] Kathryn and David; [school] Pen Mill Infant; [fav subject] Reading and drawing; [hobbies] Ballroom dancing and cycling; [pets] Cat (Spike}; [ambitions] To become a Vet or a Scientist;

TO, KENNY: [b] 24/05/89 High Wycombe; [home] Chesham Bois, Bucks; [p] William; [brother] Christopher; [sister] Sammy; [school] Elangeni Middle School; [fav subject] Maths; [hobbies] Football and tennis; [ambition] To own a Restaurant;

TOOGOOD, ALEX: [b] 24/09/88 Truro, Cornwall; [home] South Brent, Devon; [p] Robin Toogood and Jude Bishop; [brother] Richard; [school] South Brent Primary; [fav subject] Maths; [hobbies] Reading and cycling;

TOOMER, SEAN: [b] 14/01/88 Winchester; [home] Eastleigh, Hants; [p] Paul and Rae; [brother] Graham; [sister] Kirsty; [school] Crescent Primary; [fav subject] P.E.; [hobbies] Fishing, judo and football; [pets] gerbil (Shadow);

TREGEAR, DANIEL JOHN: [b] 08/03/89 Bay View; [home] Ashton, Cornwall; [p] Pauline and John; [sister] Jennifer Louise; [school] Breage C of E VP School; [fav subject] Art; [hobbies] Model Trains; [pets] 2 Dogs a cat and a bird; [ambition] To become a Train Driver;

TREMAYNE, REBECCA: [b] 25/03/93 Redhill; [home] Reigate, Surrey; [p] Frank and Claire; [school] Reigate Parish; [fav subject] English; [hobbies] Reading, computers and swimming; [ambitions] To become a Nurse or a Teacher;

TRENCHARD, JAMES: [b] 13/03/89 Plymouth; [home] South Brent, Devon; [p] Debbie and Roger; [brother] Matthew; [school] South Brent Primary; [fav subject] Reading; [hobbies] Rugby, cricket and football; [pets] Cat; [ambitions] To become a Police Officer, an Author or an Artist;

TRUDGEON, ELIZABETH: [b] 26/11/87 [home] Roche, Cornwall; [p] Kevin and Dorothy; [sister] Helen; [school] Roche CP; [fav subject] English; [hobbies] Netball and Drama; [pets] Rabbit; [ambitions] to become a Journalist or an Author of childrens books;

TRUDGEON, MARTIN: [b] 04/10/88 Truro; [home] Roche, Cornwall; [p] Stephen and Diane; [brother] Jason; [school] Roche County Primary; [fav subject] Science; [hobbies] Football and Tae Kwon Do; [ambitions] To become rich and to travel;

TRUNDLEY, DAVID JOHN: [b] 04/01/87 St Pauls Hospital; [home] Hemel Hempstead, Herts; [p] Maurice and Sandra; [brother] Ian; [sister] Rebecca; [school] The Astley Cooper School; [fav subject] Maths; [hobbies] All Sports; [pets] 2 dogs (Kallie & Bruno) 5 guinea pigs (Primrose, Lilli-Bud, Rosie, Daisy & Poppy) cat (Oliver) hamster (Marble); [ambitions] To succeeed in all that I do and to enjoy life;

TRUNKS, MATTHEW: [b] 26/06/86 Musgrove Pk Hospital; [home] Taunton, Somerset; [p] Carole and Paul; [brother] Danial; [sister] Bethany; [school] Bartletts Elm; [fav subject] English and Maths; [hobbies] Writing and music; [pets] Cat and 2 guinea pigs; [ambition] To become a famous story writer;

TURNER, GAVIN MARTIN: [b] 19/04/90 Oxford; [home] Long Crendon, Bucks; [p] Colin and Vanessa; [school] Long Crendon C.C.; [fav subject] English; [hobbies] Football; [pets] Guinea pig (Pig);

TURNER, JADE LOUISE: [b] 14/04/92 Yeovil; [home] Odcombe, Somerset; [p] Liesa Jane; [sister] Devon Jane; [school] All Saints Primary; [fav subject] Literacy; [hobbies] Horse riding and swimming; [pets] 2 cats (Dusty & Casper) and a cockatil (Cocky); [ambition] To become a Race Horse Owner;

TURNER, KATIE: [b] 09/07/87 Rochford; [home] Canvey Island, Essex; [p] Susan and Martin; [brothers] Robert and Thomas; [sister] Emma; [school] Cornelius Vermuyden; [fav subject] Science; [hobbies] Cross stitch and fishing; [pets] A dog, 4 cats and some fish; [ambition] To become an Archaeologist;

TURNER, VICTORIA: [b] 19/06/85 Basildon; [home] Canvey Island, Essex; [p] Judith and Alan; [sister] Elizabeth; [school] The Sweyne Park School; [fav subject] English; [hobbies] Dancing and playing the flute; [ambition] To have a successful career;

TWOMEY, CLARE: [b] 06/07/89 London; [home] Taunton, Somerset; [p] Monica and John; [brother] James; [sisters] Emily, Sarah and Catherine; [school] St. George's R.C. Primary; [fav subject] English and Music; [hobbies] Tap dancing, clarinet and piano; [pets] Cocker Spaniel (Max); [ambitions] To become an Author or a Musician;

TYRRELL, SARAH ELLEN: [b] Bridgwater; [home] Wembdon, Somerset; [p] Lyn and Alan; [brothers] Ian and Mark; [school] Haygrove School; [fav subject] Design and Technology; [hobbies] Dancing; [pets] Golden Retriever (Hollie); [ambitions] To dance for a major production or with a pop group;

UNDERWOOD, LEE MARTIN: [b] 25/01/91; [home] Chelmsford, Essex; [p] Amanda and Martin; [school] Perryfields Junior; [fav subject] Literacy Hour; [hobbies] Football; [pets] Rabbit and a guinea pig; [ambition] To become a Footballer;

VICKERY, EMMA: 24/12/84 Taunton; [home] Goathurst, Somerset; [school] Haygrove; [fav subject] Drama; [hobbies] Horse riding and reading; [pets] Horses, cats and a dog; [ambitions] To work with animals. preferably horses and to become a famous Poet;

VIERTEL, GRETA CARLEEN: [b] 20/08/88 Cornwall; [home] Roche, Cornwall; [p] Hans and Sandy; [brother] Karl; [school] Roche C.P.; [fav subject] English; [hobbies] Singing, netball and drama; [pets] Dog (Heidi); [ambitions] To become an Actress, Poet, or Pop Star;

WADE, DARREN: [b] 15/04/88 Truro; [home] Roche, Cornwall; [p] Mr & Mrs Wade; [brother] Matthew Tyler; [school] Roche C.P.; [fav subject] Art; [hobbies] Mini racing and rugby; [pets] Dog and a hamster; [ambition] To become a Mechanic;

WAITE, SAM SCOTT: [b] 10/04/87 Taunton; [home] West Huntspill, Somerset; [p] Paul and Lisa; [brother] Calum; [school] Haygrove; [fav subject] Rnglish; [hobbies] Writing and pop music; [pets] 4 Cats; [ambitions] To become an Author, or an RAF Pilot, or a Chef and to travel;

WALKER, HAYLEE: [b] 29/01/91 Oxford; [home] Oxford, Oxon; [p] Dean and Toni; [brothers] Lee and Jason; [school] Windmill First; [fav subject] Science; [hobbies] Swimming; [pets] A cat; [ambition] To become a Policewoman;

WASHINGTON, DANNY: [b] 09/04/90 Aylesbury; [home] Aylesbury, Bucks; [p] Alan and Majella; [brother] Wayne; [sister] Stacey; [school] William Harding Middle; [fav subject] Science; [hobbies] Playing on computers and reading; [pets] Cat (Homer); [ambition] To become a Teacher;

WATERS, GEMMA: [b] 29/03/88 Truro; [home] Heamoor, Cornwall; [p] Natasha and Shaun; [brothers] Liam and Ryan; [school] Heamoor C.P.; [fav subject] English and Art; [hobbies] Singing and dancing; [pets] Budgie, fish, hamster and 6 cats; [ambition] To become a Nurse and look after sick children;

WATERS, ROSS JAMES: 21/03/89 Truro; [home] Penryn, Cornwall; [p] Mark and Bridgit; [sister] Sally Demelza; [school] Penryn Junior; [fav subject] Art, Science and History; [hobbies] Riding my bike; [pets] Rabbit (Tinker); [ambition] To be a Monster Truck Driver;

WATKINS, FRANCES: [b] 13/11/87 Hereford; [home] Kempley Dymock, Glos; [p] Reg and Juliet; [brother] Richard; [sister] Amelia; [school] Bromsberrow St. Mary's C of E Primary; [fav subject] Sport; [hobbies] Swimming, roller blading and music; [pets] Computer pets;

WEBBER, LUKE: [b] 13/02/89 Taunton; [home] Taunton, Somerset; [p] Steven and Nikki; [school] St. Georges R.C. Primary; [fav subject] Art; [hobbies] Model making, stamp collecting and playing the clarinet; [ambitions] To become an Architect and to travel the world;

WELLS, MICHAEL: [b] 18/12/87 Aylesbury; [home] Aylesbury, Bucks; [p] Bill and Debbie; [brother] Richard; [school] Turnfurlong Middle; [fav subject] R.E. [hobbies] Football and basketball; [pets] Dog (Gaby) rabbit (Lucy); [ambition] To become a professional Footballer;

WENMAN, KIERAN JOHN: [b] 28/07/92 Branstaple; [home] Ilfracombe, N. Devon; [p] Maria and David; [brother] Oscar; [sister] Nadine; [school] Ilfracombe Infants; [fav subject] Writing and P.E.; [hobbies] Riding my bike and swimming; [pets] Cat; [ambitions] To become an Author and to work at Disneyland;

WEST, HANNAH: [b] 03/08/91; [home] Hertfordshire; [p] Kenneth and Sonia; [brother] Matthew; [fav subject] History; [hobbies] Reading, writing and walking; [pets] Cat (Suki); [ambition] Possibly to become a Vet;

WESTLAKE, MELANIE: [b] 26/01/89 Crafthole; [home] Crafthole, Cornwall; [p] Robert and Karen; [sisters] Gemma and Emily; [school] Antony CEVA School; [fav subject] English; [hobbies] Swimming, running and reading; [pets] Cat (Pickles) dogs (Solar & Bramble) and 2 ferrets; [ambitions] An Olympic Swimmer, a Writer or a Vet.;

WESTON, EMMA: [b] 01/10/87 Harlow; [home] Harlow, Essex; [p] Sue Newland; [school] St. Albans R.C. Primary; [fav subject] English and Science; [hobbies] Tennis, netball, swimming and reading; [pets] Dog (Meg); [ambition] To become a Teacher;

WHALLEY, CIARA: [b] 31/01/88 Rochford; [home] Harlow, Essex; [p] Maria and Paul; [sister] Kelly (7); [school] St. Albans R.C. Primary; [fav subject] Art; [hobbies] Music and Art; [pets] Fox Terrier (Tilly); [ambitions] To become an Artist or a professional Singer;

WHARNSBY, LAURA: [b] 23/02/87; [p] Lee and Kevin; [sister] Sarah; [school] Cornelius Vermuyden School; [pets] Rabbit (Thumper);

WHEADON, BECKIE: [b] 08/06/86 Torbay; [home] Bream, Glos; [p] Angela and David; [brother] Simon; [school] Whitecross; [fav subject] English; [hobbies] Reading and swimming; [pets] Cats (Gizmo & Tabetha); [ambition] To become famous!

WHITE, FAYE LOUISE:: [b] 24/07/88 St. Albans; [home] Harpenden, Herts; [p] Geoff and Sally; [brother] Billy; [school] Crabtree Junior; [fav subject] P.E. [hobbies] Swimming and reading; [ambition] To become famous;

WHITE, HAYLEY VICTORIA: [b] 17/10/86 Aylesbury; [home] Aylesbury, Bucks; [p] Mark and Caron; [brothers] Ashley and Archie; [sister] Georgia; [school] St. Edwards R.C.; [fav subject] English; [hobbies] Bike riding, swimming and listening to music; [pets] Fish; [ambition] To be successful in my chosen career;

WHITE, KIRSTEN: [b] 07/07/87 Great Yarmouth; [home] Winterton on Sea, Norfolk; [brothers] Paul, James and Leigh; [school] Cornelius Vermuyden; [fav subject] Drama; [hobbies] Swimming; [pets] Chinchilla and a cat; [ambition] To become a Nurse;

WHITE, LEWIS: [b] 13/11/91 Gloucester, Glos; [p] Julie and Martin; [brother] Daniel; [sister] Hollie; [school] Robinswood Primary; [fav subject] Maths; [hobbies] Football; [ambitions] To become a Policeman, Fireman or an Architect;

WHITLOCKE, LEE: [b] 29/01/90; [home] Eastleigh, Hampshire; [p] Richard and Ann; [brother] Daniel; [school] Crescent Primary;

[fav subject] English; [hobbies] Football; [pets] Cat; [ambition] To become a Policeman;

WHITWORTH, RACHEL: [b] 15/10/84 Portsmouth; [home] Southampton, Hants; [p] Alison and Trevor; [sister] Hilary; [school] The Mountbatten School; [fav subject] English; [hobbies] Music, basketball and writing; [pets] Rabbit;

WILKOPP, PHILIP STEPHEN: [b] 28/07/87 Rochford; [home] Canvey, Essex; [p] Tracy and Andreas; [brother] Ashley; [sisters] Katie and Donna; [school] Cornelius Vermuyden; [fav subject] History; [hobbies] Fishing, martial arts and rugby; [pets] 2 Cats; [ambitions] To join the Army, fish for England and to become a 5th Dan in Martial Arts and represent England;

WILLIAMS, CORY DAVID: [b] 02/09/91 Gloucester; [home] Gloucester, Glos; [p] Ann and Lindsey; [sisters] Molly and Mae; [school] Robinswood Infant School; [hobbies] Computers;

WILLIAMS, ELEANOR MAY: [b] 13/05/90 Chelmsford; [home] Danbury, Essex; [p] Alison and Nigel; [brother] Jack; [school] Danbury Park County Primary; [fav subject] Maths; [hobbies] Gym, art and craft [pets] Fish (Freddie); [ambitions] To be in the School Gym Team and reach the British Finals and to go to University, become a Teacher and have children;

WILLIAMS, FAUVE: [b] 07/10/88 Poole [home] Taunton, Somerset; [p] Andrew and Lian; [brother] Jack; [sister] Christina; [school] St. Georges R.C. Primary; [fav subject] P.E. [hobbies] Playing the flute, singing and sport; [pets] Cats (Timmy & Freddie); [ambition] To do really well as an Athlete;

WILLIAMS, KIRSTY: [b] 16/05/90 Frimley; [home] Farnham, Surrey; [p] Tony and Sarah; [sister] Carla; [school] St. Peters; [fav subject] Maths and P.E.;[hobbies] Netball, swimming and chess; [pets] 2 dogs, 2 rabbits and a budgie; [ambition] To become a Vet.;

WILSON, NICOLA: [b] 28/11/89 Dallas; [home] Gt. Haseley, Oxfordshire; [p] Alex and Belinda; [brothers] Stuart and Andrew; [sisters] Lyndsey and Fiona; [school] Great Milton Primary; [fav subject] P.E. and literacy; [hobbies] Singing and dancing; [pets] Dog, fish and a hamster; [ambitions] To become a Teacher, or Writer, or Vet, or a Secretary;

WINGENT, SUSANNAH: [b] 28/01/86 Winchester; [home] Motcombe, Dorset; [sisters] Polly and Ella; [school] King Alfred's Middle School; [fav subject] Maths; [hobbies]

Singing; [pets] 3 Cats;

WINGFIELD, KIT: [b] 05/03/90 Taunton; [home] Taunton, Somerset; [p] Timothy and Sarah-Jane; [brother] Henry; [sister] Milly; [school] St. George's R.C.; [fav subject] Art; [hobbies] Football and cycling; [pets] 4 Cats; [ambition] To play football for England;

WONNACOTT, NATHAN: [b] 26/02/92 Plymouth; [home] Tavistock, Devon; [p] Shane and Vanessa; [sister] Kayleigh; [school] St. Rumon's; [fav subject] Maths; [hobbies] Football, athletics and swimming; [ambitions] To become a Policeman and a footballer;

WOODCOCK, HEIDI: [b] 08/09/87 Exeter; [home] Taunton, Somerset; [p] Denise and Anthony; [school] Trinity; [fav subject] Art; [hobbies] Sport and shopping; [pets] Hamster, 2 goldfish and 2 cats; [ambitions] To become a Doctor or an Actress;

WRIGHT, DANIEL: [b] 20/02/90 Truro; [home] Reawla, Cornwall; [p] David and Colleen; [brother] Tom; [school] Gwinear C.P.; [fav subject] Poetry; [hobbies] Surfing; [pets] Dog (Patch); [ambitions] To become a footballer and poet;

WYATT, CHARLOTTE: [b] 28/04/90 Somerset; [home] Dulford, Devon; [p] Gary and Karen; [brother] Thomas; [school] Plymtree C of E Primary; [fav subject] Art and Technology; [hobbies] Ballet and making things; [pets] Cat (Colin) dog (Toby) and 2 goldfish; [ambitions] To become a Ballerina and a Mother;

WYTHE, SARAH: [b] 23/11/84 Winchester; [home] Chard, Somerset; [p] June and Richard; [brothers] David and Tom; [school] Holyrood; [fav subject] P.E.; [hobbies] Hockey; [pets] Hamsters (Rolo & Polo); [ambition] To play hockey for Somerset;

YEO, BENJAMIN: [b] 09/08/88 N.D.D.H. [home] Barnstaple, N. Devon; [p] Stuart and Julie; [brother] Joshua; [school] Yeo Valley Primary; [fav subject] Design Technology; [hobbies] Swimming, football and athletics; [pets] Hamster; [ambitions] To become a professsional Swimmer or a Chef;

YOUNG, HANNAH: [b] 22/02/84 Harlow; [home] Ash, Surrey; [school] Ash Manor School; [fav subject] Drama; [hobbies] Youth Theatre and Dance; [pets] Cat; [ambitions] To work and travel overseas and to work in the Theatre;

ZERVUDACHI, GEORGIA: [b] 14/04/92 Paddington; [home] Chalfont St. Giles, Bucks; [p] Clarissa and Paddy; [brother] Alexander; [school] Chalfont St. Giles First School; [fav subject] Reading; [hobbies] Swimming; [pets] Chicken; [ambitions] To become a Writer, Composer or a Vet;

INDEX
OF
POETS